Encyclopaedia of the
FLEET AIR ARM
SINCE 1945

Encyclopaedia of the
FLEET AIR ARM
SINCE 1945

Paul Beaver

PSL

Patrick Stephens
Wellingborough, Northamptonshire

First published in 1987

British Library Cataloguing in Publication Data

Beaver, Paul
  Encyclopaedia of the Fleet Air Arm since 1945.
  1. Great Britain, *Royal Navy, Fleet Air Arm*—History
  I. Title
  358.4'00941   VG95.G7

  ISBN 0-85059-760-9

Front endpapers *Sea Harrier FRS 1s of 899, 801 and 800 Squadrons* (RN).
Title page Hermes, *flagship of the Falkland Islands task force, returning to the United Kingdom* (RN/FPU).
Rear endpaper Ark Royal *in heavy Atlantic seas, 1977* (RN).

Patrick Stephens Limited is part of the Thorsons Publishing Group

Printed and bound in Great Britain

10 9 8 7 6 5 4 3 2 1

Contents

Foreword

by Captain Eric Brown CBE DSC AFC MA FRAeS RN(Ret'd)

There can be few author tasks more daunting than compiling an encylopaedia of anything, because by definition it must encompass everything on the chosen subject. Paul Beaver has at least taken the interesting subject of the Royal Navy's Fleet Air Arm, and wisely restricted it to the post Second World War period, thus avoiding the already fully documented preceding era except for continuity reference.

The history of the Fleet Air Arm has been a continually turbulent one, interwoven with political intrigue, inter-service rivalry and self-inflicted wounds by senior officers who never grasped the awesome potentional of naval airpower. In the period covered by this book, these points are illustrated by the cancellation of the new revolutionary new design aircraft carrier CVA 01, the ludicrously unsound RAF policy of Strategic Island Bases to replace naval aviation, and the phasing out of the fixed-wing carriers with their Phantoms, Buccaneers and AEW Gannets — perfectly timed to occur some three years before the Falklands campaign and thus prolong a battle which could probably have been won in two weeks if *Ark Royal* and her powerful armoury had been available.

The fascinating rise of the helicopter to a position of pre-eminence in the inventory of the Fleet Air Arm and indeed the Royal Navy is well covered. I sometimes have a wry smile to myself when I recollect how I repeatedly forecast this course of events to my sceptical fellow officers on the Joint Services Staff Course in 1956. Was it that they didn't see it, or didn't want to see it?

Although I have always preached caution about the limitations of VSTOL aeroplanes, nevertheless the magnificent British design of the Sea Harrier has saved British fixed-wing carrier aviation from extinction. These specialised VSTOL carriers were even originally called through-deck cruisers in the hope that this disguised nomenclature would fool the anti-carrier political lobby, which it obviously did, or perhaps it just helped to save face. Anyway, information on the splendid combination of the Sea Harrier and the 'Invincible' Class carriers is fully updated by the author.

Well deserved credit is given to the leading role that British ingenuity and inventiveness has played and continues to play in the development of both aircraft carrier operational technology and air equipment. Too often the British dream up superb ideas, only to see them taken up and developed to their full potential by other nations. Paul Beaver reminds us of some of our proud contributions.

This book is a mine of information, as indeed an encyclopaedia should be, but it is also a potted history of a great branch of a great Service. It has been meticulously researched and should be a 'must' in the library of every student of modern naval history.

Eric M. Brown

Preface and acknowledgements

To compile this type of book is a mammoth undertaking and many of the ideas originally considered have had to be shelved during the preparation of the text and illustrations. Nevertheless, the reader will find here an in-depth appreciation of British naval aviation since the end of the Second World War with particular attention paid to the technological improvements — the jet aircraft, guided missiles, improved flight decks and other projects.

Naturally, considerable attention is placed on the aircraft of the period and although every major in-service and experimental type has been covered, there will be a number of aeroplanes, mainly remainders from the Second World War that are not covered although they were in the Fleet Air Arm's inventory for certain second-line tasks.

The term Fleet Air Arm has been used throughout the book, even though it has not been continuously in use, but began as a Royal Air Force term for naval aviation. The first chapter explains the origins of the title and brings the reader through from the early experiments before the First World War to the modern age of the Sea Harrier and Lynx.

The second chapter examines how the Fleet Air Arm has been organized. The fixed-wing aeroplanes are described by role in the third chapter and the importance of the naval helicopter is stressed by the fact that it has a chapter to itself. Most of the Fleet Air Arm's aircraft have been organized into squadrons since the mid-1930s, and the post-1945 front-line units are introduced. The other important feature of the Fleet Air Arm in the post-1945 period has been the aircraft carrier and these are also described in detail, while the special technology used to assist aircraft to fly at sea in most weathers is presented in the next chapter. The weapons and special equipment of the Fleet Air Arm are described in a final chapter.

A little over 90,000 words in all have been compiled with the considerable assistance of the Fleet Air Arm Museum, Yeovilton and the kind assistance of former, serving and would-be Fleet Air Arm people. Four main source books to check the facts obtained from the members of such organizations as the Fleet Air Arm Officers' Association and the Telegraphist Air-Gunners' Association, and the personal accounts of over a hundred people have been used to build the picture presented in the Encyclopaedia. These source books are: *The Squadrons of the Fleet Air Arm* by Ray Sturtivant (Air Britain, 1984); *British Naval Aircraft since 1912* by Owen Thetford (Putnam, 1958), *The Fleet Air Arm History* by Jack Waterman (Fleet Air Arm Museum, c 1976) and *British Military Aircraft Serials and Markings* (British Aviation Research Group, 1980). A list of other books which the serious student is recommended to read will be found on page 261.

In acknowledging those who have so kindly assisted me in this undertaking, I would point out that whilst every reasonable care has been taken to check facts, their interpretation is mine alone. I would like to thank the following for their kind assistance: Admiral Sir Frank Hopkins KCB, DSO, DSC; Admiral Sir Derek Empson GBE, KCB; Vice Admiral Sir Donald Gibson KCB, DSC, JP; Rear Admiral Dennis Cambell CB, DSC; Rear Admiral C. K. Roberts CB, DSO; Rear Admiral H. C. N. Goodhart CB, FRAeS; Captain Eric Brown CBE, DSC, AFC, FRAeS, RN (Rtd); Captain C. V. Howard; Captain Alan Leahy CBE, DSC, RN (Rtd); Captain A. B. B. Clark RN; Captain R. L. Eveleigh DSC, RN; Captain F. Milner RN; Captain D. T. McKeown RN (Rtd); Commander Paul Madge RN; Commander Derek Monsell RN (Rtd); Commander H. E. R. Bain RN (Rtd); Commander S. N. Suthers RN; Commander Frank Bromilow; Commander P. B. Jackson RN (Rtd); Commander Barry Nation; Commander A. A. Fyfe RN (Rtd); Lieutenant Commander Cy Beattie RN; Lieutenant Commander P. M. Lamb DSC*, AFC, RN (Rtd); Lieutenant Commander M. Larcombe; Lieutenant Commander Rod Safe RN (Rtd);

Second Officer Heather Tuppen WRNS; Second Officer Sue Bradbury WRNS; Third Officer Fiona Williams WRNS (Yeovilton); Chief Wren S. D. Swain (Culdrose); Len Lovell, John Brooks and Gerry Shaw (FAA Museum); Martin Brodie (Rolls-Royce); John Baird and Ian Woodward (Westland); John Godden (British Aerospace); Mike Smith (Vickers); Michael Hill; Ken Reed; Derek Jones (Short Brothers); Derek James (Dowty); Ray Sturtivant; Robin Walker; David Warren; Mike Webber; Brian Johnstone; I. K. MacDonald; Paul Lewis MA.

To illustrate the book, a large number of photographs are used, many of which are British Crown Copyright and are credited to the unit and photographer wherever possible; others have come from the Fleet Air Arm Museum with kind permission of the curator, Graham Mottram and private collections. All photographs have been credited where possible. In addition, a number of line drawings were commissioned for the book from Ian Commin and several pieces of the late Bob Downey's work are used. Thanks also to Lynn Greenwood for the index, Patrick Allen and David Oliver for assistance with the photographs.

Paul Beaver
Old Basing, Hampshire, December 1986

From airships to air supremacy

In July 1984, as the idea for this book was being discussed between author and publisher, the Royal Navy celebrated seventy years of naval flying, for on 1 July 1914, the Royal Naval Air Service (RNAS) was founded. Naval aviation in the United Kingdom had actually begun some years before.

Initially the Admiralty, unlike their colleagues across Whitehall in the War Office, were not greatly enthusiastic about the new concept of aviation. Their Lordships even went so far as to write to the Wright brothers: 'they [aeroplanes] would not be of any practical use to the Naval Service'. This feeling took several years to amend with all initial interest being directed towards balloons and airships.

The 1909-1910 Naval Estimates were the first to include funding for aviation uses with money specially given over to the development of rigid airships and £35,000 went towards the Vickers-built No 1 Rigid Naval Airship or *Mayfly* as it became known. The same year, 1909, the Admiralty appointed an Inspecting Captain of Aircraft and by the spring of 1911 the first naval officers had been selected to fly aeroplanes.

The first aerial pioneers were destined to become famous names in the annals of the Fleet Air Arm and are considered to be amongst the ranks of the founding fathers of naval aviation. Under the auspices of the Royal Aero Club, Naval Lieutenants C. R. Samson, A. M. Longmore and R. Gregory, with Lieutenant E. L. Gerrard of the Royal Marines Light Infantry reported to Eastchurch on the Isle of Sheppey — an aerodrome which later became the primary base of the Royal Naval Air Service. Their aeroplanes were to be early Short biplanes, known as the Triple Twin (with three propellors) and the Tandem Twin (with two propellers); the latter being the first multi-engined aeroplane to be built in the United Kingdom.

In April 1912, the War Office formed its Royal Flying Corps (RFC) which in turn established a Naval Wing. At the Admiralty, there was now an Air Department and the Royal Navy had acquired sixteen of its own aeroplanes. The amount by which aviation was now being accepted within the Admiralty, just five years after that incredibly short-sighted letter to the Wright brothers, is further indicated by the fact that in 1913 aeroplanes joined the annual Fleet Manoeuvres. This paved the way for the formation of the RNAS on 1 July 1914, from the Naval Wing of the RFC, and this date is always taken as being the birth-date of naval flying, following which the first Royal Naval Air Stations and the Royal Naval Flying School were commissioned.

By the beginning of the First World War, the RNAS possessed eight air stations — Eastchurch, Isle of Grain, Felixstowe, Great Yarmouth, Killingholme, Dundee, Fort George and Calshot — plus two airship stations at Farnborough and Kingsnorth. The seaplane and landplane were in service,

Engineering training at Lee-on-solent naval air station during the First World War (RN/Daedalus).

31 and 40 of each respectively, and the RNAS had 128 officers, supported by 700 ratings.

The first major development of the war was the movement of the Eastchurch Wing to Belgium, under the command of Wing Commander Samson — this was not an air rank as such but demonstrated the small separation between naval aviators and naval officers in other branches of the Service. An eagle badge was worn on the left sleeve of the officers' jackets to signify their abilities as 'bird men'.

By now several famous manufacturers had delivered their aeroplanes to the RNAS, including Short, Maurice Farman, Bristol, Breguet, and the favoured type, the BE 2. Later other famous names such as Sopwith, Avro, Fairey and Supermarine joined the ranks.

For much of the early years of the war, the RNAS was employed as a land-based organization alongside their Army colleagues in the RFC. Although the first air-capable warship, *Hermes*, had been commissioned for the RNAS in 1913 it was not until later in the conflict that seaplanes regularly embarked aboard ship. The major exception to this was the famous Christmas raid on Cuxhaven which had gone down in the record books as the first truly naval air raid. Seaplanes from the RNAS were embarked in *Engadine*, *Riviera* and *Empress*, former Channel packets converted for the seaplane role. The target at Cuxhaven was the Zeppelin sheds and it was not until 1915 that the menace of these German rigid airships became clear; from then on the RNAS was engaged in the air defence of the United Kingdom. That year, Flight Sub-Lieutenant R. A. J. Warneford was awarded the Victoria Cross for his single-handed action against a Zeppelin.

With the sinking of the liner *Lusitania*, the RNAS was also engaged in anti-submarine patrols using mainly the Sea Scout non-rigid airships in the North Sea and English Channel. The war had also spread to the Mediterranean and the Dardanelles campaign had begun and it was here that the RNAS earned its second VC. Flight Lieutenant (later Vice Admiral) Richard Bell Davis, flying a Nieuport Scout landed behind the Turko-German lines and rescued one of his colleagues from certain death after the latter's machine, a Maurice Farman, had been shot down.

By 1916 informed naval thinkers, like Admiral Jellicoe, Commander-in-Chief of the Grand Fleet, were making the assumption that the only way that 'seaplanes' could be operated at sea satisfactorily was if they could take off directly from the deck, rather than being hoisted over the side to take-off in the water. This was the common practice with the existing seaplane carriers, like *Ark Royal*, *Campania*

and *Vindex*. The act of hoisting over usually meant that they had to stop dead in the water which was not recommended for fleet manoeuvring or in the suspected presence of German U-boats.

So the development of the aircraft carrier began. Lieutenant Samson had already successfully flown a Short Biplane off the fo'c'sle of *Africa* at Sheerness as early as 10 January 1912 but the RN's Gunnery Branch were not amused at the way in which the aeroplane's ramp incapacitated the forward turrets. Various other means of letting landplanes fly at sea were thought up, including the Porte lighter which was towed behind a speeding destroyer to allow a Sopwith Camel to be launched — recovery was a little more risky! The RN decided to convert the battlecruiser *Furious* with guns aft and a flying off ramp for'ard and in August 1917 the first trials were made by Squadron Commander E. H. Dunning. The launches were very successful. Recovery on the other hand meant the pilot flying around the funnel and being hauled down by those on deck using toggles under the wings and tail surfaces.

Sadly, Commander Dunning was killed repeating his successful experiments later that month but he did show the way for *Furious* to be convered into a sort of aircraft carrier with flat decks fore and aft, leaving just the problem of the smoke stack and masts in the centre. Besides the Camel, the Admiralty had acquired several Sopwith 1½ Strutters for shipborne work. After *Furious*' 1917-18 refit, she embarked Camels for the successful raid on the Zeppelin sheds at Tondern.

Despite continued successes at home and on the

Commander Dunning's first deck landing on 2 August 1917 in a Sopwith Pup Fighter (Fleet Air Arm Museum).

Western Front, there was continued political and military feeling that all the air services available to the country should be combined under a single authority. In the event, it was neither the Army nor the Navy, but a new, third service, named the Royal Air Force (RAF). The RNAS had, in March 1918, a little over 2,910 aircraft, 103 airships, 126 Royal Naval Air Stations and 55,000 officers and ratings — all these became part of the RAF, and even the squadron numbers changed, not to mention all the important naval traditions. The change over took place on All Fools' Day 1918!

For the next two decades, naval aviation was to suffer at the hands of masters who did not understand, nor apparently want to understand the needs of the Fleet in terms of air cover. It must also be said that there were numerous naval officers who also thought that aeroplanes belonged to trench warfare and had no place at sea.

For nearly twenty years after the end of the First World War, relations between Britain's Senior Service and the most junior service, the Royal Air Force, were to be dominated by the continued and often arduous debate about control of naval aviation and, after 1924, the Fleet Air Arm. The basic problems faced by the Royal Navy were the loss of experienced officers to the RAF and whether the new service would provide the air power necessary to defend the air above the country's sea power. This was a debate which raised its head again in the early and mid-1960s during the so-called 'carrier crisis' of the first Wilson government.

A major concern which immediately faced the Royal Navy was the terms of service for aviators in the Fleet Air Arm and later the equipment which they would fly. After any conflict, the hard-won peace is characterized by thoughts of disarmament and defence spending cuts. All three services were hit during the 1920s, and the Fleet Air Arm being a small part of the Royal Air Force was hit very hard. Morale was hit and a general feeling of malaise seems to have been prevalent.

In 1923, a House of Commons Committee was set up with the specific task of addressing the future of naval aviation, particularly in terms of command and control. The Royal Navy was especially keen on the control of naval aircraft being under local naval commanders and, even as a service, did not necessarily want to have any real responsibility for the design of aircraft and weapons systems.

In his Parliamentary Report of 1924, Lord Balfour made some far reaching recommendations which it appears went some way towards healing the rift between the RN and the RAF. The first major recommendation was that whilst the Fleet Air

Above *The Fairey Flycatcher (this is the amphibian) served as the standard Fleet fighter between 1923-34.*

Below *A deck scene aboard* Ark Royal *in 1938, with Osprey and Swordfish preparing for flying off as the carrier turns into the wind.*

Arm (as it was now to be called) would remain under Royal Air Force control, some seventy per cent of the officers (pilots and observers) would be naval officers. Secondly the Royal Navy would undertake a major part of the Fleet Air Arm's budget and so 'buy' itself more control at a policy level. Later that year amendments to the plan included the ability of the RN to request specific coverage and for the RAF to prepare the specifications of aircraft to meet those demands.

Instead of the Royal Navy seconding pilots to the Royal Air Force, a system of dual ranks would be evolved and, after some debate and high echelon political manoeuvring, seventy per cent of the pilots would anyway be naval officers by training. Naval ratings would be attached to the Fleet Air Arm and replace RAF groundcrews, but in fact it was not until the Second World War that the last RAF personnel left aircraft carriers. In the post-1945 era, RAF personnel again returned to aircraft carriers and, in her last years, *Ark Royal (IV)*'s air group had many RAF pilots and navigators flying Phantom and Buccaneer aircraft.

Until 1937, responsibility for the Fleet Air Arm was shared between the Royal Navy and the Royal Air Force, although it was not until then that naval ratings were considered suitable for pilot training. According to several sources there were chronic pilot shortages throughout the period. The bitter conflict between the RAF and RN over naval aviation continued throughout the inter-war years but it was not until 1935 that battle was again joined in earnest. The RAF saw a creeping naval take-over of its own aviation element and by December 1931, only eleven of the 26 flights at sea were commanded by RAF officers. In the meantime, the hardware side of naval aviation had been developing successfully under some forward thinking programmes.

In 1919, the Admiralty had suggested that four aircraft carriers should be commissioned, each with an air group drawn from 45 spotter, 22 reconnaissance and twelve torpedo-bomber aircraft; these aircraft would be two or three-seat types with a new profession, the Royal Naval aircrew observer, aboard. The first true aircraft carrier, *Argus*, had been commissioned and early deck landing trials were carried out by Commander Richard Bell Davies VC, a veteran of several campaigns during the First World War and considered by many to be a rising star of naval aviation.

In September 1922 Nieuport Nightjar aircraft, launched from *Argus*, were in action against Turkish nationalists threatening European interests in the Dardanelles. The carrier saw action again during the Second World War, including Malta convoy protection duties, before finally being decommissioned in 1946.

Like *Argus* (converted from the passenger liner *Conte Rosso*), the second aircraft carrier to be commissioned into the Royal Navy, *Eagle*, was a converted hull, modified with a flush deck and island superstructure on the starboard side. She had been laid down as the Chilean battleship *Almirante Cochrane* and was commissioned in 1923. Displacing 22,600 tons, *Eagle* was the only two-funnelled aircraft carrier in the Royal Navy until the commissioning of *Invincible* in 1980.

Under the terms of the 1921 Washington Naval Treaty, British aircraft carrier building programmes were limited to four 17,000 tonnes ships to be built between 1926 and 1935. Under the carrier building programme, which again suffered at the hands of the politicians, *Furious* would be converted to a full flush deck and two light battle-cruisers, *Glorious* and *Courageous*, would also be converted. In addition, the first British carrier to be designed as such from the waterline up, *Hermes*,

Above right *Furious served the Fleet Air Arm well, first as an operational carrier and later as a training ship.*

Below right *A famous naval aircraft of the inter-war period was the Fairey IIIF (Rolls-Royce).*

Below *The aircraft carrier* Argus *was the Royal Navy's first true flat-top (Fleet Air Arm Museum).*

completed in 1923, entered service in 1924.

Furious had been used for the early deck landing trials of Flight Commander Dunning but now appeared with a completely flush flight deck and two aircraft lifts to take aircraft from the flight deck to the hangar deck workshops below. During normal flying operations in the Royal Navy's aircraft carriers, it was still necessary to stow each returning aircraft below in order to give space for the next recovery. A later modification included a large metal fence which was raised when not flying to afford wind protection for those on deck. Two specially-built sponsons held the navigating bridge (starboard) and the flying control (port). The sponsons were at a level slightly below the flight deck and caused come interesting incidents when an aircraft went 'rogue' on deck. The ship's engines exhausted fumes away via special ducts just before the quarterdeck.

The Royal Navy was looking further ahead to larger, longer range aircraft which would be necessary for the Fleet Air Arm of the future. Nevertheless, *Courageous* (commissioned in 1925) and *Glorious* (1927) were designed to take the small but agile Fairey Flycatcher fleet fighter. These two near sister ships were fitted with a main flight deck running some 75 per cent of the ship's length, with a lower flying off deck on the hangar deck level below. Basically, Flycatchers operated from the latter and the larger, heavier torpedo, spotter and reconnaissance (TSR) aircraft used the top deck. Various systems of arrester gear were tried during the inter-war period and on these ships a series of fore and aft wires had been fitted. The landing aircraft was provided with hooks to catch the wires and bring it to a standstill, with the aid of deck

personnel. This was a very dangerous and operationally inefficient system which would take until the late 1930s to change into the modern arrester gear.

Naval aircraft of the period, including the Fairey IIIF (1928-36) for carrier, catapult, seaplane and shore-based spotter-reconnaissance duties and the later Blackburn Baffin (1934-37), were equipped with primitive radios and instruments, being prey to the RN/RAF arguments which often meant a complete lack of co-operation in the provision of adequate equipment. Ditching at sea, even in the relatively warm Mediterranean, was considered to be a major hazard to life.

The Mediterranean was the setting for a number of important naval exercises during the early 1930s, all designed to show how naval aircraft could influence the fortunes of a naval engagement. The Combined Fleet Exercises carried out in 1933 gave three Fleet Carriers a chance to demonstrate talents which had previously been ignored. The effect of naval air power by an enemy still took time to comprehend and the development of the torpedo bomber in the United Kingdom was not rapid enough to have anything more than a biplane available for the service against the latest monoplane fighters in 1939 when the Second World War broke out.

As aircraft improved, so the equipment aboard ship needed to be improved to cope with the new demands from the air side. *Furious* was fitted with a small island, containing the flying control position and various radio systems, including a direction finding system and primitive homing devices. By now aircraft were carrying a rating telegraphist/air gunner to communicate with the parent, other aircraft and other stations as required. A typical TSR crew complement was a pilot, observer and TAG.

Night flying operations had begun in earnest in 1927 when Squadron Leader T. B. Howe successfully landed a Blackburn Dart torpedo-bomber in *Furious* (although other sources credit Flight Lieutenant G. H. Boyce with the honour in the same ship, but earlier in 1926). No real landing lights were available but the deck could be floodlit and the 'affirmative' semaphore-type signal, used to regulate daytime operations, was illuminated.

Change in the wind

By October 1934, the Admiralty had decided to investigate the internal workings of the Fleet Air Arm and to begin political moves to wrest control of naval aviation from the air force. Admiral C. F. S. Danby was appointed to chair the investigative committee and it reported in April 1935. Amongst the Admiral's main points was the abandonment of the 'dual rank' system for naval aviators, with the Royal Navy taking full control as well as for the control of air stations ashore. The report said that RAF pilots should be specialist naval aviators with longer tours of duty in aircraft carriers or ashore, some being part of a special reserve of naval aviators equivalent to some thirty per cent of the regular aircrew force. To help with the critical pilot shortage, rating pilots should be introduced immediately, the Admiral concluded.

The government of Ramsay MacDonald was asked to give especial consideration to the development of rating pilots and the need for more commitment to naval aviation from Royal Air Force pilots. But no immediate decisions were made because of the fall of the so-called national government.

Whilst this debate was under way in 1935, the Royal Navy began to move in the right direction with the decision to order a new type of Fleet carrier of 22,000 tonnes from Cammell Laird's yard on Merseyside. The carrier was to be fitted with an flight deck armoured against most of the contemporary armour-piercing bombs and to have two

The fast two-seat biplane fighter, the Hawker Osprey, was operational from 1932 and retired in 1940.

hangars, giving an air group capacity of 72 aircraft. When completed in late 1938, *Ark Royal (III)* was equipped with two accelerators to launch aircraft too heavy for a free take-off, and the first functional hydraulic arrester wires, developed since the first trials in *Courageous* during 1931. In addition, aircraft could be moved from flight deck to hangar by three aircraft lifts and some aircraft could remain on deck, protected by a flight deck safety barrier. Three sister ships were cancelled, not through defence cuts, but to allow the monies to be spent on a larger, better class of aircraft carrier which were to become important, if not vital, assets in the naval battles of the Second World War, the 'Illustrious' Class.

By 1935, the Fleet Air Arm 'ownership' debate had reached a point where both sides were firm in their beliefs and the Royal Navy even believed that the Fleet Air Arm was the fourth arm of national defence, naval control of which was vital to the protection of trade on the high seas and to counter the growing threat of submarines. Winston Churchill enters the picture now as a champion of the naval cause which may have helped the decision by Stanley Baldwin, the newly installed Conservative premier, to reopen the matter in July 1936.

The Royal Navy's 1936 proposals were: the introduction of rating pilots; four-year tours of duty for RAF pilots; a 100 per cent FAA reserve guaranteed. For political reasons the proposals fell short of actual control of naval aviation, although that suddenly won the support of Mr Baldwin's Minister for Defence Co-ordination, Sir Thomas Inskip. Parliamentary feeling, and that echoed in the mass media, was in favour of naval control of its own

Glorious was one of the British aircraft carriers to be lost in the Second World War (Lt Cdr Richard Swift).

aviation, especially because it was being seen that the Air Ministry was not giving the Royal Navy the right types of aircraft with which to engage potential enemies — Germany was again building up its forces with modern monoplane fighters and bombers, as was expansionist Italy. In 1937, the change of ownership became inevitable.

It seems that a compromise decision was made by the Admiralty not to ask the Prime Minister to give control of shore-based (Coastal Command maritime patrol) aircraft and the supply system to the Royal Navy; Mr Baldwin (and later Neville Chamberlain) again appear to have listened to Winston Churchill's advice which sided with the Royal Navy. Much eventually hinged on whether the air group embarked in an aircraft carrier was part of the total ship's routine, or just passengers.

Sir Thomas Inskip, in the historical Inskip Award, concluded that the 'work of the Fleet Air Arm with its inevitable naval environment and having regard to the high degree of specialization in equipment' was better under naval control. Even with the Prime Minister's statement confirming that control of the Fleet Air Arm was to pass to the Royal Navy, there was much to do before naval aviation could effectively become naval again. One of the first needs was a Fifth Sea Lord (for aviation) and an aviation staff.

The Royal Air Force made over five air stations to become the first Royal Naval Air Stations — Donibristle, Eastleigh, Ford, Lee-on-Solent, Lympne and Worthy Down. In 1938 Gosport was

Above *Shore-based, carrier-based and even catapulted from naval capital ships, the Swordfish is one of the most famous naval aircraft of all time.*

Right *The first monoplane fighter in Fleet Air Arm service was the Blackburn Skua* (Rear Admiral Cambell).

added and during the next two years the list would expand considerably as naval aviation began to match the requirements dictated by war with Germany, Italy and later Japan. Personnel shortages were worse than those of shore-based facilities and they continued right into the Second World War. One solution was to attract volunteers from the rest of the Fleet but during the 1920s and 1930s the Fleet Air Arm's reputation was such that career-minded officers and senior ratings could only be attracted with some difficulty. Some RAF officers cross-trained to naval requirements transferred to the new Naval Air Branch (the term Fleet Air Arm not officially being used again until 1953). One solution was the establishment of the short-service aircrew-only commission — the 'A' branch whose officers wore the letter superimposed in the curl of the sleeve rank insignia.

By 1939, with war on the horizon, the Royal Navy possessed some 230 aircraft — only about a third of the inventory of both the United States and the other great maritime power, Japan. Naval aircraft had been in a design backwater for nearly twenty years, although certain interesting types were built — the Fairey Seafox light reconnaissance aircraft and the remarkable Swordfish from the same manufacturer. The latter aircraft became a legend in its own service life, replacing its replacement and being the only naval aircraft to operate with front line squadrons throughout the Second World War.

Second World War developments

The Fleet Air Arm had some 46 Squadrons when the Royal Navy formally took control on 24 May 1939. A naval building programme for the new 'Illustrious' Class fleet carriers was under

way and the development of naval monoplane fighters had begun. There were problems though; in his MA dissertation, Paul Lewis, a graduate student at King's College, London, concludes 'the two years between Inskip's recommendation and the outbreak of [the Second World] War, was an insufficient time to correct the two decades of mismanagement. The Fleet Air Arm entered the... War unprepared and as a result suffered much damage in the first few years of conflict.'

The 1933 reorganization had led to the formation of front line (800 series) and second line (700 series) squadrons which gave a structure on which the Fleet Air Arm built for its wartime and post-war organizational administration. With the new squadron numbers came a new breed of fleet fighters (assigned to 800-809 Squadrons) and some interesting TSR developments (810-825 Squadrons), but even as late as 1938, biplane naval fighters were still entering service. The last biplane fighter to enter the pre-war Fleet Air Arm was the Gloster Sea Gladiator which served with such distinction during the siege of Malta. The same year, the Blackburn Skua entered service as a dive-bomber and fighter, embarking in *Ark Royal* with 800 Squadron.

Fleet Carriers 1939-45

Name	Launched	Remarks
Ark Royal	April 1937	Lost after submarine attack, 1941
Argus	December 1917	Scrapped 1946
Courageous	February 1936	Lost after submarine attack, 1939

Indomitable, *one of the 'Illustrious' Class aircraft carriers* (RN).

Eagle	June 1918	Lost after submarine attack, 1942
Formidable	August 1939	Scrapped 1953
Furious	August 1916	Scrapped 1948
Glorious	April 1916	Lost after surface battle, 1940
Hermes	September 1919	Lost after air attack, 1942
Illustrious	April 1939	Scrapped 1956
Implacable	December 1942	Scrapped 1955
Indefatigable	December 1944	Scrapped 1956
Indomitable	March 1940	Scrapped 1955
Victorious	September 1939	Scrapped 1968

Significant naval aircraft 1918-39

Type	Service life	Max speed	Remarks
Cuckoo	1918-23	90 knots	First carrier TSR
Flycatcher	1923-34	115 knots	Carrier/catapult fighter
Nightjar	1920-24	104 knots	Early carrier fighter
Nimrod	1932-41	169 knots	Well-loved fighter
Osprey	1932-40	153 knots	Two-seat fighter
Ripon	1931-35	109 knots	Two-seat TSR
Seal	1933-38	119 knots	First with wheel brakes
Sea Gladiator	1939-40	213 knots	Last biplane fighter
Sea Fox	1937-43	108 knots	Catapult spotter
Skua	1938-41	195 knots	First monoplane fighter
IIIF	1928-40	104 knots	Highly successful

As the war intensified and the needs grew, the Royal Navy had to turn to the Royal Air Force for equipment, leading to the navalization of the Hurricane and Spitfire, called Sea Hurricane and Seafire respectively. Models of the Seafire remained in service until the 1950s, despite having a narrow-track undercarriage and certain weaknesses which would normally render an aircraft unfit for naval service.

Aircraft like the Sea Hurricane and Seafire were embarked in the first of the 'Illustrious' Class — *Illustrious* (launched 1939), *Formidable* (1939), *Victorious* (1939) and *Indomitable* (1940). These carriers displaced some 23,000 tons and were trend setters in their use of armoured decks and a range of anti-air gun defences. Detailed histories of these carriers, and their two near sisters, *Implacable* (1942) and *Indefatigable* (1944), are outside the scope of this chapter but specific data will be found on pages 197 to 200. Suffice to say here that the ships were to bear the brunt of the Malta convoys and British Pacific Fleet operations, all six continuing in service into the 1950s, with *Victorious* remaining in commission until 1967.

When hostilities commenced on 3 September 1939, the Royal Navy had carriers deployed with the East Indies, South Atlantic, Home and Mediterranean Fleets. It has often been said that the Fleet Air Arm was ill-prepared for the new war. Its aircraft were old-fashioned and only one aircraft

carrier, *Ark Royal (III)*, could be described as modern. According to the Fleet Air Arm booklet, *50 Years of Naval Flying,* published in 1964, naval aviators were to change the image: 'by their skill and devotion [they] finally convinced the world of the effectiveness of naval air power'.

Initially, aircraft carriers were used for anti-submarine task groups but the early loss of *Courageous* (17 September 1939) changed this policy. In the first few years of the conflict losses of aircraft, ships and men were high: *Glorious* (sunk 8 June 1940), *Ark Royal (III)* 14 November 1941, *Hermes* (9 April 1942) and *Eagle* (11 August 1942).

There were however some notable and extremely important victories for the British and the Fleet Air Arm in particular during this period. On 11 November 1940 there was the courageous attack on the Italian fleet in its heavily guarded base at Taranto when all but the most ardent and far-sighted people firmly believed that an enemy fleet could only be effectively attacked within range of (warship) guns. That November night, 22 slow biplane Swordfish flew 170 miles (274 km) from the then new aircraft carrier, *Illustrious*, and descended on the Italian battle fleet, causing more damage than the German High Seas Fleet suffered at Jutland in 1916. The action was so effective that it changed the course of the whole war in the Mediterranean.

Skuas, shore-based at the time, sank the German cruiser *Konigsburg* and in May 1941 was the *Bismarck* action in which Swordfish aircraft from *Ark Royal (III)* and *Victorious* were able to damage the German battleship and enable the Royal Navy's capital ships to move into range. During the famous 'Channel Dash' by *Scharnhorst, Gneisenau* and *Prinz*

A dramatic shot of Ark Royal *(III) sinking after being torpedoed by a German submarine in the Mediterranean* (RN).

Eugen, shore-based Swordfish were the only aircraft which were able to come into range for a torpedo attack — at a terrible cost to themselves.

From the very beginning of the war, it was evident that aircraft carriers would be needed to provide air cover for operations away from British or Allied soil. Other actions included the escort of the North Russian and Malta convoys and torpedo attacks against the German battleship *Tirpitz* in a Norwegian fjord. During the Desert Campaign in North Africa, naval fighters fought from aerodromes ashore, providing fighter cover to the troops and coastal convoys where the hard-pressed RAF could not cope. Fighters operating in this theatre included the Fairey Fulmar, one of the remarkable series of shipboard aircraft to come from that design house. The Fulmar was the first naval aircraft with eight machine guns and it could fly at 222 knots (412 km/h), powered by the famous Rolls-Royce Merlin engine. After its first flight in January 1940, some 250 Fulmar I and 350 Fulmar IIs were built, with several being converted to night fighters later in the war.

Fairey designed a replacement for the Swordfish in the shape of the Albacore, a biplane torpedo-bomber but featuring an enclosed cockpit for its crew of three rather than the open style of the earlier 'Stringbag'. The Albacore operated at sea aboard Fleet carriers and, later, based at Hal Far (Malta GC) in support of anti-shipping operating in the Mediterranean Sea. The aircraft was superceded by another Fairey model, the Barracuda (and in certain roles by the Swordfish) before D-Day. Design work on the high-wing Barracuda torpedo bomber began as far back as 1937, but the aircraft did not enter service with its first front line unit until January 1943 when 827 Squadron recommissioned with the aircraft. Barracudas took part in the *Tirpitz* raids of 1944 and served with the British Pacific Fleet until after VJ-Day. Later models of the aircraft were developed for post-war service and are described on pages 115 to 117.

Described by leading naval aviators of the day as the 'best naval aircraft of the Second World War', the Fairey Firefly first flew in December 1941 and entered service in March 1943, with some 850 of the Mk I variant alone being delivered from then until 1946. Variants included a night fighter, fighter reconnaissance and strike aircraft. Some Firefly F I aircraft remained in service after VJ-Day and the type was developed fully into anti-submarine and training variants.

With the rapid expansion of the Fleet Air Arm's aircraft and aircraft carrier forces came the expansion of personnel. The Royal Naval Volunteer Reserve (Air Branch) trained at *St Vincent*, Gosport, and its officers received the 'wavy navy' rank insignia with an 'A' in the curl. Both pilots and observers passed through the *St Vincent* courses every three months, before flying training in the UK, Canada or the United States. Rating telegraphist/air gunners were trained at Worthy Down, near Winchester.

The US training programme signalled the close liaison between the US and Great Britain which included aircraft and carrier programmes.

American involvement

The special relationship between the United Kingdom and the United States of America, particularly between the wartime leaders, made the development of naval aircraft in the Fleet Air Arm more rapid than would otherwise have been possible. Even before the US joined in the Second World war in December 1942, a lend-lease operation was under way, which brought about the transfer of aircraft to the UK.

The first type to benefit from the US Lend-Lease Act of 1941 was the Grumman Martlet (later called the Wildcat in common with the American nomenclature); the first aircraft arrived even before the act had become law and the little fighters were used extensively from Escort Carriers and from larger aircraft carriers. Malta Convoys and the invasion of Madagascar were venues for the Martlet/Wildcat operations.

The Wildcat was joined by the same manufacturer's Hellcat, a larger and developed version with the same overall appearance. Some 1,182 Hellcats were delivered to the Royal Navy after selection by the Aircraft Allocation Committee — it was to be called the Gannet in British service, but in the interests of Anglo-American co-operation the US name prevailed. A total of 74 Hellcats were converted to act as night fighters with an underwing radome carrying a simple airborne air interception radar, although the aircraft did not see action. Other Hellcats did however and were deployed to the British Pacific Fleet (BPF).

Another fighter exported to the UK, reportedly because it had proved too difficult and dangerous for the US Navy (although it was used in numbers by the US Marine Corps), was the Chance-Vought Corsair gull-winged fighter. Many of the aircraft served with the 1800-series RNVR air squadrons and some 1,977 aircraft were delivered from US production lines. In US service, the Corsair went on to fly during the Korean War but as soon as possible after VJ-Day the fighter was withdrawn from British squadrons with the BPF. Some aircraft were even dropped over the side of their parent carriers as, under the terms of the Anglo-American Lend-Lease Act, the aircraft had to be returned to the US

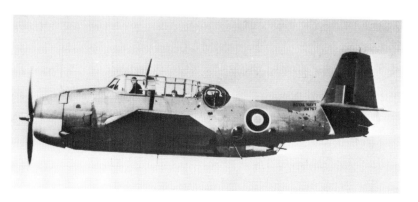

One of the major lend-lease aircraft, the Grumman Avenger I (RN).

or destroyed by the user, whichever was easier. Four marks of Corsair were flown by the Fleet Air Arm.

An outstanding American aircraft became fully operational in January 1944. The Grumman Avenger (originally called Tarpon by the British) was designed as a torpedo bomber, but proved equally efficient as an 'iron' bomber and reconnaissance aircraft. The aircraft was well loved by its aircrew and maintainers, but it could prove difficult to exit in an emergency. The aircraft achieved fame by being the first with British markings to attack the Japanese homeland islands and it continued in service until June 1946. Later, a developed model was acquired as an interim anti-submarine warfare aircraft, both with front line units and second line training squadrons.

From these American aircraft and the US-based training programmes, the Fleet Air Arm learned a great deal about new and modern techniques, so that by the end of the conflict, naval aviation in the United Kingdom was highly developed and well trained. The force which had entered the conflict so ill-prepared was now 70,000 strong with some 1,300 aircraft. More importantly, it had demonstrated in full the value of air power at sea and had caused such a revolution in naval tactics that the aircraft carrier had become the capital ship of the world's navies, taking over a role previously held by the battleship.

These new aircraft required aircraft carriers from which to operate and again the US government assisted the United Kingdom magnificently. Initially, though, the Royal Navy started to develop its own ways of getting aircraft to sea. First of the programmes was the Catapult-Aircraft Merchantship (CAM-Ship) equipped with a Hawker Hurricane or Fairey Fulmar aircraft and pilot who would take a one-way trip to, as modern fighter pilot jargon has it, 'hack the shad', destroy shadowing aircraft which could direct U-boats to the convoy in which the CAM-Ship was sailing. The idea was successful but wasteful.

In January 1941, the Admiralty ordered the conversion of the 6,000 tons *Hannover*, a captured blockade runner, and in June it was commissioned as the auxiliary aircraft carrier *Audacity*. The ship had been fitted with a small flight deck over its merchant-ship hull and a squadron of Martlets was embarked. The carrier was sunk on her third voyage but the idea had by then already proved to be highly successful and the US connection was brought into play again.

Sun Shipbuilding commenced work on a class of 8,200 to 9,000 tons 'mini' aircraft carriers of the 'Archer' Class; the small aircraft carriers were

One of the many Escort Carriers.

deployed to Russian convoy service as Escort Carriers. The design was good but the hulls were too small and the next three classes were built to 11,420 tons — 'Ruler', 'Attacker' and 'Arbiter' Classes. Some of these ships were developed into single aircraft type carriers for assault operations in the Mediterranean, carrying all Seafire or all Avenger air groups. Several of the ships served with the East Indies and British Pacific Fleets. After the war ended, the ships were immediately returned to the United States and reconverted into merchant ships.

Two other types of aircraft carrier were developed by the Admiralty planning staffs, including the merchant aircraft carriers (both grain ships and tankers) which retained merchant navy status but had a flight deck and a flight of Swordfish anti-submarine aircraft embarked. The second type was the British Escort Carrier, like *Campania*, which continued to serve after 1945 because it was not involved in lend-lease arrangements.

After the war, several US types found their way into the Fleet Air Arm inventory, including the Grumman Avenger AS 4 series and the Douglas Skyraider airborne early warning aircraft (see Chapter 3). Then, in 1969, the first McDonnell Douglas Phantom entered service as the last of the conventional fleet fighters. From the very beginnings of helicopters, however, the Royal Navy has been also completely reliant on US designed types, manufactured and developed under licence in the UK.

Post-war contraction

Despite the fact that the war in the Pacific, and to a certain extent campaigns in other theatres, had shown the world and the British Admiralty that the aircraft carrier was the capital ship of the post-war period, the Royal Navy was forced to cut its existing and planned aircraft carriers. Plans drawn up in 1942 for a new class of Fleet carriers were shelved and the Light Fleet building programme amended to allow for hulls to be diverted to Commonwealth and foreign navies. It is, of course, perfectly understandable that in the days of peace following such a conflict all thoughts of defence seem wasted but the halcyon days lasted only five years.

An immediate effect of peace was the return of the Escort Carriers to the United States along with many of the aircraft delivered under lend-lease; those aeroplanes not returned were destroyed by throwing them overboard in deep water. Existing aircraft carrier numbers were whittled down to three, with the rest in Reserve.

First jet carrier landing There was a small but concerted effort to continue development of important projects like the jet and the helicopter. Lieutenant Commander Eric Brown had succeeded in taking the Vampire single-engined fighter and the twin-jet Meteor to sea. The first of these world firsts was achieved on 3 December 1945 aboard *Ocean*, steaming off the Isle of Wight in the English Channel, and the second in the Solent on 8 June 1948 in *Implacable*.

First twin-engined carrier recovery In May 1944, Eric Brown brought a navalized Mosquito aboard the carrier *Indefatigable* for the world's first two-engined aircraft landing at sea. This programme was to lead the way for twin-engined aircraft to operate in long-range operations, particularly with the British Pacific Fleet.

It was obvious that jet aircraft would be needed at sea in the late 1940s and after, especially if the land-based air forces of the world were going to be equipped with aircraft of such potentially superior performance. Plans to acquire jets were formulated in the mid-war period and slowly came to fruition with the first front line jet, the Supermarine Attacker, which carried out shipborne trials a year after its first flight in 1946. Not completely successful, the Attacker showed the way for a whole series of naval jets from British designers — the Sea Hawk, Sea Venom, Scimitar, Sea Vixen and Buccaneer.

Rotary-winged aircraft Helicopter trials during the Second World War and immediately after suggested that the rotary-winged aircraft would be ideal for certain shipboard duties, such as anti-submarine warfare and communications, and ashore would provide liaison shore-to-ship as well as search and rescue, which has become the helicopter's non-operational forte. With a very few exceptions, the Fleet Air Arm has relied on the development of American designs manufactured and often developed by Westland. The relationship has provided some outstanding helicopters, but initially the helicopter was under-powered and quite dangerous.

The immediate post-war period saw major pro-

Below *The first twin-engined aircraft to land on an aircraft carrier was this navalized Mosquito in 1944* (RN).

Bottom *Lieutenant Commander Eric Brown brings the modified Vampire aboard* Ocean *in December 1945 to start the naval jet age.*

cedural problems for the Fleet Air Arm, trying to work closely with the US Navy, using British equipment and American-trained aircrew. One particular problem area was the fact that the RN and USN used different approach patterns and deck landing signals, causing confusion and death. The accident rate was extremely high — as much as 1 in 50 deck landings — during 1948-49. One experienced carrier aviator, Vice Admiral Sir Donald Gibson, said that the immediate post-war period was the most dangerous of his career which spanned from 1939-68: 'I can remember one morning when there were five barrier crashes. . . we were flying the most advanced propellor driven aeroplanes. . . and their large engines often obscured most of the forward view for a pilot approaching the deck. In order to protect aircraft parked for'ard, the steel barrier was erected and many accidents, not all fatal by any means, occurred. The answer to the barrier was found to be the angled flight deck, which is described on pages 228 to 230.

Ashore, the Fleet Air Arm contracted and restructured to meet the challenges of peace — a peace which was already being broken in the Dutch East Indies and Malaya, and was about to be broken in a major way in Korea.

Hoverfly I during shipboard trial (via Robin Walker).

UN operations in Korea

On 25 June 1950, the North (Communist) Koreans invaded the South (Republican) Koreans and so began a bloody and protracted campaign which still lingers on into the last quarter of the twentieth century. From July 1950 until after the 1953 ceasefire, the Fleet Air Arm maintained a carrier air group off the Korean coast in support of United Nations forces. The first carrier present was *Triumph* with Seafire FR 47 and Firefly aircraft embarked. The air group was not really up to the modern warfare methods and general conditions, but the ship assisted in the coverage of the Inchon landings and played an important part in the development of the support to be given by Light Fleet carriers. The efforts of *Triumph* are summed up in a signal to the ship from the Flag Officer Second-in-Command Far East Fleet: '*Triumph* has done very well and has kept going beyond belief'.

British carriers

In October 1950, *Triumph* was relieved by *Theseus*, another of the new Light Fleet carriers, built with the experience of early Second World War operations. This ship brought with her the new Hawker Sea Fury FB II and the Fairey Firefly AS 5, although no helicopter was yet available for plane guard duties, any downed aircrew having to wait

Fully bombed up, one of Glory's *Firefly AS 5s from 812 Squadron accelerates down the flight deck prior to firing the RATOG bottles just visible above the wing roots (Fleet Air Arm Museum).*

Sea Venom FAW 21 aircrew (pilots and observers) from 809 Squadron (Albion) *prepare for an early morning sortie during the Six Day campaign off Egypt, known as the Suez Crisis (via R.B. Wigg).*

for the faithful Sea Otter amphibian. During her first deployment off Korea, *Theseus'* aircraft flew some 384 sorties during one period of thirteen days, mainly in support of US and other UN ground forces.

To support *Theseus*, and after her *Ocean*, *Glory* and *Sydney*, the Royal Navy organized the deployment of the Maintenance Aircraft Carrier, *Unicorn*, to bring spare aircraft, engines and other parts from Singapore to Japan, where the carriers were withdrawn to rest, a voyage of about 2,500 miles (4,630 km). Even with the stresses of action, the flying operations from the Light Fleet Carriers with the Sea Fury/Firefly air groups were relatively accident free and included one two-month spell of 1,236 deck landings without incident.

Although the Korean operations, and to a certain extent the initial action against Communist guerillas fighting against the British in Malaya, were successful because of the use of propeller-driven aircraft, the advent of the jet naval aircraft could not be stopped. Korea again taught the effectiveness of the embarked naval aircraft against targets on land and, in the case of the Fleet Air Arm, some 12,000 miles (19,310 km) from the home base. Intervention in 'brush war' with naval aircraft had been proved.

Korean carrier operations

Name	Service period	Embarked squadrons
Triumph	June 1950 to October 1950	800 (Seafire) 827 (Firefly)
Theseus	October 1950 to April 1951	807 (Sea Fury) 810 (Firefly)
Glory	April 1951 to September 1951	804 (Sea Fury) 821 (Firefly)
Sydney	September 1951 to February 1952	805 (Sea Fury) 808 (Sea Fury) 817 (Firefly)
Glory	February 1952 to May 1952	804 (Sea Fury) 812 (Firefly)
Ocean	May 1952 to November 1952	802 (Sea Fury) 825 (Firefly)
Glory	November 1952 to May 1953	801 (Sea Fury) 821 (Firefly)
Ocean	May 1953 to November 1953	807 (Sea Fury) 810 (Firefly)

Notable achievements over Korea

Theseus' 17 Carrier Air Group flew 5,600.33 hours with 2,361 landings

Ocean's 802 Squadron destroyed a MiG-15 on 9 August 1952

Ocean's 17 Carrier Air Group flew 123 sorties in one day

Glory's Air Group flew 6,167 sorties in 87 days

Suez — 'Operation Musketeer'

Looked upon as a local war, 'Operation Musketeer', which ran for six days in November 1956, was the first conflict in which the Fleet Air Arm's jet aircraft and new Light Fleet Carriers had had an opportunity to show off their abilities. It gave an effective demonstration of the ability of the aircraft carrier to project air power and foreign policy — arguments which have been used for and against the aircraft carrier concept ever since. The 'police action' was taken against President Nasser's Egypt after his seizure of the Suez Canal and the inability of France and Great Britain (the builders) to gain a diplomatic solution. There is also evidence of a foreign policy alliance with Israel (an 'invasion' to keep Israel and Egypt apart) and none too

Left *Helicopters were used for commando assault for the first time at Suez, as seen here during the attack on Port Said* (Museum of Army Flying).

Right *Sea Venom fighters are launched from* Eagle *against Egyptian targets at Suez* (Fleet Air Arm Museum).

friendly motives of the United States to stop the Anglo-French action, while the USSR used the action as an international news cover to invade Hungary. In naval terms, it was a great success.

The Anglo-French carrier task groups were given three tasks: to neutralize Egyptian aircraft and airfields; to neutralize important ground targets; to support troop assaults. The Fleet Air Arm deployed Sea Hawk, Sea Venom, Skyraider and Wyvern fixed-wing aircraft, supported by naval Whirlwind helicopters with Joint Helicopter Unit (RAF/Army) Whirlwinds and Sycamores. The carriers engaged were *Albion*, *Bulwark* and *Eagle* for the strike force under Vice Admiral Power as Flag Officer Carrier Group, with *Ocean* and *Theseus* carrying the helicopters under Rear Admiral G. B. Sayer, as Flag Officer Helicopter Group.

Naval Air Squadrons engaged

Squadron	Aircraft type	Carrier
800	Sea Hawk FGA 6	*Albion*
802	Sea Hawk FB 3	*Albion*
804	Sea Hawk FGA 6	*Bulwark*
809	Sea Venom FAW 21	*Bulwark*
810	Sea Hawk FGA 6	*Bulwark*
830	Wyvern S 4	*Eagle*
845	Whirlwind HAR 3/HAS 22	*Theseus*
849A	Skyraider AEW 1	*Eagle*
849C	Skyraider AEW 1	*Albion*
892	Sea Venom FAW 21	*Eagle*
893	Sea Venom FAW 21	*Eagle*
895	Sea Hawk FB 3	*Bulwark*
897	Sea Hawk FGA 6	*Eagle*
899	Sea Hawk FGA 6	*Eagle*

812 Squadron with Gannet AS 1 (and some Gannet T 2 aircraft) was embarked in *Eagle* during the carrier's commission in the Mediterranean in 1956, but the aircraft were disembarked to Hal Far (Malta) during the Suez Crisis, presumably because no major anti-submarine threat was envisaged and the space aboard could be better used for strike and combat air patrol types. 893 Squadron, about to disband, absorbed aircraft from 890 Squadron after that unit had disbanded in June 1956, following a series of accidents. 897 Squadron exchanged its aircraft with 895 Squadron (Sea Hawk FB 3 for FGA 6) to achieve the right balance of fighter-bomber and fighter ground attack aircraft in *Albion* and *Eagle*.

A large number of Royal Air Force aircraft were also involved in the British contribution to the Anglo-French task force but they are not included in this account.

Operational calendar (1 to 6 November)

Day One At first light the aircraft carriers offshore launched raids on the Egyptian airfields at Cairo West, Cairo Almaza, Bilbeis, Dekheila, Gamil and Inchas. The airfields were destroyed with no losses to the Fleet Air Arm. Sea Venoms flew top cover but all Egyptian air cover had been eliminated in the first two strikes.

Day Two Ground targets around the canal, Port Said and Gamil were attacked, including the famous Gamil Bridge which was destroyed by rocket and cannon fire from Sea Hawk FB 3 and Wyvern S 4 aircraft. Tank concentrations were engaged.

Day Three More attacks on ground targets. First

Wyvern hit, but the pilot was rescued by helicopter from *Eagle*. *Albion* had been withdrawn to RAS (replenish at sea).

Day Four *Eagle* was withdrawn to RAS and strikes were continued by *Albion* and *Bulwark*, mainly against positions around Port Said.

Day Five An Anglo-French parachute assault was launched against Port Said and given a maximum effort naval air support.

Day Six The seaborne invasion force landed, many being transported by the Whirlwind helicopters of 845 Squadron, supported by Sea Hawk and Wyvern strikes, during which two Sea Hawks and the second Wyvern were shot down.

Some of the more interesting conclusions of 'Operation Musketeer' were that the Sea Hawk FGA 6 was a reliable operational aircraft and in the words of Lieutenant Commander P. M. Lamb DSC* AFC, the commanding officer of 810 Squadron, 'ideal for the peripheral skirmish in which we found ourselves'. 810 Squadron, part of *Bulwark*'s air group, was well worked-up and the carrier was able to mount a record number of strikes during the period, ninety per cent for ground attack with cannon and rocket projectiles, the remainder for combat air patrol; even squadron commanders flew as many as four sorties a day.

Commander Lamb's comments have been echoed by Lieutenant Commander (later Captain) Roy Eveleigh DSC who commanded 802 Squadron during the Operation. This unit was equipped with the Sea Hawk FB 3 embarked in *Albion*, although actually ear-marked for *Ark Royal*, having recently completed a work-up with *Bulwark*, the squadron 'at the peak of performance and ready for any-

thing!' 802 Squadron left most of the ground attack sorties to 800 Squadron and was tasked with air superiority: 'in the event we had little opportunity to try out the role,' says Captain Eveleigh, 'the Egyptians flew their MiGs with little verve and in spite of their undoubted advantage never mixed it with us if we looked aggressive in intent'.

The general feeling appears to have been that the carrier air groups' ability was fine in conditions of air superiority, a condition which the Fleet Air Arm had established largely through early interdiction. Carrier procedures were tested and worked well with most squadron COs being able to mount the sorties required because the maintainers were able to keep the aircraft on line.

Contemporary reports suggest three reasons for the spectacular success of the Fleet Air Arm; the long time over target because of the short carrier-to-target transmit time, excellent flight deck discipline and staggered operational cycles from three carriers mounting continued pressure.

Aircrew found that the ground defences became more accurate during the six days of conflict, prior to the United Nations ceasefire agreement. Losses to ground fire were two Wyverns (both of 830 Squadron from *Eagle*), two Sea Hawks (one pilot killed) and a Sea Venom. The Second World War 'cab rank' concept was again employed, using Sea Hawks waiting in an orbit to be called in on a strike for the ground troops.

The Wyvern was found to be vulnerable to ground fire, being relatively slow at 333 knots (616 km/h) as against the Sea Hawk's 485 knots (900 km/h). The first Wyvern from 830 Squadron was hit during a dive bombing attack on the Gamil

Westland Wyvern S 4s from 813 Squadron, shore-based at Ford. The late 1950s saw the demise of the propellor-driven strike aircraft from the the Fleet Air Arm's inventory (Westland).

Bridge which was protected by radar-controlled 37 mm guns of Soviet manufacture. The pilot was uninjured. The second pilot, the squadron's Senior Pilot, was also lucky after being hit during a low-level bombing attack on the Coastguard barracks but his engine did not stop and he managed to take the Wyvern out to sea before ejecting and was recovered in what the squadron commander, Lieutenant Commander C. V. Howard, has called 'a classic SAR recovery'.

Various statistics have been produced for the campaign, these include some figures from *Eagle* which show that the aircraft carrier's aircraft dropped 72 1,000 lb (454 kg) bombs and 157 500 lb (227 kg) iron bombs, fired 1,448 3 in rockets and some 88,000 rounds of 20 mm ammunition. 621 catapult launches were made on *Eagle*'s single serviceable catapult.

Despite the absence of enemy air activity, Anglo-French air forces were marked with yellow/black invasion stripes for ease of identification by air defence gunners. The official requirement was for two 12 in (305 mm) black stripes evenly spaced on a 5 ft (1.5 m) yellow band on the fuselage and mainplanes. The helicopters were not so marked as there was no risk of confusion.

Aircraft carriers 1954

Operational: *Eagle, Warrior* and *Glory*
Training: *Indefatigable, Implacable, Illustrious* and *Triumph*
Reserve: *Indomitable, Theseus, Ocean* and *Centaur*
Building: *Ark Royal, Albion, Bulwark* and *Hermes*
Long refit: *Victorious*
Suspended: *Leviathan*
Awaiting transfer: *Hercules (Vikrant)* and *Majestic (Melbourne)*

Aircraft carriers 1957

Operational: *Ark Royal, Eagle, Albion* and *Bulwark*
Training: *Ocean* and *Warrior*
Reserve: *Centaur, Triumph, Glory, Theseus* and *Magnificent*
Building: *Hermes*
Long refit: *Victorious*
Suspended: *Leviathan*
Awaiting transfer: *Hercules (Vikrant)*

'Operation Grapple'

In 1957 the United Kingdom carried out a number of atomic tests at Christmas Island and the support operation was called 'Grapple'. To act as the headquarters facility and floating airfield, *Warrior* was deployed from Portsmouth in February 1957. *Warrior*'s specially prepared air group included three Avenger AS 4 fixed-wing aircraft, converted for communications duties and supported by three Whirlwind HAR 5/7 helicopters for general support as the Ship's Flight.

Kuwait — commando carrier test

The US Rapid Deployment force idea is not new. After the military success of the Suez operation, the United Kingdom brought into being a Strategic Reserve Force which has been described as a 'Fire Brigade' force to intervene and prevent war. In 1961, this concept was tested by Kuwait, a country with which the UK had a successful defence agreement.

Within a day of the call for assistance by the ruler of Kuwait, threatened with Iraqi aggression, the Commando Carrier, *Bulwark*, with 848 Squadron's Whirlwind HAS 7s and 42 Commando Royal Marines embarked, was offshore. The troops were deployed by helicopters which were operating to the maximum of their performance envelope.

In the Indian Ocean, the Fleet Carrier *Victorious* was detoured from a Far East deployment to place her air group of Scimitar F 1 (803 Squadron), Sea Vixen FAW 1 (892 Squadron) and Gannet AEW 3

Victorious at sea, showing her plane guard Whirlwind off her port quarter during a Sea Hawk recovery (P.M. Lamb).

(849B Flight) at readiness for action. The prompt action of the Royal Navy and other British forces reduced the temperature of the political situation, with Kuwait and Iraq able to conclude an outline peace agreement.

This was another example of the ability of naval air power to keep the peace in a period of continued international tension and when the 'wind of change' was blowing throughout the British Commonwealth and other overseas territories of the European powers. It was a time when carrier air power showed its ability and it was a time when the whole question of British carrier air power was in debate.

It has often been said that whilst the Royal Navy congratulated itself on the excellent operational handling of such operations as Suez and Kuwait, there were elements in British politics which were totally opposed to the style of operation which the Royal Navy was capable of carrying out, particularly the ability of the Fleet Air Arm.

Events during the early and middle 1960s were to prove that the concept of organic air power did not suit every taste of political thinking and when the Labour Party returned to power in the United Kingdom, decisions were made which caused more than a ripple to pass through the Fleet Air Arm.

Post-colonial conflict

In the 1960s, the actions of the Fleet Air Arm received worldwide acclaim for the swift and efficient way in which aircraft were deployed from aircraft and commando (helicopter) carriers to such trouble spots as Kuwait (1961), Malaysia and Borneo (1962-66), the Beira Patrol (1965-66) and Aden. In fact, both commando and strike carriers were fully committed to training and operations.

Above *Early Commando helicopter operations flown by Whirlwinds; this is Borneo, 1964.*

Below *Royal Marines emplaning in Wessex helicopters of 845 Squadron during a major exercise on Masirah Island, Oman* (via Mike Webber).

By far the largest operation was the support of the Federation of Malay States, now Malaysia, where commando support helicopters transferred men and *matériel* from ship-to-shore and operated up-country to support British and Commonwealth forces fighting the insurgency of Indonesian forces. It was usual for either *Albion* or *Bulwark* to remain on station, although shore-based maintenance facilities were used for the Whirlwind and Wessex helicopters embarked.

It is usually possible to see where the action was in a certain year during this post-colonial withdrawal from the British Empire, by reading the list of Boyd Trophy winners. In 1963, 846 Squadron won the award for its support of operations in Borneo, which included nearly 4,000 operational sorties and the following year its sister squadron, 845, was awarded the trophy for a similar feat, measured as 10,000 operational flying hours. Much of this time was spent in supporting the Royal Marines, the navy's sea soldiers. The Royal Navy departed from Singapore and its East of Suez commitments on 31 October 1971.

Beira Patrol When (Southern) Rhodesia declared its own independence in 1965, the government of the day deployed the Fleet Air Arm to operate an embargo patrol in the Indian Ocean and Mozambique Channel to prevent contraband, particularly oil, reaching the illegal government.

Initially it was *Eagle* with her task group of escorts and Royal Fleet Auxiliary support which operated an air search by day and sometimes all night, using the Gannet AEW 3 and her Buccaneer, Scimitar and Sea Vixen air group to patrol the area. According to contemporary records, some 770 ships were tracked and identified during a 46 day tour of duty during which time some 1,000 operational sorties were flown. Each day the Gannets of 849D Flight were able to cover some 200,000 sq miles (518,000 sq km).

Aden Amongst the most delicate of areas from which the British withdrew in the post-colonial times was Aden and the name Radfan (the mountains within what was then the Federation) became a household name at the time. Initial support was given by *Centaur* and helicopters of 815 Squadron which put members of 45 Commando Group Royal Marines ashore in the Radfan to maintain the fragile peace. In 1967, *Albion* and *Eagle* were off Aden to cover the withdrawal of British Forces.

Carriers 1962

Fleet Carriers: *Ark Royal*
In refit: *Eagle* and *Victorious*
Light Fleet Carriers: *Centaur* and *Hermes*
Commando Carriers: *Albion* and *Bulwark*

Aircraft embarked 1962

Fleet Carriers: Scimitar, Sea Vixen, Gannet 3 and Wessex 1

Light Fleet Carriers: Scimitar, Sea Vixen, Gannet 3 and Wessex 1

Commando Carriers: Whirlwind and Wessex 5 (later *Albion* only)

Above Bulwark's *flight deck in 1979, during the carrier's second lease of life as a Commando Carrier* (Paul Beaver).

Below Hermes *at sea with a partial air group of Sea Vixen FAW 2, Gannet AEW 3 and Whirlwind HAR 9 embarked* (via Alan Kennedy).

By 1964, the Fleet Air Arm was fifty years old and at its post-Second World War peak. Its principal function was to provide air power in maritime areas which were out of effective or economic range of shore-based aircraft, either as an integral part of the Fleet or in collaboration with maritime aircraft of the UK RAF and other allied air forces — South East Asia Treaty Organization (SEATO), Central Treaty Organization (CENTO), North Atlantic Treaty Organization (NATO).

Besides the fixed-wing fighter and helicopter-borne anti-submarine warfare support to the Fleet, the Fleet Air Arm was tasked with Commando lift operations during commando assaults. Helicopters were then embarked in the converted Light Fleet Carriers *Albion* and *Bulwark*, backed up with close air support from the fixed-wing carriers such as *Eagle*, *Victorious* and *Ark Royal*. According to the 1964 booklet *50 Years of Naval Flying*, prepared by the Royal Navy public relations office, there were seven roles for the various types of naval aircraft to perform:

1 Attacks on ship and shore targets
2 Defence of surface forces and assault troops
3 Anti-submarine operations, including search, patrol and attack
4 Reconnaissance, including scouting, tracking,

photographic and radar reconnaissance
5 Land assault and support, including interdiction, close support, tactical reconnaissance and helicopter assault
6 Support of own air striking forces
7 Offensive strikes against enemy air forces

The front line aircraft were the Buccaneer S 1, Sea Vixen FAW 1, Scimitar F 1, Gannet AEW 3, Wessex HAS 1, Wasp HAS 1 and Whirlwind HAS 7. Fleet Air Arm aircraft were embarked in the aircraft carriers *Ark Royal, Eagle, Victorious, Hermes* and *Centaur,* supported by the Commando Carriers *Albion* and *Bulwark.* Great expectations were held for the forthcoming CVA-01. There were about twenty warships, destroyers and frigates, with helicopters embarked for anti-submarine warfare duties and the 'Tiger' Class cruisers were being readied for conversion into helicopter cruisers, carrying the Wessex and later the Sea King.

This was also the era of the Fleet Air Arm participation in the then-annual Farnborough Air Show.

Helicopter cruisers

As a result of the 'carrier crisis', it was realized that there would be a lack of aircraft-carrying warships available to embark the planned expansion of the ASW helicopter inventory. In the middle 1960s, the decision was made to convert three (later reduced to two) 'Tiger' Class cruisers to carry Wessex and possibly Sea King helicopters on a platform aft of the main superstructure, removing the after turrets. It was announced in the 1966 Defence White Paper that *Blake* would be taken in hand for a £5.5 million conversion at Portsmouth to be followed by *Tiger* in 1968. The latter required a half-life modernization as well which put the cost up to over £10 million. *Lion* was not converted.

The original air group consisted of four Wessex

HAS 1/3 helicopters but the Sea King HAS 1 was introduced in 1969/70. During the three years 1972-75 four Sea Kings from 826 Squadron in *Tiger* and from 820 Squadron in *Blake;* the latter upgraded its Sea Kings to Mk 2A standard in January 1977.

By 1980, the use of the cruisers had been overshadowed by the planned commissioning of light aircraft carriers of the 'Invincible' Class and the ships were paid off by 1981. So ended an interesting but short era of the Fleet Air Arm.

The 'carrier crisis'

Just 25 years after the power of carrier-borne aviation had been shown to the world at Taranto, the new Labour government in the United Kingdom took a series of major steps which almost completely destroyed the morale and the actual being of the Fleet Air Arm. The so-called 'carrier crisis' in the mid-1960s has had a profound influence on the Fleet Air Arm. Although the service has never forgotten the period, it is obvious that it did not take long to bounce back.

The 'carrier crisis' centred around the replacement of the British fixed-wing conventional strike aircraft carriers, all of which were in need of eventual replacement. By 1960, it had been established that the Royal Navy's peacetime and war roles and that of the aircraft carrier were heavily intertwined. Carriers performed the following roles:

1 Showing the Flag and influencing foreign governments
2 'Fire brigade' operations during 'brushfire war'
3 Provision of mobile air bases
4 Protection of sea routes
5 Part of the NATO striking fleet

By 1962, there were five fixed-wing strike carriers in commission, with two converted Light Fleets to act as helicopter-only commando carriers. The Royal Navy's replacement programme was centred

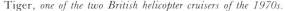

Tiger, one of the two British helicopter cruisers of the 1970s.

Right Eagle *in 1966 with Sea Vixen FAW 2 (899 Squadron), Gannet AEW 3 (849D Flight) and Wessex HAS 1 (820 Squadron) embarked. Note the ship's Seacat missile defences and 3-D radar (via Brian Johnstone).*

Below Hermes *operated as a joint Amphibious/Anti-Submarine Warfare Carrier in the late 1970s, prior to her refit for Sea Harrier operations.*

around the CVA-01 concept for a fast, modern and powerful aircraft carrier class which would replace *Ark Royal, Eagle, Hermes* and *Victorious*. It had been conceived as a project by the staff of Director Naval Air Warfare. There was a requirement for a minimum of three carriers of this type to maintain commitments and the programme had been endorsed by the outgoing Tory government.

The modern aircraft carrier is expensive and many observers now believe that the project was doomed from the start because of the rising feeling against intervention abroad, especially in the newly independent nations east of Suez and because, with the Polaris submarine programme under way, the funds were simply not available for two types of capital ship. The matter was further complicated by the VTOL (Vertical Take-Off and Landing) aircraft programme, centred around the Hawker P 1154 project. The Royal Navy was being offered

the aircraft on the back of an RAF contract when in fact most naval advisers felt that its development was too far behind the modern needs of the Fleet which would be better served by the McDonnell-Douglas F-4 Phantom fighter-bomber then entering service with the US Navy and Marine Corps.

In 1966, the British government decided to scrap the CVA-01 programme and other specialist programmes, indicating that within five years there would also be a withdrawal from East of Suez as an operational area, with the Royal Navy, and therefore the Fleet Air Arm, operating in support of NATO in the Eastern Atlantic.

The RAF had made a good case to the government that it could operate almost anywhere in the world with land-based aircraft and give cover to British forces and other interests, including the Royal Navy. The RN did not agree with that point of view, being proved right in 1982 when it is

certain that the successful operations in the South Atlantic could not have been undertaken without the support of shipborne aircraft.

The decision to cancel CVA-01 and therefore to complete the eventual phasing out of British conventional carrier aviation brought aboard a howl of protest. It cause a large number of Senior Service resignations and had a bad effect on morale.

The first aircraft carrier to go was *Victorious*, under refit in Portsmouth after a minor fire in a mess water heater. She was due to be replaced by the first CVA-01 in 1970-72, followed by *Ark Royal* (1974-76) and *Eagle* (1978-80). In addition, *Centaur* was planned to pay off and *Hermes* converted to replace *Albion* and *Bulwark* (later) in the helicopter-carrier commando role, with added anti-submarine warfare capability.

As a result of the 1966 decision, *Ark Royal* was to remain in service following a major modernization and refit to operate the F-4K Phantom fighter-bomber, whilst *Eagle* (reportedly in better condi-

tion) would be paid off in the early 1970s, leaving *Hermes* and possibly *Bulwark* to maintain the Royal Marines support role for the Northern and Southern Flanks of NATO.

The last aircraft carriers

The government's decision to phase out fixed-wing aircraft carriers led to a considerable dip in service morale, especially for the Fleet Air Arm. Many had hoped that the incoming Conservative government of 1970 would bring back the carrier concept but by then the foreign policy decision to concentrate on the Eastern Atlantic and European Central Region and the technology cuts of the previous administration had already taken the matter too far.

Eagle's last commission was in 1971, when she left Britain for a passage to Singapore via Cape Town for her final operational training cruise. That year, the Far East Fleet was disbanded and on 31 October 1971, the ship sailed from Singapore harbour on the day the naval base was handed over to local government. *Eagle* returned to Portsmouth harbour in 1972 and was paid off to await the breaker's yard at Devonport where most of her useable equipment was stripped away for use in *Ark Royal*, which still had another six years of service.

Ark Royal was the only aircraft carrier to be fitted for the Phantom and for over eight years the ship's air group of Phantom FG 1 (892 Squadron), Buccaneer S 2 (809), Gannet AEW 3 (849B Flight) and Sea King HAS 1/2 (824 Squadron) was the most powerful naval aviation force that the Fleet Air Arm had ever embarked in an aircraft carrier. During various naval exercises, the air group functioned well and was able to take on all-comers.

Somewhere in the Mediterranean Sea, on 27 November 1978, the last Phantom was launched from *Ark Royal* to return to RAF St Athan in South Wales, where its unit, 892 Squadron, would disband and transfer its aircraft to the Royal Air Force. Disbandment was also the fate of the Buccaneer and Gannet squadrons, but the Sea King has gone on to operate from a variety of ships. The Gannet's demise led to the end of airborne early warning for the Royal Navy, a fact which was pressed home hard in May 1982 when the guided missile destroyer *Sheffield* was sunk off the Falkland Islands by a sea skimming missile. The aircraft which launched the missile and the missile itself could well have been detected by an airborne early warning aircraft covering the task group, which in any case would have meant that *Sheffield* would not have been assigned to a radar picket role in a vulnerable position.

Between March 1971 and August 1973, *Hermes* was under dockyard hands for a conversion to com-

Below Eagle *leaves Singapore in 1971, the last British aircraft carrier to be stationed East of Suez* (Fleet Air Arm Museum).

Bottom *The last conventional fixed-wing fighter in the Fleet Air Arm was the McDonnell Douglas Phantom FG 1, seen here recovering aboard* Ark Royal. *Note the Acquisition Sidewinder installation* (RN/L.A. Pratt).

Right Ark Royal *in heavy Atlantic weather in 1977; note the Phantom (892 Squadron), Buccaneer (809 Squadron), Gannet AEW 3 (849B Flight) and Sea King HAS 2 (824 Squadron) ranged on the flight deck for flying operations* (RN).

Below Hermes *was the flagship for the Falkland Islands task force and is seen here returning to the United Kingdom with Sea Harrier FRS 1 (809 Squadron) and a mixture of Sea King types embarked* (RN/FPU).

mando carrier, which meant that her steam catapults and arrester gear were removed. In 1976-77, Hermes was taken in hand again, as a result of NATO pressure, for additional modernization to undertake an anti-submarine warfare role with both Wessex HU 5 and Sea King HAS 2 helicopters embarked. Later, 1979-81, the ship was modified for Sea Harrier operations and given a ski-jump ramp. It was in this configuration that she went to the South Atlantic in 1982, as flagship for Rear Admiral Sandy Woodward's task group.

The Falklands campaign

The Fleet Air Arm played an important and vital role in the Falklands campaign of April to July 1982, using the carriers Hermes and Invincible, as well as other warships making the following contributions:

1 Fleet air defence and beachhead air defence with the Sea Harrier FRS 1, carrying the Sidewinder missile
2 Fleet anti-submarine warfare protection with the

Above *One of the merchant ships taken from trade (STUFT) to assist the Falklands task force was the ill-fated* Atlantic Conveyor, *seen here with Sea Harrier FRS 1s aboard.*

Below *Flight deck scene aboard* Hermes *in the South Atlantic, with an electronic warfare Lynx in the centre.*

Wasp HAS 1, Lynx HAS 2, Wessex HAS 3 and Sea King HAS 5 helicopters
3 Stores and personnel lift with Sea King and Wessex helicopters

4 Anti-surface vessel warfare with the Lynx/Sea Skua and the Wasp/AS 12 combinations

During the conflict, the Fleet Air Arm lost some six Sea Harriers (although none in aerial combat), two Sea King HAS 5, three Sea King HC 4 (including one 'intentionally destroyed in Chile'), three Lynx HAS 2, one Wessex HAS 3 and eight Wessex HU 5 helicopters (two on South Georgia and six in *Atlantic Conveyor*). The successes of the remaining aircraft made that loss acceptable, although the sinking of the converted merchant ship *Atlantic Conveyor* meant that there was a shortage of logistical support helicopters and technical supplies. Nevertheless, the Fleet Air Arm and indeed the other services involved in 'Operation Corporate', the overall name for the Falklands campaign, served their country well.

The Sea Harrier proved to be the star of the campaign, effective in all its assigned roles, including aerial reconnaissance and combat air patrol. Because there were not enough Sea Harriers available, complete air superiority was not established over the beachhead and the task force, which meant that Argentine aircraft were allowed to penetrate to attack ships and land positions. Overall, however, the fighter support was adequate and accounted for 20 enemy aircraft, 16 destroyed by the use of the Sidewinder missile.

Airborne early warning As a direct result of the Falklands campaign, two Sea King HAS 2 airframes were taken in hand by Westland and converted to carry the Thorn EMI Electronics Searchwater radar, being embarked in the rapidly completed light aircraft carrier, *Illustrious*. This ship sailed south on 2 August and relieved *Invincible*. The helicopters were initially assigned to D Flight of 824 Squadron, before the reformed 849 Squadron came into being.

A future direction By 1986, the Royal Navy had commissioned three 'Invincible' Class light aircraft carriers and decommissioned *Hermes* which was sold to India as a Sea Harrier and Sea King carrier. The plan is now to keep two carriers at any one time, with the other in refit. *Invincible*'s first major refit and modernization was from 1986-87, to be followed by *Illustrious* and then *Ark Royal*. This way, the Fleet Air Arm is only tasked with providing two air groups of Sea Harrier and Sea King aircraft, allowing another potential air group to be formed from the training units ashore.

Right *The first two Sea King AEW 2 helicopters for the Fleet Air Arm, developed during the Falklands conflict but which did not see active service (RN/Culdrose).*

Below Illustrious *on her way home from Falklands duty in December 1982, seen arriving at Fort Lauderdale, Florida* (RN).

The Fleet Air Arm 1986

The following are official figures published by Flag Officer Naval Air Command:

Type	Number in service	Remarks			
Sea Harrier FRS 1	35		Lynx HAS 3/8	none	7 on order
Sea Harrier T4(N)	2	9 on order	Wasp HAS 1	36	
Sea Harrier T4	1		Gazelle HT 2	31	
Sea King AEW 2	10		Wessex HU 5	18	
Sea King HC 4	24	9 on order	Jetstream T2	16	
Sea King HAS 5	78	11 on order	Jetstream T3	1	3 on order
Lynx HAS 2	45 ⎫	18 being	Canberra	9	
	⎬	modernized,	Hunter	33	
Lynx HAS 3	33 ⎭	some for trials	Sea Devon/Sea Heron	8	
			Chipmunk T 10	16	
			BAe 125	2	

Command structure and organization

At the end of the Second World War, the Royal Navy was the largest in terms of manpower and equipment that it had ever been; on VJ-Day there were 72 front-line squadrons, many with the British Pacific Fleet in carrier air groups. Within a matter of a year, after the return or destruction of American-built lend-lease aircraft that number had halved.

In addition to the front-line units, there were several dozen second-line and specialist units, as well as 34 aircraft carriers in commission. The 1940s were a time to take stock and, so many believed, reduce the forces until only three aircraft carriers remained. Just five years after VJ-Day the Royal Navy, and particularly the Fleet Air Arm, was in combat again in Korea.

By the middle 1950s, the peacetime structure of the Fleet Air Arm was becoming established and the command organization in 1956 is described below.

Based in Whitehall, the air member on the Admiralty Board was the Fifth Sea Lord. He was responsible for the fighting effectiveness of the Fleet Air Arm, including operational tactics and technical policy, but not personnel, which came (as it still does) under the control of the Second Sea Lord. Reporting to the Fifth Sea Lord was the Director of Naval Air Warfare (DNAW) and the Director Naval Air Organization and Training, the latter also having a reporting responsibility to the Second Sea Lord.

Within the Admiralty, the supply, procurement and maintenance of naval aircraft came under the Director Air Equipment and the Director Aircraft Maintenance and Repair, but they reported to the Controller of the Navy, the Third Sea Lord. There was also a Captain RN on the staff of the Ministry of Supply to act as Deputy Controller of Aircraft, responsible for meeting the naval staff requirements for aircraft and equipment.

The implementation of the policy laid down by the Admiralty Board was the responsibility of the Flag Officer Air (Home), for all United Kingdom (and certain other locations), and Flag Officer Aircraft Carriers (FOAC), for the Fleet Air Arm afloat, reporting to Commander-in-Chief Home Fleet in respect of the operational effectiveness of task groups. Carriers operating East of Suez were nominally the responsibility of Commander-in-Chief Far East, a 'four star' appointment (but not necessarily Royal Navy). Operationally, he dele-

'Father' of the modern Fleet Air Arm, the late Admiral Sir Casper John (centre), at the opening of the Fleet Air Arm Museum, Yeovilton, Somerset (RN).

gated to Flag Officer Far East Fleet (FOFEF) and Flag Officer Second-in-Command Far East Fleet (FO2FEF). The Commander-in-Chief Mediterranean Fleet, until the post lapsed, also had an operational control over aircraft carrier groups.

A generalized command structure was:

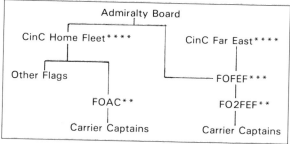

The appointment of FAOC was first announced in October 1954, taking the responsibilities of Flag Officer Heavy Squadron (1952-54), which in turn had replaced Flag Officer Third Aircraft Carrier Squadron (1948-52). FOAC continued until the beginning of the demise of the conventional fixed-wing aircraft carrier in the Royal Navy and it lapsed in June 1968.

The Home Air Command was tasked with providing the aircraft carriers and other air capable ships with trained personnel and equipment capable of fulfilling the operational role. The headquarters was at Lee-on-Solent.

To provide the training facilities, two further Flag Officers reported to FOA(H) for flying training, Flag Officer Flying Training (FOFT) and Flag Officer Reserve Aircraft (FORA); in addition, ground training was the responsibility of a staff officer (a Captain RN) on the staff of FOA(H). In 1957, there were six Fleet Air Arm establishments concerned with flying training, three with ground training and six with maintenance.

The six naval air stations under the control of FOFT were Yeovilton (his headquarters), Culdrose (observer training), Lossiemouth (fighter training), Eglinton (anti-submarine training), Ford (carrier trials) and Brawdy (fighter and fighter ground attack).

FORA was in charge of the supply of aircraft to the units, with a headquarters at Arbroath; in addition, there were three aircraft repair yards, at Fleetlands, Donibristle and Belfast, three aircraft holding stations, at Abbotsinch, Anthorn and Stretton, whilst two naval air stations, Lossiemouth and Lee-on-Solent, had aircraft holding sections. These stations were responsible for the delivery, repair, overhaul and modernization of naval aircraft.

With the lapse of the Fifth Sea Lord appointment, the Fleet Air Arm was assured of direct access to the Admiralty Board through the Assistant Chief of Naval Staff (Operations and Air), but by 1984 the most senior naval aviator in the Ministry of Defence (successor to the Admiralty from 1965) was Director Naval Air Warfare not even Flag Officer Naval Air Command (FONAC) was necessarily an aviator.

Command at sea

Although there had been a Flag Officer designated to command the aircraft carrier forces of the Royal Navy during the First World War, the appointment lapsed in 1919. In September 1931, with the resurgence of carrier aviation, the post of Rear Admiral Aircraft Carriers was established and this continued until 1940, when the Aircraft Carrier Squadron was transferred to the Mediterranean Fleet, and again to the Eastern Fleet in 1943, returning to the Mediterranean command structure in 1944, until the formation of another aircraft carrier squadron in 1948.

Flag Officer Third Aircraft Carrier Squadron was a post for Rear Admirals established in July 1948 and which functioned afloat until January 1951. In January 1952, the Admiralty Board created the post of Flag Officer Heavy Squadron to control the aircraft carrier element of the Home Fleet, this post becoming Flag Officer Aircraft Carriers in October 1954. The period until June 1968, when the post was changed to that of Flag Officer Carriers and Amphibious Ships (FOCAS), marks the heyday of British carrier aviation, but with the demise of the conventional fixed-wing aircraft carrier, it was an obvious move to include the converted commando carriers as 'amphibious ships'.

For the next ten years, until the establishment of Flag Officer Third Flotilla's (FOF3's) post on 1 January 1979, the complexion of the aircraft and commando carrier forces changed considerably with the demise of *Eagle*, conversion of *Hermes* and eventually the decommissioning of the last British conventional aircraft carrier, *Ark Royal*.

The post of FOF3 is responsible for the Royal Navy's major surface ships, including the 'Invincible' Class aircraft carriers, as well as for the aviation element at sea in all ships of the Fleet. In addition, FOF3 has a NATO hat as Commander Anti-Submarine Warfare Group 2, in direct support of the NATO Striking Fleet Atlantic. FOF3 is the Fleet Aviation Authority.

Left Eagle, *the only twin-funnelled aircraft carrier until* Invincible *commissioned in 1980* (Harry Liddle).

Right *Fairey Firefly AS 5s during 'summer camp' for the RNVR Air Branch's Channel Air Division in the carrier* Triumph *during June 1952* (Eric Bond).

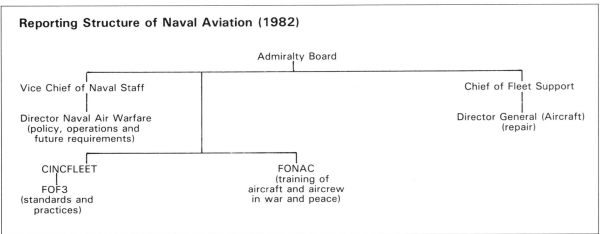

Reporting Structure of Naval Aviation (1982)

Admiralty Board

Vice Chief of Naval Staff

Director Naval Air Warfare
(policy, operations and
future requirements)

Chief of Fleet Support

Director General (Aircraft)
(repair)

CINCFLEET

FOF3
(standards and
practices)

FONAC
(training of
aircraft and aircrew
in war and peace)

Flag Officers Aircraft Carriers

Rear Admiral W. T. Couchman	October 1954-December 1954
Rear Admiral A. R. Pedder	December 1954-May 1956
Vice Admiral M. L. Power	May 1956-January 1958
Vice Admiral Bingley	January 1958-January 1959
Rear Admiral C. L. G. Evans	January 1959-March 1960
Rear Admiral R. M. Smeeton	March 1960-January 1962
Rear Admiral F. H. E. Hopkins	January 1962-January 1963
Rear Admiral D. C. E. F. Gibson	January 1963-April 1964
Rear Admiral H. R. B. Janvrin	April 1964-February 1966
Rear Admiral W. D. O'Brien	February 1966-April 1967
Rear Admiral L. D. Empson	April 1967-June 1968
Rear Admiral M. F. Fell	June 1968-September 1968

Flag Officers Carriers & Amphibious Ships

Rear Admiral M. F. Fell	September 1968-July 1970
Rear Admiral J. D. Treacher	July 1970-May 1972
Rear Admiral R. D. Lygo	May 1972-February 1974
Rear Admiral A. D. Cassidi	February 1974-May 1975
Rear Admiral J. H. F. Eberle	May 1975-March 1977
Rear Admiral W. D. M. Staveley	March 1977-July 1978
Rear Admiral P. G. M. Herbert	July 1978-December 1978

Right *One of the RNVR Sea Hawk F 2 fighters based at Benson in September 1955; note the Sea Furies in the background* (Brain M. Service).

The Royal Naval Volunteer Reserve

From 1938, when an air branch of the Royal Naval Volunteer Reserve (RNVR) was formed with 33 aircrew who were trained at weekends and during annual training camps, until 1945, there was a steady growth in numbers. During the two-week continuous training sessions, the squadrons would move to new environments, including that of an aircraft carrier in the Fleet Carriers, *Implacable* and *Illustrious.*

During the last war years, coincidental with the establishment of American-equipped squadrons in the United States, the number of RNVR(A) pilots and observers had grown to 94 per cent of the total aircrew officer complement. At the same time, there were a large number of hostilities-only telegraphist/air gunners in the Fleet Air Arm.

During the Korean War, some forty Royal New Zealand Naval Volunteer Reserve aircrew flew with the Fleet Air Arm squadrons with the United Nations forces and later a number of Australian volunteers were in the complement of *Sydney* during her spell of duty.

With the cessation of hostilities, it was obvious that not all the RNVR personnel would be required but in 1947 the decision was made to reinstate the RNVR for anti-submarine warfare and fighter duties. The re-formation was linked to the use of wartime-trained aircrew and in June 1947 1831 Squadron, based at Stretton, received a Harvard T 3 and a mixed batch of Seafire F 15 and F 17 fighters.

The unit to form in August 1947 was 1830

Avenger AS 5 aircraft of 1844 Squadron RNVR based at Bramcote (Fleet Air Arm Museum).

Squadron, which had flown Corsair II fighters with the British Pacific Fleet and it re-formed at Abbotsinch. The new aircraft were a mixture of Seafire F XVII and Firefly FR 1, with later mounts including several more Firefly marks, the Sea Fury T 20 and the Avenger. 1832 Squadron was re-formed on 1 July 1947 at Culham, with aircrew from the Home Counties and London. Its fighter role was supported by Seafires, including the FR 46 but later, from 1952, it flew the Sea Fury FB 11, some 27 being on strength in 1955.

In 1951, the need for greater numbers of anti-

Firefly AS 5s of the Channel Air Division over Malta during an Annual Camp in 1954.

submarine aircraft and aircrews led to the formation of five new RNVR squadrons with Firefly and later Gannet aircraft. In addition, two fighter units were raised, giving a total of eleven squadrons in commission, seven of which took part in the Queen's Coronation Naval Review flypast in 1953.

RNVR Air Divisions

A reorganization of the RNVR Air Branch took place in 1952 and this led to the creation of RNVR Divisions:

Channel Air Division Based at Ford, with 1840 and 1842 Squadrons, both of which flew the Firefly and later the Gannet AS 1; pooled for administrative reasons.

Midland Air Division Based at Bramcote, this division, formed in July 1953, was host to 1833 Squadron (Seafire FR 47 and Sea Fury FB 11), operating from grass. The anti-submarine warfare role was undertaken by 1844 Squadron (Fireflies and Avengers). When the Attacker FB 2 replaced the Sea Fury with 1833, the unit moved to the concrete runways of RAF Honiley as a lodger.

Northern Air Division 1831 Squadron (Sea Fury FB 11, later being equipped with the Attacker FB 2) and 1841 Squadron (Firefly FR 1, later AS 6 and eventually with the Avenger AS 5). This division was also famous for its aerobatic display team, also based at Stretton.

Scottish Air Division 1830 and 1843 Squadrons, at Abbotsinch, shared Firefly AS 6 aircraft, later being equipped with the Avenger for anti-submarine warfare duties. Other aircraft such as the Sea Balliol T 21 and Sea Prince T 1 were on strength with 1830 Squadron during 1953-57.

Southern Air Division Based at Culham, 1832, 1834, 1835 and 1836 Squadrons (Sea Fury FB 11); the latter two were formed in October 1952, moving with 1832 Squadron to RAF Benson in July 1953. 1834 Squadron operated the Sea Fury throughout its short re-formation, moving to Yeovilton for a short while before disbanding in April 1955, about two years prior to the rest of the RNVR Air Branch.

There can be little doubt that the Royal Naval Volunteer Reserve Air Branch was efficient and well-trained, and consistently scored marks equal to front-line regular units during practice camps, which were held at such locations as Hal Far (Malta) and the near European continent. The aircrew and the supporting groundcrew would train twice a month for a long weekend, with additional commitments to exercises and voluntary attendance dependent on the availability of aircraft and train-

ing commitments.

In March 1957 came a major blow. The infamous Defence White Paper of that year brought about the immediate disbandment of the Air Branch and its Air Divisions and squadrons. Part of the decision was linked to cost-cutting to pay for new and costly high technology projects like guided missiles and part was the need to convert anti-submarine warfare squadrons to helicopters, rather than using fixed-wing aircraft. Training requirements for that demanding task were thought to be higher than for fixed-wing.

Royal Naval Reserve

By 1980, the RNVR had also disappeared, being replaced by an all-embracing Royal Naval Reserve which has been able to provide continuation training for Fleet Air Arm pilots who have left the Royal Navy for aviation related jobs in industry. Temporarily, one or two squadrons were formed to host these pilots and observers, but since 1982, aircrew have been trained with front-line units.

Fleet Air Arm afloat

Despite continued pressure on defence spending in the United Kingdom since 1945 with the immediate decline until the Korean War, the temporary upswing when the Soviet government's expansionist foreign policies saw a development of the Russian Navy from a coastal defence force to a powerful tool of policy and the decline which followed the 'carrier crisis', the Fleet Air Arm has continually proved the importance of its position in the present and future defence strategy. Since the decommissioning of *Ark Royal (IV)* in 1978, it has continued to play a vital and increasingly successful role in the defence of the United Kingdom and the

Today's Royal Naval Reserve air branch flies helicopters such as the Sea King HAS 5 with front line units like 810 Squadron (RN/Culdrose).

North Atlantic Alliance. Central to this role is the part played by embarked aviation during the 1982 Falklands campaign, which has greatly contributed to the current well-being of the Fleet Air Arm.

Small ships' flights

The Royal Navy has been the leader in this field of

The use of light helicopters at sea revolutionized anti-submarine warfare, starting with the Westland Wasp and the 'Leander' Class frigate (Brian M. Service).

maritime aviation and the first trials were conducted in the late 1940s, resulting in the first frigate detachments being embarked in 1964-65 flying the Westland Wasp HAS 1 — known then as the MATCH (Medium range Anti-submarine Torpedo Carrying Helicopter). This form of naval aviation was developed in the 'Tribal', 'Rothesay' and 'Leander' Classes of frigate and eventually led to the development of the Lynx helicopter for both anti-submarine and anti-shipping operating. From March 1964 until September 1986, 829 Squadron solely parented the Wasp flights of the Fleet Air Arm, adding survey ships, Royal Fleet Auxiliaries and the Ice Patrol Ship *Endurance* to the list of Wasp users.

In 1964, 829 Squadron began an association with the Wessex HAS 1 and the 'County' Class guided missile destroyers which lasted until 1970, when the eight destroyer flights were parented by 737 Squadron at Portland. The first of the 'Counties' was *Devonshire*, commissioned in 1962 with a helicopter to carry the anti-submarine battle away from the ship and to act as an autonomous hunter-killer air vehicle. The Wessex had entered service in November 1961 for aircraft carrier use and the embarkation of the type in the DLG (Destroyer Large Guided Missile) was very much an after-thought and the hangar accommodation was cramped. The Wessex HAS 3 — known affectionately as the Camel — replaced the HAS 1 from 1969. 737 Squadron adopted a joint role of DLG Flight parent and the training of ASW pilots, observers and aircrewmen until December 1982 when the last of the Wessex HAS 3 was phased out of service; the remaining 'Counties' embarked either the Wessex HU 5 or Lynx HAS 2/3 until paid off in 1987.

By the time that 829 Squadron recommissioned with a mixture of Lynx HAS 2/3 and Wasp HAS 1,

there were only sixteen flights of the latter remaining but at one time, with all the 'Leanders' and 'Rothesays' equipped with the helicopter, fifty flights had been established. Wasp training were carried out by 703 Squadron from 1972 to 1980 but as the Lynx entered service this duty was transferred to 829 Squadron.

The Lynx HAS 2/3 has a significantly improved anti-shipping role, armed with the British Aerospace Sea Skua missile, as compared to the Wasp with the AS 12 wire-guided missile; Lynx is also capable of carrying the more traditional anti-submarine weapons like the Mk 44, Mk 46 and Stingray lightweight torpedoes or Mk II depth bombs.

In March 1986, the Type 22 frigates started to be complemented with two Lynx helicopters which has increased the flight's personnel level from an average of eight to eleven maintainers and two complete aircrews of pilots and observers. As before, the Flight Commander can be either a pilot or observer, although the latter is becoming more common, as the role is more tactical than 'straight' pilotage. A Wasp flight has usually no more than a pilot, an aircrewman and seven maintainers.

Antarctic air arm

In February 1955, the Admiralty Board announced that *Protector* would be brought out of reserve and converted for duties as the Falkland Islands guard-ship, carrying two Whirlwind HAR 3 helicopters. The ship commissioned in September that year, two months after the flight had been formed at Gosport. The helicopters to be embarked were to be the first off the Westland production line, modified to carry HF (high frequency) radio, a simple radio homing aid, a cabin heater and a windscreen de-icing system designed by the Royal Naval Air Yard at

Fleetlands. Production problems at Yeovil eventually necessitated the adoption of the Whirlwind HAR 1 (with the Pratt & Whitney Wasp engine) for the flight rather than the Wright Cyclone-powered HAR 3.

Besides search and rescue, the helicopters were assigned to survey support and trooping duties; the latter with the Royal Marines of the Falklands garrison. For a while, the Flight operated as a detached unit of 701 Squadron, being formed and disbanded to correspond to the Antarctic calendar.

In 1966, the Whirlwind HAR 9 was introduced and two years later *Protector* was paid off and the Flight embarked in the newly converted Ice Patrol Ship, *Endurance*. When ashore, the HAR 9 helicopters operated from Lee-on-Solent, often in support of the Lee SAR Flight. In 1976, the Whirlwind was superseded by the Wasp HAS 1.

Endurance Flight was prominent in 'Operation Paraquat', the recapture of the South Georgia dependency in April and May 1982, when the ship's two Wasps engaged, with other helicopters, the Argentine submarine, *Santa Fé*. The helicopters, usually unarmed for the Antarctic role, were equipped with the Nord/Aerospatiale AS 12 wire-guided missile and this action is said to be the first operational use of a guided missile by a Royal Navy helicopter. The action resulted in the scuttling of the submarine and led directly to the liberation of South Georgia by British forces.

In 1986, *Endurance* was taken in hand for con-

Until 1986, the ice patrol ship Endurance *carried Wasp helicopters and the ship's flight, armed, took part in Operation Paraquat, the recapture of South Georgia* (RN/FPU).

Hecla's Wasp with red cross markings during the Falklands conflict.

version to re-equip the ship for the embarkation of Westland Lynx HAS 2/3 helicopters and the Flight will remain in being until *Endurance* decommissions in the mid-1990s.

Survey Ships

Initially the Hydrographic Survey Ship, *Vidal*, was the only one of seven ocean-going craft to be equipped to operate a helicopter, the Whirlwind

Dragonfly SAR provided by Theseus' *ship's flight.*

which was parented by 701 Squadron until 1958. In the mid-1960s, a new class of three (later an improved ship was added) Ocean Survey Ships of the 'Hecla' Class was commissioned in response to the needs of the nuclear-powered ballistic missile submarines then entering service. These ships of 2,733 tons were only capable of carrying a light helicopter and so when available the Wasp was allocated for their use.

During the Falklands conflict, some of the ships and their respective helicopters were used for ambulance duties and carried casualties to Uruguay. In the mid-1980s, with defence spending curbs, some of these ships were phased out and their helicopter flights disbanded.

SAR and ships' flights

During the Korean War it was seen that helicopters were perfect for search and rescue tasks associated with flying operations from carriers. In the past it had been the practice to station a destroyer on the port quarter for 'plane guard' duties, especially during night flying. The US Navy lent the Fleet Air Arm a number of Sikorsky S-51 Dragonfly helicopters and these soon replaced the embarked Sea Otter amphibious aircraft.

With the licence production of the Dragonfly HR 1, 3 and 5 helicopter for the Royal Navy by Westland, each carrier and naval air station was equipped with a rescue helicopter flight from about 1956. For daylight flying operations, the Dragonfly replaced the destroyer on 'plane guard' but the helicopter's performance was limited at night.

By 1958, the Dragonfly was beginning to be replaced by the various marks of Whirlwind — HAR 1, HAR 3 and HAS 7. Again naval air stations and aircraft carriers were complemented for the helicopter with administrative control being exercised by 701 Squadron (until September 1958) and the various ships (including air stations) themselves. In 1966, the piston-engined Whirlwinds were replaced by the HAR 9 which had been specially designed for search and rescue duties, but this single-engined helicopter was replaced by the more reliable Wessex HU 5 from 1977. In 1987, the Wessex HU 5 still operates a 24-hour SAR stand-by at Culdrose (771 Squadron) as well as Lee-on-Solent and Portland (772 Squadron).

Aboard aircraft carriers, with space at a premium, the specialist ships' helicopter flight was only embarked in *Eagle* and *Ark Royal* from 1970, with the last flight in *Ark Royal* being disbanded in 1978. The Commando Carriers and the later 'Invincible' Class CVSs were not complemented for such specialist helicopters when they entered

Right *Until 1978, the Wessex HAS 1 has remained in service as* Ark Royal's *plane guard helicopter, the last of a thirty-year line of ship's flight SAR machines* (RN).

Below *A full strength Sea Vixen FAW 1 squadron — 890 at Yeovilton — in September 1961; aircrew and engineering officers in the foreground, then the technical senior rates in the mid-ground with the junior ratings at the back* (Commander Derek Monsell).

service, using instead the embarked operational squadrons to provide SAR cover for the ship, task group and *ad hoc* humanitarian duties. Occasionally, Wessex HU 5 helicopters are embarked in CVSs for temporary duties.

Typical squadron organization

The basic unit of the Fleet Air Arm is the squadron, based ashore when disembarked and parented by an aircraft carrier or other ship when embarked.

Histories of the front line air squadrons can be found in Chapter 5.

The squadron can be organized into flights, sections or divisions, depending on the type of aircraft used and the theatre in which the squadron is operating. With the advent of the helicopter for small ship operations, the squadron was used as a collective entity and Wasp or Lynx units do not operate as a squadron but as separate flights assigned to the ship's captain when embarked. In the same way, the ship's flight SAR helicopters for plane guard duties were administered by the ship rather than a squadron.

Above *During flight deck operations in* Ark Royal, *the ship's plane guard helicopter stays close by as a bombed-up Buccaneer is manoeuvred by the all-wheel drive tractor* (RN/FPU).

Above right *Wessex 3 team, 1979.* Antrim *flight in working rig — aircrew in survival/immersion suits and the flight deck crew in coveralls and life jackets* (Paul Beaver).

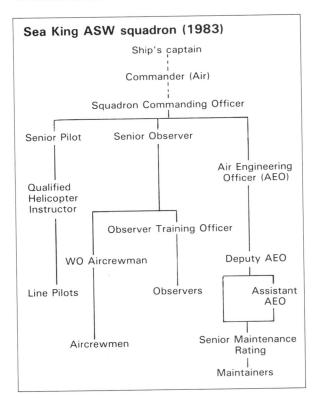

Sea King ASW squadron (1983)

Ship's captain

Commander (Air)

Squadron Commanding Officer

Senior Pilot — Senior Observer

Air Engineering Officer (AEO)

Qualified Helicopter Instructor

Observer Training Officer

WO Aircrewman — Deputy AEO

Line Pilots — Observers — Assistant AEO

Aircrewmen

Senior Maintenance Rating

Maintainers

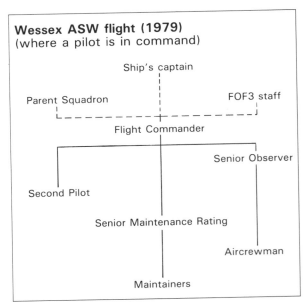

Wessex ASW flight (1979)
(where a pilot is in command)

Ship's captain

Parent Squadron — FOF3 staff

Flight Commander

Second Pilot — Senior Observer

Senior Maintenance Rating — Aircrewman

Maintainers

Fleet Air Arm ashore

Although naval aircraft were obviously mainly operational from aircraft carriers and some, but an increasing number, of smaller warships, there were several naval air stations at home and overseas in the 1950s and 1960s. These are described in greater detail elsewhere in this chapter but as a general rule their primary role was the training of ships' air complements, the development and trials of new and improved aircraft, aircraft weapon system development, aircraft repair, storage and maintenance, accommodation for disembarked aircraft and the administration of aircraft and squadron/flight personnel in transit.

During this period, naval air stations and naval aircraft repair yards in the United Kingdom were under the command of the Flag Officer Naval Air Command with a headquarters at Lee-on-Solent. FONAC then delegated the supervision and training of flying personnel and the formation of squadrons to the Flag Officer Flying Training at Yeovilton. This post lapsed in 1966 and FONAC moved to a purpose-built headquarters complex at Yeovilton.

As the number of air stations increased and developed requirements for many and varied tasks, the number of Women's Royal Naval Service personnel — Wrens — increased and by the 1970s

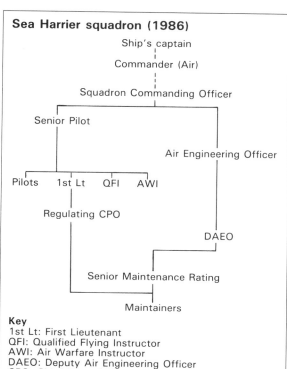

Sea Harrier squadron (1986)

Ship's captain

Commander (Air)

Squadron Commanding Officer

Senior Pilot

Air Engineering Officer

Pilots   1st Lt   QFI   AWI

Regulating CPO

DAEO

Senior Maintenance Rating

Maintainers

Key
1st Lt: First Lieutenant
QFI: Qualified Flying Instructor
AWI: Air Warfare Instructor
DAEO: Deputy Air Engineering Officer
CPO: Chief Petty Officer

Above *A Wren aircraft engineering technician working on a helicopter engine at Culdrose* (RN/Culdrose).

Below *Culdrose tower's visual control room during routine flying operations; radar controllers are normally positioned on the floor below* (RN/Culdrose).

many of the important groundcrew and support positions had been filled by women. Examples include aircraft handlers, meteorological observers, photographers and air traffic controllers.

Royal Naval Air Stations

The Fleet Air Arm is as much at home ashore as afloat and over the years a number of Royal Naval Air Stations (RNASs) have been established. The permanent stations have been given ship's names in true naval tradition. These establishments trace their histories back to the formation of the Royal Naval Air Service in a few cases, but mainly to the development of the Fleet Air Arm once it left the control of the RAF, immediately before and during the Second World War. In the 1950s, there was a major contraction and since the demise of the fixed-wing conventional aircraft the number has been reduced to four (Culdrose, Lee-on-Solent, Portland, and Yeovilton) with their respective satellite airfields. Prestwick is a shared facility with the Scottish international airport.

The average Royal Naval Air Station is commanded by a Captain RN, usually but not always a naval aviator. To support him and to run the main divisions, there are four Commanders: the Executive Officer (day-to-day manager); the Commander (Air) (all flying, squadron and airfield activities); the Base Supply Officer (supply and secretarial back-up); and often the Commander (Training) who co-ordinate those facilities. The medical unit would normally be headed by a Commander in his specialist branch.

In addition, Yeovilton has housed the Fleet Air Arm's Flight Safety Centre and other specialist areas, which had been a Commander's appointment.

Air Department Headed by the Commander (Air), usually called 'Wings' and supported by the Lieutenant Commander (Flying), usually called 'Little F', the officer responsible for the airfield and its circuit. Subordinate sections include air traffic control, airfield fire service, flight planning and weather forecasting.

Air Engineering Department This section provides engineering assistance to the squadrons and visiting aircraft, as well as looking after the technical considerations of ground radio and radar, fuel bowsers and workshops. Several naval air stations have been the host to a Naval Aircraft Support Unit where deep aircraft maintenance, storage and conversions are undertaken.

Air Traffic Control Comes under the auspices of Commander (Air) but it is an important part of the efficient running of a naval air station. At various times there have been special training units associated with particular air stations, such as the Fighter Direction School at Yeovilton. Modern naval air stations even have a falconry unit for bird scare duties.

For the sake of completeness, the following entries include air stations, air yards, unit bases and other air facilities which have been used by the Fleet Air Arm on a permanent or semi-permanent basis. The entries are split into two sections, the United Kingdom and Overseas. They do not include the small number of bases which lingered on for a short time after the close of the Second World War, but which did not contribute to active naval aviation.

United Kingdom

Abbotsinch (*Sanderling*) Situated close to Glasgow, Abbotsinch was used throughout its career as a naval aircraft storage, administration and training establishment. It is now Glasgow International Airport.

Anthorn (*Nuthatch*) This naval air station opened in 1944 for aircraft preparation purposes and closed in 1957.

Arbroath (*Condor*) Situated near Dundee, Arbroath was a famous Second World War naval air station. It was transferred to the Royal Marines in 1970 as a training centre and base for 45 Commando. The Air Engineering School moved to Lee-on-Solent.

Belfast (*Gadwall*, later *Gannet III*) Until 1973 there was a naval air repair facility at Belfast, a location famous for the Sea Vixen conversions and early steam catapult testing. It was commissioned in 1943.

Bramcote (*Gamecock*) A centre for the Royal Naval Volunteer Reserve (Air Branch) in the 1950s.

Brawdy (*Goldcrest*) The Royal Naval Air Station at Brawdy was situated in what used to be called Pembrokeshire but was transferred from the RAF in 1946 and returned to RAF care in 1974.

Culham (*Hornbill*) Now the site of the National Physical Laboratory, Culham was naval training establishment and home to RNVR squadrons in the 1940s until September 1953.

Culdrose (*Seahawk*) Commissioned on 17 April 1947, Culdrose is situated close to the Cornish market town of Helston. The original task of the air station was to act as the Naval Air Fighter School, operating Seafire, Sea Fury, Meteor and Vampire aircraft. In 1952, Culdrose became the home of the

Fleet Air Arm's first airborne early warning unit, 849 Squadron, and a year later the Observer School was formed at the air station, but the association was brief, the school moving to Eglinton in 1954. AEW flying moved away to Brawdy during 1964-70, before moving to Lossiemouth and then back to Culdrose.

Helicopter pilot training moved from Lee-on-Solent to Culdrose in 1959 and ever since the air station has been very involved in naval helicopter flying, being the largest and busiest maritime helicopter facility in Europe. The same year, the School of Aircraft Handling moved from Lee-on-Solent, but Culdrose lost the Observer School to Hal Far until it returned in 1972, via Lossiemouth.

From 1962, advanced flying training for helicopter aircrew in anti-submarine warfare has been undertaken at Culdrose, pilots, observers and aircrewmen being trained there. Commando pilot advanced flying training was also carried out at the air station until 707 Squadron took its Wessex HU 5 to Yeovilton in 1970.

By 1981, Culdrose was host to the Royal Navy's Schools of helicopter flying, observer training, aircrewman, meteorology and oceanography, aircraft handling, telephony, motor transport driving, naval air command firefighting and some engineering tasks.

Search and rescue flying has always played an important part in the air station's life and Culdrose continues to provide a 24 hour helicopter rescue service for military aircrew in the South-Western Approaches and for the Department of Trade, HM Coastguard and in liaison with the Royal National Lifeboat Institution. Culdrose has also been home to 705 Squadron and the famous 'Sharks' helicopter display team.

Dale (*Goldcrest*) This naval air station was only active from 1943 to December 1947.

Donibristle (*Merlin*) Famous as a disposal point and storage establishment for naval aircraft, Donibristle closed in 1959.

Eglinton (*Gannet*) The former naval air station near Londonderry was commissioned on 15 May 1943 and continued as an anti-submarine training school until 1958 when it was closed in one of the post-war defence cuts and Home Air Command restructuring. The last front line squadron to be based there departed in 1956, the same year that major improvements were carried out to the airfield facilities, including a major installation of runway lighting. Less than two years later, the naval air station closed, such was the Sandys Axe. In 1971, the ship's name *Gannet* was transferred to Prestwick.

Ford (*Peregrine*) In 1955, Ford was the base of the Jet Fighter Pilot Pool which allowed aircrew

awaiting transfer to front line units an opportunity to undergo refresher and continuation training. This moved to Lossiemouth in 1957.

Gosport *(Siskin)* The home of naval helicopter aviation, the first evaluation unit forming there in 1945. It is now a housing estate.

Henstridge *(Dipper)* The air station was operational between 1943 and 1957.

Hinstock *(Godwit)* Commissioned in 1943, this naval air station closed in February 1947.

Lee-on-Solent *(Daedalus)* The seaplane base between Portsmouth and Southampton was returned to the Royal Navy in 1939 and named *Daedalus,* the fifth ship to bear the name. It was temporarily called *Ariel* in 1959-65. It is the *alma mater* for all maintenance ratings in the Fleet Air Arm, having been the Air Engineering School (previously at Arbroath) since 1970.

An SAR flight was formed in February 1973 with three Whirlwind HAR 9 helicopters, replaced in April 1977 with three Wessex HU 5 under the control of 772 Squadron at Portland. Using the sea-plane ramp, the Royal Navy formed its hovercraft trials unit at Lee-on-Solent in January 1975, with men and equipment from the Inter-Service Hovercraft Unit which had already been at *Daedalus* since February 1962. The NHU disbanded in June 1982.

Providing an inter-service assistance programme, the Mobile Aircraft Repair, Transport and Salvage Unit is based at Lee-on-Solent, surveying and recovering some 200 downed, wrecked or disabled helicopters a year.

Associated with Lee-on-Solent is the Royal Naval Air Medical School, the Survival Equipment School and various examination boards at Seafield Park, Hill Head.

Lossiemouth *(Fulmar)* In 1953, the Naval Air Fighter School at Culdrose was decommissioned and the jet element moved up to Lossiemouth and from 1959 jet air warfare training was carried out

A typical morning scene at Lossiemouth in 1959 as a morning's flying practice gets under way; the aircraft are Sea Hawk FGA 4/6 of 738 Squadron (Commander Derek Monsell).

at the air station, mainly by 764 Squadron flying the Hunter GA 11, T 8C and some Scimitar F 1s; this role remained until 1972. During this period of Fleet Air Arm expansion, the Royal Navy formed several training, trials and evaluation units at Lossiemouth.

Lossie was also home to a number of front line squadrons over the years, particularly fighters. Like all aircraft operating from the Scottish airfield, they found the mild climate (often snow free in the middle of winter) extremely useful for training and flight safety.

Machrihanish *(Landrail)* Used for naval anti-submarine warfare during the Second World War, Machrihanish (on the Firth of Clyde) is now a stand-by naval air station with a NATO role.

Merryfield *(Satellite of Yeovilton)* This airfield in Somerset is used for training associated with Yeovilton.

Milltown *(Fulmar II)* Operational between 1946 and 1972 for a variety of purposes, including training.

Portland *(Osprey)* The first helicopters were flown in the Portland area during 1946, but it was not until 1957 that a helicopter ASW squadron was regularly based at Chickerell and two years later 737 Squadron was formed when the Air Anti-Submarine School moved from Eglinton. The naval air station was formally commissioned on 24 April 1959.

A major airfield development took place in 1969-74 and, by 1983, the air station was the base of the Lynx and Wasp (with 772 Squadron providing transportation for Flag Officer Sea Training and SAR). In 1986, the only front line units at Portland were 815 (Lynx) and 829 (Lynx/Wasp) Squadrons.

Predannack The tiny airfield of Predannack is a satellite of Culdrose naval air station and has been used for aircraft training since the Second World War, being built in 1941. It closed in 1946, was reopened for the Royal Air Force, and taken on strength by Culdrose in December 1958.

Prestwick (*Gannet*) Part of the international airport is used for naval helicopter operations and is the home base of 819 Squadron with Sea King helicopters. It was commissioned in November 1971.

St Merryn (*Vulture*) / **St Merryn** (*Curlew*) A satellite for Culdrose, used from August 1940 until January 1956.

Stretton (*Blackcap*) Built during the Second World War as a training base, from 1947 to 1951 this naval air station was the home of 1831 Squadron, an RNVR fighter unit which originally flew piston-engined types such as the Seafire and Sea Fury before converting to the Attacker F 1 in 1955. 1841 flew Avengers from the airfield. In 1952, Stretton became a Northern Air Division air station.

The last front line unit to be home based at Stretton was 898 Squadron, but for several years the air station was used for the receipt and dispatch of Sea Hawk, Sea Vampire and Sea Venom aircraft coming from base maintenance or the manufacturer; a few Wyvern aircraft passed through in the mid 1950s.

Worthy Down (*Kestrel* and *Ariel III*) A naval rating aircrew training establishment from 1939, Worthy Down was paid off in 1947 but re-opened in June 1952. It was transferred to the Royal Army Pay Corps in 1960.

Yeovilton (*Heron*) Built just before the Second World War, Yeovilton was home of the All-Weather Fighter Pool from 1955 until 1957, when the designation appears to have changed to that of the All-Weather Fighter School, a task which continued for some years. Until 1974, it was the home of the Royal Navy's Phantoms.

Today, Yeovilton is the home of the Fleet Air Arm with a number of hosted squadrons, units and special facilities. It is the home of naval command helicopter flying. Co-located is the headquarters of Flag Officer Naval Air Command.

Royal Naval Air Station tail codes

A	Arbroath (*Condor*)
AC	Abbotsinch (*Sanderling*)
AH	Anthorn (*Nuthatch*)
AO	Arbroath (*Condor*)
AR	Arbroath (*Condor*)
BL	Belfast (*Gadwall* and *Gannet III*)
BR	Bramcote (*Gamecock*)
BW	Sembawang (Singapore) (*Seagull*)
BY	Brawdy (*Goldcrest*)
CF	Church Fenton

One of the most important summer events for the Fleet Air Arm is the Yeovilton Air Day which attracts thousands of visitors. This picture also shows the layout of a typical naval air station with squadron hangars and workshops on either side of the taxiways (RN/Heron).

CH	Culham (*Hornbill*)
CM	Culham (*Hornbill*)
CU	Culdrose (*Seahawk*)
CW	Culdrose (*Seahawk*)
DL	Dale (*Goldcrest*)
DM	Dartmouth (*Norton*)
FD	Ford (*Peregrine*)
FL	Fleetlands
GJ	Gosport (*Siskin*)
GN	Eglinton (*Gannet*)
HF	Hal Far (Malta) (*Falcon*)
JA	Stretton (*Blackcap*)
JB	St Merryn (*Vulture* and *Curlew*)
JR	Eglinton (*Gannet*)
LM	Lossiemouth (*Fulmar*)
LO	Linton-on-Ouse
LP	Lee-on-Solent (*Daedalus*)
LS	Lee-on-Solent (*Daedalus*)
LU	Leuchars
MA	Machrihanish
MF	St Merryn (*Vulture* and *Curlew*)
MV	Milltown (*Fulmar II*)
PO	Portland (*Osprey*)
PQ	Belfast (*Gadwall*)
PW	Prestwick (*Gannet*)
SJ	Syerston
SR	St Merryn (*Vulture* and *Curlew*)
SZ	Belfast (*Gadwall*)
VL	Yeovilton (*Heron*)
VM	Worthy Down (*Kestrel*)
WU	Wroughton

Overseas

In the true traditions of the Fleet Air Arm and Royal Navy, even overseas naval air stations were given ship's names and became an integral part of the naval air command logistical and operational chain.

Falklands Islands Although various helicopters from Ice Patrol, Survey and other warships had made use of the facilities at Port Stanley and other locations in the period since the end of the Second World War, it was not until after the cessation of hostilities with the Argentine forces that a more permanent Fleet Air Arm presence was established.

From 1982 to 1986, a detached flight from 826 Squadron with Sea King HAS 5 helicopters was based at RAF Stanley and Mount Pleasant to provide anti-submarine warfare, search and rescue and surface search capability to the garrison commander.

Gibraltar The RAF airfield at Gibraltar has been used for naval flying since before the Second World War, but recently a Lynx helicopter flight has been based there permanently.

Hal Far (*Falcon*) Situated on Malta GC, Hal Far, with its record of fine weather and good flying conditions, was an important Fleet Air Arm base until 1970. At different times there were various aircraft attached to the naval air station, including Dragonfly and Whirlwind helicopters.

Hal Far was the home from home for naval air squadrons operating in the Mediterranean, many of whom used the range and gunnery facilities on the island.

Sembawang (*Seagull*) The Fleet Air Arm re-commissioned Sembawang (Singapore) in 1950 and various aircraft were allocated to the naval air station from time to time; in 1956, three Fireflies were allocated for local flying and refresher training. The air station was handed over to the Malaysian authorities in 1971.

Above right *All ASW Sea King squadrons are equipped with the HAS 5 version, seen here in the markings of 826 Squadron* (RN/Culdrose).

Left *Since the 1970s, the Fleet Airm Arm has had no overseas naval air stations, but in the past much work was carried on at such places as Hal Far, Malta, where these 728 Squadron Sea Hornet F 20s were based. Note the HF tail code* (Fleet Air Arm Museum).

Fleet Air Arm today

The number of warships which can operate helicopters at sea has increased dramatically in the past twenty years. Today, no surface escort or modern Royal Fleet Auxiliary would be built without the provision of helicopter flight deck and hangar. Within the current Fleet Air Arm structure, squadrons are assigned to various types and classes of modern warship and RFA:

Squadron	Aircraft	Primary platform
800	Sea Harrier	'Invincible' Class CVS
801	Sea Harrier	'Invincible' Class CVS
814	Sea King HAS	'Invincible' Class CVS
815	Lynx	Type 42 DLG and other escorts
820	Sea King HAS	'Invincible' Class CVS
824	Sea King HAS	RFA
826	Sea King HAS	RFA
829	Wasp/Lynx	Type 22 frigates and older escorts
849	Sea King AEW	'Invincible' Class CVS

In the 'quick dash' role the CVSs would embark Sea King HC 4 helicopters from 845 and/or 846 Squadrons.

There has been a marked increase in the use of Royal Fleet Auxiliaries in recent years which has been brought about by the development of large replenishment ships with hangar and flight deck facilities, and by a change in operational doctrine which requires more helicopters over a greater area; this is not unconnected with the development of towed array frigates.

The 'Fort' Class have and the new *Fort Victoria* will have facilities for up to four Sea King HAS 5 helicopters, keeping them fuelled and armed, as well as providing a base facility for other helicopters operating with the same task group. It is not thought that Sea King AEW 2 helicopters will be embarked in RFAs until the operational doctrine has been fully established.

The aircraft

The period since the end of the Second World War has seen a tremendous revolution in aircraft design and their operational abilities. This revolution in forty years is however only equivalent to that of the preceeding period to the first attempts at naval aviation, except that now a single carrier-borne aircraft is capable of delivering the same firepower as almost all that available to a squadron in the Royal Naval Air Service of 1918 vintage.

The post-1945 revolution has brought the naval aircraft into the jet age and during the last two decades into the vertical take-off and landing age. The helicopter too has entered service and developed into the status of almost a mini-frigate. The aircraft of the Fleet Air Arm are its heart and everything revolves around them.

Naval aircraft development

From the earliest days, the naval aeroplane (although not the naval helicopter) has almost without exception been developed from a land-based type, optimized to face the demands of prolonged over water flight. For example, the Bristol Scout C with its 80 hp Gnome engine was the navalized, over water version of the Army's Scout. The later Fairey Nimrod was a developed Royal Air Force Fury while the Seafire was a navalized Spitfire; in fact most of the post-war naval aircraft developed from or with land-based counterparts.

In one form or another specialized gear has always been carried by naval aircraft making them different from their shore-based brethren. Perhaps most important amongst this equipment has been flotation and survival gear and the various pieces of apparatus for deck landing and take-off, the arrester hook and the catapult slings. Folding wings have been developed, in various forms, over the years to allow the aircraft on the carrier deck to be struck below, bearing in mind the narrow confines of flight deck lifts. Some aircraft have even needed folding tails, and helicopters, of course, can usually fold their main rotor blades and tail booms for ease of stowage and lift transportation.

Left *Fairey Fulmar, the first eight-gun Fleet fighter* (Fleet Air Arm Museum).

Above right *The last fixed-wing airborne early warning aircraft was the Gannet AEW 3, seen here with 849 Squadron's headquarters flight, then at Brawdy.*

Right *Corsair fighter from the British Pacific Fleet's carrier,* Vengeance (Peter George).

Most aircraft have their wing folds about one-third to one-half of the way along the wing, allowing the formation of a triangle when the wings are folded. Examples include the Hawker Sea Fury, Hawker Sea Hawk and Blackburn Buccaneer; the latter also folded its nose cone back. Other naval aircraft were developed with specially folding wings, particularly if the triangular design meant that their height was greater than the wartime constructed carriers. The Fairey Firefly is one example of a special wing fold, with the main planes lying back alongside the fuselage, or the Fairey/Westland Gannet with its double fold mechanism, giving an Indian dancer effect.

Like all aircraft, those used by the Fleet Air Arm have grown in weight, size, performance, ability and cost over the years. Since the end of the Second World War in particular the weights have increased, for example the Buccaneer and Phantom heavyweights in the conventional fixed-wing school and the Sea King HAS 6 and proposed EH 101 in helicopters. To give an idea of the growth in naval aircraft, some selected examples are shown below and it should be borne in mind that continued growth also meant continued and costly improvements to aircraft design, especially to the strengthening of flight decks, lifts and arrester gear.

Type	Date in service	Max AUW lb (kg)
Propellor-driven aircraft		
Seafire 47	1948	11,615 (5,269)
Sea Fury FB 11	1948	12,500 (5,670)
Gannet AS 1	1954	19,600 (8,891)
Gannet AEW 3	1960	25,000 (11,340)
Jet aircraft		
Attacker F 1	1951	11,500 (5,217)
Sea Hawk FGA 6	1956	16,200 (7,348)
Sea Vixen FAW 1	1959	35,000 (15,876)
Buccaneer S 1	1962	45,000 (20,412)
Phantom FG 1	1969	56,000 (25,402)
Sea Harrier FRS 1	1980	23,000 (10,433)
Helicopters		
Dragonfly HR 3	1950	5,870 (2,663)
Whirlwind HAS 7	1957	7,800 (3,538)
Wessex HAS 1	1961	12,600 (5,715)
Sea King HAS 1	1970	20,500 (9,299)

Fighter development

The first naval fighter aircraft, like the Bristol Scout, which first flew on 23 February 1914, were primarily scout types, used for army co-operation. During the inter-war period, the naval fighter developed into beautiful designs like the Hawker

Nimrod with the sole aim of defending the carrier as part of the Fleet at sea (the capital ships being the battleships).

The Nimrod was replaced in service by the Blackburn Skua (monoplane) and Gloster Sea Gladiator (biplane) which had been designed as a dive-bomber and land-based fighter respectively. The role of the fleet carrier-borne fighter had become one of reconnaissance and observation. Great strides were made however with the introduction of the Seafire and Sea Hurricane, developed from the top rank land-based fighters of the day. During the Second World War, the Fleet Air Arm was also the operator of fast, sleek and specially designed American-built naval fighters, starting with the

Wildcat and including the Corsair (still in limited service until 1946). The two-place fighter had become more specialized as a strike fighter (Firefly FR 1) and night fighter (Firefly NF 1).

With the war in the Pacific really showing the need and worth of the fleet fighter, the Allies had designed, built and tested several twin-engined types which offered both greater range and better over water safety. The Sea Mosquito was pressed into limited service as fighter-bomber and torpedo bomber, leading to the Sea Hornet. The heavier fighters, optimized for strike missions, proceeded in the direction of the Sea Fury (developed from the RAF's Typhoon/Tempest programme) and the Firefly, the latter then being further developed into the anti-submarine field (see below).

With the coming of the jet age, the naval fighter at last began to catch up with its land-based cousins; with the Sea Vixen and Scimitar the Fleet Air Arm was certainly a match for all comers. Later, *Ark Royal*'s air group of Buccaneer and Phantom aircraft was the best equipped 'mini air force' in the world. In the following pages the fighter aircraft of the Fleet Air Arm in service since 1945 are listed alphabetically for ease of reference and the list includes those naval aircraft already in service at the end of the war and which continued in use for the immediate post-war years.

Fleet fighters

Firefly I/F 1/FR 1/NF 1

Manufacturer Fairey Aviation; **Purpose** Fleet fighter and fighter-reconnaissance; **Crew** 1 pilot, 1 observer/aircrewman; **Maiden flight** 22 December 1941; **Service entry** 4 March 1943; **Squadrons** (Mk I & F 1) 700 (1945-49), 706 (1945-46), 768

(1948-49), 772 (1944-46), 780 (1946), 783 (1945-46), 790 (1944-47), 837 (1945-47), 860 (1946-50), 861 (1946-47), 1772 (1944-46); (FR 1) 703 (1945-49), 719 (1946-47), 736 (1946-50), 737 (1949-50), 741 (1946-47), 766 (1944-54), 767 (1945-52), 771 (1950-55), 778 (1943-48), 781 (1949-54), 782 (1945-53), 783 (1945-46), 795 (1946-47), 796 (1947-51), 799 (1945-52), 805 (1946-47), 812 (1946-48), 814 (1945-48), 816 (1945-48), 822 (1945-46), 824 (1945-46), 825 (1945-47), 826 (1946-50), 837 (1945-47), 1830 (1945-51), 1842 (1952-54); (NF 1) 805 (1946-47), 812 (1948-51), 816 (1946-48), 1790 (1945-46); **Phased out of service** 1954; **Range** 1,130 nm (2,090 km); **Max speed** 275 knots (508 km/h); **Cruising speed** 225 knots (417 km/h); **Service ceiling** 28,000 ft (8,535 m); **Rate of climb** 2,000 ft/min (10.2 m/sec); **Length** 37.6 ft (11.46 m), (NF 1) 39.1 ft (11.9 m); **Height** 13.58 ft (4.14 m); **Wing span** 44.5 ft (13.6 m), (folded) 13.25 ft (4.04 m); **Wing area** 328 sq ft (30.47 sq m); **Power plant** 1 × Rolls-Royce Griffon IIB (1,730 hp) or Griffon XII (1,990 hp); **All-up weight** 14,020 lb (6,360 kg); **Empty weight** 9,750 lb (4,423 kg); **Weapons** 4 × Hispano 20 mm cannon in wings, 8 × 3 in rocket projectiles with 60 lb (27 kg) warheads or 2 × 1,000 lb (454 kg) bombs underwing; **Sensors** Mk I none, F 1 none, NF 1 AI Mk X, FR 1 ASV Mk II.

The Firefly Mk I was developed during the Second World War as a Fleet fighter for carrier operations to replace the Fulmar which had been successful in the Mediterranean Sea. Some 850 Firefly Mk Is were built between 1943 and 1946, with later aircraft being modified to F 1 standard with new windscreens and canopies.

The NF 1 night fighter version can be identified by its radar housings close to the wing roots, exhaust shrouds and because extra fuselage length was required for the centre of gravity. The NF 2

Right *Firefly FR 5, during a pilot familiarization* (Vice Admiral Gibson).

Left *Firefly NF 1s of 1792 Squadron embarked in Ocean, 1946; note the shrouded exhausts* (Fleet Air Arm Museum).

variant was in limited wartime production and did not see service after early 1945.

With a new radar available, the fuselage modifications were unnecessary and costly, so the last variant of the Mk I series was the FR 1 with pod-mounted ASV radar beneath the fuselage. This variant saw service over Korea and against Communist terrorists in Malaya, as well as equipping RNVR, Dutch and Canadian units.

Serials include *Z1832* (Mk 1), *Z1833* and *Z1836*, *DT333* (NF 1), *DT934* (FR 1).

Firefly FR 4

Manufacturer Fairey Aviation; **Purpose** Shipborne reconnaissance; **Crew** 1 pilot, 1 observer; **Maiden flight** 25 May 1945; **Service entry** August 1947 (825 Squadron); **Squadrons** 810 (1947-50), 812 (1948), 814 (1948-49), 816 (1948-51), 825 (1947-49); **Phased out of service** 1950; **Range** 600 nm (1,111 km); **Max speed** 329 knots (610 km/h) at altitude; **Cruising speed** 200 knots (370 km/h); **Service ceiling** 28,000 ft (8,543 m); **Length** 27.92 ft (8.51 m); **Height** 14.33 ft (4.37 m); **Span** 41.17 ft (12.55 m); **Wing area** 330 sq ft (30.66 sq m); **Power plant** 1 × Rolls-Royce Griffon 74 (2,245 hp); **All-up weight** 15,615 lb (7,083 kg); **Empty weight** 9,674 lb (4,388 kg); **Weapons** 4 × 20 mm Aden cannon in wings.

The first of the post-Second World War variants of the Firefly and the first with a radically different shape. The famous under nose air scoop had been replaced by air intakes/radiators in the wing roots. The wings themselves had been clipped and a new four-bladed Rotol propellor fitted to the aircraft. They were delivered to five front-line fixed-wing squadrons and used in combination with anti-submarine aircraft in mixed air groups. The FR 4 was used for army co-operation tasks and fleet

Firefly FR 4, the last production aircraft, (Vice Admiral Gibson).

fighter defence exercises, serving aboard *Implacable, Theseus* and the Canadian carrier, *Warrior*.

Some 160 airframes were completed, including some forty for the Royal Netherlands Navy and part of the batch was taken from the last 43 Firefly Mk 1s on the Hayes line. The last Firefly FR 4 was delivered in February 1948 and work concentrated on strike variants of the Firefly design.

Variants NF 4 converted for night fighting trials; TT 4 converted for target-towing.

Firefly FR 5

Manufacturer Fairey Aeroplane; **Purpose** Shipborne fighter reconnaissance; **Crew** 1 pilot, 1 observer; **Maiden flight** 12 December 1947; **Service trials entry** January 1948; **Squadrons** 810 (1951-53), 817 (1950-52), 821 (1952-53), 825 (1951-52) **Phased out of service** 1953; **Range, Max speed, Cruising speed, Service ceiling, Length, Height, Span, Wing area, Power plant, All-up weight, Empty Weight** and **Weapons** as Firefly FR 4.

This version of the Firefly was developed with

power folding wings for ease of handling aboard aircraft carriers. Some 352 of the model were built. The bulk of these were internally configured for anti-submarine warfare but fourteen went to the Royal Netherlands Navy. ASW variants are dealt with separately.

Variants FR 5 was the day fighter-reconnaissance variant; NF 5 was the night fighter type; AS 5 was the ASW variant (see page 118).

Seafire F XV

Manufacturer Vickers Supermarine; **Purpose** Shipborne Fleet fighter; **Crew** 1 pilot; **Naval Staff Requirement** N 4/43; **Maiden flight** 1944; **Service entry** May 1945 (802 Squadron); **Squadrons** 736 (1946-48), 773 (1950), 800 (1946-47); 801 (1945-46), 802 (1945-48), 803 (1945-47), 805 (1945-46), 806 (1945-47), 1832 (1949-51), 1833 (1949-51); **Phased out of service** March 1950; **Range** 556 nm (1,030 km); **Max speed** 333 knots (616 km/h); **Cruising speed** 290 knots (537 kmh); **Service ceiling** 35,500 ft (10,820 m); **Rate of climb** 2,857 ft/min (14.5 m/sec); **Length** 32.25 ft (9.8 m); **Height** 10.67 ft (3.3 m); **Span** 36.83 ft (11.23 m); **Wing area** 242 sq ft (22.48 sq m); **Power plant** 1 × Rolls-Royce Griffon 1,850 hp; **All-up weight** 8,000 lb (3,630 kg); **Empty weight** 6,200 lb (2,812 kg); **Weapons** 2 × 20 mm cannon and 4 × 0.303 in Browning guns.

Produced by Westland and Cunliffe-Owen, the Seafire F XV did not see active service during the Second World War although earmarked for the British Pacific Fleet. Instead it joined six front line squadrons for service in Escort and Light Fleet Carriers.

Seafire XV in flight, circa 1946 (Fleet Air Arm Museum).

The first of the Fleet Air Arm's Griffon-engined Seafires, the fighter was well liked by its pilots apart from the perennial Seafire deck handling problems attributed to the narrow track undercarriage and long engine nacelle. Unlike previous marks of Seafire, it had folding wings, a single (sting) type arrester hook and good internal fuel capacity. The final squadron to fly this mark of Seafire did so in 1950 when the nomenclature had changed to Seafire F 15.

Serials include *SW781-SW828; SW844-SW875.*

Seafire F XVII/FR XVII

Manufacturer Vickers Supermarine; **Purpose** Shipborne Fleet fighter; **Crew** 1 pilot; **Maiden flight** 1945; **Service entry** May 1947 (883 Squadron); **Squadrons** 736 (1946-51), 738 (1950-51), 759 (1951-54), 800 (1947-49), 807 (1945-47), 883 (1947-48), 1831 (1947-51), 1832 (1948-53), 1833 (1947-52), **Phased out of service** 1954; **Range** 378 nm (700 km) (internal fuel), 747 nm (1,384 km) (underwing tanks); **Max speed** 336 knots (623 km/h); **Cruising speed** 295 knots (545 km/h); **Service ceiling** 35,200 ft (10,730 m); **Rate of climb** 2,778 ft/min (14.1 m/sec); **Length, Height, Span, Wing area, Power plant, All-up weight** and **Empty weight** as Seafire F XV; **Weapons** 2 × 20 mm cannon and 4 × 0.303 in Browning machine guns, plus 8 × 3 in rocket projectiles (60 lb warhead).

Basically a refined Seafire F XV/F 15 model, the Seafire F XVII/FR XVII (F 17) was a stalwart mount of the Royal Naval Volunteer Reserve air branch. It features a teardrop cockpit canopy and improved pilot's vision aft across the top of the fuselage. It served with the Fleet Air Arm and assisted the Royal Canadian Navy in the development of its naval aviation.

The FR XVII/F 17 model was used for training photographic reconnaissance aircrew and was fitted with two Vinten F 24 cameras in place of the fighter model's extra internal fuel tank. 759 Squadron operated this mark of Seafire as the last of the type in Fleet Air Arm service, 232 having been built.

Serials include *SW986-SW993; SX111-SX139; SX386-SX389.*

Seafire F 45

Manufacturer Vickers Supermarine; **Purpose** Fleet fighter; **Crew** 1 pilot; **Naval Staff Requirement** N 7/44; **Maiden flight** 1945; **Service entry** June 1945 (778 Squadron); **Squadrons** 771 (1947-50), 778 (1945-47); **Phased out of service** September 1950; **Range** 378 nm (700 km); **Max speed** 381 knots (705 km/h) at 25,000 ft (7,620 m);

Seafire F 45 commences free take off from Ocean (RN/Yeovilton).

Cruising speed 300 knots (555 km/h) at 20,000 ft (6,096 m); **Service ceiling** 41,000 ft (12,500 m); **Length** 33.58 ft (10.24 m); **Height** 12.75 ft (3.89 m); **Span** 36.92 ft (11.25 m); **Wing area** 244 sq ft (22.67 sq m); **Power plant** 1 × Rolls-Royce Griffon 61 (2,035 hp); **All-up weight** 9,400 lb (4,264 kg); **Empty weight** 7,100 lb (3,220 kg); **Underwing load weight** 500 lb (227 kg); **Weapons** 4 × 20 mm Aden cannon; 1 × 500 lb iron bomb under fuselage.

Developed directly from the RAF's Spitfire

Seafire F 46 photographed at Culdrose (RN/Culdrose).

Mk 21 fighter, the Seafire F 45 was fitted with a five-blade propeller (although a number of production aircraft are reported to have been fitted with a six-bladed contra-rotating propellor for trials). The production ran to fifty airframes for second line duties.

Serials include *TM379.*

Seafire F 46/FR 46

Manufacturer Vickers Supermarine; **Purpose** Fleet fighter; **Crew** 1 pilot; **Maiden flight** October 1945; **Service entry** January 1946 (737 Squadron); **Squadrons** (F 46) 736 (1946), 781 (1947); (FR 46) 1832 (1947-50); **Phased out of service** January 1950; **Range, Max speed, Cruising speed, Service ceiling, Length, Height, Span, Wing area** and

Power plant as Seafire F 45; **All-up weight** 9,730 lb (4,414 kg); **Empty weight** and **Weapons** as Seafire F 45.

This mark of Seafire did not see front line service with the Fleet Air Arm and only 24 production aircraft were built, with the prototype being converted from the second prototype F 45. Several of the airframes were modified to take the F 24 camera and were thus designated the FR 46; it seems that most if not all of this sub-variant was flown by the RNVR at Culham and Benson.

Serials include *TM383.*

Seafire FR 47

Manufacturer Vickers Supermarine; **Purpose** Shipborne Fleet fighter; **Crew** 1 pilot; **Maiden flight** Not available; **Service entry** February 1948 (804 Squadron); **Squadrons** 759 (1952-53), 800 (1949-50), 804 (1948-49), 1833 (1952-54); **Last delivery** 1949; **Phased out of service** November 1953; **Range** 817 nm (1,512 km); **Max speed** 393 knots (727 km/h) at 20,500 ft (6,250 m); **Cruising speed** 332 knots (615 km/h) at sea level; **Service ceiling** 43,100 ft (13.140 m); **Rate of climb** 4,800 ft/min (24.4 m/sec); **Length** 34.33 ft (10.46 m); **Height** 12.75 ft (3.89 m); **Span** 36.92 ft (11.25 m); **Wing area** 244 sq ft (22.67 sq m); **Power plant** 1 × Rolls-Royce Griffon 85 (2,375 hp); **All-up weight** 11,615 lb (5,269 kg); **Empty weight** 7,625 lb (3,459 kg); **Weapons** 4 × 20 mm cannon, plus 8 × 3 in rocket projectiles (60 lb warheads) or 3 × 500 lb (227 kg) iron bombs under fuselage and each wing.

The last of the magnificent Spitfire/Seafire family, the Seafire FR 47 was designed to operate

Seafire FR 47 (possibly 804 Squadron) collects an arrester wire (Fleet Air Arm Museum).

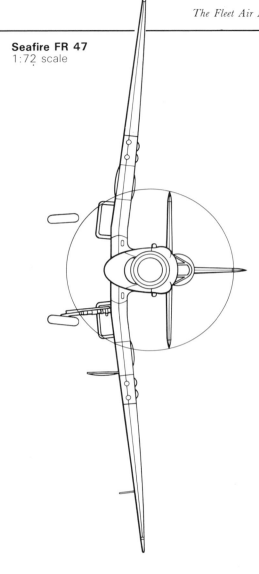

Seafire FR 47
1:72 scale

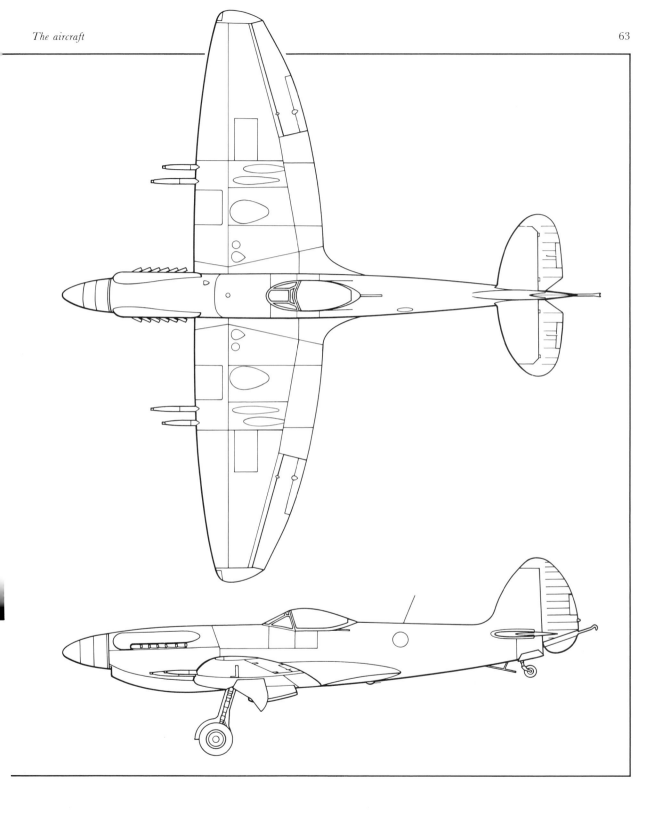

as a fighter-reconnaissance fighter for Fleet support operations from the deck of the Light Fleet aircraft carriers. It was the ultimate in designer ability to squeeze every drop of performance and internal storage from an old airframe.

However, by the late 1940s it was outclassed as a fighter and the continued handling problems of the narrow track undercarriage made it less successful as a Fleet fighter than might have been expected. In the end only ninety of the original order for 150 were completed. Nevertheless the aircraft served with two front line units, an RNVR unit and a training squadron.

The aircraft saw action twice during its short front line service life. Embarked in *Triumph*, 800 Squadron was active in the air offensive against Communist bandit sanctuaries in the hills and jungles of Malaya during the winter of 1949-50. With the outbreak of the Korean War, 800 Squadron, still embarked in *Triumph*, deployed from Hong Kong to the operational area in support of the US-led United Nations forces which had come to the aid of the South Koreans after the North (Communists) invaded. *Triumph* and the Seafires arrived on station on 2 July 1950. The Seafire FR 47 flew some 360 sorties from the carrier in Korean waters. It was replaced in service by the Sea Fury FB 10/11.

Serials include *VP427-VP465; VP471-VP495.*

Sea Hornet F 20

Manufacturer de Havilland Aircraft; **Purpose** Medium-range shipborne strike fighter; **Crew** 1 pilot; **Naval Specification** N 5/44; **Maiden flight** 19 April 1945; **Production maiden flight** 13

Sea Hornet F 20 landing (with plane guard Dragonfly in the background); it is possibly wearing an incorrect serial (Fleet Air Arm Museum).

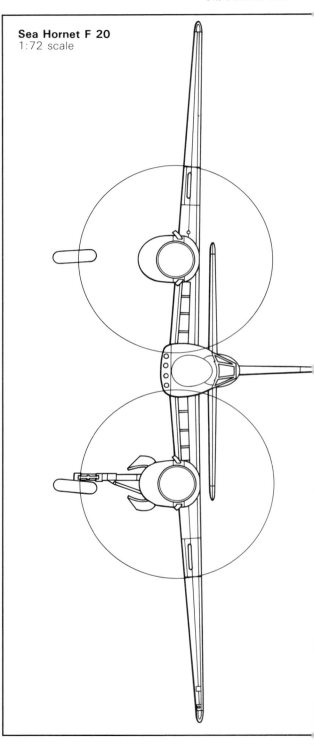

Sea Hornet F 20
1:72 scale

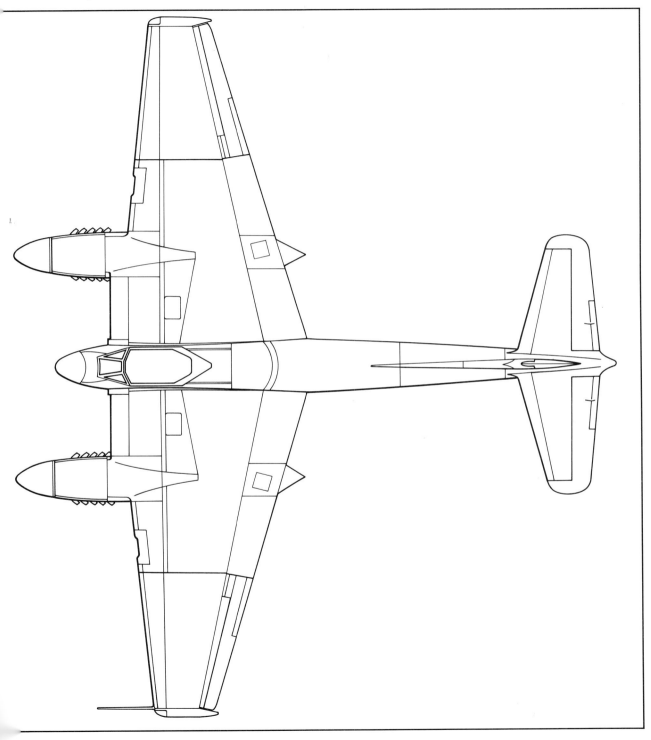

Sea Hornet F 20
1:72 scale

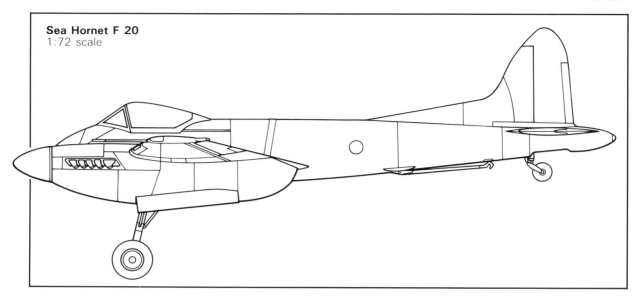

August 1946; **Service trials entry** (703 Sqn) April 1947; **First front line squadron formed** (801) 1 July 1947; **Embarked** (*Implacable*) March 1948; **Squadrons** 806 (1948 display), 809 (1949-52 — one Flight), Fleet Requirements and Training units; **Last delivery** 21 June 1951; **Phased out of service** 1957; **Radius of action** 750 nm (1,390 km) with aux tanks; **Max endurance** 3 hours **Max speed** 374 knots (693 km/h); **Cruising speed** 300 knots (556 km/h); **Service ceiling** 35,000 ft (10,668 m); **Rate of climb** 4,000 ft/min (1,219 m/min); **Length** 36.67 ft (11.2 m); **Height** 14.17 ft (4.3 m); **Span** 45 ft (13.7 m); **Wing area** 361 sq ft (33.5 sq m); **Power plant** 2 × Rolls-Royce Merlin 133/134 piston engines (2,030 hp); **All-up weight** 18,250 lb (8,279 kg); **Empty weight** Not available; **Weapons** 4 × 20 mm Aden guns; 8 × 60 rockets; 2 × aerial mines.

The Sea Hornet, described by world-famous naval test pilot, Captain Eric 'Winkle' Brown, as his favourite aeroplane, was designed to fulfil a need for a medium-range fighter, with two-engine safety, to operate from carriers in the Pacific and Indian Oceans. The design, directly stemming from the RAF's Hornet, shows clear descent from the Mosquito and was made of composite plywood and light alloy (wing structure) with a wooden fuselage.

In March 1951, the only full-strength front line unit, 801 Squadron, was re-equipped with the Sea Fury, with the aircraft being ferried to Malta for 728 Fleet Requirements Unit service (1952-57), mainly for radar duties for visiting warships.

Serials include *PX212* and *PX214* (prototypes);

PX219 (naval development); *TT186* and *TT210*; *VR856-VR893*.

Sea Hornet NF 21

Manufacturer de Havilland Aircraft; **Purpose** Shipborne night figher; **Crew** 1 pilot, 1 observer; **Naval Staff Requirement** N 21/45; **Maiden flight** 9 July 1946; **Service entry** 20 January 1949 (809 Squadron); **Squadrons** 771 (1950-52); 792 (1950); 809 (1949-54); **Phased out of service** October 1955; **Range** 1,305 nm (2,415 km); **Max speed** 374 knots (692 km/h) at 22,000 ft (6,705 m); **Cruising speed** 300 knots (556 km/h); **Endurance** about 5 hours; **Service ceiling** 36,500 ft (11,125 m); **Rate of climb** 4,400 ft/min (22.4 m/sec); **Length** 37 ft (11.28 m); **Height** 14 ft (4.27 m); **Span** 45 ft (13.7 m); **Wing area** 361 sq ft (33.54 sq m); **Power plant** 2 × Rolls-Royce Merlin 134 (2,030 hp); **All-up weight** 19,530 lb (8,860 kg); **Empty weight** 14,230 lb (6,455 kg); **Weapons** 4 × Hispano 20 mm cannon (night fighter); 8 × 3 in rocket projectiles with 60 lb (27 kg) warheads or 2 × 1,000 lb (454 kg) or 500 lb (277 kg) iron bombs (strike); **Sensor** 1 × AI Mk 15 (later AN/APS-6) radar.

In May 1950, the Fleet Air Arm's first all-weather air group was formed to embark in *Vengeance*, with the Sea Hornet making up the long-range fighter element. The aircraft, developed from the single seat Hornet concept, was superceded by the Sea Venom but not before it had demonstrated the ability of the airframe and the systems carried aboard. Considerable work had been carried out on the radar system, the observer's rear-facing cockpit

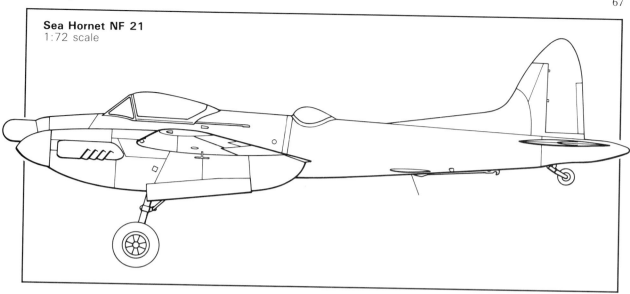

Sea Hornet NF 21
1:72 scale

and the flame-dampened Rolls-Royce Merlin engines. It was the only two-seat version of the Hornet.

Besides a fixed Hispano cannon armament, the Sea Hornet NF 21 was capable of carrying iron bombs and rocket projectiles, to operate in a strike role if require. In the event, there was only one front line squadron but good use was made of the

Sea Hornet NF 21 prior to delivery (Fleet Air Arm Museum).

aircraft in second line roles, including fleet requirements and night fighting radar training with 792 Squadron.

A remarkable record is quoted in Owen Thetford's *British Naval Aircraft since 1912* when it is said that a Sea Hornet NF 21 of 809 Squadron flew from Gibraltar to Lee-on-Solent non-stop at an average speed of 328 knots (608 km/h).

Serials include *PX230; PX239; VV430-VV441; VX245-VX252; VZ672; VZ699.*

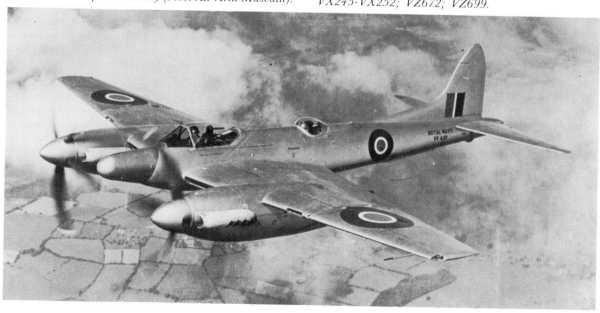

Sea Hornet PR 22

Manufacturer de Havilland Aircraft; **Purpose** Medium-range photo-reconnaissance; **Crew** 1 pilot; **Maiden flight** 1949; **Service entry** 1949; **Squadrons** 703 (1950-53), 738 (1950-51), 739 (1950-51), 759 (1951-52), 787 (1949), 801 (1949-50), 809 (1949-52), 1833 (1951-52); **Phased out of service** 1953; **Range** 2,050 nm (3,797 km); **Max speed** 406 knots (751 km/h) at altitude; **Cruising speed** about 350 knots (648 km/h); **Service ceiling** 37,500 ft (11,430 m); **Length, Height, Span, Wing area** and **Power plant** as Sea Hornet F 20; **All-up weight** 18,230 lb (8,269 kg); **Empty weight** about 14,000 lb (6,350 kg); **Special equipment** 2 × Royal Aircraft Establishment F 52 daylight camera or 1 × Fairchild K 19B low-light/IR system.

A total of 43 specially modified photo-reconnaissance Sea Hornet PR 22 fighters were built for the Fleet Air Arm, but served a limited time in front line service. The night time operating limits of the aircraft meant a reduced all-up weight of 16,804 lb (7,622 kg) when only one camera was carried.

Serials *VW930-VW939; VW946-VW978; VZ655-VZ664; WE245-WE249.*

Jet fighters

Attacker F 1

Manufacturer Vickers Supermarine; **Purpose** Shipborne fighter; **Crew** 1 pilot; **Naval Staff Requirement** E10/44; **Maiden flight** (naval prototype) 17 June 1947; **Embarked trials** October 1947 (*Illustrious*); **Service entry** 22 August 1951 (800 Squadron); **Squadrons** 702 (1952), 767 (1953-54), 736 (1952-54), 787 (1951-52), 800 (1951-52), 803 (1951-53), 890 (1952); **Phased out of service** 1954; **Range** (normal) 513 nm (949 km), (max) 1,034 nm (1,915 km); **Max speed** 513 knots (950 km/h) at sea level; **Cruising speed** 308 knots (571 km/h); **Service ceiling** 45,000 ft (13,716 m); **Rate of climb** 6,350 ft/min (32.3 m/sec); **Length** 37.5 ft (11.43 m); **Height** 9.92 ft (3.02 m); **Span** 36. 92 ft (11.25 m); **Wing area** 226 sq ft (21 sq m); **Power plant** 1 × Rolls-Royce Nene 3 (5,100 lb thrust); **All-up weight** 11,500 lb (5,216 kg); **Empty weight** 8,434 lb (3,826 kg); **Weapons** 4 × 20 mm Aden cannon in wings.

The Supermarine division of Vickers-Armstrong built the Fleet Air Arm's first jet fighter, although the aircraft was actually destined to have been a land-based fighter. The Attacker was liked by its pilots, except by those who engaged the aircraft carrier flight deck barrier, because the cockpit was

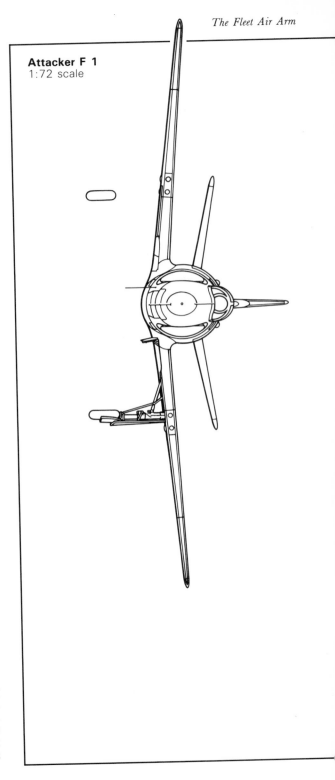

Attacker F 1
1:72 scale

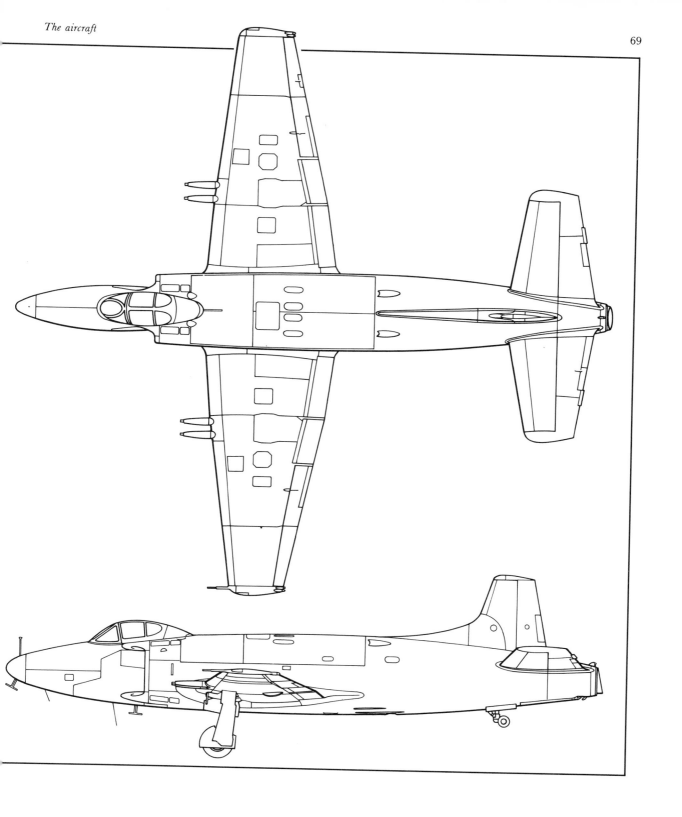

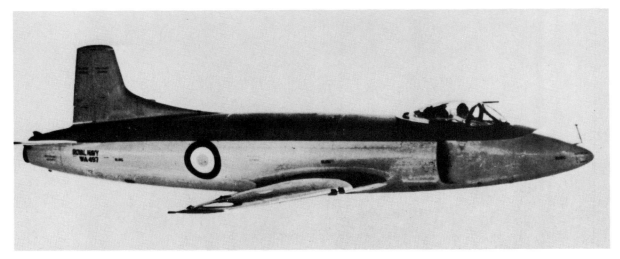

Attacker F 1 from the first production batch (Fleet Air Arm Museum).

so close to the nose that severe injury or death was likely from the steel hawser. To some eyes, the Attacker was a jet-power Spiteful (a development of the Seafire) and the designers had used some components from that ill-fated programme.

The type pioneered the introduction of the Martin Baker ejection seat but still used RATOG in certain weight configurations, especially when carrying the 250 Imp gal belly slipper tank. The first squadron commander, Lieutenant Commander (now Captain) George Baldwin described the Attacker as being better as a gun platform than the later Sea Hawk, and should have been developed further. Most of his contemporaries, including the world-famous naval test pilot, Captain Eric Brown, do not agree with him. In this assertion, Captain Brown is supported by the A&AEE Boscombe Down report on the aircraft's handling trials prior to service acceptance, and it seems that the Attacker F 1 was an extremely bad gun platform at altitude. Nevertheless the Attacker was a useful addition to the Fleet Air Arm inventory but too primitive to be considered for duties in the Korean War and so did not see action.

Serials *WA469-WA498; WA505-WA526.*

Attacker FB 1

Manufacturer Vickers Supermarine; **Purpose** Shipborne fighter-bomber; **Crew** 1 pilot; **Maiden flight** 1950; **Service entry** February 1952 (800 Squadron); **Squadrons** 767 (1953), 787 (1952-54), 800 (1952-53); **Phased out of service** 1954; **Range,**

Max speed, Cruising speed, Service ceiling, Rate of climb, Length, Height, Span, Wing area, Power plant, All-up weight and **Empty weight** as Attacker F 1; **Weapons** 4 × 20 mm Aden cannon in wings, 8 × 3 in rocket projectiles (60 lb warheads), or 2 × 1,000 lb (454 kg) iron bombs.

A modified version of the Attacker fighter, the FB 1 was designed to bring a strike role to the aircraft and thus widen the operational tasking possible aboard ship.

Serials include *WA527-WA534.*

Attacker FB 2

Manufacturer Vickers Armstrong; **Purpose** Shipborne fighter-bomber; **Crew** 1 pilot; **Maiden flight** 1951; **Service entry** September 1952 (800 Squadron); **Squadrons** 787 (1954), 800 (1952-54), 803 (1952-54), 1831 (1955-57), 1832 (1955-56), 1833 (1955-57); **Phased out of service** 1957; **Range, Max speed, Cruising speed, Service ceiling, Rate of climb, Length, Height, Span** and **Wing area** as Attacker F 1; **Power plant** 1 × Rolls-Royce Nene 102; **All-up weight, Empty weight** and **Weapons** as Attacker F 1.

The final variant of the Attacker went to sea in *Eagle*, but was mainly used by the RNVR Air Branch units around the country and did not leave second line service until 1957 when the RNVR was disbanded. The aircraft differed from the other two marks in having a more rugged cockpit canopy and modified ailerons which increased the safety of the aircraft in certain flight regimes.

Serials   *WK319-WK342;   WP275-WP304; WT851; WZ273-WZ302.*

Attacker FB 2 in September 1955 (Brian Service).

Phantom FG 1

Manufacturer McDonnell Douglas; **Purpose** Shipborne general purpose fighter; **Crew** 1 pilot, 1 observer; **Maiden flight** (F-4K) 27 June 1966; **Service entry** 30 April 1968 (700P Squadron); **First carrier deployment** June 1970; **Squadrons** 700P (1968-69), 767 (1969-72), 892 (1969-78); **Phased out of service** 15 December 1978 (aircraft transferred to the RAF); **Range** (combat) 1,000 nm (1,850 km), (ferry) 2,500 nm (4,630 km); **Max speed** Mach 2.1 at sea level; **Cruising speed** about 500 knots (926 km/h); **Service ceiling** 70,000 ft (21,335 m); **Rate of climb** 32,000 ft/min (162 m/sec); **Length** 57.58 ft (17.6 m); **Height** 16.08 ft (4.9 m); **Span** 38.42 ft (11.71 m); **Wing area** 530 sq ft (49.24 sq m); **Power plant** 2 × Rolls-Royce Spey 201 turbofans (12,250 lb static thrust dry, 20,515 lb with re-heat); **All-up weight** 56,000 lb (25,400 kg); **Empty weight** 30,000 lb (13,610 kg); **Weapons** 4 × Sparrow and 4 × AIM-9 Sidewinder air-to-air missiles; up to 10,000 lb (4,536 kg) underwing stores, including iron bombs and rockets; **Sensors** Air interception radar (radar warning receivers fitted in 1974).

During the 1964-66 'carrier crisis', the Fleet Air Arm ordered the Phantom fighter-bomber for service in *Ark Royal* and *Eagle*, for later embarkation in *CVA-01*. The cancellation of the *CVA-01* and early phase out of *Eagle* meant that only twelve operational Phantoms would be embarked in *Ark Royal*, with 892 Squadron, carrying the Omega fin emblem — the last of the conventional front line fixed-wing squadrons of the Fleet Air Arm.

Trials of the US design, which was partly fabricated and assembled at British Aircraft Corporation, Preston, and Shorts of Belfast, began in April 1968 at Yeovilton where the 700 series trials and intensive flying unit was based. It was soon found that the British engines gave greater power to the aircraft and in May 1969 a Phantom from the newly formed 892 Squadron won the *Daily Mail* Trans-Atlantic Air Race, averaging a true air speed of some 956 knots (1,770 km/h). The record stood until the USAF SR-71 spy plane visited Farnborough in 1974.

Trials were carried out in *Eagle* but could not be sustained because that carrier's deck was not strong enough to withstand the heat of the engines. *Ark Royal* was substantially modernized to take the new aircraft, which itself received considerable modifi-

Right *Phantom FG 1, 892 Squadron, with centreline fuel tank* (RN/Heron).

F-4K Phantom FG 1
1:72 scale

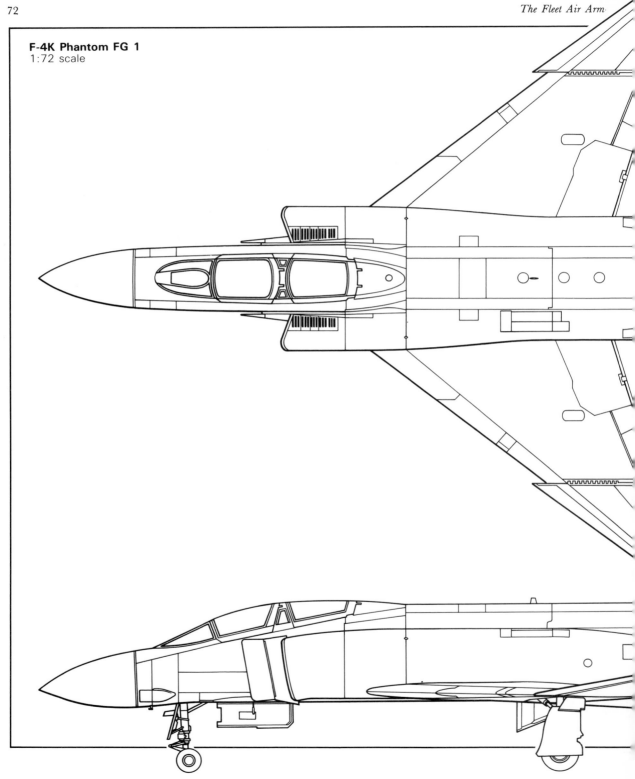

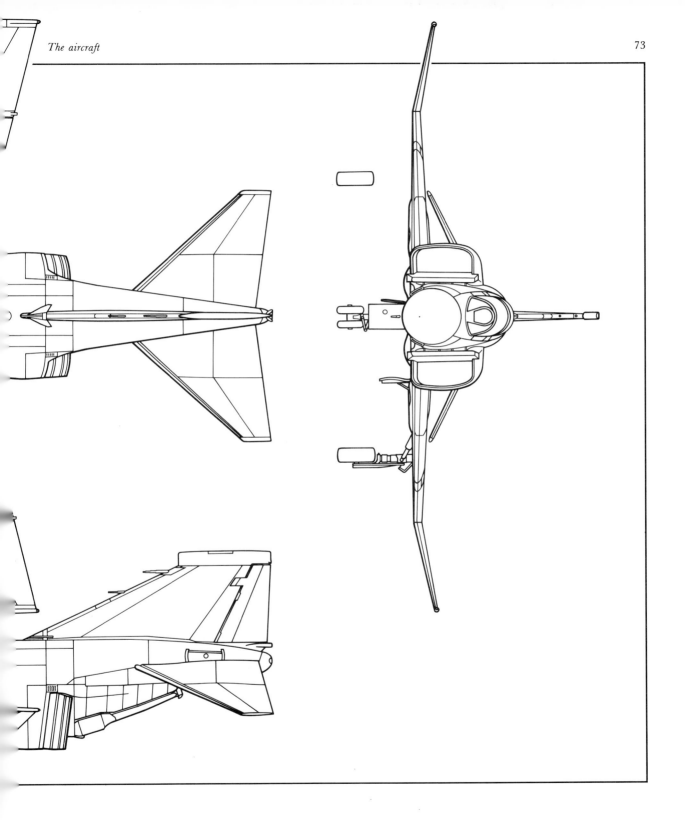

Flight deck activity in Ark Royal, *February 1978. Note the Phantom FG 1 on the waist catapult has its nose wheel leg oleo extended; the FDO is ready to signal the launch* (RN/Ark Royal/LA, S. Pratt).

cation including the adoption of an extendable nose leg oleo (to give a better angle of attack on launch) and a folding radar nose cone to allow the aircraft to use *Ark Royal*'s deck lifts. The Phantom was

The first production Scimitar F 1 in January 1957 (Vickers, via Gordon Roberts).

phased out of Fleet Air Arm service in December 1978 and most of the airframes were transferred to the RAF for air defence duties; many still remain in service.

Serials *XT857-XT876; XV565-XV592* (RAF airframes included); a further batch of seven aircraft cancelled.

Scimitar F 1

Manufacturer Supermarine; **Purpose** Shipborne fighter; **Crew** 1 pilot; **Naval Staff Requirement** N 113D; **Maiden flight** 27 April 1954 (Type 544), 11 January 1957 (production); **Service entry** August

Right *Scimitar in-flight refuelling under way* (RN).

Below *Scimitar F 1 tanker from 800B Squadron in* Eagle, *1964-65* (RN).

1957 (700X Squadron); **Squadrons** 700X (1957-58), 764B (1959), 800 (1959-64), 800B (1964-66), 804 (1960-61), 807 (1958-62), later with the Fleet Requirements Unit; **Phased out of service** 1966; **Range** 1,500 nm (2,778 km); **Max speed** 617 knots (1,140 km/h) at 10,000 ft (3,050 m); **Cruising speed** about 460 knots (833 km/h); **Service ceiling** 50,000 ft (15,240 m) **Rate of climb** 12,000 ft/min (61 m/sec); **Length** 55.33 ft (16.9 m); **Height** 15.25 ft (4.65 m); **Span** 37.17 ft (11.33 m); **Wing area** 484.9 sq ft (45.05 sq m); **Power plant** 2 × Rolls-Royce Avon 202 turbojets (11,250 lb st each); **All-up weight** 40,000 lb (18,145 kg); **Empty weight** 23,962 lb (10,869 kg); **Weapons** 4 × 30 mm Aden cannon or 4 × AIM-9B Sidewinder or 12 × 2 in unguided rockets (air defence); 4 × 500 lb (227 kg) or 4 × 1,000 lb (454 kg) bombs, or 24 × 3 in (50 mm) rockets; 4 × Bullpup missiles (strike); **Sensors** A1 radar.

The remarkable and beautiful Scimitar was the first Fleet Air Arm aircraft capable of supersonic flight, the first with swept wings, the first with power-assisted flying controls and the first to be nuclear-weapon capable. It was derived from a number of Vickers Armstrong Supermarine projects, including the butterfly-tailed Type 508. It entered service during a period when naval aircraft were equalling the ability of land-based aircraft for the first time.

Unfortunately, the Scimitar did not enter service on a good note as the CO of 803 Squadron, Lieutenant Commander J. D. Russell, was killed carrying out the first embarkation aboard *Victorious*. The aircraft was, however, the strike component of *Ark Royal, Eagle, Hermes* and *Victorious'* air groups at the beginning of the 1960s. Ashore, the Scimitar was a good aerobatic aircraft, performing at Farnborough and other venues. The aircraft saw service in the Far East and during the Kuwait crisis.

It was replaced by the Buccaneer in service, although a number continued in training, in-flight refuelling (800B Squadron) and fleet requirement roles for several years after the last front line unit had phased out the Scimitar.

Serials *XD212-XD250; XD264-XD282; XD316-XD333.*

Scimitar F 1
1:72 scale

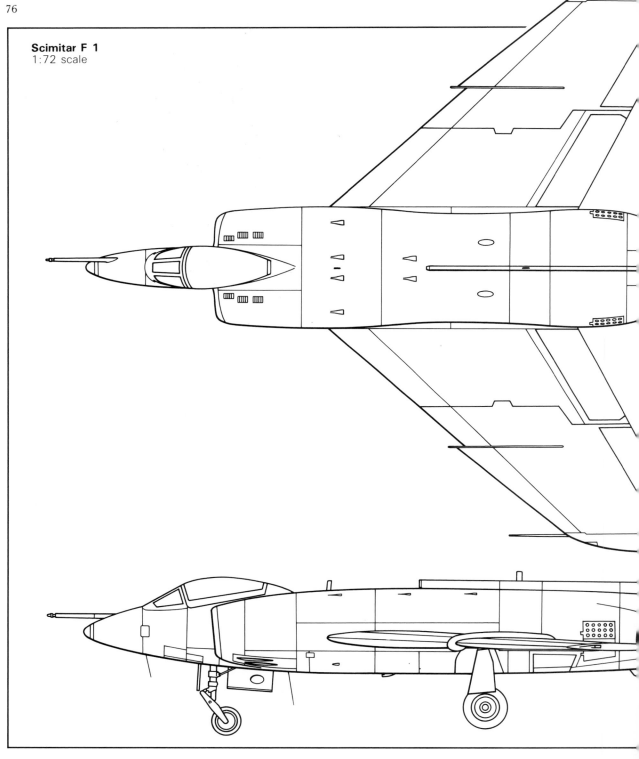

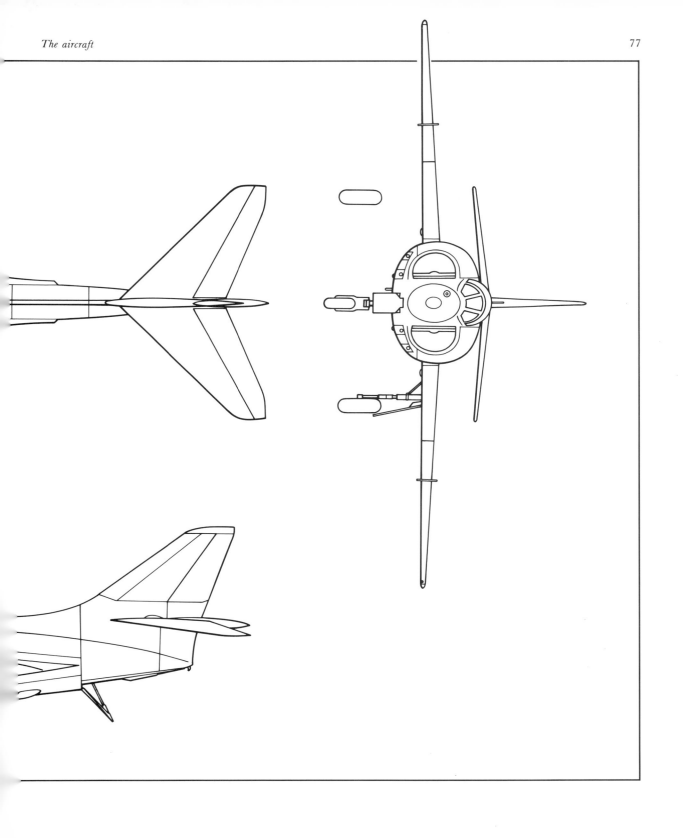

Sea Harrier FRS 1 from 700A Squadron, 1979 (RN/Heron).

Sea Harrier FRS 1

Manufacturer British Aerospace (formerly Hawker); **Purpose** Shipborne STOVL strike fighter; **Crew** 1 pilot; **Naval Staff Requirement** 1969; **Ordered** May 1975; **Maiden flight** 20 August 1978; **Trials Unit formed** (700A Sqn) 19 September 1979; **Sea trials** (*Hermes*) November 1979; **First front line squadron formed** (800) 31 March 1980; **First front line squadron embarked** (800) 13 May 1981; **Squadrons** 800 (1981-), 801 (1981-), 809 (1982 only), 899 (1980-); Still active; **Radius of action** 250 nm (463 km); **Max speed** 642 knots (1,189 km/h); **Cruising speed** 485 knots (898 km/h); **Max endurance** 7.3 hours (with one in-flight refuel); **Service ceiling** 50,000 ft (15,240 m); **Rate of climb** Classified; **Length** 47.6 ft (14.5 m), folded 42.3 ft (12.9 m); **Height** 12.2 ft (3.7 m); **Span** 25.3 ft (7.7 m); **Wing area** 201 sq ft (18.67 sq m); **Power plant** 1 × Rolls Royce Pegasus 104 vectored-thrust turbofan (21,500 lb static thrust); **All-up weight** 26,000 lb (11,794 kg); **Operational weight** 23,000 lb (10,433 kg); **Empty weight** 12,950 lb (5,874 kg); **Fuel capacity** 5,010 lb (2,273 kg); **Underwing load weight** 5,000 lb (2,268 kg); **Weapons** 2 × 30 mm Aden under fuselage gun pack; 4 × AIM-9L Sidewinder AAM; 5 × 1,000 lb (454 kg) iron bombs; 5 × 600 lb (272 kg); 2 × Sea Eagle ASM; 4 × 68 mm rocket pods; 5 × Cluster bombs; 10 × Lepus flares; 1 × 600 lb centreline + 2 × 100 Imp gal (363 l) wing tanks; 2 × 330 Imp gal (1,500 l) ferry tanks (2,340 nm range); **Sensors** Blue Fox radar and radar warning receiver.

It took the Sea Harrier a considerable time to reach operational service with the original ideas being discussed in the Admiralty in the middle 1960s, with light aircraft carriers in mind. The aircraft's antecedence dates to the Hawker P 1127 vertical take-off and landing (VTOL) aircraft which

Sea Harrier FRS 1
1:72 scale

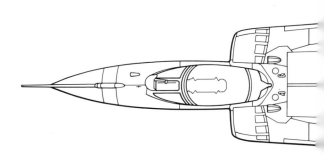

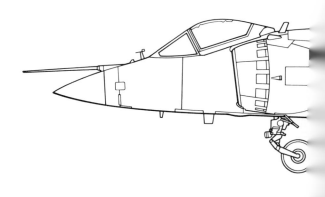

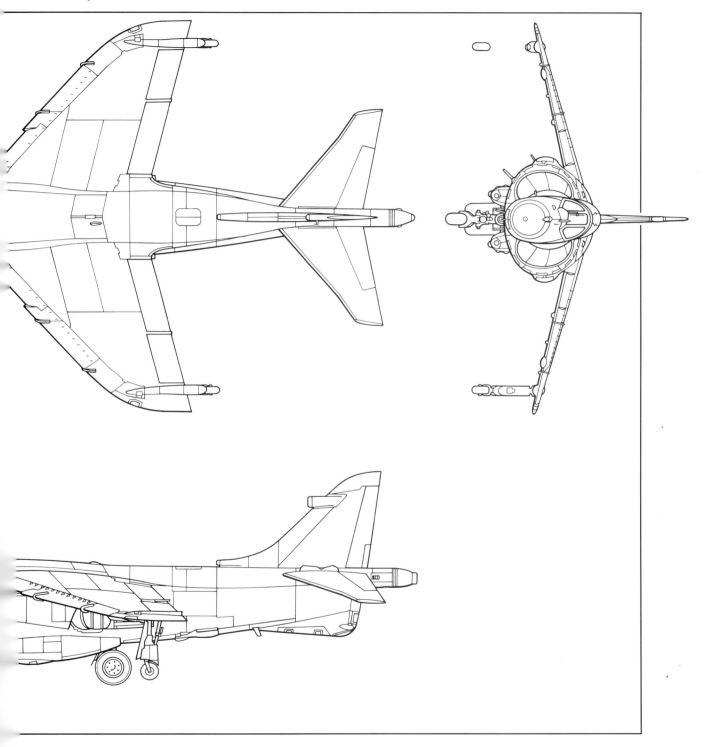

undertook sea trials in *Ark Royal* in 1963.

The major differences between the Sea Harrier FRS 1 and the RAF's Harrier GR 1, from which the former is directly descended, are centred around the cockpit area which has been completely redesigned to accommodate a fighter radar and other naval-orientated avionics. The radar originally fitted was Ferranti Blue Fox which is due to be replaced by Blue Vixen during the aircraft's mid-life update.

The Sea Harrier's electrical equipment differs from that of the land-based Harrier and the flying characteristics have been improved by providing increased roll reaction for 'dog-fighting' and allowing 2° more nose-down pitch control via greater tailplane positive travel. The engine and many other structural components have been replaced to give just four magnesium items — the Pegasus accessory gearbox, nosewheel and two outrigger legs. In addition, the ejection seat is the Martin Baker Type 10 zero-zero rocket type. The weight penalty for the navalized aircraft is less than 100 lb (45 kg).

In May 1975, 24 single-seat Sea Harrier FRS 1s and a single Harrier T 4 were ordered from British Aerospace and an additional ten were ordered in May 1978. Following the Falklands campaign, fourteen Sea Harriers were ordered as attrition replacements and in 1984 a further nine were procured. In addition, three Harrier T 4(N)s have been delivered.

In 1982, 28 Sea Harriers were deployed to the Falklands, including the temporarily re-formed 809 Sqn which flew to Ascension Island in formation. These aircraft, operating from *Invincible* and *Hermes*, flew over 1,100 combat air patrols and undertook ninety offensive support operations; 99 per cent of all planned missions were flown and six Sea Harriers were lost, but none in air combat.

As a result of the lessons learned in the South Atlantic, improvements were ordered for the radar (Blue Vixen), radar warning receivers, enlarged drop-tank facilities and the ability to carry four rather than two AIM-9L Sidewinder missiles. The wing is to be modified to give a leading edge root extension and designated Sea Harrier FRS 2.

The Sea Harrier uses the ski-ramp to increase its load carrying capability and to recover the aircraft hovers 'helicopter fashion' alongside the carrier for a vertical landing.

Serials *XZ438-XZ440* (Pre-production/development aircraft); *XZ450-XZ460; XZ491-XZ500; ZA174-ZA177; ZA190-ZA195; ZD578-ZD582; ZD607-ZD615.*

Sea Harrier FRS 2 with ASRAAM
1:72 scale

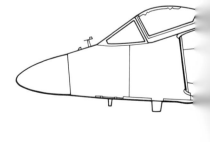

Right *Sea Harrier FRS 2, an artist's impression prior to the conversion programme* (British Aerospace).

Left *Sea Harrier FRS 1 from 800 Squadron, embarked in* Illustrious, *1985.*

Sea Harrier FRS 2 (mid-term update)

Following the Falklands experience, the Royal Navy has been authorized to begin a mid-term update of the Sea Harrier force from 1987. There were certain modifications carried out during and immediately after the conflict, including giving the aircraft clearance to carry four AIM-9L Sidewinder missiles instead of two.

The full update to FRS 2 standard is to be carried out using the existing Sea Harrier FRS 1 airframes (when the full complement of 44 will have been delivered). The new aircraft will have returned to service from British Aerospace and the Naval Aircraft Support Unit by 1989.

The major changes to the current aircraft will include the capability to carry up to four AIM-120 Advanced Medium Range Air-to-Air Missiles (AMRAAM), with the installation of Ferranti Blue Vixen pulse-doppler radar to give a 'look-down, shoot-down' ability over land or water. Secure voice communications for contact between the Sea Harrier pilot and controller in either warships or AEW helicopters and improved Thorn EMI Electronics Guardian radar warning receivers will be fitted. Twin colour CRT displays will be fitted and the aircraft will conform to the HOTAS (Hands-On Throttle And Stick) philosophy. But the American JTIDS (Joint Tactical Information and Distribution System) which was planned has been ruled out on cost grounds.

Serials include *ZE690-ZE698.*

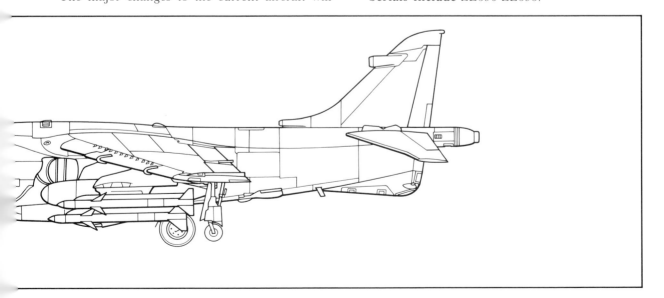

Sea Hawk F 1 during final approach to a Light Fleet carrier (Fleet Air Arm).

Sea Hawk F 2 from 1832 Squadron, pictured at Benson in October 1955 (Brian Service).

Sea Hawk F 1

Manufacturer Hawker Aircraft (Armstrong Whitworth); **Purpose** Shipborne Fleet fighter; **Crew** 1 pilot; **Naval Staff Requirement** N 7/46; **Maiden flight** 3 September 1948; **Service entry** March 1953 (806 Squadron); **Squadrons** 802 (1954), 804 (1953-55), 806 (1953-54), 807 (1954), 898 (1953-54), 1832 (1955-57); **Phased out of service** 1957; **Range** 490 nm (907 km) with drop tanks; **Max speed** 455 knots (843 km/h) at altitude; **Cruising speed** Approx 350 knots (648 km/h); **Service ceiling** 44,500 ft (13,564 m); **Rate of climb** 5,700 ft/min (29 m/sec); **Length** 39.83 ft (12.14 m); **Height** 8.75 ft (2.67 m); **Span** 39 ft (11.9 m); **Wing area** 278 sq ft (25.83 sq m); **Power plant** 1 × Rolls-Royce Nene 101 (with starting cartridge); **All-up weight** 13,200 lb (5,988 kg); **Empty weight** 9,560 lb (4,377 kg); **Weapons** 4 × 20 mm Hispano Mk V nose-mounted cannon; provision for drop tanks and rocket projectiles under wing.

Designed as the Hawker P 1040, the Sea Hawk is perhaps the most beautiful and graceful British naval aircraft of all time. Initial deck landing trials were carried out aboard *Eagle* during 1952 when the fighter was given the accolade of 'excellent' deck landing characteristics. Following the production of the first 35 airframes, production was transferred to Armstrong Whitworth, the company also developing the basic airframe through another five variants for the Fleet Air Arm and several more for foreign naval air arms.

The specification for this jet fighter called for the installation of contemporarily modern radios, approach and homing aids, as well as bullet proof windscreen, RATOG gear and wing folding gear to enable the aircraft to be struck below after flying operations.

In the Fleet fighter role, Naval Staff Requirement N 7/46 called for 285 nm (528 km) radius of opera-

tion, with 15 minutes combat at 35,000 ft (10,668 m) and enough fuel to allow for a loiter time of 20 minutes awaiting a recovery slot aboard ship. It was fitted with pressurized cockpit and ejection seat.

The aircraft's primary role was fighter (combat air patrol), but included the secondary roles strike, reconnaissance, ground attack (improved in later versions) and forward air control/naval gunfire support control. Some 95 Sea Hawk F 1s were built. After front line service, the aircraft flew with the RNVR Southern Air Division at Ford, Sussex.

Serials *VP413* (prototype); *WF143-WF192; WF196-WF235; WF901-WM905.*

Sea Hawk F 2

Manufacturer Armstrong Whitworth; **Purpose** Shipborne Fleet fighter; **Crew** 1 pilot; **Maiden flight** 24 February 1954; **Service entry** December 1952 (803 Squadron); **Squadrons** 802 (1954-55), 803 (1952-54), 807 (1954-55); **Range, Max speed, Cruising speed, Service ceiling, Rate of climb, Length, Height, Span, Wing area, Power plant, All-up weight, Empty weight** and **Weapons** as Sea Hawk F 1; **Phased out of service** 1956.

This version of the Sea Hawk was the first to be produced totally at the Armstrong Whitworth factory at Baginton, near Coventry. The aircraft had a relatively short service life but introduced power-assisted ailerons for better combat manoeuvring as a fighter. Forty were built.

Sea Hawk FB 3

Manufacturer Armstrong Whitworth; **Purpose** Shipborne Fleet strike fighter; **Crew** 1 pilot; **Maiden flight** 13 March 1954; **Service entry** July 1954 (806 Squadron); **Squadrons** 800 (1954-55), 802 (1956-57), 803 (1954-55), 806 (1954-55), 807 (1954-55), 895 (1956), 897 (1955-56), 898 (1954-55) and second line units; **Phased out of service** 1957.

Right *Sea Hawk FB 3 and FGA 4 aboard* Eagle.

Below *Sea Hawk FGA 4 from 898 Squadron,* Ark Royal, *in 1955.*

Range as Sea Hawk F 2; **Max speed** 520 knots (963 km/h); **Max speed** (fully armed) 440 knots (815 km/h); **Cruising speed** about 375 knots (695 km/h); **Service ceiling** as Sea Hawk F 2; **Rate of climb** 3,333 ft/min (17 m/sec); **Length** 40.23 ft (12.28 m); **Height** as Sea Hawk F 2; **Span** 39 ft (11.9 m); **Wing area** as Sea Hawk F 2; **Power plant** 1 × Rolls-Royce Nene 101 (15,000 lb st); **All-up weight** 8,926 lb (4,049 kg); **Empty weight** Not available; **Weapons** 4 × 20 mm Hispano cannon; 2 × 1,000 lb (454 kg) or 4 × 500 lb (277 kg) bombs or 30 × 25 (11 kg) or 20 × 60 lb (27 kg) rocket projectiles underwing.

Developed from the original design to have strengthened main wings for the carriage of heavy underwing stores, including 500 lb (277 kg) iron bombs and up to 10 rocket projectiles. Like all Sea Hawks, the FB 3 maintained the four Hispano cannon in the nose for self-defence and strike tasks, being almost equally good as a fighter and ground attack aircraft.

The Sea Hawk FB 3 was considered by its pilots to be a good platform for ground strafing with its four front guns and during the Suez action both squadrons operating the type fired thousands of rounds at targets ranging from radar stations and aircraft on the ground to gun positions, armoured cars and infantry support vehicles.

738 Squadron, one of the several second line units which flew the Sea Hawk FB 3, used the aircraft, painted bright red, as a demonstration aerobatic team during the 1957 Farnborough Air Show. Altogether 116 of this version were built.

Serials include *WM906-WM945; WM960-WM999.*

Sea Hawk FGA 4

Manufacturer Armstrong Whitworth; **Purpose** Shipborne ground attack fighter; **Crew** 1 pilot; **Maiden flight** 26 August 1954; **Service entry** November 1954 (802 Squadron); **Squadrons** 800 (1955-56), 801 (1955-56), 802 (1954-55), 804 (1954-55), 806 (1955), 807 (1955), 895 (1956), 898 (1955-57) and second line units; **Phased out of service** 1960; **Range** as Sea Hawk F 2; **Max speed** 520 knots (963 km/h); **Cruising speed** 300 knots

(556 km/h); **Service ceiling** and **Rate of Climb** as Sea Hawk FB 3; **Length** as Sea Hawk FB 3; **Height** as Sea Hawk F 2; **Span** as Sea Hawk FB 3; **Wing area** as Sea Hawk F 2; **Power plant** 1 × Rolls-Royce; **All-up weight** 8,995 lb (4,088 kg); **Empty weight** Not available; **Weapons** 4 × 20 mm Hispano cannon; underwing stores (see text).

In the early 1950s, with the experience of Korea, the Fleet Air Arm wanted a strike aircraft which was capable of giving close support to troops, particularly Royal Marines, on the ground. The main difference in the FGA (Fighter Ground Attack) version was the provision of various underwing offensive stores, including rocket projectiles, bombs and napalm-filled drop-tanks. A total of 97 of this variant were built.

Serials include *XE327-XE338.*

Sea Hawk FB 5

Manufacturer Armstrong Whitworth; **Purpose** Shipborne fighter-bomber; **Crew** 1 pilot; **Maiden flight** 1956 (converted FB 3); **Service entry** January 1957 (806 Squadron); **Squadrons** 802 (1957-58), 806 (1957-58); **Phased out of service** 1960; **Range** as Sea Hawk F 2; **Max speed** 500 knots (926 km/h); **Cruising speed** 425 knots (787 km/h); **Service ceiling** as Sea Hawk F 2; **Length, Height, Span** and **Wing area** as Sea Hawk FB 3; **Power plant** 1 × Rolls-Royce Nene 103 (5,200 lb st); **All-up weight, Empty weight** and **Weapons** as Sea Hawk FB 3.

This Sea Hawk variant was a reworked FB 3, modified with certain performance-related features, and it gradually replaced the FB 3s in 806 Squadron and two months later in 802 Squadron. The former only kept its Sea Hawk FB 5s for a little over a year, soon receiving the FGA 6, its last aircraft.

Sea Hawk FGA 6

Manufacturer Armstrong Whitworth; **Purpose** Shipborne strike fighter; **Crew** 1 pilot; **Maiden**

Sea Hawk FB 5s from 806 Squadron, Eagle, *1957-58.*

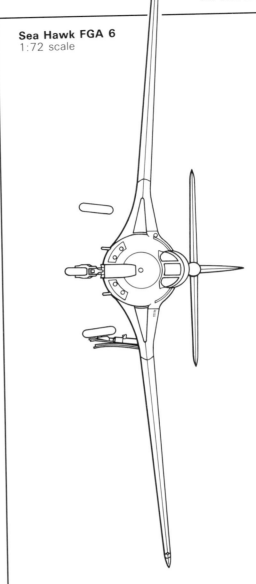

Sea Hawk FGA 6
1:72 scale

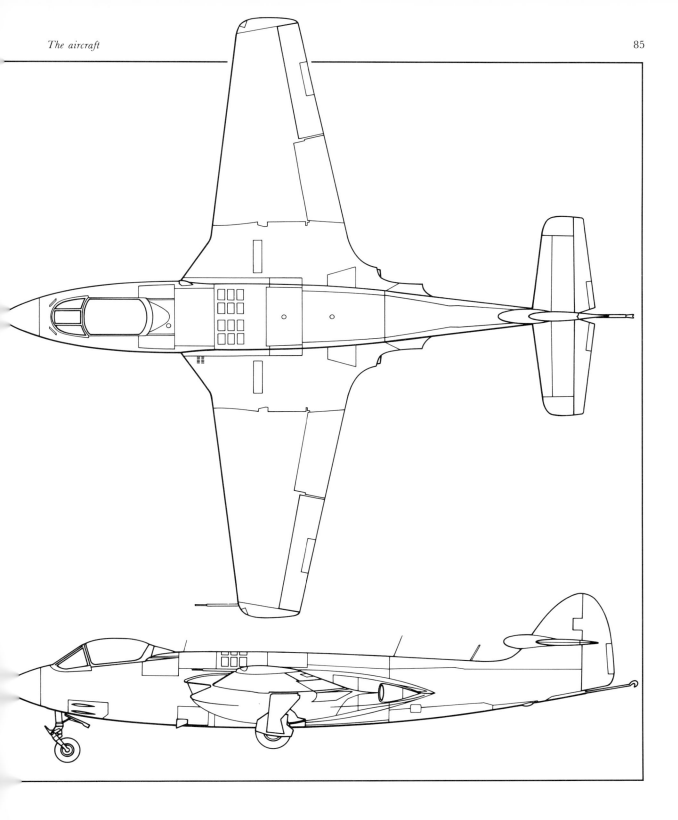

Left *Sea Hawk FGA 6 from 806 Squadron, Eagle, prior to disbandment in 1960* (Fleet Air Arm Museum).

Right *Sea Venom FAW 20 in prototype form in January 1953* (RAF Museum).

flight 1955; **Service entry** June 1955 (800 Squadron); **Squadrons** 800 (1955-59), 801 (1957-60), 803 (1957-58), 804 (1956-59), 806 (1958-60), 896 (1956), 897 (1956-57), 898 (1957-59), 899 (1955-57) and various second line units, including 738 Squadron; **Phased out of service** 1966; **Range** 600 nm (1,111 km); **Combat radius** 250 nm (463 km); **Max speed** 450 knots (833 km/h) at sea level; 460 knots (853 km/h) at altitude; **Cruising speed** Approx 300 knots (556 km/h); **Service ceiling** 44,500 ft (13,564 m); **Rate of climb** 5,700 ft/min (29 m/sec); **Length** 39.83 ft (12.14 m); **Height** 8.75 ft (2.67 m); **Span** 39 ft (11.89 m); **Width** (folded) 13.33 ft (4.06 m); **Wing area** 278 sq ft (25.83 sq m); **Power plant** 1 × Rolls-Royce Nene 103 (5,200 lb thrust); **All-up weight** 13,600 lb (6,170 kg); **Attack configuration weight** 16,200 lb (7,348 kg); **Empty weight** 9,560 lb (4,336 kg); **Weapons** 4 × 20 mm Aden cannon; 10 × 3 in rocket projectiles (60 lb warhead) or 25 × 3 in RP (25 lb warhead) plus 2 × 500 lb (277 kg) iron bombs and 2 × 100 Imp gal drop tanks, or 4 × 500 lb bombs, or 2 × 1,000 lb (454 kg).

The ultimate and perhaps best loved version of the Sea Hawk was the FGA 6; used operationally at Suez (along with the FB 3), this aircraft remained in front line service with 806 'Ace of Diamonds' Squadron. Many of the Baginton-built and Bitteswell-tested Sea Hawk FGA 4s were converted to FGA 6 standard at the Royal Naval Aircraft Yard at Fleetlands, using the Lee-on-Solent airfield.

After front line and some active service, the Sea Hawk was posted to a number of second line units such as the Lossiemouth-based Operational Flying Training School (738 Squadron), being replaced by Hunter GA 11 aircraft in 1962. During the Sea Hawks' operational service, pilots were trained by another second line unit, 736 Squadron, also at Lossiemouth, although most of the front line units were based at Brawdy.

The Sea Hawk lacked the radar-ranging equipment of, and carried less fuel than, its closest rivals, the US Navy's Cougar and Fury fighters; however the British fighter was able to fly higher and, in some configurations, to climb higher than the two swept-wing types. The advantage of a multi-role fighter (the term had yet to be invented) to smaller Fleet Air Arms was simply flexibility of roles. Proof of the aircraft's ability is easily told from the fact that the Indian Navy retired the aircraft from active embarked service in 1984 after the arrival of the country's first batch of Sea Harrier fighters.

Serials include *XE362-XE411; XE435-XE463.*

Sea Venom FAW 20

Manufacturer de Havilland Aircraft; **Purpose** Shipborne all-weather strike fighter; **Crew** 1 pilot, 1 observer; **Naval Specification** N 107/1950; **Prototype maiden flight** 19 April 1951; **Initial deck trials** 9 July 1951 (*Illustrious*); **Production maiden flight** 27 March 1953; **First front line squadron formed** (890 Sqn) 20 March 1954; **Last delivery** 6 June 1955; **Squadrons** 809 (1954-55), 890 (1954-55), 891 (1954-55); **Phased out of service** 1955; **Radius of action** 500 nm (926 km); **Max endurance** 2 hours; **Max speed** 547 knots (1,014 km/h); **Cruising speed** Approx 400 knots (741 km/h); **Service ceiling** 49,000 ft (14,935 m); **Rate of climb** 5,000 ft/min (1,524 m/min); **Length** 36.33 ft (11.1 m); **Height** 7.58 ft (2.3 m); **Span** 42.83 ft (13.1 m); **Wing area** 279.76 sq ft (25.99 sq m); **Power plant** 1 × de Havilland Ghost 103 (4,850 lb thrust); **All-up weight** 15,400 lb (6,985 kg); **Empty weight** 9,709 lb (4,413 kg); **Weapons** 4 × 20 mm Aden guns; provision for bomb and 8 × 60 lb rocket projectiles; tip tanks; **Sensors** AI Mk X (later AN/APS-57) radar.

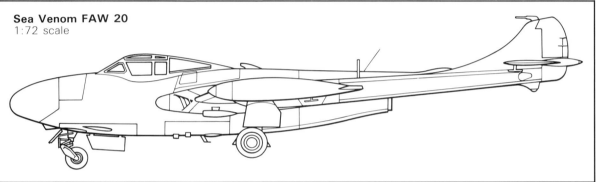

Sea Venom FAW 20
1:72 scale

The first carrier-borne all-weather fighter for the Fleet Air Arm, the Sea Venom FAW 20 was developed from a private-venture land-based aircraft, the Venom NF 2 and the first two prototypes were only partially navalized. Although fifty examples of the first model were built, they proved relatively unsuccessful during the sea trials in *Albion* and the front line squadron was renumbered 766 Squadron, to await the improved FAW 21. 809 and 891 Squadrons were also equipped (10 May and 12 November respectively) but did not embark.

Serials *WP277* (for evaluation); *WK376, WK379* and *WK385* (prototypes); *WM500-WM523; WM542-WM567.*

Sea Venom FAW 21

Manufacturer de Havilland Aircraft; **Purpose** Shipborne all-weather strike fighter; **Crew** 1 pilot, 1 observer; **Maiden flight** 22 April 1954; **Service entry** May 1955 (809 Squadron); **Sea trials** (*Bulwark*) July 1955; **Squadrons** 809 (1955-56; 1956-59), 891 (1955-56), 892 (1955-56), 893 (1956-59), 890 (1956), 736 (1957), 738 (1957-60),

750 (1960-61), 766 (1956-60); **Last unit disbanded** January 1959 (893); **Radius of action** 500 nm (926 km); **Max endurance** 2 hours; **Max speed** 547 knots (1,014 km/h); **Cruising speed** Approx 350

Sea Venom FAW 21, 894 Squadron, ready to launch from Eagle *in 1957 (Fleet Air Arm Museum).*

knots (648 km/h); **Service ceiling** 49,200 ft (14,996 m); **Rate of climb** 5,000 ft/min (1,524 m/min); **Length** 36.67 ft (11.18 m); **Height** 8.5 ft (2.6 m); **Span** 42.83 ft (13.1 m); **Power plant** 1 × de Havilland Ghost 104 (4,950 lb thrust); **All-up weight** 15,400 lb (6,985 kg); **Empty weight** 10,853 lb (4,933 kg); **Weapons** as Sea Venom FAW 20; **Sensors** AI 21 radar (later as part of AN/APS-35 system).

This was a considerable improvement on the earlier FAW 20, with features developed at A&AEE Boscombe Down including power-operated ailerons and the Martin-Baker Mk 4 ejection seat, working through a new clear-glass cockpit canopy. For better performance from the deck, the FAW 21 was fitted for RATOG and had long-stroke undercarriage (hence the increased height). According to Lieutenant Commander M. A. Birell DSC, the CO of 891 Squadron in 1954-56, writing in *Flight Deck* magazine, the Sea Venom FAW 21 'although not a brilliant performer, [its] 0.82 Mach in level flight left the day fighters behind as did its climb'.

The generally poor flight performance limited the aircraft effectiveness as an interceptor, mainly because of the time needed to reach 40,000 ft (12,192 m) and the model's inability to remain on combat air patrol.

On the flight deck, the FAW 21 was easier to handle, although the large radome, housing the AI

Sea Venom FAW 21, 893 Squadron, returned aboard Eagle *having been damaged by Egyptian anti-aircraft fire at Suez, November 1956.*

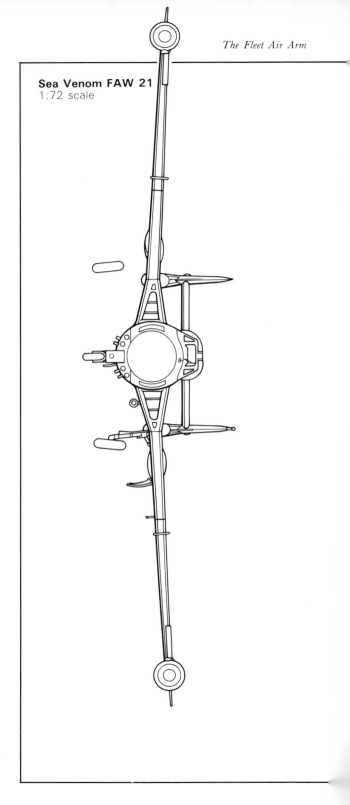

Sea Venom FAW 21
1:72 scale

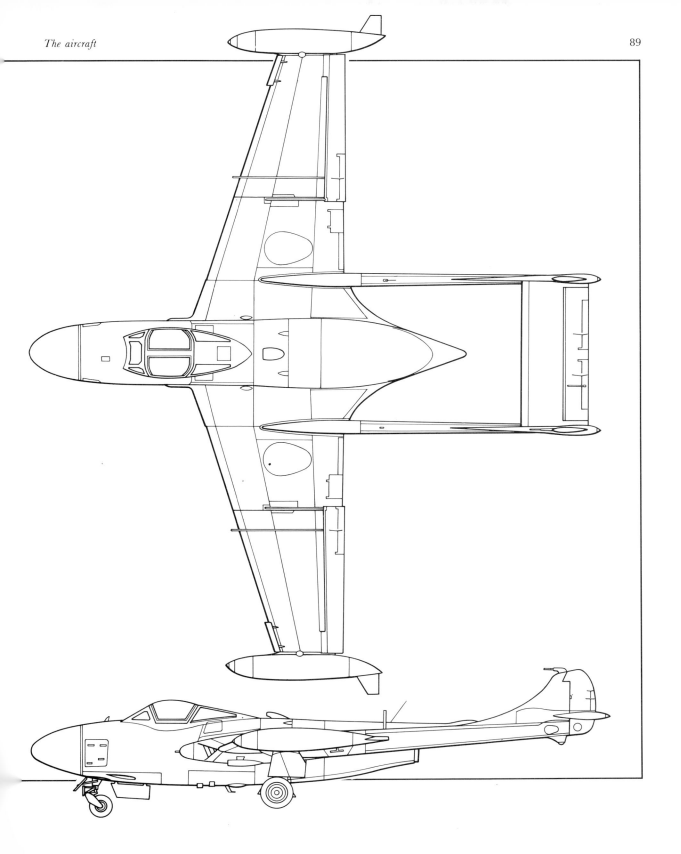

21 radar (AN/APS-57), made deck manoeuvring difficult and, again according to Commander Birell, 'it takes several shots to learn how to approach the catapult when loading...'

As a strike aircraft, the Sea Venom showed its abilities during the Suez Campaign ('Operation Musketeer') in November 1956, when four embarked squadrons in *Albion, Bulwark* and *Eagle* engaged targets in Egypt. Only one Sea Venom FAW 21 was lost during 'Musketeer', being saved from total destruction by the newly installed nylon crash barrier in *Eagle*. The incident is now famous as a result of the splendid photographs taken at the time and almost anything in print about the Sea Venom shows the aircraft, from 893 Squadron, taking the barrier after a wheels-up recovery.

A special sub-variant, the Sea Venom FAW 21ECM, was operated by 831 Squadron from 1 May 1958 until April 1960 (when the type was replaced by the FAW 22ECM), to investigate the use and operational abilities of electronic warfare. The aircraft embarked from RNAS Ford, from time to time, to engage in Fleet exercises; this role has been continued to the present day, with the joint RN/RAF unit, 360 Squadron, based at RAF Wyton and operating the Canberra T 17.

The Royal Australian Navy purchased 39 production aircraft of a modified FAW 21 form, known as the FAW 53 for service in Sydney. The French company, Sud Aviation (now part of Aerospatiale), produced the Sea Venom under licence in France, where the aircraft was called the Aquilon.

Serials *WM568-WM577; WW137-WW154; WW186-WW225; WW261-WW298; XG606-XG638; XG653-XG680; WZ893-WZ911; WZ927-WZ946* (for RAN).

Sea Venom FAW 22

Manufacturer de Havilland Aircraft; **Purpose** Shipborne all-weather strike fighter; **Crew** 1 pilot, 1 observer; **Service entry** January 1957 (893 Squadron); **First front line squadron formed** (894 Squadron) 17 January 1957; **Sea trials** (*Eagle*) August 1957; **Squadrons** 831 (1960-66), 891 (1957-61), 893 (1959-60), 894 (1957-60); **Phased out of service** (front line) 17 December 1960, (FRU airwork) 6 October 1970; **Radius of action** and **Endurance** as FAW 21; **Max speed** 500 knots (926 km/h); **Ceiling, Rate of climb** and **Length** as FAW 21; **Height** 8.52 ft (2.6 m); **Span** as FAW 21; **Wing area** 279.8 sq ft (26 sq m); **Power plant** 1 × de Havilland Ghost 105 (5,300 lb thrust); **All-up weight** 15,800 lb (7,167 kg); **Empty weight** Not available; **Weapons** as Sea Venom FAW 20 except development aircraft 2 × Firestreak; **Sensors** as Sea Venom FAW 21.

The improved power of the FAW 22 gave better performance through most of the flight envelope, but by the time the aircraft was entering service, eyes were on the Sea Vixen. In any case, the Sea Venom had always been regarded by the Fleet Air Arm as an interim aircraft between the Sea Hornet and the Sea Vixen. The FAW 22 assisted the Sea Vixen programme with Firestreak missile trials in the Mediterranean, which resulted in the first live firings of a guided missile from aircraft of an operational squadron, when 893 Squadron (*Victorious*) achieved eighty per cent hits against unmanned Firefly U 8 drones operating from Hal Far, Malta.

Sea Venom FAW 22 at Yeovilton (Fleet Air Arm Museum).

Sea Vixen FAW 1, probably 890 Squadron, carrying out deck landing practice in Hermes, *June 1960.*

The Sea Venom FAW 22 was superceded by the Sea Vixen FAW 1 from the middle of 1959 and the last aircraft was withdrawn from use in 1970.

Serials *XG681-XG702; XG721-XG737.*

Sea Vixen FAW 1

Manufacturer de Havilland Aircraft; **Purpose** All-weather interception and strike fighter; **Crew** 1 pilot, 1 observer; **Naval Specifications** N40/46 and N14/49; **Prototype maiden flight** (*WG236*) 26 September 1951; **Production maiden flight** (*XJ474*) 20 March 1957; **First carrier landing** (*XF828*) 5 April 1956 in *Ark Royal*; **Trials Unit commissioned** 4 November 1958 (700Y); **First front line squadron commissioned** 2 July 1959 (892); **First embarked** March 1960; **Second unit commissioned** 1 February 1960 (890); **Squadrons** 890 (1960-66), 892 (1959-65), 893 (1960-65), 899 (1961-64) and 766B (1959-68); **Phased out of service** 7 October 1966; **Range** 1,200 nm (2,222 km); **Max speed** 560 knots (1,038 km/h) at 10,000 ft (3,048 m); **Ceiling** 48,000 ft (14,630 m); **Rate of climb** 5,714 ft/min (29 m/sec); **Time to height** 7 min to 40,000 ft (12,192 m); **Length** 55.58 ft (16.9 m); **Height** 10.75 ft (3.28 m); **Span** 51 ft (15.54 m); **Wing area** 648 sq ft (60.2 sq m); **Power plant** 2 × Rolls-Royce Avon 208 turbojets (11,230 lb static thrust); **All-up weight** 35,000 lb (15,876 kg); **Empty weight** 24,500 lb (11,113 kg); **Weapons** 4 × Firestreak AAM, or 4 × Microcell 51 mm rocket packs, plus 28 × 51 mm rockets (internal); 2 × 1,000 lb (454 kg) iron bombs; 2 × Bullpup missiles.

Developed from an RAF requirement, based on the DH 110, for a swept-wing two-seat fighter aircraft. The Sea Vixen FAW 1 was the Fleet Air Arm's first swept-wing fighter, the first British aircraft with an integrated weapon system and the first to carry guided missiles rather than a gun armament. From 1961, the Sea Vixen squadrons changed from eight aircraft on strength to fifteen Sea Vixens, with seventeen crews, to make better use of the carriers' accommodation, having one Sea Vixen and one Scimitar squadron per ship; 890 Squadron was the first Sea Vixen unit so established. From the aircrew point of view, the Sea Vixen FAW 1 was a great step forward, having two engines, good radios and radar, but the aircraft had poor aileron control at deck landing speed and was difficult to line up and keep straight, thus was a difficult machine to deck land at night, leading to a 'fairly high accident rate' in the words of one former CO.

The Sea Vixen had an advantage over the Scimitar in that the former could carry two drop tanks and four weapon stations, whereas the latter had four stations in total; in addition, the Sea Vixen with Firestreak was an all-weather fighter as against the Scimitar's day only performance. In 1962, *Centaur* became an all-Sea Vixen aircraft carrier, with thirteen aircraft and fifteen crews embarked. Later 67 Sea Vixen FAW 1s were converted to FAW 2 standard.

Serials *WG236* (DH 110 prototype); *WG240; XF828* (navalized prototype); *XJ474* (navalized production); *XJ513-XJ528; XJ556-XJ611; XN647-XN658; XN683-XN710; XP918.*

Sea Vixen FAW 2

Manufacturer Hawker Siddeley; **Purpose** All-weather interceptor and strike fighter; **Crew** 1 pilot, 1 observer; **Interim prototype maiden flight** (*XN684*) 1 June 1962; **Production maiden flight**

Sea Vixen FAW 2
1:72 scale

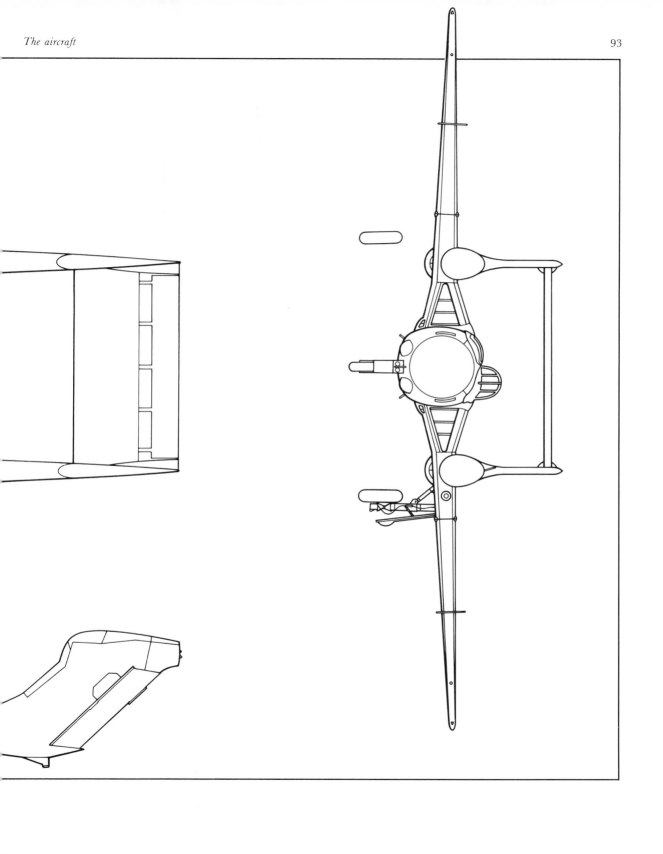

Sea Vixen FAW 2 of 899 Squadron, the last Fleet fighter unit, embarked in Eagle, *1971 (Brian Service).*

(*XP919*) 8 March 1963; **First front line squadron formed** (899) December 1963; **Embarked** December 1964 in *Eagle*; **Squadrons** 890 (1967-71), 892 (1965-68), 893 (1965-70), 899 (1964-72), 766 (1965-70); **Phased out of service** January 1972 (899); **Range** Not available; **Max speed** 556 knots (1,030 km/h); **Cruising speed** about 450 knots (833 km/h); **Endurance** 3 hours; **Service ceiling, Rate of climb, Time to height, Length, Height, Span, Wing area** and **Power plant** as FAW 1; **All-up weight** 37,000 lb (16,783 kg); **Empty weight** 28,000 lb (12,727 kg); **Weapons** 4 × Red Top AAM, plus 2 × 14 51 mm rocket pods (retractable), (strike) 4 × 500 lb (227 kg) iron bombs; Bullpup missiles could be carried.

The Sea Vixen FAW 2 was a direct development of the FAW 1 and although 29 new-built aircraft were manufactured between 1964-66, the bulk of the Fleet Air Arm strength came from conversions carried out at Chester and RNAY Belfast. The first fourteen aircraft were remanufactured on the production line from the third production contract at Chester where the final production run was also completed.

The FAW 2 had a number of important advantages over the FAW 1, starting with the intro-

Sea Vixen FAW 2, 893 Squadron from Hermes, *at Yeovilton Air Day in September 1969. Note the frangible observer's hatch cover to allow for straight-through ejection (Philip Birtles).*

duction to the Fleet Air Arm of the Red Top air-to-air guided missile which allowed enemy aircraft to be engaged from a wider aspect than the astern-only Firestreak. Lepus flares were also introduced to replace the Gloworm in the air-drop inventory.

In terms of appearance, the FAW 2 is characterized by the permanent fitting of the overwing boom extension slipper tanks, increasing the Sea Vixen's fuel capacity by some 2,000 lb (907 kg). A fuel jettison system was also introduced, together with new fuel pumps for better fuel management. These, linked with a new auto throttle system, allowed for very slightly slower landing speeds, but this was not to every pilot's liking. From the aircrew point of view, the improved underwater escape system, frangible escape hatch for the observer and command ejection, initiated by the pilot only, were particularly welcome.

To go with the Red Top missiles, the AI 18 interceptor radar was improved to give full engagement envelopes for the missile, with the pilot having an indication. Also in the electronics suite was a Wide Band Homer to allow detection of enemy S and X band radar sets.

The aircraft achieved fame on the Beira Patrols in the Indian Ocean, forming part of the British 'blockade' of Rhodesia, and during one patrol a Sea Vixen from *Ark Royal*, with 890 embarked, was lost after an engine flamed out, the observer being unable to escape despite the valiant efforts of the pilot. The Beira Patrol, through no fault of its own, was unable to bring Rhodesia to 'its knees'. The aircraft was also involved in operations in Aden in support of British security forces, but with the

demise of the fixed-wing aircraft carrier, the Sea Vixen FAW 2 was short lived and many were withdrawn with many hundreds of hours of useful life remaining. A number were taken in hand by Flight Refuelling Limited and converted into D 3 drones for guided weapons research.

Serials *XP919-XP925; XP953-XP959; XS576-XS590* built as FAW 2; *XJ489-XJ491; XJ494; XJ516-XJ518; XJ521; XJ524 and XJ526; XJ558-XJ561; XJ564 and XJ565; XJ570-XJ572; XJ574-XJ576; XJ578-XJ582; XJ584; XJ602 and XJ604; XJ606-XJ610; XN647, XN649-XN658; XN683-XN694; XN696 and XN697; XN699 and XN700; XN702; XN705-XN707; XP918* converted to FAW 2.

Sea Vampire F 20

Manufacturer de Havilland Aircraft; **Purpose** Shipborne fighter; **Crew** 1 pilot; **Maiden flight** October 1948; **Service entry** April 1949; **Squadrons** 700 (1955-56), 702 (1949-52), 787 (1949-53); **Phased out of service** 1956; **Range** 783 nm (1,450 km) at sea level; **Max speed** 457 knots (846 km/h); **Cruising speed** 302 knots (560 km/h); **Endurance** 2.35 hours at altitude; **Service ceiling** 35,000 ft (10,668 m); **Rate of climb** 2,500 ft/min (12.7 m/sec); **Length** 30.75 ft (9.37 m); **Height** 8.83 ft (2.69 m); **Span** 38 ft (11.58 m); **Wing area** 266 sq ft (24.7 sq m); **Power plant** 1 × de Havilland Goblin 2 (3,000 lb st); **All-up weight** 12,660 lb (5,743 kg); **Empty weight** 7,623 lb (3,458 kg); **Weapons** 4 × 20 mm Aden cannon.

Developed directly from the converted Vampire I which was used to make the world's first pure jet aircraft carrier landing in December 1945, the Sea Vampire F 20 was the navalized version of the Royal Air Force's Vampire FB 5 fighter-bomber. To fulfil the naval role, the aircraft was modified to take catapult and arrester gear fittings.

Only eighteen of the type were built and they were used only by second line training units to give potential jet fighter pilots an idea of the problems and advantages of the jet, especially at sea.

A number of specialist trials were carried out by the Ford-based Naval Jet Evaluation Unit (702 Squadron) for carrier trials embarked in *Implacable* and *Theseus* during 1949-50. Further trials in jet evaluation were carried out with Meteor and Attackers, but the Sea Vampire F 20 is reckoned by many of those first jet fighter pilots to have made the greatest contribution to advancing jet operations at sea.

Serials *VV136; VV141; VV152; VV165.*

Other Vampire variants:

Vampire I The third prototype was converted

Sea Vampire F 20 trials aboard Implacable (Brian Clark).

for deck landing trials and assessed in May 1945 by Lieutenant Commander Eric Brown. For deck landing trials in late 1945 the aircraft (*LZ551/G*) was modified with a tear-drop canopy and an uprated Goblin 2 engine. Trials were carried out in *Ocean*.

Sea Vampire F 21 This was the experimental undercarriageless trials aircraft for the rubber/flexible flight deck trials in 1949; two airframes were converted from F 20 standard and attached to 764 Squadron, serials *VG701* and *VT803*.

Strike aircraft

Firebrand TF 4

Manufacturer Blackburn Aircraft; **Purpose**

Firebrand TF 4 showing off its robust but not ungraceful lines (Rolls-Royce).

Shipborne torpedo/strike fighter; **Crew** 1 pilot;
Maiden flight 17 May 1945; **Service entry**
September 1945; **Squadrons** 736 (1948), 738
(1950-51), 813 (1945-46); **Phased out of service**
1951; **Range** 643 nm (1,190 km); **Max speed** 295
knots (547 km/h); **Cruising speed** 222 knots (412
km/h); **Service ceiling** 31,000 ft (9,450 m); **Rate of
climb** 2,600 ft/min (13.2 m/sec); **Length** 38.75 ft
(11.8 m); **Height** 13.25 ft (4.04 m); **Span** 51.29 ft
(15.6 m); **Wing area** 383 sq ft (35.58 sq m); **Power
plant** 1 × Bristol Centaurus IX (2,250 hp); **All-up
weight** 17,500 lb (7,938 kg); **Empty weight** 11,835
lb (5,368 kg); **Weapons** 4 × Hispano Mk 8 cannon
(wing-mounted), 1 × 1,850 lb (839 kg) torpedo
under fuselage or 2 × 1000 lb (454 kg) iron bomb
or 32 × rocket projectiles underwing.

The idea of a single-seat, carrier-borne torpedo
strike fighter was first considered in 1939 but the
pressures of the Second World War brought design
work to a halt until Specification N 11/40 was issued
to Blackburn. During the next five years, considerable time and energy was expended on the design,
the powerplant and operational doctrine of the aircraft, which eventually did not see active service.
The fin/rudder design and the airframe/engine
interfaces caused most of the problems.

Towards the end of 1944, development of the aircraft had progressed to a stage where a successful
airframe, with enlarged fin and rudder, could be
produced and the TF 4 entered service in 1945, the
first single-seat torpedo aircraft since the Blackburn
Dart of 1923-33. Some 102 were built.

One pilot's impression of the aircraft reads 'being
considerably larger (with a fin that looked as if it
had been made in the dockyard), much heavier and
somewhat slower than contemporary naval fighters
it was not popular. With some 15 ft (5.5 m) of metal
between the pilot's eye and the engine cowling it
was difficult to deck land and there were many
accidents. Only pilots with above average ability
were appointed to the two front line squadrons and
eleven out of twelve squadron pilots had at least one
accident each.'

Firebrand F I first flew in 1942 but was
abandoned before 1945.

Firebrand TF II first flew in 1943 and saw
limited service with 708 Squadron.
Firebrand III first flew in 1943 and saw limited
service.

Serials include *EK601-EK740*.

Firebrand TF 5/5A

Manufacturer Blackburn Aircraft; **Purpose**
Shipborne torpedo/strike fighter; **Crew** 1 pilot;
Maiden flight 1947; **Service entry** April 1947;

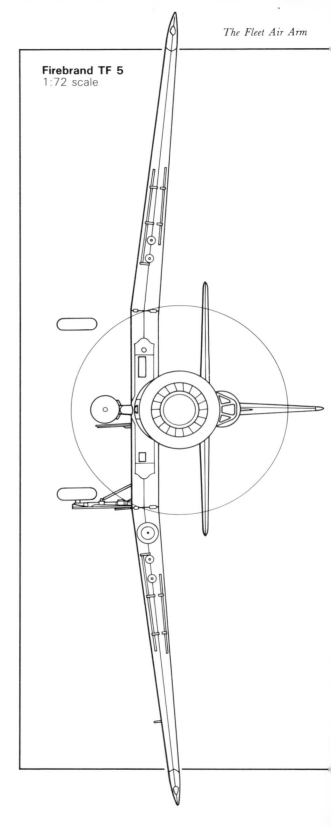

Firebrand TF 5
1:72 scale

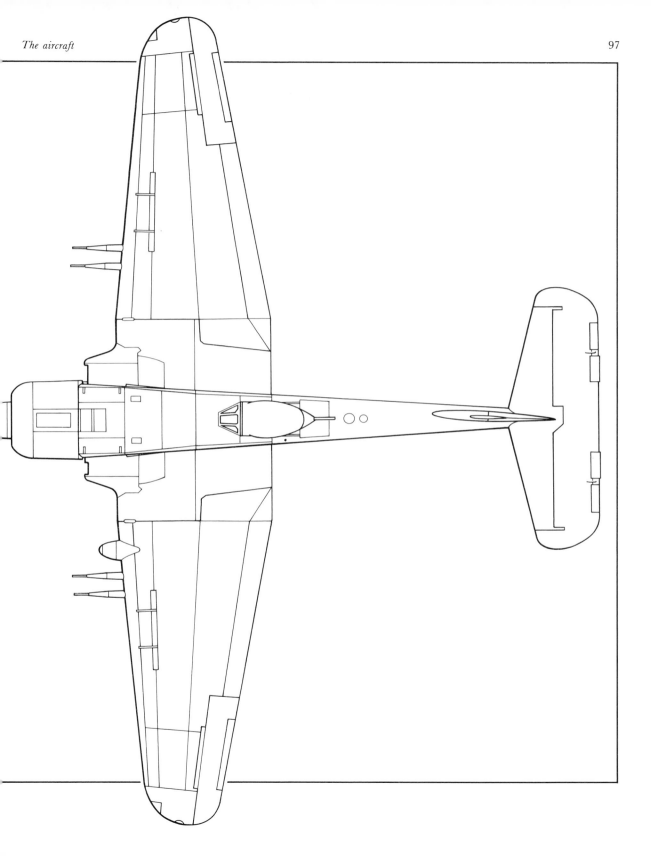

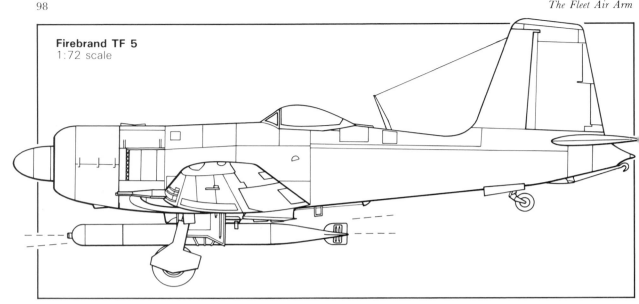

Firebrand TF 5
1:72 scale

Squadrons 759 (1951-53), 813 (1947-53), 827 (1950-52); **Phased out of service, Range, Max speed, Cruising speed, Service ceiling, Rate of climb, Length, Height, Span, Wing area, Power plant, All-up weight, Empty weight** and **Weapons** as Firebrand TF 4.

The Firebrand TF 5 was a developed version of the TF 4 with horn-balanced elevators and longer aileron tabs for fine trimming the aircraft for certain flight regimes, including deck operations. Some forty modifications were undertaken in service and production line TF 4s to bring them up to the required standard and 68 new-built aircraft were delivered.

To improve handling further, the TF 5A was introduced with powered ailerons but little detail of

the operational service of this variant is available, because it was absorbed into service synonymously with the TF 5.

The aircraft embarked in several aircraft carriers, including *Illustrious* for Arctic trials in 1952, before 827 Squadron disbanded in December of that year. The Firebrand was replaced by the Westland Wyvern.

Serials *EK741-EK850.*

Sea Mosquito TR 33

Manufacturer de Havilland Aircraft; **Purpose** Shipborne strike aircraft; **Crew** 1 pilot, 1 observer; **Maiden flight** 10 November 1945; **Service entry** August 1946; **Squadrons** 703 (1946-50), 771 (1947-50), 787 (1946), 790 (1946-49), 811 (1946-47); **Phased out of service** 1950; **Range** 1,095 nm (2,025 km); **Max speed** 334 knots (620 km/h) at altitude; **Cruising speed** Approx 250 knots (463 km/h); **Service ceiling** 30,000 ft (9,145 m); **Rate of climb** 3,000 ft/min (15.27 m/sec); **Length** 42.25 ft (12.88 m); **Height** 13.5 ft (4.11 m); **Span** 54.17 ft (16.5 m), 27.25 ft (8.31 m) folded; **Wing area** 454 sq ft (42.18 sq m); **Power plant** 2 × Rolls-Royce Merlin 25 (1,640 hp); **All-up weight** 22,500 lb (10,205 kg); **Empty weight** 17,165 lb (7,786 kg); **Weapons** 4 × 20 mm Hispano Mk 6 cannon in nose; (strike) 8 × 3 in rocket projectiles with 60 lb (27 kg) or 2 × 5000 lb (277 kg) bombs internally plus 2 × 500 lb underwing; (torpedo attack) 1 × 18 in torpedo below fuselage; **Sensors** Surface US-manufactured search radar.

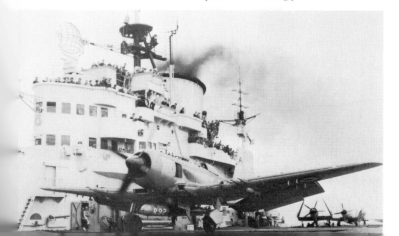

Firebrand TF 5, 813 Squadron, launching from Indomitable.

The Fleet Air Arm saw the need for a twin-engined strike aircraft, capable of operating from aircraft carriers, about midway through the Second World War. Development trials were carried out in 1944 (see below) with the highly successful Mosquito fighter-bomber design. A navalized version was ordered.

The aircraft's role would be to take a lightweight aerial torpedo to a target about 500 nm (925 km) from a carrier battle group, with twin-engined safety as demanded by the Fleet Air Arm for over-water operations in the North Atlantic and Pacific Oceans where alternative land airfields were not available. The end of the Pacific war took away much of the need, but the aircraft entered service with 811 Squadron for a short period of front line service before being moved to second line tasks.

Underwing fuel tanks were used to extend the range of the aircraft and trials were carried out at Ford to seek good fuel/ordnance combinations for the aircraft and its successors in service.

Serials include *TW227-TW257; TS444; TS449; TW256; TW268.*

Sea Mosquito TR 37

Manufacturer de Havilland Aircraft; **Purpose** Shipborne torpedo/strike; **Crew** 1 pilot, 1 observer; **Maiden flight** 1948; **Service entry** December 1948; **Squadron** 703 (1948-50); **Phased out of service** 1950; performance as Sea Mosquito TR 33 except **Range** 972 nm (1,800 km); **Max speed.**300 knots (555 km/h) at sea level; **Cruising speed** and **Service ceiling** as Sea Mosquito TR 33; **Length** 43 ft (13.1 m) approx; **Height, Span, Wing area, Power plant, All-up weight, Empty weight** and **Weapons** as Sea Mosquito TR 33; **Sensors** UK-designed ASV radar in nose.

Only six of this version of the Sea Mosquito were delivered to the Fleet Air Arm, being used for anti-shipping, anti-submarine and carrier training. The best recognition feature is the large thimble radome on the nose for the UK-designed ASV radar.

Sea Mosquito TR 33; note the thimble nose (via R.C. Sturtivant).

Serials *VT724-VT729.*
Other Mosquito variants:
Mosquito VI (Navalized) Two airframes were converted for naval trials of twin-engined aircraft and equipped with arrester hook in 1944; successful trials were carried out in *Indefatigable* in March with Lieutenant Commander Eric Brown at the controls. **Serials** *LR359* and *LR387.*

Other Mosquito VIs were used to train pilots and observers in twin-engined aircraft techniques and to prepare the way for multi-engined carrier flying. The aircraft was operational with 811 Squadron in 1945-46.

Mosquito FB 6 Later version operated by 771 Squadron for liaison and training tasks.
Mosquito PR 16 Used for Fleet requirements and fighter direction duties in 1948-52.
Mosquito B 25 Used by the Northern Fleet Requirements Unit, 1945-46.
Mosquito PR 34 Used for requirements and training duties, 1948-50.

Sea Mosquito TR 37; the first production aircraft at Hatfield, March 1948 (Fleet Air Arm Museum.

Sea Fury Mk 10

Manufacturer Hawker; **Purpose** Shipborne strike
fighter; **Crew** 1 pilot; **Naval Specification** N 7/43;
Maiden flight 21 February 1945; **Service entry** 31
July 1947 (807 Squadron); **Squadrons** 703
(1948-52), 778 (1947), 781 (1948-50), 802 (1948),
803 (1947-50), 805 (1948-49), 807 (1947-48);
Phased out of service 1950; **Range** 617 nm (1,142
km); **Max speed** 404 knots (748 km/h) at altitude;
Cruising speed 350 knots (648 km/h); **Service
ceiling** 36,180 ft (11,030 m); **Rate of climb** 3,060
ft/min (15.6 m/sec); **Length** 34.25 ft (10.44 m);
Height 15.88 ft (4.84 m); **Span** 38.4 ft (11.7 m),
16.08 ft (4.9 m) folded; **Wing area** 280 sq ft (26 sq
m); **Power plant** 1 × Bristol Centaurus 18 radial
(2,480 hp); **All-up weight** 10,660 lb (4,835 kg);
Empty weight 9,070 lb (4,114 kg); **Weapons** 4 ×
20 mm Hispano Mk 5 cannon in wings; 1,000 lb
(454 kg) of underwing stores.

The Mark 10 was developed from a requirement
for a long-range, single-engined fighter for both the
RAF and the Fleet Air Arm, especially in the
presumed island-hopping campaign against the
Japanese in the Pacific Ocean and surrounding
seas. The first production Sea Fury Mk 10
(originally F X) was first flown from Langley, near
Slough, on 30 September 1946 and the aircraft
allocated, with the production batch of fifty, to front
line fighter squadrons. Early production aircraft
were fitted with a four-bladed propellor and a short
arrester hook.

With the service entrance of the Seafire FR 47,
the Sea Fury was designated as a strike or fighter
bomber aircraft, designated the FB 11.

Serials *TF895-TF928; TF940-TF955.*

Sea Fury FB 11

Manufacturer Hawker; **Purpose** Shipborne strike
fighter/fighter-bomber; **Crew** 1 pilot; **Maiden
flight** 1947; **Service entry** May 1948 (802
Squadron); **Squadrons** 700 (1955-56), 736
(1949-52), 738 (1950-55), 739 (1948), 759 (1952),
767 (1949-52), 781 (1953-55), 787 (1949-54), 799
(1949-51), 801 (1951-55), 802 (1948-54), 803
(1948-51), 804 (1949-54), 805 (1948), 807
(1948-54), 808 (1950-54), 810 (1954-55), 811
(1953-54), 871 (1951-56), 898 (1951-53), 1831
(1951-55), 1882 (1951-55), 1833 (1954-55), 1834
(1953-55); **Phased out of service** 1956; **Range** 904
nm (1,674 km) with two 90 Imp gal tanks; **Max
speed** 400 knots (740 km/h) at altitude; **Cruising
speed** 300 knots (556 km/h); **Service ceiling** 35,800
ft (10,912 m); **Rate of climb** 2,778 ft/min (14.14
m/sec); **Length** 34.67 ft (10.6 m); **Height, Span,**

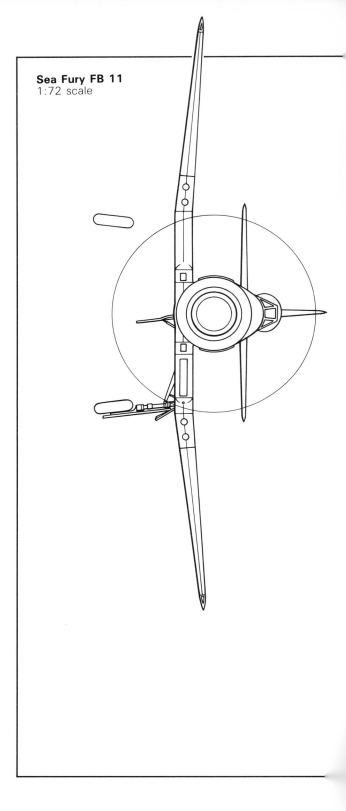

Sea Fury FB 11
1:72 scale

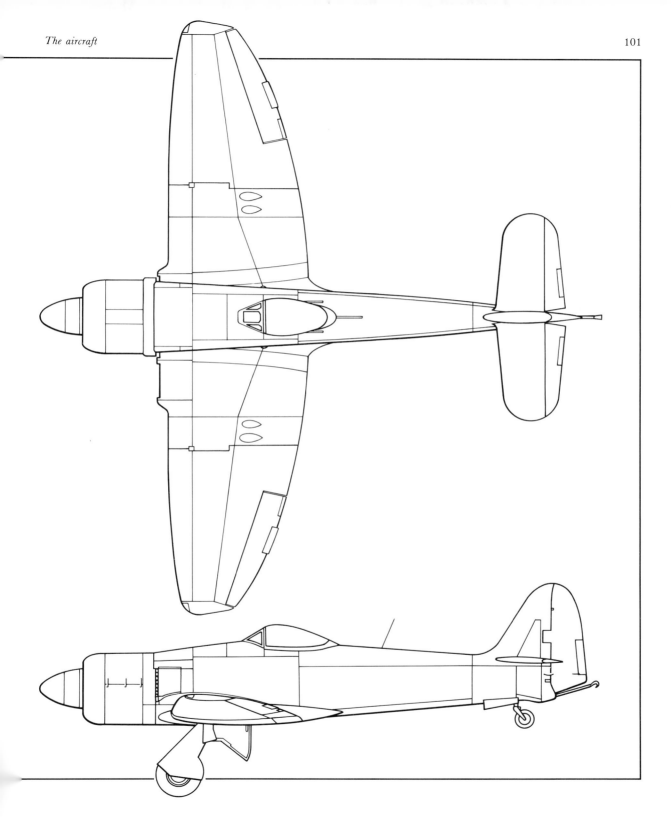

Sea Fury FB 11, the first production example of that mark (RN).

Wing area and **Power plant** as Sea Fury Mk 10; **All-up weight** 14,650 lb (6,645 kg); **Empty weight** 9,240 lb (4,190 kg); **Weapons** as Sea Fury Mk 10, plus 2,000 lb (907 kg) of underwing ordnance including bombs and rocket projectiles.

The last Fleet Air Arm propeller driven fighter and arguably the most beautiful, certainly from the pilot's point of view. The veteran naval test pilot Captain Eric Brown has described the aircraft's flying characteristics as 'delightful' and 'a handsome aircraft imparting an impression of strength'.

The aircraft served the Fleet Air Arm well in the

Sea Fury FB 11, 802 Squadron, embarked in Ocean *during the Korean War; note the 500 lb bomb underwing* (Captain Paddy Kckeown).

late 1940s and the early 1950s, especially during the Korean War when it was used in air groups for fighter-bomber, strike interdiction tasks. It was also good as a fighter aircraft as demonstrated on 9 August 1952 when a flight of four Sea Furies led by Lieutenant Peter Carmichael of 802 Squadron (*Ocean*) was 'jumped' by eight MiG-15s over Korea. In the short engagement which followed, Lieutenant Carmichael is credited with destroying a MiG-15, the Royal Navy's first jet 'kill', and another of the flight damaged a MiG before the Communist pilots broke off the engagement. The next day, the same flight damaged another MiG, again without loss.

The last FB 11 was delivered to the Fleet Air Arm in November 1952, completing a run which had included rates of ten airframes a month from the production line to the Fleet Air Arm.

Serials include *TF956-TF973; VW224-VW243; VX608-VX643; WE673-WE694; WG564-WG575; WH581-WH594; WN474-WN479; WZ627-WZ656.*

Wyvern TF 1

Manufacturer Westland; **Purpose** Shipborne torpedo/strike fighter; **Crew** 1 pilot; **Naval Staff Requirement** N·11/44; **Maiden flight** 12 December 1946; **Range** 1,025 nm (1,900 km); **Max speed** 396 knots (735 km/h) at 20,000 ft (6,100 m); **Service ceiling** 23,000 ft (7,010 m); **Length** 39.25 ft (12 m); **Height** Not available; **Span** 44 ft (13.4

m); **Wing area** Not available; **Power plant** 1 × Rolls-Royce Eagle 22 piston engine (2,690 hp); **All-up weight** 21,879 lb (9,924 kg); **Empty weight** 15,500 lb (7,830 kg); **Weapons** 4 × 20 mm Hispano Mk 5 cannon; 3,000 lb (1,361 kg) underwing stores or underfuselage torpedo.

Designed as a piston-engined torpedo and strike fighter, with a requirement dating back to the Second World War, the Wyvern took some years to come to fruition as an operational aircraft; in that respect it was quite typical of the naval aircraft projects of the time.

In 1945, the project became a purely naval programme to be powered by a turbine engine, either the Rolls-Royce Clyde or the Armstrong-Siddeley Python. Amongst the options given to the Admiralty was a long-range fighter, armed with four 20 mm cannon and having an endurance of five hours over 1,180 nm (2,185 km). The proposed carrier-borne torpedo bomber role was based on a performance of 700 nm (1,296 km) and an endurance of three hours.

The prototype Wyvern TF 1 was first flown at Boscombe Down (Wiltshire) with an Eagle 22 piston engine and a new eight-blade contra-rotating propellor. It was not successful and development continued with the TF 2 (see below).

The Wyvern TF 1 was deck landed aboard *Eagle* in 1952.

Serials *TS371; TS375; TS378; TS380; TS384; TS387; VR131-VR140* (pre-production).

Wyvern TF 2 with trial underwing tanks (Westland).

Wyvern TF 2

Manufacturer Westland; **Purpose** Shipborne torpedo/strike fighter; **Crew** 1 pilot; **Maiden flight** 19 January 1945 (RR Clyde), 22 March 1949 (AS Python); **Range, Max speed, Cruising speed, Service ceiling, Rate of climb, Length, Height, Span** and **Wing area** as Wyvern S 4; **Power plant** 1 × Rolls-Royce Clyde (4,030 ehp) or 1 × Armstrong Siddeley Python (4,110 ehp) turbine; **All-up weight, Empty weight** and **Weapons** as Wyvern S 4.

The Python-engined Wyvern was tested at sea in January 1950, following modifications to the Rotol propellor system; in addition, handling characteristics were improved with a taller fin. Of the twenty ordered into production, seven were converted to TF 4 standard (see below).

Serials *VP109* (Python); *VP120* (Clyde); *VW867-VW887.*

Wyvern T 3 A dual-seat trainer version first flew in February 1950 but was not adopted by the Fleet Air Arm and only *VZ739* was completed.

Wyvern S 4 (TF 4)

Manufacturer Westland; **Purpose** Shipborne strike fighter; **Crew** 1 pilot; **Maiden flight** May 1951; **Service entry** May 1953 (813 Squadron);

Wyvern S 4
1:72 scale

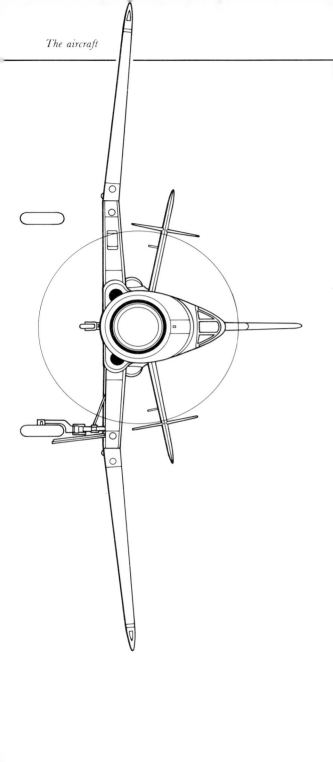

Wyvern S 4 during trials at Ford, but embarked in Eagle.

Squadrons 700 (1955-57), 703 (1954-55), 764 (1955-57), 787 (1954), 813 (1953-55 and 1956-58), 827 (1954-55), 830 (1955-57), 831 (1955-57); **Range** 785 nm (1,454 km); **Max speed** 333 knots (617 km/h) at sea level, 331 knots (613 km/h) at 10,000 ft (9,145 m); **Cruising speed** 303 knots (561 km/h) at 20,000 ft (6,100 m); **Service ceiling** 28,000 ft (8,534 m); **Rate of climb** 2,350 ft/min (12 m/sec); **Length** 42.002 ft (12.8 m); **Height** 15 ft (4.6 m); **Span** 44 ft (13.41 m); **Wing area** 355 sq ft (32.98 sq m); **Power plant** 1 × Armstrong Siddeley Python ASP 3 (4,110 ehp); **All-up weight** 24,500 lb (11,113 kg); **Empty weight** 15,608 lb (7,080 kg); **Weapons** 4 × 20 mm Hispano Mk 5 cannon in wings, up to 16 × 98 lb (45 kg) rocket projectiles, or 1 × 1,850 lb (839 kg) torpedo, or 3 × 1,000 lb (454 kg) bombs (two underwing, one on the centreline); **Sensors** None

Wyvern S 4 of 813 Squadron, a 'bolter' past Eagle*'s catwalk* (RN).

except provision of cameras (fuselage and wing tank); IFF.

The Wyvern S 4 was a modified variant of the TF 2, with a reshaped cowling to allow for cartridge starting of the Python engine, a new canopy, modified ailerons and auxiliary finlets on the tailplane. In 1953, the designation was changed from TF 4 to S 4, when the torpedo role was abandoned.

813 Squadron took its Wyverns to *Eagle* in 1954 and later several other front line squadrons embarked with the type, which was operational during the Suez Crisis with only one unit (830 Squadron). The aircraft had a good deck landing record, even during 'Operation Musketeer', but it was not suitable for ground attack operations against a well-prepared enemy. However, the former squadron commander at Suez, Commander C. V. Howard, says 'the Wyvern performed well as a steady weapons platform. On army support patrol... it could offer a fully loaded 20 mm cannon, sixteen 3 in rockets with 60 lb HE heads and a 1,000 lb bomb; with such a configuration we were able to give the Para [Parachute Regiment] effective support.' He also comments that the Wyvern was 'a good photo-reconnaissance vehicle, in both vertical and oblique modes'.

Some 98 Wyvern S 4s were produced even though it was arguably obsolete when it arrived in the first front line squadron.

Serials *VW880-VW886; VZ745-VZ766; VZ772-VZ799; WL876-WL888; WN324-WN336; WP336-WP346.*

Jet strike aircraft

Buccaneer S 1

Manufacturer Blackburn Aircraft; **Purpose** Shipborne low-level strike; **Crew** 1 pilot, 1 observer; **Naval Staff Requirement** NA 39; **Maiden flight** 30 April 1958; **Service trials** June 1959 (*Victorious*); **Service entry** March 1961 (700Z Flight); **Operational** July 1962 (801 Squadron); **Squadrons** 700Z (1961-63), 736 (1965-70), 800 (1964-66), 801 (1962-65), 809 (1963-65); **Phased out of service** December 1970; **Range** 1,200 nm (2,222 km); **Radius of action** 500 nm (926 km); **Max speed** 626 knots (1,158 km/h) at sea level; **Cruising speed** Approx 450 knots (833 km/h); **Service ceiling** Approx 50,000 ft (15,240 m); **Length** 63.42 ft (19.33 m), 51.83 ft (15.8 m) folded; **Height** 16.25 ft (4.95 m); **Span** 44 ft (13.4 m), 20 ft (6.1 m) folded; **Wing area** 515 sq ft (47.84 sq m); **Power plant** 2 × de Havilland Gyron Junior 101 turbojets (7,100 lb st each); **All-up weight** 45,000 lb (20,412 kg); **Empty weight** 24,500 lb (11,113 kg); **Weapons** 4,000 lb (1,814 kg) internal, 4 × 1,000 lb (454 kg) external underwing; nuclear-capable.

The Buccaneer is held in great affection by the Fleet Air Arm as it was one of the aircraft types which it embraced in the heyday of carrier-borne aircraft when the naval air group was equal to the land-based equivalent in performance and capability. In fact, the updated S 2 model remains in operational service with the Royal Air Force and the South African Air Force and is scheduled to do so until the fortieth anniversary of the prototype Blackburn NA 39's first flight.

The Buccaneer S 1 was designed to deliver nuclear or conventional bombs against sea or land targets by flying at subsonic speed under the enemy radar and thus achieving surprise. Designed to carry a good payload and without the need for airframe stressing for high supersonic flight, the aircraft was also fitted with advanced avionics systems to ensure precision navigation and accurate weapons delivery. Much of that equipment is still classified.

Half of the weapons payload is held in a rotating bomb-bay (later used for fuel in buddy-pack inflight refuelling trials) and weapons delivery was by conventional bombing run over the target or the more survivable 'toss bombing' technique of allowing the released bomb to follow a ballistic trajectory to the target whilst the aircraft remained

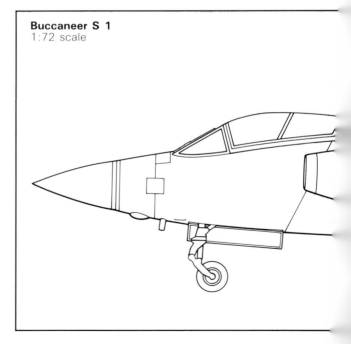

Buccaneer S 1
1:72 scale

Buccaneer S 1, painted in flash-reflective white for the nuclear strike role.

at a comparative stand-off range. This also allowed for the use of nuclear weapons and the Buccaneer fleet was painted reflective white for much of its career when tasked with the nuclear strike role.

The Buccaneer S 1 was also capable of photographic reconnaissance and 'deep' visual surface search. These roles were employed during the 1965 Beira Patrol in the Indian Ocean enforcing the Rhodesian oil sanctions. Production ran from October 1959 until the last S 1 was delivered in December 1963, after some twenty pre-production and forty production aircraft had been delivered.

During May 1963, the Blackburn Aircraft Company was absorbed into the Hawker Siddeley Group.

Specially converted Scimitar F 1 tankers of 800B Squadron were embarked in *Eagle* to provide operational and emergency in-flight services for the Buccaneer S 1 from 1964-66. Tasks included topping up heavily-loaded operational aircraft prior to setting of on a strike and topping up returning aircraft waiting to recover on a busy deck.

Serials *XK486 (prototype); XK523-XK536 (pre-production); XN922-XN935; XN948-XN973.*

Buccaneer S 2

Manufacturer Hawker Siddeley; **Purpose** Shipborne low-level strike; **Crew** 1 pilot, 1

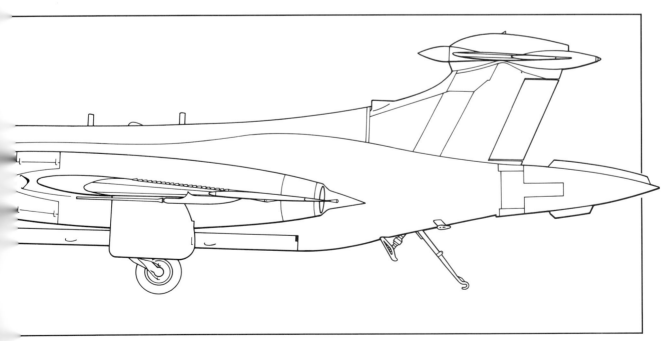

Buccaneer S 1
1:72 scale

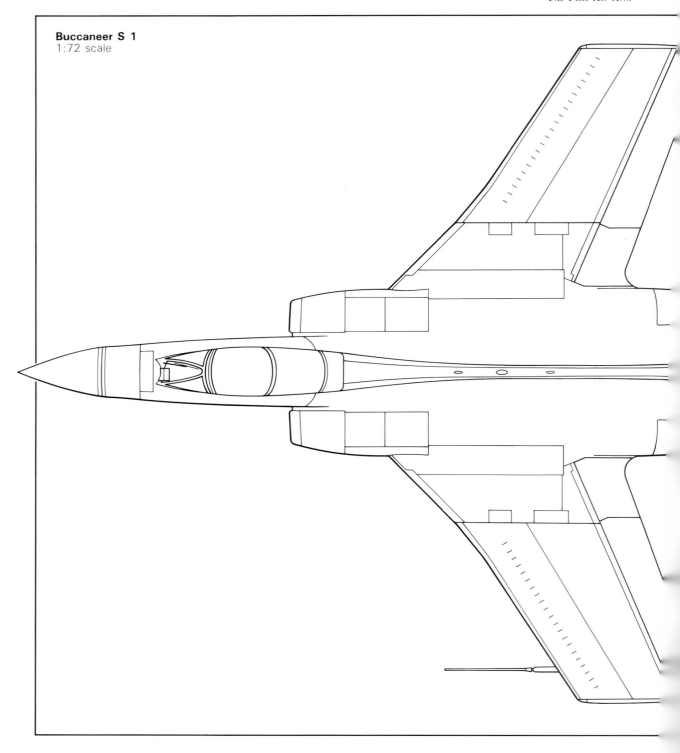

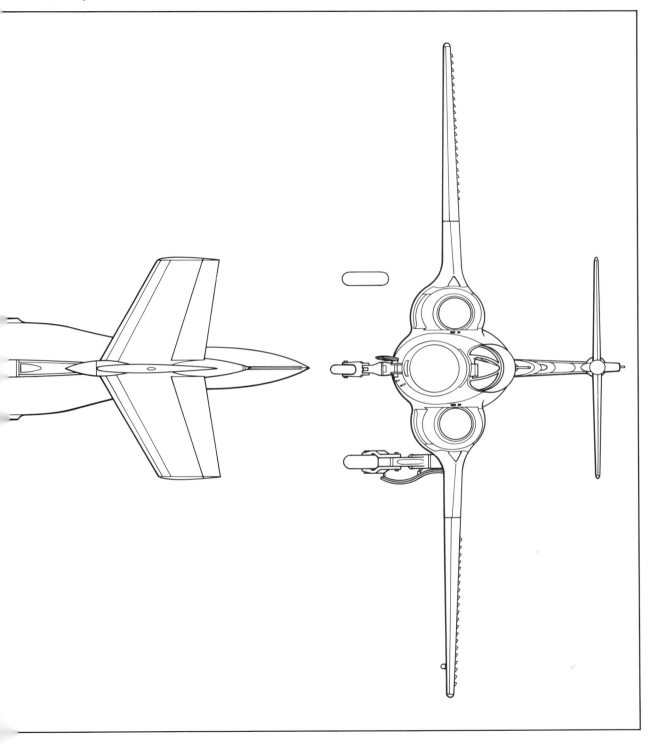

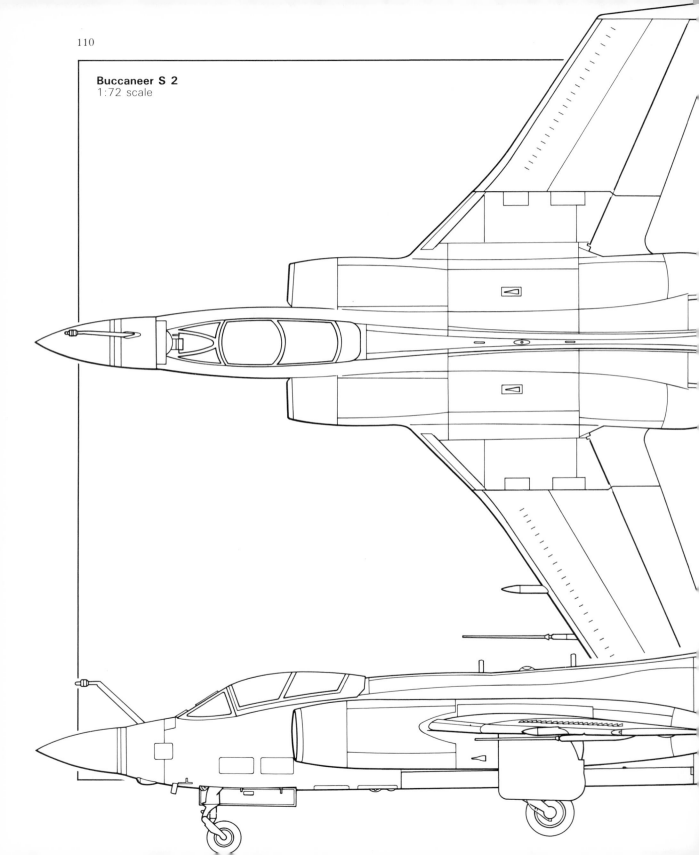

Buccaneer S 2
1:72 scale

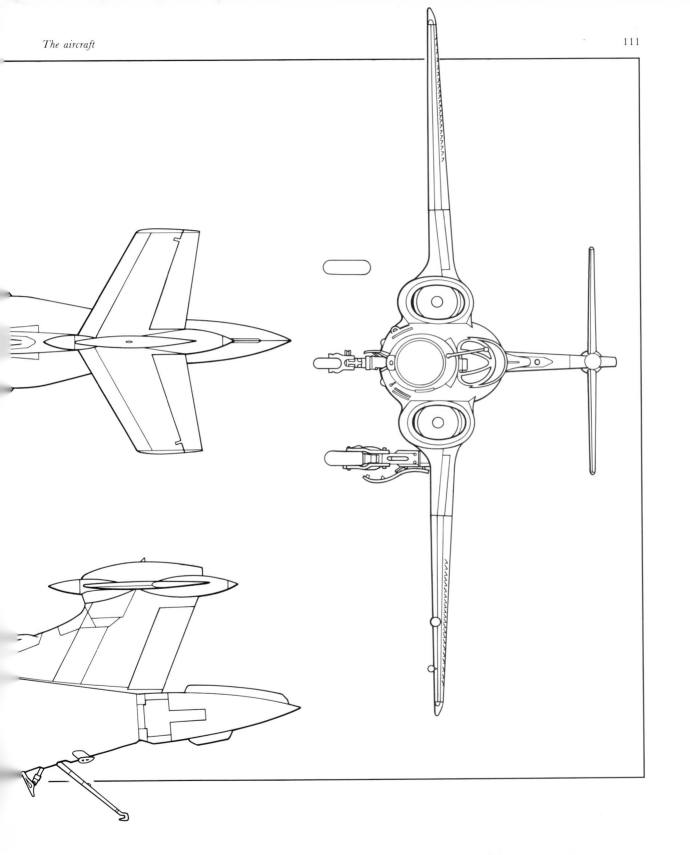

observer; **Conversion maiden flight** 17 May 1963; **Production maiden flight** 6 June 1964; **Service entry** 14 October 1965 (801 Squadron); **Squadrons** 736 (1966-72), 800 (1966-72), 801 (1965-70), 803 (1968-69), 809 (1966-78); **Phased out of service** 1978 (transferred to RAF); **Range** 3,000 nm (5,556 km); **Max speed** Mach 0.85 at 200 ft (61 m); **Cruising speed** and **Service ceiling** Classified because the aircraft is still active with the RAF; **Length** 63.42 ft (19.33 m); **Height** 16.25 ft (4.95 m); **Span** and **Wing area** as Buccaneer S 1; **Power plant** 2 × Rolls-Royce Spey 101 turbojets (11,100 lb st each); **All-up weight** 45,000 lb (20,412 kg); **Empty weight** 30,901 lb (14,017 kg); **Weapons** 16,000 lb (7,258 kg) ordnance, including 500 lb and 1,000 lb bombs, 18 × 68 mm SNEB rockets, 36 × 2 in rockets, Martel air-to-ground missiles (S 2D).

Using the original Buccaneer airframe, Hawker Siddeley Aviation achieved an increase in power (by fitting the Spey turbojets) and range (by increasing the internal fuel capacity). The Buccaneer S 2 was rated as the best low-level strike aircraft of the 1960s and it remained in production until December 1968.

The Buccaneer S 2 achieved some notable feats during its service career with the Fleet Air Arm, including the first non-stop crossing of the Atlantic Ocean on 4 October 1965. The aircraft did not use in-flight refuelling and covered the distance of 1,950 nm (3,611 km) in four hours. In March 1967, the Buccaneer again hit the headlines when aircraft from 800 and 736 Squadrons took part in the *Torrey*

Buccaneer S 2, 809 Squadron, during Ark Royal's *last deployment* (RN/FPU).

Left *Buccaneer S 2 of 800 Squadron, Eagle, in 1970.*

Right *Avenger AS 4, 815 Squadron; note the ASV radar radome.*

Canyon operations to destroy the oil cargo of a tanker aground off the Welsh coast, using Brawdy as a base for operations.

The Buccaneer S 2 was equipped for in-flight refuelling to extend its range for rapid reinforcement and for flight safety reasons if a flight deck was fouled during flying operations.

The last Buccaneer S 2 unit, 809 Squadron, also the last conventional strike unit in the Fleet Air Arm, was disbanded in December 1978 and its aircraft transferred to the RAF, having been shore-based at RAF Honington since October 1972.

Serials *XK526* and *XK527* (prototypes); *XN974-XN983; XT269-XT288; XV152-XV168; XV332-XV361; XV863-XV869.*

Buccaneer S 2A was the former naval S 2/S 2B aircraft modified for RAF use.

Buccaneer S 2C was the naval aircraft without Martel missile capability.

Buccaneer S 2D was the naval aircraft equipped for Martel.

Anti-submarine aircraft

Avenger AS 4/AS 5/AS 6

Manufacturer Grumman; **Purpose** Shipborne anti-submarine; **Crew** 1 pilot, 1 observer, 1 rating operator; **Delivery** 30 March 1953; **Service entry** May 1953 (815 Squadron); **Squadrons** 814 (1954-55), 815 (1953-55), 820 (1954-55), 824 (1953-55); Special duties (AS 6) 831 (1958-59); RNVR (AS 5) 744 (1955-56), 1830 (1955-57), 1841 (1955-57), 1844 (1956-57); **Phased out of service** 1960; **Range** 982 nm (1,820 km); **Max speed** 227 knots (420 km/h) at low level; **Cruising/patrol**

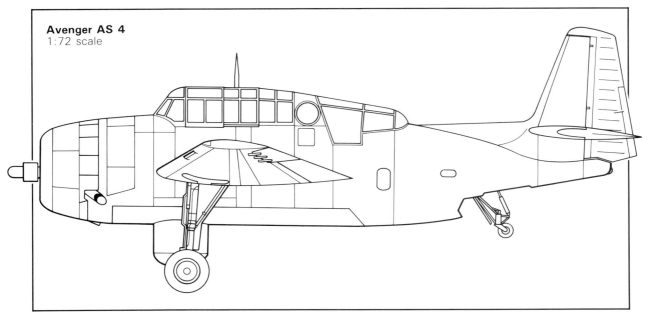

Avenger AS 4
1:72 scale

Avenger AS 4
1:72 scale

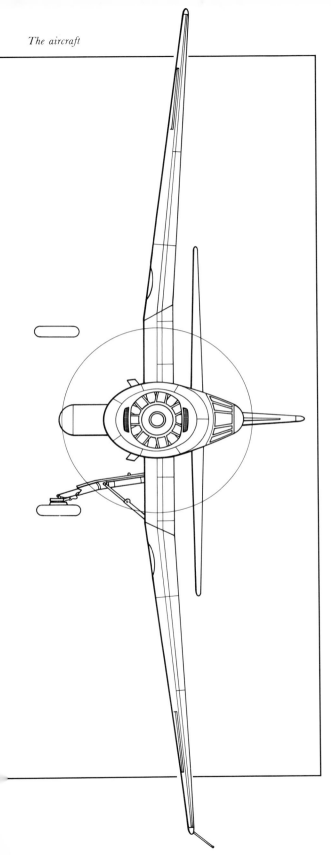

speed 131 knots (243 km/h); **Service ceiling** 22,600 ft (6,888 m); **Length** 40 ft (12.2 m); **Height** 15.67 ft (4.78 m); **Span** 54.17 ft (16.5 m); **Wing area** 490 sq ft (45.52 sq m); **Power plant** 1 × Wright Cyclone R-2600-20 (1,750 hp); **All-up weight** 16,761 lb (7,603 kg); **Empty weight** 10,700 lb (4,854 kg); **Weapons** 2,000 lb (907 kg) of iron bombs or depth charges underwing, or 8 × 3 in rocket projectiles (60 lb warhead) underwing.

Brought into Fleet Air Arm service in 1953 to serve as a stop gap before the first Gannet AS 1 units were ready to be formed in 1955. The aircraft were supplied under the auspices of the Mutual Defence Assistance Program and were basically the TBM-3E version.

The first aircraft arrived in the carrier *Perseus* in March 1953 and were later supplemented by eighty Avenger AS 4 and AS 5 which had been modified for British requirements. The aircraft were operational in time for the 1953 Coronation Naval Review Flypast at Spithead on 15 June.

In front line units, the AS 4 was operational first and later supplemented and eventually replaced by the AS 5. The aircraft were embarked for sea duties, including *Eagle*. In 1958 the electronic countermeasures unit, 831 Squadron, was equipped with several Avenger AS 6 variants, used for testing Fleet defences and other electronic warfare tasks. These were the last Avengers in British service. After front line service, the aircraft were deployed to RNVR (AS 5) and second line units for trials, training and other duties.

881 Squadron, Royal Canadian Navy, operated the Avenger TBM-3E during 1951-57, including embarkation in *Magnificent* and shored-based in Canada.

Serials *XB296-XB332; XB335-XB404; XB437-XB449.*

Barracuda TR 3

Manufacturer Fairey Aviation; **Purpose** Shipborne torpedo bomber; **Crew** 1 pilot, 1 observer; **Service entry** January 1943 (Mk III), December 1947 (TR 3); **Squadrons** (III) 744 (1951-53), 783 (1946); (TR 3) 750 (1952-53), 815 (1947-53); **Phased out of service** 1953; **Range** 977 nm (1,810 km) at altitude; **Max speed** 208 knots (385 km/h) at altitude; **Cruising speed** 148 knots (274 km/h); **Service ceiling** 20,000 ft (6,096 m); **Length** 39.75 ft (12.11 m); **Height** 15.08 ft (4.6 m); **Span** 49.17 ft (14.99 m); **Wing area** 367 sq ft (34 sq m); **Power plant** 1 × Rolls-Royce Merlin 32 (1,640 hp); **All-up weight** 14,100 lb (6,396 kg); **Empty weight** 9,407 lb (4,267 kg); **Weapons** 1 × 1,572 lb (713 kg) torpedo or 4 × 250 lb (113 kg)

depth charges; **Sensors** ASV Mk 11 radar under rear fuselage.

In December 1947, the Barracuda Mk III/TR 3 was returned to squadron service from storage for front line anti-submarine warfare training with 815 Squadron at Eglinton (Northern Ireland) and later others were used by second line units. Only about fifteen aircraft are thought to have returned to

Above *Barracuda III, later modified to TBR 3, standard,* (RN/Heron).

Below right *Firefly AS 5 from* Glory; *note the lack of wing guns* (Fleet Air Arm Museum).

Below *Barracuda V, probably aboard* Indomitable.

active service and they were replaced by Avengers in due course.

Serials include *RJ759-RJ799; RJ902-RJ948; RJ963-RJ966.*

Barracuda 5

Manufacturer Fairey Aviation; **Purpose** Shipborne reconnaissance/strike; **Crew** 1 pilot, 1 observer; **Maiden flight** November 16 1944; **Service entry** 27 October 1947; **Squadron** 783 (1947-48); **Phased out of service** 1950; **Range** 970 nm (1,800 km); **Max speed** 220 knots (407 km/h) at altitude; **Cruising speed** 180 knots (333 km/h); **Service ceiling** 24,000 ft (7,315 m); **Length** 41.08 ft (12.52 m); **Height** 13.2 ft (4.02 m); **Span** 53.04 ft (16.17 m); **Wing area** 435 sq ft (40.41 sq m); **Power plant** 1 × Rolls-royce Griffon 37 (2,020 hp); **Weapons** 2,000 lb (907 kg) underwing stores, no guns; **Sensors** ASV Mk 9 radar in wing-mounted pod.

Designed as a replacement for the older Barracudas with the British Pacific Fleet, the Mk V (Mk 5) did not see front line service and records indicate that only Lee-on-Solent based 783 Squadron was equipped with the type in the immediate post-war years. Only some thirty airframes were completed.

Serials *DT845, PM944, PM941, PM940* (conversions for prototypes); *RK530-RK574.*

Firefly AS 5

Manufacturer Fairey Aviation; **Purpose** Shipborne ASW; **Crew** 1 pilot, 1 observer; **Maiden flight** 12 December 1947; **Service entry** 9 January 1948; **Squadrons** 810 (1949-51), 812 (1948-51), 814 (1949-50), 816 (1949-54), 817 (1950-52), 820 (1951), 825 (1949-51, 1953-54) and various second line units; **Phased out of service** 1956; **Range** 573 nm (1,062 km); **Max speed** 335 knots (620 km/h) at 14,000 ft (4,627 m); **Cruising speed** 191 knots (354 km/h); **Endurance** 6.5 hours; **Service ceiling** 28,400 ft (8,656 m); **Rate of climb** 1,450 ft/min (7.4 m/sec); **Length** 27.92 ft (8.51 m); **Height** 14.33 ft (4.37 m); **Span** 41.17 ft (12.5 m); **Wing area** 330 sq ft (30.7 sq m); **Power plant** 1 × Rolls-Royce Griffon 74 (2,250 hp); **All-up weight** 16,096 lb (7,300 kg); **Empty weight** 9,674 lb (4,388 kg); **Weapons** 4 × 20 mm Aden cannon in wings, 16 × 3 in rocket projectiles (60 lb warhead) or 2 × 1,000 lbs (454 kg) bombs underwing; **Sensor** ASV Mk 9 in wing-mounted pod.

The Firefly AS 5 entered Fleet Air Arm service in time for the outbreak of the Korean War and many thousands of successful strike sorties were flown by these aircraft in the period 1950-53. In 1954, the Firefly was in action again with 825 Squadron (*Warrior*) hunting down Communist bandits in Malaya.

Although identified as an ASW aircraft, the

AS 5 could undertake strike tasks ashore, being armed with the four Aden cannon, as well as carrying rockets and bombs. It was often possible to see mixed sorties of Firefly FR 5, AS 5 and later AS 6 operating together from one aircraft carrier or shore station. Besides the Fleet Air Arm and the Dutch naval air service, the Firefly AS 5 was flown by the Royal Australian and Canadian navies.

Serials include *VX371-VX436.*

Firefly AS 6

Manufacturer Fairey Aviation; **Purpose** Shipborne ASW; **Crew** 1 pilot, 1 observer; **Maiden flight** 23 March 1949; **Service entry** 26 May 1950; Squadrons 812 (1951-53), 814 (1951-54), 816 (1951-55), 817 (1950-55), 820 (1950-54), 821 (1951-52), 824 (1952-53), 826 (1951-55), 1830 (1951-55), 1841 (1955), 1844 (1955-56) and second line units; **Phased out of service** 1956; **Range, Max speed, Cruising speed, Endurance, Service ceiling, Rate of climb, Length, Height, Span, Wing area, Power plant, All-up weight** and **Empty weight** as Firefly AS 5; **Weapons** Provision for 2 × 1,000 lb (454 kg) underwing stores, including 16 × 3 in rocket projectiles (60 lb warhead); **Sensor** ASV Mk 9 radar in wing-mounted pod.

The penultimate Firefly was a version of the Mk 5 but without the wing-mounted Aden cannon and using only underwing stores. The aircraft was designed to act as an anti-submarine weapon, directed on to the target by the radar of the mother ship or escorts. It had only the ASV Mk 9 radar to detect a submarine, although some aircraft were also fitted with the Leigh Light searchlight system for night-time operations.

737 Squadron operated the aircraft in 1954-55 to train observers in anti-submarine warfare which, following the development of the Soviet Navy, was seen in the early 1950s to be an important future threat to the United Kingdom. The continued build-up of Soviet and Warsaw Pact submarines has proved this policy correct. Another observer training unit was 796 Squadron which used the AS 6 and the T 3 trainer in the 1951-53 period. To accommodate the various requirements of the Royal Navy in the Channel exercise areas in the period 1950-53, 771 Squadron was equipped with a variety of aircraft, including the Firefly AS 6.

The Firefly AS 6 was replaced by the Avenger and Gannet, not by the three-seat Firefly AS 7 (see below) which saw only limited front line service.

Serials include *WD824-WD872; WD878-WD923; WJ104-WJ121.*

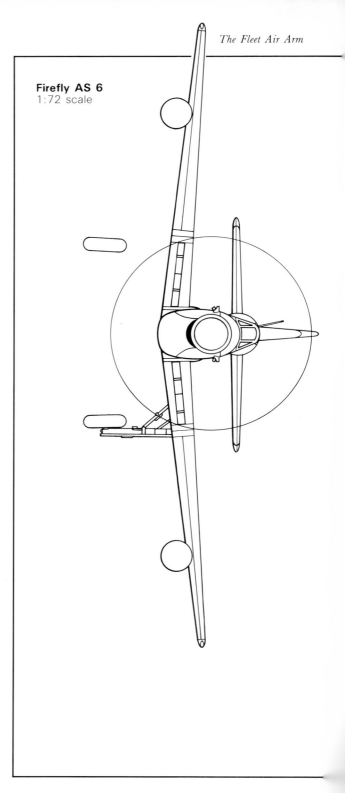

Firefly AS 6
1:72 scale

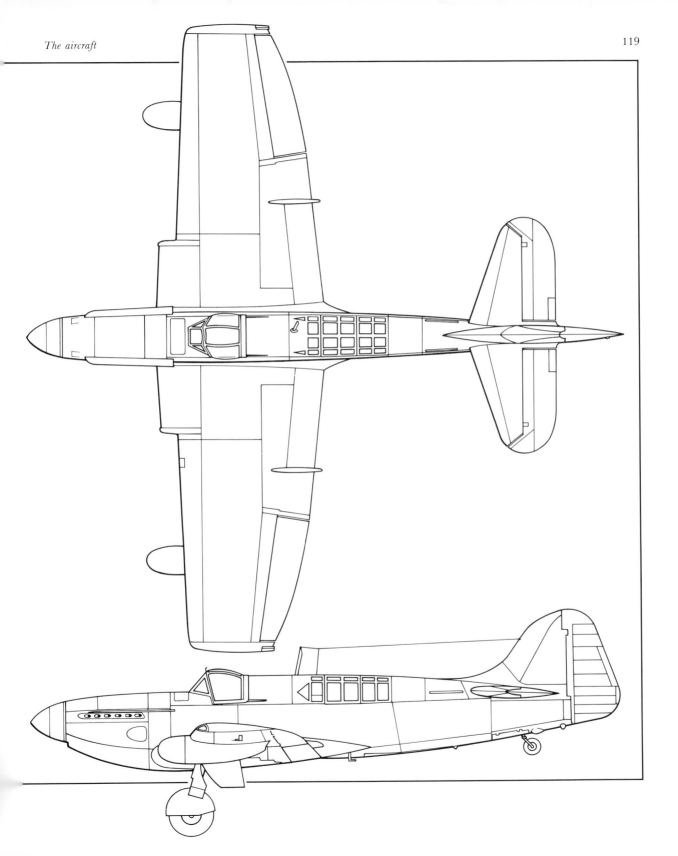

Firefly AS 6 on approach to the deck (Fleet Air Arm Museum).

Firefly AS 7

Manufacturer Fairey Aviation; **Purpose** Shipborne ASW; **Crew** 1 pilot, 2 observers (radar operators); **Maiden flight** 22 May 1951; **Service entry** March 1953; **Squadrons** 719 (1953-56), 750 (1953-55), 765 (1955-57), 796 (1953-57); **Phased out of service** 1957; **Range** 747 nm (1,380 km); **Max speed** 261 knots (483 km/h) at 10,750 ft (3,277 m); **Cruising speed** 223 knots (414 km/h); **Service ceiling** 25,500 ft (7,772 m); **Rate of climb** 1,550 ft/min (7.9 m/sec); **Length** 38.25 ft (11.66 m); **Height** 13.25 ft (4.04 m); **Span** 44.5 ft (13.6 m); **Wing area** 342.5 sq ft (31.82 sq m); **Power plant** 1 × Rolls-Royce Griffon 59 (1,965 hp); **All-up weight** 13,970 lb (6,337 kg); **Empty weight** 11,016 lb (4,997 kg); **Weapons** None; **Sensors** ASV Mk 9 radar in wing-mounted pod.

The ultimate variant of the Firefly series, but not the last to see service. The aircraft had major changes of airframe structure, including the new fin and rudder and the two-observer rear cockpit canopy, similar to that used later for the Gannet. The older type air intake scoop under the nose was revived. No accurate record can be found of the aircraft having served with front line squadrons,

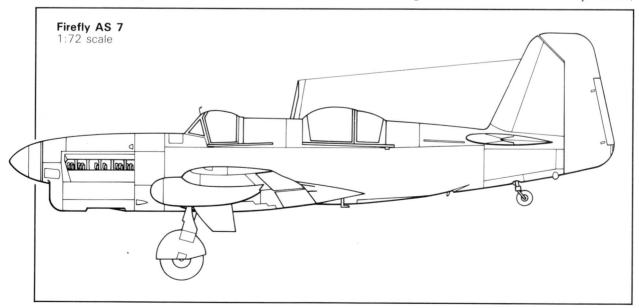

Firefly AS 7
1:72 scale

Firefly AS 7 in flight (Fleet Air Arm Museum).

despite material previously published to that effect. The Firefly AS 7 did fly with several second line training and support squadrons, taking part in the 1953 Coronation Naval Review flypast at Spithead.

Airframes previously destined for the AS 7 programme were converted to T 7 (see page 139) and U 8 drone (page 148) standards.

Serials includes *WJ154-WJ174; WJ215-216.*

Gannet AS 1, the third prototype.

Gannet AS 1

Manufacturer Fairey Aviation; **Purpose** Shipborne ASW/strike; **Crew** 1 pilot, 1 observer, 1 rating radar operator; **Naval Staff Requirement** N16/45; **Maiden flight** 19 September 1949; **Ordered** 14 March 1951; **Service trials** October 1953; **Service entry** April 1954 (703X Flight); **Squadrons** 703 (1953-56), 719 (1955-59), 737 (1955-57), 796 (1957-58), 812 (1955-56), 815 (1956-57), 824 (1955-56), 825 (1955-56), 826 (1955), 831 (1958), 847 (1956-58); RAN 816 (1955-57), 817 (1955-58); RNVR 1840 (1956-57); **Range** 600 nm (1,111 km); **Max speed** 270 knots (500 km/h) at altitude; **Cruising speed** 190 knots

(352 km/h); **Endurance** 4.5 hours; **Service ceiling** 25,000 ft (7,620 m); **Rate of climb** 2,000 ft/min (10.2 m/sec); **Length** 43 ft (13.1 m); **Height** 13.71 ft (4.18 m); **Span** 54.33 ft (16.6 m); **Wing area** 482.8 sq ft (44.9 sq m); **Power plant** 1 × Armstrong Siddeley Double Mamba 100 turboshaft (2,950 ehp); **All-up weight** 19,600 lb (8,891 kg); **Empty weight** 15,069 lb (6,835 kg); **Weapons** (external) 16 × 3 in rocket projectiles (60 lb warheads); (internal) 2 × ASW torpedoes or mines, depth charges and iron bombs; **Sensors** Ferranti ASV radar in retractable under fuselage radome.

The Fairey Gannet was the last of a long line of aircraft types designed for the Fleet Air Arm by that company. It was also the first turboprop-powered aircraft in the world to land on an aircraft carrier and the first in the world to fly with a double turbine engine configuration driving a single-engine configuration. In Fleet Air Arm terms, it was the first in the inventory to combine the hunting (search) and the killing (strike) in one airframe, with most of the weapons carried in the weapons bay.

The Gannet's first carrier landing and the world's first by a turboprop was made on 19 June 1950, using the first prototype and with *Illustrious* , the trials carrier, as the venue. 826 Squadron was the first front line squadron to equip with the Gannet AS 1. Further trials were carried out in *Bulwark*, *Eagle* and *Ark Royal* as squadrons were equipped with the aircraft and commenced work-up. The aircraft had some major teething problems with airframe and systems integration, causing the government of the day to order some 100 Avengers (see above) as an interim measure prior to the full development of the Gannet.

Serials *VR546-VR557, WE488* (prototypes); *WN339-WN364; WN366-WN378; WN390-WN429; WN445-WN464; XA319-XA364; XA387-XA409; XA434; XA436; XD898; XG784; XG785; XG787; XG789; XG791; XG792; XG795.*

Gannet AS 4

Manufacturer Fairey Aviation; **Purpose** Shipborne ASW/strike; **Crew** 1 pilot, 1 observer, 1 rating operator; **Maiden flight** 13 April 1956; **Service entry** 1956; **Squadrons** 810 (1959-60), 815 (1957-58), 824 (1956-57), 825 (1957-58), 847 (1958-59); RNVR 1841 (1955-57); **Phased out of service** 1960; **Range** 575 nm (1,065 km); **Max speed** 260 knots (481 km/h) at low level; **Cruising speed** 130 knots (241 km/h); **Endurance** 4.9 hours; **Service ceiling** 25,000 ft (7,620 m); **Rate of climb** 2,000 ft/min (10.18 m/sec); **Length, Height, Span,**

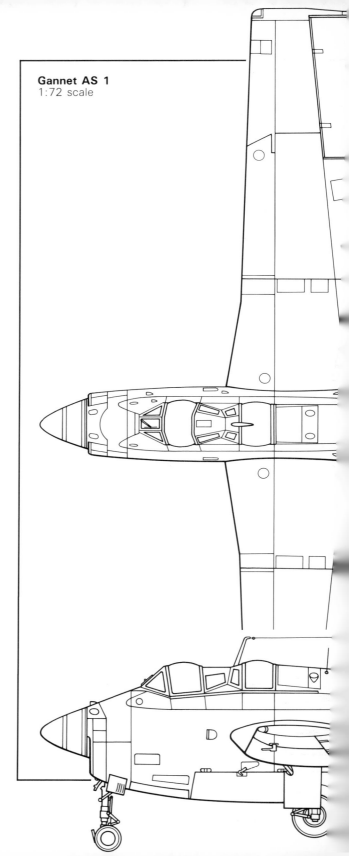

Gannet AS 1
1:72 scale

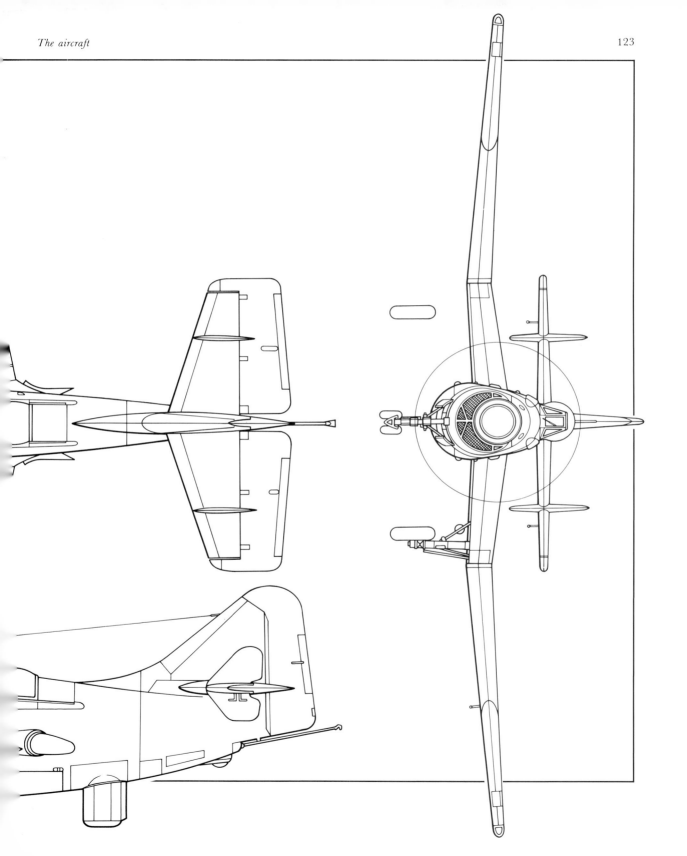

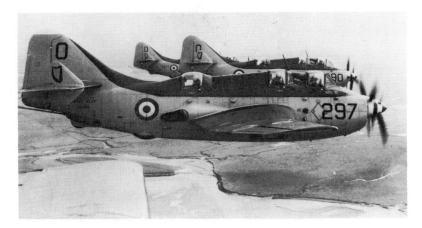

Left *Gannet AS 4, 815 Squadron, en route to embark in* Ark Royal *(RN/ FPU).*

Right *Gannet AEW 3 and Sea King 2; the old and the new, 1984* (Thorn EMI Electronics).

and Wing area as Gannet AS 1; **Power plant** 1 × Armstrong Siddeley Double Mamba 101 (3,035 ehp); **All-up weight** 23,446 lb (10,635 kg); **Empty weight** 14,069 lb (6,382 kg); **Weapons** as Gannet AS 1.

With continued service trials, it was seen that the Double Mamba 100 engine was not powerful enough to cater for the increase in both empty and mission weights. In March 1956, the first uprated Double Mamba was test flown and the engine entered service in the remaining Gannet ASW airframes.

This was the last of the fixed-wing anti-submarine warfare aircraft as the Fleet Air Arm was about to rethink its ASW doctrine in view of the development of dipping sonar by the United States. The Gannet AS 4 was paid off in July 1960 when 810 Squadron disbanded at Culdrose.

Serials *WN372* (development aircraft); *XA410-XA433; XA435; XA454-XA473; XG783; XG786; XG788; XG790; XG793; XG784; XG797; XG798; XG827-XG829.*

Skyraider AEW 1 of 849B Flight embarked in Ark Royal.

Airborne early warning

The art and science of airborne early warning (AEW) is a development of the post-war era and directly stems from the experiences of the US and Royal navies in the Pacific Ocean at the end of the Second World War. The Fleet Air Arm has operated three specific AEW aircraft since the reformation of 849 Squadron at Brawdy on 7 July 1952 (778 Squadron had been carrying out service trials since November 1951 at Culdrose); all three aircraft have been modified versions of types designed for other uses.

The first AEW aircraft was the Skyraider, equipped with the AN/APS 20 radar, and the combination filled a serious gap in the radar defence of the Fleet at sea. Until the arrival of the Skyraider, low-flying attack aircraft could close in on the Carrier Task Group undetected by shipborne radar until the very last minute. Initial trials of Skyraider and APS 20 showed that a very high proficiency could be developed, even against smaller jet aircraft, such as the Seahawk or Sea Venom, which did not present the best of radar targets.

Once the technique and effectiveness of AEW had been proved, Flights from 849 Squadron became an integral part of the Fleet's radar defence system. A Flight embarked in *Eagle* during January 1953 with four Skyraider AEW 1. In 1960, the Gannet AEW 3 was supplied to the Fleet Air Arm and again 849 A Flight was the first to embark, again to *Eagle,* in March 1960. The Gannet AEW 3 remained in service with basically the same radar, but different processors and displays, until the paying off of *Ark Royal* in 1978; 849 Squadron disbanded in December 1978.

The RAF was then given the AEW role for the Fleet using aged Shackleton AEW 2 aircraft, but

the idea was never really effective as the aircraft were almost always on call for the defence of the UK fighter squadrons. In 1982, the lack of carrier-borne AEW aircraft was amply illustrated following the demise of the Type 42 destroyer *Sheffield* to low flying aircraft attack with sea skimming missiles. This again demonstrated that AEW must be locally controlled and operated for defence of warships at sea. To provide naval task forces with long-range AEW, thus extending radar cover beyond ships' radar horizons and allowing time for effective defensive measures to be taken, two Sea King HAS 2 helicopters were fitted with Thorn EMI Search-water radars. The system was developed in just eleven weeks for planned embarkation in *Illustrious,* but in the event the Falklands hostilities ceased before the programme was completed. Neverthe-less, the Fleet Air Arm took delivery of the first pro-duction Sea King AEW 2 in February 1985, after the reformation of 849 Squadron on 1 November 1984 at RNAS Culdrose (previously service development had been carried out by D Flight of 824 Squadron). This is the first helicopter AEW squadron to be operational in the world and the current plans are for the helicopters to be embarked in 'Invincible' Class aircraft carriers and perhaps Royal Fleet Auxiliaries for 'Out of Area Opera-tions' where local land-based AEW is not available.

849 A Flight reformed in May 1985 and em-barked with the normal complement of three Sea King AEW 2 (and five complete crews) in *Illustrious* in August that year. 849 B Flight is due to form in 1986 and embark with the same complement in *Ark Royal,* when that ship has been fully worked-up with the Fleet.

Tactical doctrine

Following the formation of 849A Flight for service

in *Illustrious* in 1985, the helicopters were given their operational debut in 'Exercise Ocean Safari' in September 1985, when they proved most successful, especially as they were able to provide a screen against 'attacking' aircraft (and Soviet snoopers) when the USN's fixed-wing aircraft were unable to be launched because of the bad weather. In April 1986, 849B Flight was formed for service in *Ark Royal.* A normal sea going flight in a CVS is three helicopters and five complete crews (fifteen officers plus the Squadron AEO).

The standard *modus operandi* of the Sea King AEW 2 is to provide coverage against low flying air-craft and missiles, whilst the controlling ship takes care of the medium and high level 'trade'. The AEW observers hope to put the Sea Harrier combat air patrols on collision course to intercept the enemy, from where the Sea Harrier's own Blue Fox radar system takes over. The Sea King AEW 2 is assisted in its work by the use of Cossor Jubilee Guardsman IFF (Identification, Friend or Foe) and Racal MIR-2 Orange Crop electronic surveillance measures.

As an aid to the naval force commander, the Sea King AEW 2 can be used to search for, identify and classify surface ship targets, such is the power and processor ability of the Searchwater radar. Radar information can be passed to command ships via Link 11 and other NATO standard data link systems, with future modifications to the helicopters including secure speech for commonality with the Sea Harrier FRS 2 when it comes into service.

Gannet AEW 3

Manufacturer Fairey/Westland; **Purpose** Airborne early warning; **Crew** 1 pilot, 2 observers; **Maiden flight** 20 August 1958; **Service entry** 18 August 1959; **Squadrons** 700G (1959-60), 849A (1960-70),

Gannet AEW 3
1:72 scale

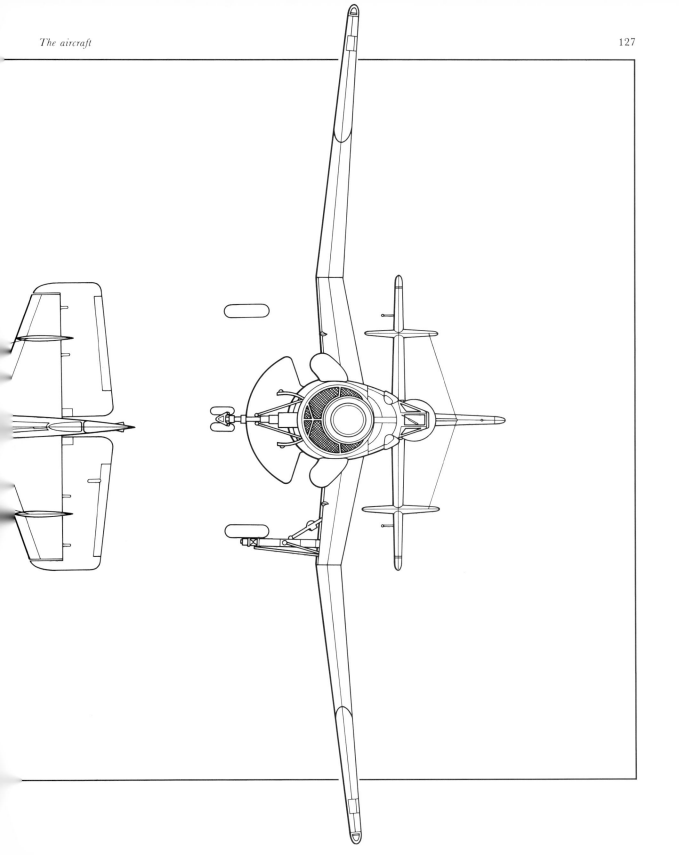

Gannet AEW 3
1:72 scale

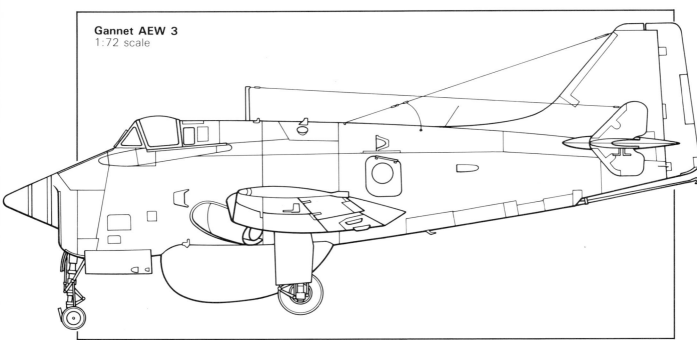

Above *Gannet AEW 3, showing the double wing-folding sequence* (RN/Ark Royal/Rod Safe).

Left *Gannet AEW 3, 849B Flight, in the setting sun aboard Ark Royal, 1978* (RN/Ark Royal/LA, J. Anderson).

849B (1960-65 and 1966-78), 849C (1960-66), 849D (1964-72), 849E (1964); **Phased out of service** December 1978; **Range** 700 nm (1,296 km); **Max speed** 217 knots (402 km/h) at altitude; **Cruising speed** 175 knots (324 km/h); **Endurance** 6 hours; **Service ceiling** 25,000 ft (7,620 m); **Length** 44 ft (13.41 m); **Height** 16.83 ft (5.13 m); **Span** 54.33 ft (16.56 m); **Wing area** 490 sq ft (42.7 sq m); **Power plant** 1 × double Mamba 102 (3,875 ehp); **All-up weight** 25,000 lb (11,340 kg); **Empty weight** Not available; **Weapons** none (but see accompanying picture); **Sensors** AN/APS 20F radar.

Developed from the carrier-borne anti-submarine aircraft, the Gannet AEW 3 was modified to carry the generic APS 20 radar which had been previously flown in the Skyraider (see below). Considerable work was carried out by Westland on the Gannet design, including a completely new fuselage arrangement to allow the aircraft's two observers to sit together in a cabin which also held the radar consoles and associated controls. The pilot was placed high on the fuselage in a separate compartment.

Initial deck landing trials were successfully carried out in *Centaur* during November 1958, some months before the first fully-equipped Gannet AEW 3 was ready for test flying after its first flight in January 1959. The intensive flying trials unit, 700G Squadron, was formed at Culdrose and later became the headquarters element of 849 Squadron, the only front line unit to operate fixed-wing airborne early warning aircraft. In 1964, the squadron moved to Brawdy and again to Lossiemouth in 1970; the squadron's remaining small headquarters element and the last operational flight, 849B Flight, remained there until disbanded in December 1978.

Each flight was embarked in a specific carrier, many keeping a parent carrier for a number of years — 849D Flight was associated with *Eagle* from the time it reformed with the Gannet until the carrier's paying off in 1972. When the Gannet flights paid off, their APS 20 radar was transferred to the RAF Shackleton airborne early warning fleet and is destined to continue in service until 1990. Most Gannet airframes were broken up.

Serials *XJ440; XL449-XL456; XL471-XL482; XL493-XL503; XP197-XP199; XP224-XP229.*

Sea King AEW 2

Manufacturer Westland; **Purpose** Shipborne airborne early warning; **Crew** 1 pilot, 2 observers; **Maiden flight** June 1982; **Service entry** June 1982

Sea King AEW 2, 849A Flight, embarked in Illustrious, *1986*
(Rolls-Royce).

(824D Flight); **Squadrons** 824D (1982-84); 849A
(1984-), 849B (1985-); Still active; **Range** 420 nm
(778 km); **Max speed** 140 knots (259 km/h);
Cruising speed 112 knots (207 km/h); **Endurance**
Over 4 hours; **Service ceiling** 10,000 ft (3,050 m);
Length 47.24 ft (14.4 m) folded; **Height** 16.83 ft
(5.13 m); **Rotor diameter** 62 ft (18.9 m); **Power
plant** 2 × Rolls-Royce Gnome H-1400 (1,660 shp);
All-up weight 21,500 lb (9,752 kg); **Sensors**
Searchwater radar, Orange Crop ESM, Jubilee
Guardsman IFF.

Within days of the loss of *Sheffield* to sea skimming missile attack in the South Atlantic, the Fleet
Air Arm with considerable assistance from British
industry, including Westland and Thorn EMI Electronics, produced and AEW radar-carrying version
of the Sea King Mk 2 medium anti-submarine
helicopter.

Trials were carried out throughout June and
flying trials were carried out in the carrier *Illustrious*
in August; the ship with the Sea King AEW 2s
embarked was deployed to the South Atlantic,
where further trials were carried out. The aim of the
conversion is to provide the task commander with
organic airborne early warning and surface
search/classification, especially when out of range of
land-based AEW cover.

The Sea King AEW 2s of 849A Flight (*Illustrious*)
were first tested during Ocean Safari '85 when they
proved to be very effective against incoming raids,
being able to direct Sea Harrier combat air patrols
onto targets before the latter were able to acquire
the task group. 849B Flight (*Ark Royal*) exercised
during 1986 with various NATO naval forces.

The helicopter's Searchwater radar, which stands
up well against the E-2 Hawkeye, is a development of the maritime patrol radar found in the
Long Range Maritime Patrol version of the
Nimrod. It is mounted on the starboard side of the
helicopter and is retracted for landing, with its

Skyraider AEW 1, 849B Flight, takes a long free take-off launch from Ark Royal *(RN/FONAC).*

protective bag deflated.

In November 1984, the Fleet Air Arm reformed 849 Squadron to parent the two operational flights and to provide a training nucleus for the Fleet. By 1986, both *Illustrious* and *Ark Royal* had been equipped to support equipment and after refit *Invincible* will have similar facilities.

In December 1986, it was announced that Ferranti Defence Systems had won a contract to supply sixteen sets of FIN 1110 gyro navigation systems for the Sea King AEW 2 to assist with accurate position keeping.

Serials include *XV649; XV650; XV656; XV671; XV672; XV697; XV704; XV707; XV714.*

Skyraider AEW 1

Manufacturer Douglas Aircraft Corporation; **Purpose** Shipborne airborne early warning; **Crew** 1 pilot, 2 observers; **Naval Staff Requirement** December 1943; **Delivered** 9 November 1951; **Service entry** 1 October 1951 (778 Squadron);

First front line squadron formed 7 July 1952 (849 Squadron): **Squadrons** 849A (1952-), 849B (1952-), 849C (1953-), 849D (1953-), 849E (1953-); **Phased out of service** December 1960; **Range** (internal fuel) 868 nm (1,608 km), (maximum) 1,250 nm (2,315 km) with 2 × 150 Imp gal tanks; **Max speed** 305 knots (565 km/h); **Endurance** 7.8 hours at 115 knots (213 km/h); **Service ceiling** 36,000 ft (10,975 m); **Length** 38.83 ft (11.8 m); **Height** 15.63 ft (4.76 m), 16.67 ft (5.08 m) (folded); **Span** 50 ft (15.24 m); **Wing area** 400 sq ft (37.2 sq m); **Power plant** 1 × Wright Double Cyclone R-3350-26WA piston engine (3,300 hp); **All-up weight** 18,300 lb (8,300 kg) catapult launch; **Operational weight** 17,311 lb (7,852 kg); **Empty weight** 13,614 lb (6,175 kg); **Weapons** None; **Sensors** AN/ APS 20A pulse search radar.

The Skyraider was developed by the US Navy as

Skyraider AEW 1
1:72 scale

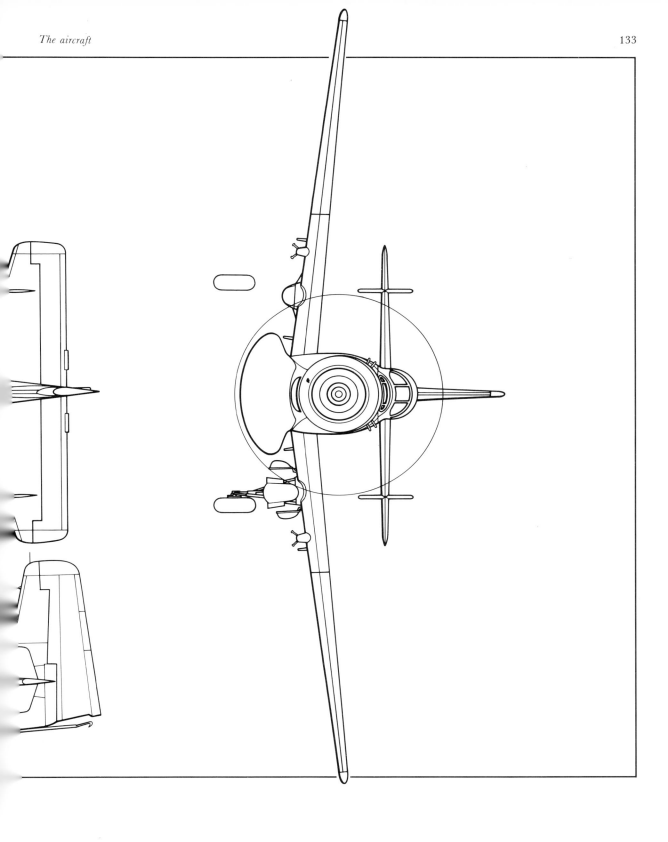

an airborne radar station to protect a carrier strike force, but when the aircraft and its radar was delivered to the Fleet Air Arm, under the Mutual Defense Assistance Program in 1951, it was decided that the British operational role would be that of airborne control station. The aircraft were delivered in two batches of four and 46 aircraft.

Initial training was carried out at Culdrose and aboard *Eagle* under the aegis of 778 Squadron, which although a second line unit was not a regular special flying trials unit; nor did the Skyraider undergo the long A&AEE Boscombe Down trials.

The Skyraider AEW 1 provided the Fleet Air Arm with airborne early warning against low flying enemy strike aircraft, with a secondary role of surface surveillance and fighter control. The aircraft were deployed at sea in flights of four aircraft each, with a larger headquarters element at Culdrose to provide training facilities. The first flight to commission was 849A Flight on 3 November 1952. The Skyraider was replaced by the Gannet AEW 3.

Serials *WT097; WT112; WT121; WT761; WT849; WT944-WT969; WT984-WT987; WV102-WV107; WV177-WV185.*

Communications and transport aircraft

Immediately following the Second World War and during the next thirty years, the Fleet Air Arm was very active with a communications and transport aircraft network which spanned the world. As the Empire contracted, the need for commuter services, even around the United Kingdom, decreased and by the late 1970s only a small unit, 781 Squadron at Lee-on-Solent, remained. This squadron disbanded in March 1981.

Basically, Fleet Air Arm communications aircraft were almost identical to their air force counterparts and carried the mark prefix C, the exception being the Gannet COD 4 for carrier on-board delivery of spares, high value supplies and personnel.

Dominie MkI

Manufacturer de Havilland Aircraft; **Purpose** Communications and training; **Crew** 2 pilots, 10 passengers; **Maiden flight** Not available; **Service entry** April 1940; **Last delivery** December 1946; **Squadrons** 700 (1962), 701 (1946-47), 703 (1947), 739 (1948-50), 744 (1951-53), 767 (1950-51), 778 (1947-48), 781 (1946-63), 782 (1941-53), 790 (1945-46), 799 (1945-46), 1832 (1955), 1844 (1956-57); **Phased out of service** 1958 (one survived with 781 until 1963); **Range** 570 nm (1,056 km); **Max speed** 136 knots (253 km/h) at 1,000 ft (330 m); **Cruising speed** 121 knots (225 km/h); **Service ceiling** 16,000 ft (4,875 m); **Length** 34.5 ft (10.52 m); **Height** 10.25 ft (3.1 m); **Span** 48 ft (14.6 m); **Wing area** 336 sq ft (31.2 sq m); **Power plant** 2 × DH Gipsy Six (200 hp each); **All-up weight** 5,500 lb (2,495 kg); **Empty weight** 3,230 lb (1,465 kg).

Impressed into service for UK communications duties during the Second World War, the DH 89 Dominie was a cost-effective and highly successful transport aircraft which continued in communications squadron service until 1958, despite the biplane design which originated in 1934. Early service tasks also included wireless telegraphy training (Mk I) and some 65 were delivered to the Royal Navy.

Station flights (including Culdrose, Culham and Lossiemouth) as well as squadrons were equipped with aircraft. After service in the Fleet Air Arm a large number of aircraft were sold to airline and other commercial operators.

Serials include *RL936-RL946.*

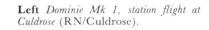

Left Dominie Mk 1, station flight at Culdrose (RN/Culdrose).

Above right Gannet COD 4 aboard Ark Royal (Brian Service).

Right Sea Devon C 20, 781 Squadron, at Lee-on-Solent, 1978.

Gannet COD 4

Manufacturer Fairey Aviation; **Purpose** Carrier on-board delivery; **Crew** 1/2 pilots, 1 aircrewman or passenger; **Maiden flight** 1960; **Service entry** September 1961; **Squadron** 849; **Phased out of service** September 1964; **Range** 578 nm (1,070 km); **Max speed** 260 knots (481 km/h); **Cruising speed** 130 knots (241 km/h); **Service ceiling** 25,000 ft (7,620 m); **Rate of climb** 2,000 ft/min (10.2 m/sec); **Length** 43 ft (13.1 m); **Height** 13.71 ft (4.18 m); **Span** 54.33 ft (16.6 m); **Wing area** 490 sq ft (45.5 sq m); **Power plant** 1 × Armstrong Siddeley Double Mamba 101 turbine engine (3,035 hp); **All-up weight** 19,600 lb (8,890 kg); **Empty weight** 15,069 lb (6,835 kg).

Converted from five Gannet AS 4 airframes with the ASW surface search radar removed (see page 122), the COD 4 was an ideal carrier deck-landing communications aircraft. High value cargo could be flown out to a carrier at sea, either for that ship or for onward transfer to other ships in a task group.

Serials *XA430; XA454; XA466; XA470; XG790.*

Sea Devon C 20

Manufacturer de Havilland Aircraft; **Purpose** Communications and patrol aircraft; **Crew** 2 pilots, 8 passengers; **Maiden flight** 25 September 1945 (as Dove); **Service entry** 1955; **Squadrons** 750 (1957-61), 765 (1957), 771 (1983-), 781 (1955-81); **Range** 765 nm (1,417 km); **Max speed** 200 knots (370 km/h) at 8,000 ft (2,438 m); **Cruising speed** 170 knots (315 km/h); **Endurance** 3 hours; **Service ceiling** 19,685 ft (6,000 m); **Rate of climb** 850 ft/min (4.3 m/sec); **Length** 39.24 ft (11.96 m); **Height** 13.32 ft (4.06 m); **Span** 57 ft (17.37 m); **Wing area** 335 sq ft (31.1 sq m); **Power plant** 2 × DH Gipsy Queen 70 (340 hp each); **All-up weight** 8,950 lb (4,060 kg); **Empty weight** 6,500 lb (2,948 kg).

The Sea Devon is the navalized version of the highly successful de Haviland Dove which was the first British aircraft to fit reversible-pitch propellors. It is a low wing monoplane which was first acquired by the Fleet Air Arm to replace the Dominie Mk I in communications duties but has also been used for air ambulance, training, VIP transport, weather flights and fishery patrols.

Ten aircraft were delivered to 781 Squadron but the survivors are now flown by Culdrose Station Flight. The aircraft were originally manufactured in 1953 for the North American market but sold to the Royal Navy in 1954 after being kept in storage.

Left Sea Heron C 1, 781 Squadron and Yeovilton station flight.

Right Sea Prince C 2 of Culdrose Station Flight (RN/Culdrose).

Three additional aircraft built for the Royal Navy were handed over in April 1956.
Serials *XJ319-XJ324, XJ347-XJ350* (first batch); *XK895-XK897* (second batch).

Sea Heron C 1

Manufacturer de Havilland Aircraft; **Purpose** Transport, communications and patrol; **Crew** 2 pilots (1 flight attendant), 14 passengers; **Maiden flight** 10 May 1950 (as Heron); **Service entry** March 1961; **Squadron** 781 (1961-81); Still active; **Range** 400 nm (741 km); **Max speed** 175 knots (324 km/h); **Cruising speed** 159 knots (295 km/h); **Endurance** 2 hours; **Service ceiling** 18,500 ft (5,639 m); **Rate of climb** 1,060 ft/min (5.4 m/sec); **Length** 48.5 ft (14.8 m); **Height** 14.17 ft (4.32 m); **Span** 71.5 ft (21.8 m); **Wing area** 499 sq ft (46.4 sq m); **Power plant** 4 × DH Gipsy Queen 30 (250 hp each); **All-up weight** 13,500 lb (6,124 kg); **Empty weight** 8,150 lb (3,697 kg).

Five Sea Heron C 1 four-engined monoplane communications aircraft were purchased second-hand from de Havilland Aircraft having originally flown with Jersey Airlines and West African Airways. The five were delivered to 781 Squadron at Lee-on-Solent for communications duties which in-

cluded the 'Naval Clipper' service to airports, air stations and port facilities around the UK.

With the disbandment of 781 Squadron, the aircraft remaining in service were transferred to Culdrose Station Flight for offshore patrol and surveillance duties in the Irish Sea and South-West Approaches. This role ceased in 1985 and the aircraft continue in the communications role.
Serials *XR441-XR445.*
Variants Sea Heron C 4 was first delivered as a Heron C 4 (*XM296*) under an RAF contract for the Queen's Flight in April 1958 and handed over to the Fleet Air Arm as an Admiral's barge in July 1972 under the new designation of Sea Heron C 4 to replace the Sea Heron C 1 (*XR444*) and to supplement the Hunter T 8 for FONAC's VIP flights; Sea Heron C 20 was an alternative designation for Sea Heron C 1.

Sea Prince C 1

Manufacturer Hunting Percival; **Purpose** VIP and communications; **Crew** 2 pilots, 8 passengers; **Naval Specification** C18/49; **Maiden flight** 24 March 1950; **Service entry** 1953; **Squadron** 781 (1950-65); **Phased out of service** 1965; **Range** 1,150 nm (2,130 km); **Max speed** 194 knots (359 km/h); **Cruising speed** 159 knots (294 km/h); **Service ceiling** 22,000 ft (6,706 m); **Length** 46 ft (14 m); **Height** 16.1 ft (3.3 m); **Span** 64.5 ft (19.7 m); **Wing area** 365 sq ft (33.9 sq m); **Power plant** 2 × Alvis Leonides 125 (550 shp each); **All-up weight** 13,500 lb (6,124 kg); **Empty weight** 8,850 lb (4,104 kg).

The Fleet Air Arm ordered three C 1 transports for VIP duties at the same time as the first order for T 1 trainers was announced. Based on the civilian Pembroke, one was fitted out as an Admiral's barge (green parrot) and another flew the Atlantic Ocean to Washington DC to be used by the Joint Services Mission. 781 Squadron, the Communication Unit, used the C 1 until 1965 when it was replaced by the Sea Devon and Sea Heron.

Sea Heron C 4, Flag Officer Naval Air Command.

Serials *WF136-WF138; WJ348* (later converted to C 2 standard).

Sea Prince C 2

Manufacturer Hunting Percival; **Purpose** and **Crew** as for C 1; **Maiden flight** 1 April 1953; **Service entry** July 1953; **Squadron** 781 (1953-61); **Phased out of service** 1970; **Range, Max speed, Cruising speed, Service ceiling, Length, Height, Span, Wing area, Power plant, All-up weight** and **Empty weight** as for C 1.

The C 2 version was produced to give improved reliability and better cost-effective service. The last of four was delivered in September 1953.

Serials *WJ348-WJ350; WM756.*

Training aircraft

Rarely during its long history, and never since 1945, has the Fleet Air Arm been able to bring into service its own aeroplane which has been designed for training aircrew — pilot or observer officers, or rating grades for sonar operation and winching. Most of the types in this section are either derived from RAF needs, the front line type variants or a special modification after front line service. Nevertheless, there are seventeen different training aircraft in this section; helicopters are covered in the next chapter.

Canberra T 4

Manufacturer English Electric/BAC; **Purpose** Fleet requirements training; **Crew** 1/2 pilots, 1 observer; **Service entry** December 1972 (FRADU); Still active with FRADU; **Range** 3,300 nm (6,110 km); **Max speed** 500 knots (926 km/h); **Cruising speed** 450 knots (833 km/h); **Endurance** about 6 hours; **Service ceiling** 25,000 ft (7,620 m); **Length** 65 ft (19.8 m); **Height** 16.08 ft (4.9 m); **Span** 64 ft (19.5 m); **Wing area** 1,045 sq ft (97.1 sq m); **Power plant** 2 × Rolls-Royce Avon turbojets; **All-up weight** 54,563 lb (24,750 kg); **Empty weight** 20,342 lb (9,227 kg).

The Canberra was the first British jet bomber and appeared in many forms during its production life, and afterwards as airframes were modified to other tasks. The T 4 trainer was developed in response to an RAF need in the 1950s and aircraft were supplied to the Fleet Air Arm from RAF surplus stocks for Fleet requirement and air direction tasks, as well as for training aircrew on an airframe similar to others in service, the Canberra TT 18 and T 22.

Serials *WJ861; WJ865-WJ867; WJ869* and *WJ870; WJ874.*

Canberra T 22

Manufacturer English Electric/BAC; **Purpose** Fleet requirements and air direction; **Crew** 1 pilot, 1 observer; **Maiden flight** (conversion) June 1973; **Service entry** November 1973 (FRADU); Still active with FRADU; **Range, Max speed, Cruising speed, Endurance, Service ceiling, Length, Height, Span, Wing area** and **Power plant** as for Canberra T 4; **All-up weight** 54,500 lb (24,720 kg); **Empty weight** Not available.

Canberra T 4 from FRADU at Yeovilton.

Canberra T 22 from FRADU at Yeovilton, 1980 (Robin Walker).

When the RAF updated its photographic reconnaissance fleet, a number of Canberra airframes were made available to the Fleet Air Arm and con-

Below *Chipmunk T 10 from Britannia RNC Flight, Plymouth.*
Bottom *Firefly T 1 of 1840 Squadron in 1953* (MAP via R.C. Sturtivant).

verted for the special training role by British Aircraft Corporation at Samlesbury. Initially six Canberra PR 7s were converted and later additional aircraft were delivered to Yeovilton for the Fleet Requirements and Air Direction Unit.

Serials *WH780; WH797; WH801; WH803; WT510; WT525; WT535.*

Chipmunk T 10

Manufacturer de Havilland Canada; **Purpose** Training and air experience; **Crew** 1 pilot, 1 student; **Naval Specification** 8/48; **Maiden flight** 1 January 1947; **Service entry** June 1966; **Squadrons** 771 (1983-), 781 (1971-81); Still active with BRNC Flight and station flights; **Range** 260 nm (482 km); **Max speed** 120 knots (222 km/h); **Cruising speed** 100 knots (185 km/h); **Service ceiling** 9,845 ft (3,000 m); **Rate of climb** 800 ft/min (4 m/sec); **Length** 25.66 ft (7.82 m); **Height** 7.09 ft (2.16 m); **Span** 34.35 ft (10.47 m); **Wing area** 172 sq ft (15.97 sq m); **Power plant** 1 × DH Gipsy Major 8 piston engine (145 hp); **All-up weight** 2,014 lb (914 kg); **Empty weight** 1,425 lb (646 kg).

Designed in Canada to succeed the Tiger Moth (see below), the UK-built Chipmunk T 10 was ordered in quantity for the RAF and later some examples were passed to the Fleet Air Arm for air experience and flight training with Britannia Royal Naval College Flight at Roborough (Plymouth). Some have been used as 'hacks' by station flights including Culdrose and Yeovilton. For a time 781 Squadron had the aircraft on strength for RNR (Air Branch) experience flying. Miscellaneous duties include glider towing.

Serials include *WB575; WK511; WK574; WK608; WK634; WK635; WP801; WP809; WP859.*

Firefly T 1

Manufacturer Fairey Aviation; **Purpose** Dual-control deck-landing trainer; **Crew** 1 pilot, 1 student; **Maiden flight** 1 September 1947; **Service entry** 1948; **Squadrons** 736 (1948-50), 781

(1950-54), 1830 (1948-49); **Phased out of service** 1954; **Range** 700 nm (1,295 km); **Max speed** 265 knots (490 km/h) at 16,500 ft (5,030 m); **Cruising speed** 245 knots (455 km/h) at sea level; **Service ceiling** 28,000 ft (8,545 m); **Rate of climb** 1,740 ft/min (8.9 m/sec); **Length** 37.6 ft (11.46 m); **Height** 13.58 ft (4.14 m); **Span** 44.5 ft (13.56 m); **Wing area** 328 sq ft (30.47 sq m); **Power plant** 1 × Rolls-Royce Griffon II piston engine (1,735 hp), or 1 × Rolls-Royce Griffon XII piston engine (1,735 hp); **All-up weight** 12,300 lb (5,580 kg); **Empty weight** 9,647 lb (4,376 kg); **Weapons** First nine carried 2 × 20 mm cannon in wings, remainder unarmed.

Developed directly from the highly successful carrier-borne fighter of the Second World War, the Firefly T 1 was a conversion from Firefly I airframes, modified by means of a second, high-mounted cockpit in the fuselage centre section for an instructor pilot. The cockpit was mounted high so that the instructor had a good view of the flight deck during an approach.

In the late 1940s, the Deck Landing Training School was at Milltown (Scotland) and training carriers would operate in Scottish waters during flying practice. In addition, the Royal Naval Volunteer Reserve operated the Firefly T 1 for training from Bramcote, Ford and Abbotsinch.

In all 34 Firefly T 1 conversions were completed, all with folding wings and deck landing arrester gear. The first was *MB473.*

Firefly T 2

Manufacturer Fairey Aviation; **Purpose** tactical weapon trainer; **Crew** 1 pilot, 1 student; **Maiden flight** 12 August 1949; **Service entry** July 1950 (781 Squadron); **Squadrons** 765 (1955-57); 781 (1950-56); 1830 (1950-55), 1841 (1952-55), 1844 (1954); **Phased out of service** 1957; **Range, Max speed, Cruising speed, Service ceiling, Rate of climb, Length, Height, Span** and **Wing area** as for Firefly T 1; **Power plant** 1 × Rolls-Royce Griffon XII piston engine (1,735 hp); **All-up weight** 12,300 lb (5,579 kg); **Empty Weight** as Firefly T 1; **Weapons** 2 × 20 mm cannon in wings.

As with the T 1, this variant of the Firefly was developed from the Mk I airframe and all 54 aircraft completed were directly rebuilt from the original fighter. Like the T 1, the rear cockpit was raised to give a good view forward but unlike the T 1, the aircraft was designed to operate as a weapons trainer, with cannon armament in the wings and a gyro gunsight in both cockpits. All aircraft had folding wings and arrester gear. The first conversion was *MB543.*

Firefly T 3

Manufacturer Fairey Aviation; **Purpose** Observer and ASW training; **Crew** 1 pilot, 1 student observer; **Maiden flight** 1951; **Service entry** 1951; **Squadrons** 796 (1950-54), 1830 (1950-51), 1831 (1952), 1833 (1952-54), 1841 (1952-53), 1844 (1954); **Phased out of service** 1954; **Range, Max speed, Cruising speed, Service ceiling, Length, Height, Span** and **Wing area** as Firefly FR 4 (see page 59); **Power plant** as Firefly T 2; **All up weight** and **Empty weight** as Firefly FR 4.

The third and final Firefly trainer to be based around the Mk I airframe, the T 3 was converted from the Firefly FR 1 airframes declared surplus by the introduction of the Sea Fury FB 10 and FB 11. The T 3 was designed to train observers in the relatively new art of anti-submarine warfare (ASW) and was therefore unarmed.

From 1953, the Firefly T 3 was superceded by the Firefly T 7 (see below) and the airframes were scrapped.

Serials include *PP485; PP523; PP609; PP657.*

Firefly T 7

Manufacturer Fairey Aviation; **Purpose** Observer and ASW training; **Crew** 1 pilot, 1 observer, 1 student observer; **Maiden flight** 16 October 1951 (as AS 7); **Service entry** 1953; **Squadrons** 719 (1953-56), 744 (1952-54), 750 (1953-55), 765 (1955-57), 796 (1953-57); **Phased out of service** 1957; **Range** 745 nm (1,380 km); **Max speed** 260 knots (483 km/h) at 10,750 ft (3,275 m); **Cruising speed** 223 knots (414 km/h); **Service ceiling** 25,500 ft (7,772 m); **Rate of climb** 1,550 ft/min (7.9 m/sec); **Length** 38.25 ft (11.7 m); **Height** 13.25 ft (4.04 m); **Span** 44.5 ft (13.6 m); **Wing area** 342.5

Firefly T 7 training aircraft converted from a Firefly AS 7 (see picture on page 121) (Fleet Air Arm Museum).

sq ft (31.8 sq m); **Power plant** 1 × Rolls-Royce Griffon 59 piston engine (1,965 hp); **All-up weight** 13,970 lb (6,337 kg); **Empty weight** 11,016 lb (4,997 kg).

The last of the Firefly trainers, the T 7 was a direct follow-on from the AS 7 carrier-borne ASW search aircraft. It was built at Hayes (Middlesex) and Stockport (Cheshire). The aircraft served with training units ashore and was not armed or equipped for deck landing. Like the AS 7, the two observers (which might include a rating radar operator under training) were accommodated in the enlarged rear cockpit with a bubble canopy; this could be screened off with curtains. With the introduction of the Gannet AS 1, several of the AS 7 airframes were diverted to training units, but retained the AS 7 variant classification (see page 120).

Gannet T 2

Manufacturer Fairey Aviation; **Purpose** Pilot training; **Crew** 1 pilot, 1 student, 1 aircrewman; **Maiden flight** 16 August 1954; **Service entry** February 1955 (*XA508* to 737); **Squadrons** 719 (1955-59), 737 (1955-57), 796 (1957-58), 1840 (1956-57); **Phased out of service** 1959; **Range** 572 nm (1,060 km); **Max speed** 259 knots (480 km/h); **Cruising speed** 130 knots (240 km/h); **Endurance** 5 hours; **Service ceiling** 25,000 ft (7,620 m); **Rate of climb** 2,000 ft/min (10.2 m/sec); **Length** 43 ft (13.1 m); **Height** 13.71 ft (4.2 m); **Span** 54.33 ft (16.6 m); **Wing area** 490 sq ft (45.5 sq m); **Power plant** 1 × Armstrong Siddeley Double Mamba 100 turbine engine (2,950 hp); **All-up weight** 19,600 lb (8,891 kg); **Empty weight** 15,069 lb (6,835 kg).

When production of the Gannet AS 1 was completed, the T 2 dual-control trainer was put into production at Hayes and Stockport to fulfil a need primarily for pilot training. The T 2 is outwardly similar to the AS 1 except that the second cockpit has a retractable periscope visor for the instructor pilot to see over the student's head and the ASW radar and its radome is not fitted.

Like most fixed-wing naval aircraft, the Gannet T 2 was fitted with folding wings, which in the Gannet's case doubled back over the fuselage but did not increase the aircraft's height or width. Deck landing equipment was retained.
Serials *WN365* (converted AS 1 for trials); *XA508-XA530; XG869-XG881.*

Gannet T 5

Manufacturer Fairey Aviation; **Purpose** Pilot training; **Crew** 1 pilot, 1 student pilot, 1 aircrewman; **Maiden flight** 1 March 1957 (*XG882*); **Service entry** September 1961; **Squadrons** 745 (1956-57), 849 (1961-76); **Last delivery** 1958 (*XG889*); **Phased out of service** 1976; **Range, Max speed, Cruising speed, Endurance, Service ceiling, Rate of climb, Length, Height, Span,** and **Wing area** as Gannet T 2; **Power plant** 1 × Armstrong Siddeley Double Mamba 101 turbine engine (3,035 hp); **All-up weight** and **Empty weight** as Gannet T 2.

Developed as the companion to the Gannet AS 4, the T 5 model was basically similar to the T 2 (see above), other than having the more powerful Double Mamba 101 engine installed. The aircraft were modified from T 2 standard at Hayes. These aircraft were used for initial and refresher pilot training at Culdrose with 849 Squadron.
Serials *XG882-XG889.*

Harrier T 4(N)

Manufacturer British Aerospace; **Purpose** Sea Harrier conversion training; **Crew** 1 pilot, 1 student; **Maiden flight** 1982; **Service entry** 1982;

Gannet T 2 on pre-delivery flight; note the second pilot's periscope.

Gannet T 5 during deck landing practice aboard Ark Royal, *1955.*

Squadron 899; Still active; **Range** 2,000 nm (3,704 km); **Max speed** 625 knots (1,158 km/h); **Cruising speed** 480 knots (889 km/h); **Endurance** 2 hours; **Service ceiling** 16,400 ft (5,000 m); **Length** 55.8 ft (17 m); **Height** 12.17 ft (3.71 m); **Span** 25.3 ft (7.7 m); **Wing area** 201 sq ft (18.7 sq m); **Power plant** 1 × Rolls-Royce Pegasus 104 vectored thrust turbojet; **All-up weight** 13,600 lb (6,168 kg); **Empty weight** Not available.

The Harrier T 4(N) is the navalized version of the RAF's Harrier T 4 training aircraft and three were procured for the Fleet Air Arm to assist with conversion, operational and refresher training for naval pilots. The aircraft are operated by 899 Squadron at Yeovilton.

In addition, a Harrier T 4 was purchased from BAe for conversion training in 1980, coming from an RAF batch, while a decision was made about the navalized Harrier trainer.

Serials include *XZ445* (Harrier T 4); *ZB604-ZB608.*

Harvard T 2/T 3

Manufacturer North American; **Purpose** Trainer; **Crew** 1 student, 1 instructor; **Maiden flight** April 1935; **Service entry** 1938; **Squadrons** Various training units; **Phased out of service** 1960; **Range** 643 nm (1,191 km); **Max speed** 183 knots (338 km/h); **Cruising speed** 150 knots (278 km/h); **Endurance** 8 hours; **Service ceiling** 21,500 ft (6,550 m); **Rate of climb** 1,350 ft/min (6.9 m/sec); **Length** 28.99 ft (8.84 m); **Height** 11.75 ft (3.57 m); **Span** 42 ft (12.8 m); **Wing area** 253.7 sq ft (23.57 sq m); **Power plant** 1 × Pratt & Whitney Wasp R-1340 radial (600 hp); **All-up weight** 5,250 lb (2,380 kg); **Empty weight** 4,020 lb (1,823 kg).

The highly successful North American Harvard (Texan) was used for training Fleet Air Arm aircrew and has the distinction of being the first US

Harrier T 4(N), 899 Squadron, used for continuation and operational conversion of Sea Harrier pilots at Yeovilton (RN/Yeovilton).

design to be purchased by the United Kingdom.
Serials include *EX847-EX999; EZ459-EZ799.*

Hunter T 8/T 8B/T 8C

Manufacturer Hawker; **Purpose** Trainer; **Crew** 1 pilot, 1 student; **Maiden flight** 1958; **Service entry** July 1958; **Squadrons** 738 (1962-70), 759

Below *Harvard T 2B, 1949.*
Bottom *Hunter T 8, FONAC.*

(1963-69), 764 (1958-72), FRU (1969-71), FRADU (1972-); **Still active**; **Range** 200 nm (370 km); **Max speed** 540 knots (1,000 km/h); **Cruising speed** Not available; **Service ceiling** 47,000 ft (14,325 m); **Rate of climb** 3,600 ft/min (18.3 m/sec); **Length** 48,875 ft (14.9 m); **Height** 13.17 ft (4.01 m); **Span** 33.67 ft (10.3 m); **Wing area** 349 sq ft (32.42 sq m); **Power plant** 1 × Rolls-Royce Avon 122 turbojet (7,550 lb st); **All-up weight** 17,200 lb (7,800 kg); **Empty weight** 13,360 lb (6,060 kg); **Weapons** Provision for cannon, bombs and other underwing stores (see text); **Sensors** AI radar; TACAN.

Some 41 Hunter T 8 variants were supplied to the Fleet Air Arm after conversion from redundant Hunter F 4 airframes, plus another ten aircraft which were new-built and based on the RAF's Hunter T 7 dual-seat trainer. Changes included the provision of an arrester hook, variable weapons fit (including Bullpup missiles at one stage) and practice weapons. Initially used for weapons and advanced operational training, the aircraft (in three sub-variants) is now used by FRADU for training and calibration duties.

Variants Hunter T 7, a small number of which were transferred to FRADU in 1981; Hunter T 8B has full TACAN (Tactical Air Navigation) receiver

equipment; Hunter T 8C has partial TACAN fitting; Hunter T 8M is a special sub-variant designed to take the Ferranti Blue Fox radar for the Sea Harrier FRS 1 training programme, for which the two aircraft are based at Yeovilton with 899 Squadron.
Serials include *WT701-WT702; WW661; XL602-XL604.*

Jetstream T 2

Manufacturer British Aerospace (Scottish Division); **Purpose** Navigation trainer; **Crew** 1/2 pilots, 2 instructors, 3 students; **Maiden flight** 1978; **Service entry** April 1979; **Squadron** 750 (1979-); Still active; **Range** 1,200 nm (2,225 km); **Max speed** 248 knots (459 km/h) at 12,000 ft (3,658 m); **Cruising speed** 245 knots (454 km/h); **Service ceiling** 26,000 ft (7,925 m); **Rate of climb** 2,500 ft/min (12.7 m/sec); **Length** 47.125 ft (14.36 m); **Height** 17.46 ft (5.32 m); **Span** 52 ft (15.8 m); **Wing area** 270 sq ft (25 sq m); **Power plant** 2 × Turbomeca Astazou XVI turboprops (940 shp each); **All-up weight** 12,550 lb (5,692 kg); **Empty weight** 8,741 lb (3,965 kg); **Sensors** Navigation radar in nose radome.

Brought back into service to replace the Sea Prince T 1, the Jetstream T 2 is a development of the RAF's twin-engined trainer and serves with the Royal Naval Observer School at Culdrose. The aircraft is used to train ASW and AEW observers, by making use of the 'classroom' rear cabin for

Left Hunter T 8M, 899 Squadron, operated for radar training at Yeovilton.

Below Jetstream T 2, 750 Squadron, during a training flight to Gibraltar.

navigation exercises, including 'land aways' to foreign countries.
Serials *XX475-XX481; XX483-XX490.*

Jetstream T 3 Four PT-6A-powered Jetstreams were delivered to the Fleet Air Arm in 1986, equipped with the Racal Avionics ASR 360 radar to train observers in techniques using the 360° radar system and display, prior to the introduction of the EH 101 and Lynx Mk 8; Sea King ASW and AEW aircrew also benefit from the new system.
Serials *ZE438-ZE441.*

Meteor T 7

Manufacturer Gloster; **Purpose** Jet trainer; **Crew** 1 pilot, 1 student; **Maiden flight** Not available; **Service entry** February 1955; **Squadrons** 728 (1955-67), 759 (1952-54), station flights LM (1956-65), FRU (1967-71); **Phased out of service** 1971; **Range** 820 nm (1,520 km); **Max speed** 508

Jetstream T 3, 750 Squadron, features Racal ASR 360 radar (Robin Walker).

knots (941 km/h); **Cruising speed** 464 knots (860 km/h); **Service ceiling** 35,000 ft (10,668 m); **Rate of climb** 7,600 ft/min (38.6 m/sec); **Length** 43.5 ft (13.26 m); **Height** 13 ft (3.96 m); **Span** 37.17 ft (11.33 m); **Wing area** 350 sq ft (32.5 sq m); **Power plant** 2 × Rolls-Royce Derwent 5 (or 8) jet engines (3,600 lb st); **All-up weight** 14,000 lb (6,350 kg); **Empty weight** 10,600 lb (4,808 kg).

Used as a shore-based training aircraft, especially for propellor-driven aircraft pilots to convert to the fast growing fleet of jet aircraft in the late 1940s and

Meteor T 7 of Yeovilton Station Flight, painted black with dayglo red nose, wing tips and fuselage band, at Odiham in September 1966 (Robin Walker).

early 1950s. The Meteor T 7 (unusually designated the same numeral as its RAF counterpart) was in service until 1967.

Serials include *WS103-WS117; WS140-WS141.*

Meteor U15/U16 A remotely-piloted aircraft, variants of which were operated by 728B Squadron in connection with guided missile trials from 1959-61.

Serials include *VT310* (U15), *WK870* (U16).

Mosquito T 3

Manufacturer de Havilland Aircraft; **Purpose** Dual-seat trainer; **Crew** 1 pilot, 1 student; **Maiden flight** 1945; **Service entry** 1945; **Squadrons** 728 (1945-46), Airwork FRU (1950-56); **Phased out of service** 1956; **Range** 1,050 nm (1,940 km); **Max speed** 324 knots (600 km/h) at altitude; **Cruising speed** 300 knots (556 km/h); **Service ceiling** 36,000 ft (10,975 m); **Length** 40.5 ft (12.3 m); **Height** 15.25 ft (4.65 m); **Span** 54.17 ft (16.5 m); **Wing area** 454 sq ft (42.2 sq m); **Power plant** 2 × Rolls-Royce Merlin XXV (1,230 hp each); **All-up weight** 17,240 lb (7,820 kg); **Empty weight** as Meteor T 7.

To provide dual-engine training for the Fleet Air Arm, the RAF provided a number of Mosquito T 3 trainers for shore-based duties; the aircraft were fitted with side-by-side controls. In the early 1960s, the civilian company Airwork Limited undertook the Heavy Twin Conversion Courses for the Fleet Air Arm at Brawdy.

Serials include *VT622; VT626-VT631.*

Sea Balliol T 21

Manufacturer Boulton Paul; **Purpose** Deck landing trainer; **Crew** 1 pilot, 1 student; **Maiden flight** October 1952; **Service entry** 1953; **Squadrons** 702 (1957-58), 765 (1957), 781 (1954-58), 796 (1957-58), 1830 (1954-57), 1831 (1954-57), 1840 (1954-55), 1844 (1954-57), several station flights; **Phased out of service** 1958; **Range** 650 nm (1,204 km); **Max speed** 250 knots (463 km/h); **Cruising speed** 200 knots (370 km/h); **Service ceiling** 32,500 ft (9,910 m); **Rate of climb** 1,790 ft/min (9.1 m/sec); **Length** 35.125 ft (10.7 m); **Height** 12.5 ft (3.81 m); **Span** 39.33 ft (11.98 m); **Wing area** 250 sq ft (23.2 sq m); **Power plant** 1 × Rolls-Royce Merlin 35 (1,280 hp); **All-up weight** 8,410 lb (3,815 kg); **Empty weight** 6,730 lb (3,053 kg).

The Sea Balliol was designed to give junior officers air experience and provide a training aircraft for deck landing experience. Various specialist uses were made of the tiny aircraft, including the transition of Gannet aircrew. The last Sea Balliol was delivered to the Fleet Air Arm on 7 December 1954 and one of the last users was the Royal Naval Volunteer Reserve air branch.

Serials include *WL715-WL734; WP324-WP333.*

Sea Fury T 20

Manufacturer Hawker; **Purpose** Fighter training; **Crew** 1 pilot, 1 student; **Maiden flight** 15 January 1948 (prototype); **Service entry** October 1950; **Squadrons** 1830 (1952-54), 1831 (1950-55), 1832 (1950-56), 1833 (1950-55), 1834 (1953-55); **Phased out of service** 1956; **Range** 817 nm (1,512 km); **Max speed** 387 knots (716 km/h) at 18,000 ft (5,486 m); **Cruising speed** 252 knots (467 km/h); **Service ceiling** 35,600 ft (10,850 m); **Rate of climb** 2,970 ft/min (15.1 m/sec); **Length** 34.58 ft (10.94 m); **Height** 15.67 ft (4.78 m); **Span** 38.4 ft (11.7 m), 16.08 ft (4.9 m) folded; **Wing area** 280 sq ft (26 sq m); **Power plant** 1 × Bristol Centaurus 18 radial (2,480 hp); **All-up weight** 11,930 lb (5,411 kg); **Empty weight** 8,700 lb (3,946 kg); **Weapons** 2 × 20 mm Hispano Mk 5 cannon, plus provision for 2,000 lb (907 kg) underwing stores.

This was the shore-based training aircraft for conversion of pilots to the Sea Fury FB 11, as well as role conversion/refresher for the fighter-bomber strike tactics. Its major role was for the conversion of Second World War pilots to the new RNVR squadrons. The aircraft had two 20 mm cannons

Right *Sea Prince T 1, 750 Squadron, flying off the Cornish coast* (RN/ Culdrose).

Left *Sea Balliol T 21, used to train pilots in deck landings (note the hook) and other air experience* (Dowty Boulton Paul).

Sea Fury T 20 WG655/GN-910 of the Royal Naval Historic Aircraft Flight at Yeovilton on 5 August 1978 (Robin A. Walker).

removed and was fitted with a periscope sight for the instructor in the rear cockpit to be given an adequate view of the landing/approach which the student in the front cockpit was carrying out. Production of the Sea Fury T 20 ran to 60 airframes.

Serials include *VX280-VX292; VX297-VX310; WE820-WE826.*

Sea Prince T 1

Manufacturer Hunting Percival; **Purpose** Radar and navigation trainer; **Crew** 2 pilots, 1 instructor, 3 pupils; **Naval Specification** T17/49; **Maiden flight** 28 June 1951; **Service entry** February 1953; **Squadrons** Front line 831 (1962-66); Second line 750 (1953-79), 744 (1953-54), 781 (1953-57), 727 (1956-60), 702 (1957-58); 1830, 1840, 1841 and 1844 also equipped; **Phased out of service** May 1979; **Range** 400 nm (741 km); **Max speed** 194 knots (359 km/h); **Cruising speed** 159 knots (294 km/h) at operational altitude; **Service ceiling** 22,000 ft (6,706 m); **Rate of climb** 1,400 ft/min (427 m/min); **Length** 46.33 ft (14.1 m); **Height** 16.08 ft (3.3 m); **Span** 56 ft (17.1 m); **Wing area** 365 sq ft (34 sq m); **Power plant** 2 × Alvis Leonides 125 (550 hp each); **All-up weight** 11,850 lb (5,375 kg); **Empty weight** 8,850 lb (4,014 kg).

Three orders were placed for the Sea Prince T 1, the first in 1949 for eighteen aircraft, followed by eight in 1951 and another fifteen in the same year. The aircraft replaced several marks of Barracuda in training service and was itself replaced by the Jetstream T 2 in 1979, after having been resparred in the early 1970s. The change in naval equipment

Sea Vampire T 22, prior to delivery in June 1957 (Philip Birtles).

and the disbandment of the RVNR (Air Divisions) led to several T 1s being scrapped in the 1960s.

Serials *WF118-WF133; WF934; WF949; WM735-WM742; WP307-WP321.*

Sea Vampire T 22

Manufacturer de Havilland Aircraft; **Purpose** Jet trainer; **Crew** 1 pilot, 1 student; **Maiden flight** May 1953; **Service entry** 1953; **Squadrons** 700 (1957), 702 (1957-58), 736 (1953-58), 738 (1954-55 and 1958-62), 750 (1962-65), 759 (1953-54), 764 (1955-57), 766 (1956), 781 (1953-64), 893 (1956-57), 1831 (1955-57), 1832 (1955-57) and various

Tiger Moth T 2 XL714/VL of HMS Heron *Flight at Yeovilton on 5 September 1970* (Robin A. Walker).

special/station flights; **Phased out of service** 1964; **Range** 730 nm (1,350 km); **Max speed** 467 knots (856 km/h) at sea level; **Cruising speed** Not available; **Service ceiling** 35,000 ft (10,670 m); **Rate of climb** 4,500 ft/min (22.9 m/sec); **Length** 34.42 ft (10.49 m); **Height** 6.17 ft (1.88 m); **Span** 38 ft (11.6 m); **Wing area** 261 sq ft (24.25 sq m); **Power plant** 1 × de Havilland Goblin 35 turbojet (3,500 lb st); **All-up weight** 11,150 lb (5,058 kg); **Empty weight** Not available.

Developed from the RAF's Vampire T 11 trainer, the Sea Vampire was used in several second line roles in support of the Fleet Air Arm's jet fighter programme. 736 Squadron, for example, was teaching US Navy-trained pilots to use British deck procedures and flying regimes, as well as training piston engine pilots to operate a jet fighter, a role which was also carried out by the Naval Fighter School at Culdrose.

In the late 1950s, the Junior Officers Air Course was undertaken by 781 Squadron with a variety of aircraft, including the Sea Vampire T 22, which remained at Lee-on-Solent until 1964. Several front line jet fighter units flying the Sea Venom had their own Sea Vampire T 22 training/refresher flight in the middle 1950s. In all 73 of this aircraft were ordered for Fleet Air Arm service, and from 1956 they were fitted with ejection seats.

Serials *XA100-XA103; XA152-XA172; XG742-XG777.*

Tiger Moth T 2

Manufacturer de Havilland Aircraft; **Purpose** Basic training; **Crew** 1 pilot, 1 student; **Maiden flight** October 1931; **Service entry** 1943; **Squadrons** 700 (1945), 701 (1945-46), 721 (1946), 727 (1946-50), 733 (1947), 767 (1948), 781 (1960-72), 796 (1950), 799 (1945-46), 1833 (1953), BRNC Flight (1960- 66) and station flights (1965-73); **Phased out of service** 1973; **Range** 262 nm (485 km); **Max speed** 95 knots (175 km/h); **Cruising speed** 75 knots (139 km/h); **Service ceiling** 13,600 ft (4,145 m); **Rate of climb** 673 ft/min (3.4 m/sec); **Length** 23.92 ft (7.29 m); **Height** 8.75 ft (2.67 m); **Span** 29.33 ft (8.94 m); **Wing area** 239 sq ft (22.2 sq m); **Power plant** 1 × de Havilland Gypsy Major (130 hp); **All-up weight** 1,770 lb (803 kg); **Empty weight** 1,115 lb (506 kg).

Probably the most famous training aircraft in the history of aviation, the Tiger Moth remained in Fleet Air Arm service for longer than would be imagined; certainly there were glider tugs at several Naval Air Stations in the late 1960s. Post-war use of the Tiger Moth included basic training, air experience and liaison duties.

Serials include *NM148; XL714-XL717.*

Canberra TT 18, used for target towing and seen here at Gibraltar.

Special duties aircraft

Canberra TT 18

Manufacturer English Electric (BAC); **Purpose** Target-towing and training; **Crew** 1 pilot, 1 observer/aircrewman; **Maiden flight** Converted from B 2; **Service entry** September 1969; **Squadrons** FRU (1969-72); FRADU (1972-); Still active; **Range** 1,200 nm (2,222 km); **Max speed** 524 knots (970 km/h) at altitude; **Cruising speed** Not available; **Service ceiling** 48,000 ft (14,600 m); **Length** 65.5 ft (20 m); **Height** 15.58 ft (4.75 m); **Span** 64 ft (19.5 m); **Wing area** 960 sq ft (89.2 sq m); **Power plant** 2 × Rolls-Royce Avon turbojets (7,500 lb st); **All-up weight** 54,675 lb (24,800 kg); **Empty weight** 22,265 lb (10,100 kg).

Some eighteen Canberra B 2 bombers were converted by the British Aircraft Corporation at Salmesbury for target-towing duties (including several transferred from the RAF in 1981). It can have target-towing winches and other target equipment fitted to its wings and is operated by Flight Refuelling for the Fleet Air Arm. The Canberra TT 18 replaced the Meteor TT 20 (see below).

Canberra B 2 One was ordered by FRADU for a short time.

Canberra U 10/D 14/U 14

Manufacturer English Electric (BAC); **Purpose** Manned/unmanned targets; **Maiden flight** 1960; **Service entry** May 1961; **Squadron** 728B (1961-62); **Phased out of service** 1962; **Range, Max speed, Cruising speed** and **Service ceiling** remain classified but thought to be similar to Canberra TT 18; **Length, Height, Span** and **Wing area** as Canberra TT 18; **Power plant** 2 × Rolls-Royce Avon 109 turbojets (7,500 lb st); **All-up weight** Not available; **Empty weight** as Canberra TT 18; **Sensors** For guided missile experiments.

The Canberra U 10 was developed from the RAF's Canberra B 2 bomber by Short Brothers of Belfast to carry out guided missile and remotely-piloted vehicle trails. The D 14 (a later designation of the U 14 conversion) was used for trials with Seaslug and Seacat surface-to-air missiles, especially from Hal Far (Malta) with the trials ship, *Girdlenęss*. Trails were completed in December 1961.

Serials include *WH704; WH876.*

Firefly TT 4

Manufacturer Fairey Aviation; **Purpose** Target towing; **Crew** 1 pilot, 1 aircrewman; **Maiden flight**

Canberra U 14 of 728B Squadron in Malta during Seaslug missile trials with Girdleness. *This aircraft later served with A&AEE Boscombe Down for a number of years (via Robin Walker).*

Firefly TT 4 aboard Illustrious *in 1950.*

1949; **Service entry** November 1951; **Squadron** 771 (1951-55); **Phased out of service** 1955; **Range, Max speed, Cruising speed, Service ceiling, Length, Height, Span, Wing area, Power plant, All-up weight** and **Empty weight** as Fairey Firefly FR 4 (page 59).

An unspecified number of Firefly FR 4 aircraft were converted retrospectively for the Fleet Air Arm to act as target-towing aircraft. They operated from various locations, such as Ford. The aircraft were fitted with the propeller-driven ML Aviation Type G winch under the fuselage centre-section from which a number of targets, including the standard gunnery banner, could be flown.

Serials include *VH127; VH132.*

Firefly TT 5 A small number of AS 5s were converted for target towing, including WB 406.

Firefly U 8/U 9

Manufacturer Fairey Aviation; **Purpose** Unmanned target drone; **Maiden flight** 1957; **Service**

Firefly U 9 of 728B Squadron, Hal Far (via Robin Walker).

entry January 1958; **Squadron** 728B (1958-61); **Phased out of service** 1961; **Range, Max speed, Cruising speed, Endurance, Service ceiling, Rate of climb, Length, Height, Span, Wing area, Power plant, All-up weight** and **Empty weight** as Firefly AS 5; **Sensors** None, but some early telemetry equipment.

Some forty of these pilotless drones were converted from stock AS 5 airframes, probably by Short Brothers of Belfast, to assist in the proving trials for the Firestreak air-to-air guided missile and the Seaslug medium range surface-to-air missile system. Most of the trials were carried out in the Mediterranean Sea from Hal Far and using *Girdleness.*

Serials include *VX416; VX418; VX421; WB257; WJ188.*

Gannet ECM 4/ECM 6

Manufacturer Fairey Aviation; **Purpose** Shipborne electronic warfare; **Crew** 1 pilot, 2 observers; **Maiden flight** Not available; **Service entry** February 1959; **Squadron** 831 (1959-66); **Phased out of service** 1966; **Range, Max speed, Cruising speed, Endurance, Service ceiling** and **Rate of climb** as Gannet AS 4 (page 122); **Length, Height, Span** and **Wing area** as Gannet AS 1 (page 121); **Power plant, All-up weight** and **Empty weight** as Gannet AS 4 (page 122); **Sensors** Remain classified.

A number of early AS 4 and some AS 6 airframes were converted for electronic warfare trials and training in the 1958-66 period, with aircraft being deployed to aircraft carriers as and when required.

Exact details of the aircraft and their service lives remain difficult to come by even with the time laspe, such is the secrecy of the electronic warfare world. However it is known that 831 Squadron

Gannet ECM 6 of 831 Squadron, Culdrose, 1961 (Fleet Air Arm Museum).

Meteor TT 20, 728 Squadron, at Hal Far, Malta, in 1965 (Brian Johnstone).

received the Boyd Trophy for 1960 in respect of the unit's efficiency in training other elements of the Fleet Air Arm in electronic warfare.

Serials include *WN464* (ECM 4); *XG798* and *XG831* (ECM 6).

Meteor TT 20

Manufacturer Gloster; **Purpose** Target towing; **Crew** 1 pilot, 1 aircrewman; **Maiden flight** October 1957; **Service entry** 1958; **Squadron** FRU (1958-71); **Phased out of service** 1971; **Range** 800 nm (1665 km); **Max speed** 480 knots (891 km/h); **Cruising speed** 400 knots (741 km/h); **Service ceiling** 30,000 ft (9,145 m); **Length** 48.5 ft (14.8 m); **Height** Not available; **Span** 43 ft (13.1 m); **Wing area** 374 sq ft (34.7 sq m); **Power plant** 2 × Rolls-Royce Derwent; **All-up weight** 22,000 lb (9,979 kg); **Empty weight** 12,000 lb (5,443 kg).

Redundant Meteor airframes were used in the late 1950s to provide the service with aircraft for second line tasks, such as target towing. Several dozen NF 11 airframes which had formerly been used by the RAF to provide night fighter defence for the United Kingdom and other Nato locations were taken in hand and converted to TT 20 standards.

Serials include *WM159*.

Mosquito TT 39

Manufacturer de Havilland Aircraft; **Purpose** Target towing; **Crew** 1 pilot, 1 aircrewman; **Maiden flight** 1946; **Service entry** March 1949; **Squadron** 728 (1949-52); **Phased out of service** 1952; **Range** 626 nm (1,160 km); **Max speed** 243 knots (450 km/h) towing; **Cruising speed** 272 knots (504 km/h); **Endurance** 1 hour; **Service ceiling** 31,800 ft (9,690 m); **Length** 43.33 ft (13.2 m); **Height** 15.25 ft (4.65 m); **Span** 54.17 ft (16.5 m); **Wing area** 454 sq ft (42.2 sq m); **Power plant** 2 × Rolls-Royce Merlin 73 engine (1,650 hp); **All-up weight** 23,000 lb (10,433 kg); **Empty weight** 16,330 lb (7,407 kg).

A number of Second World War Mosquito B XVI airframes were converted to the high speed target-towing role by General Aircraft. They had a longer nose with a redesigned window, a target towing winch system and a dorsal turret to view the performance of the target during its operation. The aircraft was not converted for shipborne service.

Mosquito PR 16 Some redundant RAF airframes were used for target towing from Hal Far by 728 Squadron during 1948-52.

Serials include *PF606; RV295.*

Sea Otter

Manufacturer Supermarine; **Purpose** Shipborne/shore-based SAR; **Crew** 1 pilot, 1 observer, 1/2 aircrewmen; **Maiden flight** July 1943; **Service entry** November 1944; **Squadrons** 772 (1944-45), 781 (1946-52), 1700 (1944-46), 1701 (1944-46), 1703 (1944-46), 1703 (1945) and ship's flights; **Phased out of service** 1952; **Range** 630 nm (1,170 km); **Max speed** 130 knots (241 km/h) at 5,000 ft (1,524 m); **Cruising speed** 87 knots (161 km/h); **Rate of climb** 870 ft/min (4.42 m/sec); **Service ceiling** 16,000 ft (4,880 m); **Length** 39.42 ft (12.02 m); **Height** 16.17 ft (4.93 m); **Span** 46 ft (14.02 m); **Wing area** 610 sq ft (56.7 sq m); **Power plant** 1 × Bristol Mercury 30 (855 hp); **All-up weight** 10,000 lb (4,536 kg); **Empty weight** 6,805 lb (3,090 kg); **Weapons** 3 × 0.303 in machine guns carried.

Developed from the famous Walrus amphibian, the Sea Otter was used for search and rescue operations as well as communications and liaison flights.

Left *Sea Otter aircraft was used as plane guards until the helicopter entered service* (Fleet Air Arm Museum).

Below *Sturgeon TT 2, 728 Squadron operating from an aircraft carrier during Fleet firing exercises* (Shorts).

It was embarked in aircraft carriers and went to Korea with *Triumph* and *Theseus* before being replaced by the Westland Dragonfly/Sikorsky S-51 helicopter. The last Sea Otter was withdrawn from service in October 1952.

   Serials include *JM831; RD878.*

Sturgeon TT 2

Manufacturer Short Brothers; **Purpose** Shipborne target tug; **Crew** 1 pilot, 1 observer/aircrewman; **Maiden flight** 1 September 1949; **Service entry** August 1951; **Squadrons** 703 (1951), 728 (1951-56), 771 (1950-52); **Phased out of service** 1956; **Range** 1,390 nm (2,575 km); **Max speed** 320 knots (595 km/h); **Cruising speed** 250 knots (463 km/h); **Target towing speed** 215 knots (400 km/h); **Endurance** 1 hour; **Service ceiling** 32,900 ft (10,030 m); **Length** 48,875 ft (14.9 m); **Height**
13.21 ft (4.03 m); **Span** 59.75 ft (18.2 m); **Wing area** 564 sq ft (52.4 sq m); **Power plant** 2 × Rolls-Royce Merlin 140S (1,660 hp each); **All-up weight** 22,350 lb (10,138 kg); **Empty weight** 17,647 lb (8,005 kg); **Sensors** Target towing equipment only.

   The Short Sturgeon is an interesting but often overlooked aircraft. It was the first British twin-engined aircraft designed especially for aircraft carrier operations, being proposed under specification S 11/43 as a long-range reconnaissance bomber for the British Pacific Fleet operating against Japan.

   The dimensions, when folded, were so constructed to allow hangar stowage aboard the newly-proposed Fleet carriers of the 'Ark Royal' Class and the improved Light Fleet design which became *Hermes*. With the cessation of hostilities against Japan, the aircraft's first prototype had not flown and so the design was modified for second line

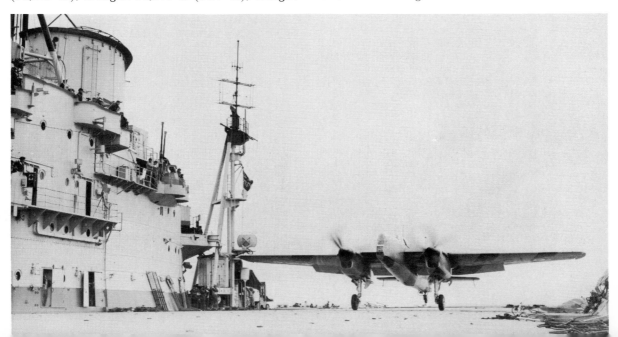

duties, specifically for high speed target towing, using aircraft carriers if required.

The first production Sturgeon TT 2, with carrier specification, was flown at Belfast on 8 June 1950 and some 23 were delivered to the Fleet Air Arm, mainly operating from Hal Far (Malta), being flown by 728 Squadron and other units.

Serials *RK787; RK791; RK794; VR363; VR371; TS475-TS497.*

Sturgeon TT 3

Manufacturer Short Brothers; **Purpose** High speed target towing; **Crew** 1 pilot, 1 observer/aircrewman; **Maiden flight** 1954; **Service entry** May 1954; **Squadron** 728 (1954-58); **Phased out of service** 1958; **Range, Max speed, Cruising speed, Target towing speed, Endurance** and **Service ceiling** as Sturgeon TT 2; **Length** 44 ft (13.4 m) approx; **Height, Span, Wing area, Power plant, All-up weight, Empty weight** and **Sensors** as Sturgeon TT 2.

The Sturgeon TT 3 was a shore-based only development of the TT 2 with no deck landing arrester gear and manually folding wings for hangar stowage. Nineteen of the variant were delivered to the Fleet Air Arm between 1954 and 1957 for service around the United Kingdom and at Hal Far. The aircraft was replaced by the Meteor TT 20 target tug in the late 1950s.

Experimental fixed-wing aircraft

This section looks at several projects which were planned either during the Second World War or immediately prior to the 'carrier crisis' in 1964-66; subsequently all were abandoned in favour of other solutions, not always completely successful in themselves. In several cases it has not been possible to give full technical details of projects, especially those only conceived on paper.

Firecrest

Manufacturer Blackburn; **Purpose** Shipborne torpedo bomber; **Crew** 1 pilot; **Naval Specification** S 28/43; **Maiden flight** 1948; **Abandoned** 1953.

Developed from the Firebrand TF 5, the unofficially-named Firecrest was produced by Blackburn under the guise of the B-48 and six prototypes were in various forms of production when the Fleet Air Arm chose the Westland Wyvern in its place.

Serials *RT561; RT656; VF172; VF254; VF257; VF262.*

P 139B

Designer Hawker Siddeley; **Purpose** Carrier AEW/COD; **Crew** 2 pilots; **Abandoned** 1966.

This project was to provide airborne early warning and carrier on-board delivery for the proposed CVA-01 aircraft carrier, but when that was cancelled in 1966 the P 139B went the same way.

P 1154

Designer Hawker; **Purpose** Shipborne V/STOL fighter; **Crew** 1 pilot (later modified to include 1 observer).

In about 1961, Sydney Camm, the great Hawker designer, began work on a NATO requirement for a vertical/short take-off and landing (V/STOL) fighter aircraft and by 1963 a single seat version had been designed. The Fleet Air Arm was interested in the project but needed a higher specification than the RAF, including two aircrew, Mach 2 performance, conventional undercarriage, catapult gear, a primary high altitude performance and complete marinization. It would be a vectored thrust powered aircraft.

In 1963, the project was cancelled because the RAF and Fleet Air Arm requirements could not be reconciled. The Fleet Air Arm subsequently acquired the Phantom FG 1, having to wait until 1980 for a subsonic V/STOL aircraft, the Sea Harrier FRS 1.

Future plans for an Anglo-American V/STOL fighter with supersonic performance were announced in 1986 and preliminary design work is thought to be under way by British Aerospace and McDonnell Douglas.

Seafang F 31/F 32

Manufacturer Supermarine; **Purpose** Shipborne fighter; **Crew** 1 pilot; **Naval Staff Requirement**

Seafang Mk 32 experimental fighter (Fleet Air Arm Museum).

N 5/45; **Maiden flight** 1946; **Abandoned** 1947.

Developed as the naval version of the Spiteful, the Seafang F 31 was a fixed (non-folding) wing version powered by the Griffon 61 engine, and the F 32 was the carrier-rated, Griffon 89-powered fighter, with contra-rotating propellors.

Ten F 31s were built, eight were delivered and although several F 32s were also built, none is thought to have flown. The latter had a proposed range of 1,120 nm (2,075 km), a maximum speed of 413 knots (764 km/h) and a service ceiling of 42,000 ft (12,800 m).

Serials *VB893-VB895; VG471-VG480* (F 31); *VG481-VG482; VG486-VG505* (F 32).

Seamew AS 1

Manufacturer Shorts; **Purpose** Shipborne anti-submarine; **Crew** 1 pilot, 1 observer; **Maiden flight** 13 August 1953; **Cancelled** 1957.

This ungainly looking aircraft was a rival bid to the Fairey Gannet as an anti-submarine warfare aircraft with the pilot and observer sitting in tandem above the main fuselage. Although the aircraft was not selected for front line service, two of the prototypes were operated by 700 Squadron in 1956-57.

Serials *XA209; XA213; XA216; XE169-XE172; XE177-XE179; XE181-XE186; XE205-XE211.*

Spearfish TDB 1

Manufacturer Fairey Aviation; **Purpose** Shipborne torpedo bomber; **Crew;** 1 pilot, 1 observer; **Naval Staff Requirement** 05/43; **Maiden flight** 5 July 1945; **Service entry** 1946; **Phased out of service** 1952; **Range** 900 nm (1,667 km); **Max speed** 254 knots (470 km/h) at altitude; **Cruising speed** 170 knots (315 km/h) at altitude; **Service ceiling** 25,000 ft (7,620 m); **Length** 44.58 ft (13.56 m); **Height** 16.33 ft (4.97 m); **Span** 60.25 ft (18.36 m); **Wing area** 530 sq ft (49.2 sq m); **Power plant** 1 × Bristol Centaurus 60 (2,320 hp); **All-up weight** 22,083 lb (10.017 kg); **Empty weight** 15,200 lb (6,895 kg); **Weapons** 2 × 20 mm defensive cannon, 1 × ASV/ASW torpedo or 4 × 500 lb (227 kg) bombs or 4 × depth charges in bomb bay; 8 × Mk VIII rockets underwing; **Sensors** ASV Mk XV retractable dome; camera in outer wing.

Designed as a replacement for the Barracuda in the Pacific War, the Spearfish was cancelled as a front line production project at the end of the Second World War, but three prototypes were flown and used for trials and training tasks until 1952.

Serials *RA356; RA360; RA363.*

SR 177

Designer Saunders Roe; **Purpose** Shipborne fighter; **Crew** 1 pilot; **Abandoned** 1957.

A unique aircraft design, the Saunders Roe SR 177 was a rocket-jet with a fast interception role; the rocket motor was housed in the tail and the reheated Gyron Junior engine in the belly of the fuselage. The design called for a naval fighter which could intercept Soviet manned nuclear bombers at 60,000 ft (18,290 m) some 55 nm (110 km) from the parent carrier or naval air station. Because the project could not be continued as a joint NATO project, it was cancelled by the UK Ministry of Supply on Christmas Eve 1957 and the Cowes (Isle of Wight) production line was terminated.

Serials allocated *XL905-XL907; XL920-XL925.*

Seamew, the first prototype during flying trials in August 1953.

The helicopters

From the early days of Igor Sikorsky's first helicopter experiments with the US Navy and Coast Guard off Long Island, New York, the Royal Navy has been very interested in the pursuit of submarines using helicopters. Even towards the end of the Second World War, a lend-lease deal for the supply of 52 Sikorsky R-4 Hoverfly I helicopters was entered into by the British government. The first Hoverflies arrived in the United Kingdom before VE Day and were assigned to 771 Squadron and by late 1945 the helicopters had moved to Portland.

Some trials were carried out by 771 Squadron but it was not until 1947 and the formation of 705 Squadron that the helicopter began to develop in earnest. The major thrust of the helicopter evaluation changed from being primarily anti-submarine to include SAR (search and rescue), Fleet requirements, transportation and other general duties. The American influence continued with the delivery of the Westland/Sikorsky S-51 Dragonfly in January 1950 and the Hiller HT-1 in 1953.

The first major development was the evaluation of the Sikorsky S-55 helicopter which was to be manufactured under licence by Westland Helicopters at Yeovil under the name Whirlwind. The first Whirlwind HAS 22 was delivered to 705 Squadron in October 1953.

In 1957, the trials role was handed over to 701 Squadron, leaving 705 Squadron to move to Culdrose and set up as the helicopter training squadron, which it is to date. During this time, training helicopters have been the Whirlwind HAR 3 and HAS 7, Dragonfly HR-3 and HR-5, the Wasp HAS 1 and Hiller HT-2; since March 1974, the Fleet Air Arm's training helicopter has been the Gazelle HT 2. 701 Squadron only had a short run as helicopter requirements unit, before being disbanded in 1958, when it was deemed that the frontline squadrons could undertake much of the work and a few, select, second line units could be used for trials, evaluation and training. Some 700 series flights have also been formed since then for the intensive flying trials of particular helicopters, such as the Sea King (700S) and Lynx (700L).

The need for twin-engined helicopters to operate over water was demonstrated during the service time of the Whirlwind and gradually piston-engined types were replaced by turbine-powered helicopters. Even by 1980 there were still two types of single-engined turbine helicopters in front line

Early helicopter shipborne trials were carried out by the Fleet Air Arm with the American designed S-51 Dragonfly and Fort Duquesne *in 1951.*

Whirlwind HAS 7, Lossiemouth SAR Flight, during a wet winching exercise in the Moray Firth, 1962 (Brian Johnstone).

Anti-submarine helicopters

The first real attempt by the Fleet Air Arm to use the helicopter for anti-submarine warfare came with the Whirlwind HAS 7, but there were initial problems. For example, in one period during 1961-62 *Centaur,* with 824 Squadron embarked, lost thirteen of the type out of a standard complement of eight helicopters — even the replacements were lost — in flying accidents, mainly caused by engine problems. Nevertheless, the Whirlwind showed the way for future helicopter anti-submarine warfare.

The normal *modus operandi* for the Whirlwind squadrons was to embark eight helicopters, six of which would be configured to carry the American AN/AQS-4 dipping sonar. This was operated from the helicopter's main cabin by an observer (officer) and an aircrewman (rating). The helicopter's role was to detect submarines for prosecution by fixed-wing or frigate ASW systems; in the event of close-range contact, especially that which could engage the parent aircraft carrier, one of the other two Whirlwinds would be launched to investigate.

One was nominally the plane guard and the other the stand-by helicopter, armed with a single 21 in (53 cm) Mk 30 passive ASW torpedo. Such were the weight limitations of the Whirlwind HAS 7 that it could either carry a torpedo and rescue winch, or just the dipping sonar and sonics suite.

service and regularly operating over water — the Wasp HAS 1 and the Wessex HAS 3. Both helicopters were actively involved in the Falklands campaign and achieved success and fame there.

A major change for the Fleet Air Arm's helicopter force came in 1969 with the introduction of the Sea King HAS 1 aboard aircraft carriers and the 'Tiger' Class helicopter cruisers. The basic American-designed airframe has been developed fully into the world's best medium-range, medium-weight anti-submarine helicopter in its Mk 5 state. In addition, Westland has developed the helicopter for airborne early warning duties and commando assault tasks.

Wessex HAS 1, 771 Squadron, recovering the SAR diver (RN/Culdrose).

By 1961, the front line Fleet Air Arm helicopter anti-submarine warfare squadrons were being re-equipped with the Wessex HAS 1 which not only had night hover ability and an automatic flight control system, but carried the up-to-date Type 195 sonar and two Mk 44 lightweight torpedoes as well as the rescue winch. The Wessex 1 was embarked in aircraft carriers for ASW support (what is now called 'inner zone' protection in NATO), in the 'Tiger' Class helicopter cruisers and for use by the Portland-based training units. By the late 1960s, the Fleet Air Arm was beginning to use Royal Fleet Auxiliaries as ASW helicopter operating platforms, a programme which has continued through the Wessex HAS 3, Sea King variants and will presumably still be an operational option for the EH 101.

The Wessex HAS 3 was a natural progression to bring together a tactical display system (radar), sonar and weapons delivery. The helicopters were mainly converted from Mk 1 airframes and it was considered a smooth helicopter to fly, having a duplex AFCS with linked doppler inputs. From an operational point of view it carried the more advanced Type 5955 radar and the Type 195 dipping sonar, together with the ability to carry Mk 44 and Mk 46 homing torpedoes.

In the mid 1960s, it was decided that the Fleet Air Arm would adopt the Sikorsky SH-3 anti-submarine helicopter for its primary ASW helicopter to replace the Wessex and to undertake more outer zone screening tasks within the redefined NATO role of the Royal Navy. Westland again undertook the licence production of the Sea King and it remains in production in 1987.

Small ships' flights were equipped with the Wasp HAS 1 during 1964-65 and later with the Westland-designed Lynx HAS 2, which combined the surface search ability of radar and the ability to carry a variety of ASW weapons. Following the Falklands, the Lynx has started to follow the anti-shipping warfare road, leaving the older frigates to soldier on with the Wasp until 1988. Small ship ASW could well go to the EH 101 in the next decade, leaving the Lynx to concentrate on the anti-surface vessel role.

Small ship helicopter operations for the modern Fleet Air Arm centre around the Lynx HAS 2/3 helicopter and the frigate (this is Brazen*) or destroyer. The Union Flag was worn for operations off Lebanon in 1984 (RN).*

EH 101

Manufacturer E H Industries; **Purpose** Long-range ASW; **Crew** 1 pilot, 2 observers, up to 8 passengers; **Maiden flight** May 1987; **Service entry** 1993; **To be embarked** Type 22 and Type 23 frigates; **Range** 1,100 nm (2,035 km); **Max speed** 167 knots (309 km/h); **Cruising speed** 164 knots (304 km/h) **Endurance** 5 hours; **Service ceiling** 4,000 m; **Rate of climb** Not available; **Length** Not available; **Height** 6.5 m; **Rotor diameter** 18.6 m; **Power plant** 3 × General Electric T700-GE-401 or 3 × RR/Turbomeca RTM 322-01 (2,000 shp each); **All-up weight** 28,000 lb (12,700 kg); **Empty weight** Not available; **Weapons** Various including 4 × Mk 46 or Stingray torpedoes, 4 × Mk 11 depth bombs, nuclear depth charges.

Designed and produced by the Anglo-Italian consortium of Westland Helicopters and the helicopter division of Gruppo Agusta, the EH 101 is the first long-range medium anti-submarine helicopter to have complete three-engine safety, the ability to operate from a flight deck irrespective of wind and to have been built on an exact 50:50 share by two nations.

The Italian MMI will operate the helicopter in a

Above EH 101, in model form, is destined to be the Sea King replacement in the 1990s.

Left Lynx HAS 3, 815 Squadron, armed with two MK 46 torpedoes and equipped with Orange Crop electronic surveillance measures.

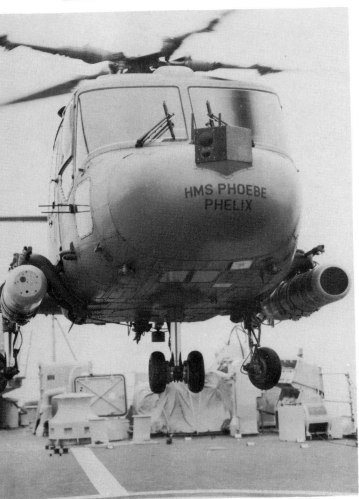

dipping sonar role from large warships, whilst the current Royal Navy thinking appears to be the use of the helicopter from small ships, such as the Batch 2 and 3 Type 22 frigates and the Type 23 towed array frigates, without dipping sonar but using sonobuoys linked to a special GEC Avionics computerized processor unit.

The helicopter's prototype is due to make a first flight at Westland's Yeovil plant in May 1987 and service deliveries could begin in 1993, with the first trials unit being formed at RNAS Yeovilton that year.

Lynx HAS 2/3

Manufacturer Westland; **Purpose** Shipborne ASVW/ASW; **Crew** 1 pilot, 1 observer, (1 aircrewman), up to 10 passengers; **Maiden flight** 20 May 1972; **Service entry** HAS 2 September 1976 (700L Squadron), HAS 3 June 1982 (702 Squadron); **Squadrons** HAS 2 700L (1976-77), 702 (1978-), 815 (1981-), 829 (1986-); HAS 3 702 (1982-), 815 (1982-), 829 (1986-); Still active; **Range** 320 nm (593 km); **Max speed** 146 knots (270 km/h); **Cruising speed** 125 knots (232 km/h), 122 knots (226 km/h) on one engine; **Endurance** 2.5 hours; **Service ceiling** (HIGE) 9,678 ft (2,950 m); **Length** 38.25 ft (11.66 m); **Height** 11 ft (3.66 m); **Rotor diameter** 42 ft (12.8 m); **Power plant** 2 × Rolls-Royce Gem 41-1 (1,120 shp each); **All-up weight** 10,500 lb (4,767 kg); **Empty weight** 6,836 lb (3,101

Lynx HAS 2 XZ239/VB-375 of 815 Squadron on board HMS Beaver as it sails from Portsmouth on 14 April 1986 at the start of Exercise 'Global '86' (Robin Walker).

kg); **Weapons** 2 × Mk 44, Mk 46 or Stingray torpedoes; 4 × Sea Skua; 4 × Mk 11 depth charges; 1 × nuclear depth bomb; 1 × 7.62 mm cabin-mounted machine gun; **Sensors** Sea Spray Mk 1 radar, Racal Avionics MIR-2 Orange Crop.

The Westland Lynx was the third of the Anglo-French helicopter projects of the late 1960s and was specifically designed to meet the Fleet Air Arm's need for a second generation helicopter to operate from small ships in extreme sea states. The Lynx, using the Fairey Harpoon deck restraint, can in fact operate from a Type 22 frigate in high sea states and make allowance for the wind by manoeuvring on deck to face into it for launch.

The original role for the helicopter was to deliver an anti-submarine weapon with speed and accuracy, but that was developed into surface search using the Sea Spray radar and Orange Crop ESM. From 1982, the primary role of the helicopter has been in anti-surface vessel warfare using the Sea Skua missile.

From 1986, Type 22 frigates of 9th Frigate Squadron have been complemented for two Lynx HAS 2/3 and parented by 829 Squadron, the former Wasp operational unit.

The HAS 2 was the first production model with tricycle undercarriage for shipborne operations and was uprated to HAS 3 standard in June 1982 by fitting the Gem 41 engine. The data above relates to the HAS 3.

The Lynx can transfer 4.5 tonnes of stores between two ships some 50 nm (93 km) apart in 2.5 hours without the need to refuel, using the under-slung load hook. The Lynx can therefore be used for a variety of non-combat roles, including SAR, vertrep (vertical replenishment) and cargo carrying.

Serials include *XX469, XX510* and *XX910* (prototypes); *XZ227-XZ252; XZ254-XZ257; XZ689-XZ700; XZ719-XZ736; ZD250-ZD258; ZD565-ZD567.*

Lynx HAS 8

Although it appears that the 'sonics Lynx' update, to equip the helicopter with dipping sonar or active sonobuoys and an onboard processor, has been cancelled, the Lynx HAS 8 helicopter will probably enter service for the Type 23 frigates in 1990.

The helicopter will be remodelled by Westland Helicopters, using the existing airframes and some new-built machines, with the GEC Avionics Sea Owl Passive Identification Device System (for the surface search role), the Racal Avionics Tactical Management System, the Rolls-Royce Gem 43 engine, reverse direction tail rotor and the Ferranti Sea Spray Mk III 360 degrees radar, which will

Advanced Lynx mock-up shows the new rotor blades, 360 degrees radar and Sea Owl passive identification system.

Sea King HAS 1, 706 Squadron, armed with Mk 11 depth charges.

allow Sea Skua anti-shipping attacks from a wider engagement envelope.

Work will be carried out by Westland at Weston-super-Mare and Yeovil, with funding probably being made available for the BERP (British Experimental Rotorcraft Programme) main rotor blades to be fitted. These blades were a contributing factor in the success of G-LYNX in August 1986 when it took the world's absolute helicopter speed record from the Soviet A-10 (Mi-24 Hind) helicopter with a speed of 216.45 knots (400.87 km/h).

Sea King HAS 1

Manufacturer Westland; **Purpose** Shipborne medium ASW; **Crew** 2 pilots, 1 observer, 1 sonar operator, up to 25 passengers (depending on internal configuration); **Maiden flight** 7 May 1969; **Service entry** 19 August 1969 (700S Squadron); **Squadrons** 700S (1969-70), 706 (1970-78), 737 (1970-75), 814 (1973-77), 819 (1971-78), 820 (1972-77), 824 (1970-77), 826 (1970-76); **Phased out of service** 1978 (conversion to HAS 2); **Range** 600 nm (1,111 km); **Max speed** 112 knots (207 km/h); **Cruising speed** 100 knots (185 km/h); **Endurance** 4 hours; **Service ceiling** 10,500 ft (3,200 m); **Rate of climb** 3,000 ft/min (15.3 m/sec); **Length** 55.8 ft (17.01 m); **Height** 16.3 ft (4.91 m); **Rotor diameter** 62 ft (18.9 m); **Power plant** 2 × Rolls-Royce Gnome H 1400 (1,500 shp each); **All-up weight** 20,500 lb (9,300 kg); **Empty weight** 12,170 lb (5,520 kg); **Weapons** 4 × Mk 44 torpedoes, 4 × Mk 11 depth charges, 1 × nuclear depth bomb; **Sensors** Type 195 sonar, ARI 5955 radar.

Unlike many other ASW helicopters, the Sea King is capable of automonous operations without requiring the back-up of shipborne systems.

Developed from the Sikorsky S-61 Sea King helicopter, the Westland Sea King HAS 1 was the first in a line of medium anti-submarine helicopters using the common airframe. For the first time, the Fleet Air Arm was able to take a helicopter afloat with power folding, five-blade main rotor system and a platform capable of long-range co-ordination

Sea King HAS 2, 814 Squadron, embarked in Hermes.

of the anti-submarine battle. The first Sea Kings went to sea in *Eagle* during 1970, later embarking in *Ark Royal* and the two 'Tiger' Class helicopter cruisers; each type of warship having six and four helicopters respectively.

Sea King HAS 2/2A

Manufacturer Westland; **Purpose** Shipborne medium ASW; **Crew** 2 pilots, 1 observer, 1 rating sonar operator, up to 25 passengers depending on internal configuration; **Maiden flight** 18 June 1976; **Service entry** December 1976 (826 Squadron); **Squadrons** 706 (1978-85), 814 (1977-82), 819 (1977-85), 820 (1977-80), 824 (1977-85), 825 (1982), 826 (1976-84); **Phased out of service** 1985 (conversion to HAS 5 and AEW 2); **Range** 664 nm (1,230 km); **Max speed** 144 knots (267 km/h); **Cruising speed, Endurance, Service ceiling, Rate of climb, Length, Height** and **Rotor diameter** as Sea King HAS 1; **Power plant** 2 × Rolls-Royce Gnome H 1400-1 turboshafts (1,660 each); **All-up weight** 21,000 lb (9,525 kg); **Empty weight** 13,000 lb (5,896 kg); **Weapons** as Sea King HAS 1, plus Mk 46 torpedo; **Sensors** as Sea King HAS 1 but some aircraft fitted with MIR-2.

A development of the Sea King HAS 1 following the result of initial squadron service aboard ship; amongst the basic modifications was a six-bladed tail rotor for better lateral stability in the hover and when working around the confines of the ship's flight deck. The power plant was improved, giving greater power for take-off and continuous operations, although as with all previous naval helicopters the power was transmission limited.

To supplement the existing commando lift during the Falklands conflict, the Fleet Air Arm reformed 825 Squadron to operate the HAS 2 but with the dipping sonar equipment and other ASW electronics removed.

819 Squadron was the only shore-based front line Sea King squadron with the type, a role in support of the nuclear submarines based at Faslane, which it maintains with the Sea King HAS 5 which was developed from the HAS 2.

A number of Mk 2 airframes have been modified in the 1982-87 period to provide the basis for the Sea King AEW 2 (see page 00) helicopter which carries the Searchwater airborne early warning radar.

Besides its anti-submarine role, the Sea King was operated in the surface search, over-the-horizon targeting and SAR roles, achieving fame in the latter with various sorties from Culdrose and Prestwick. As a result of this ability, the RAF purchased

Sea King HAS 2, 849A Flight, over Illustrious, *1986* (RN/Illustrious).

the basic airframe for its SAR flights, under the designation Sea King HAR 3.

Sea King HAS 5

Manufacturer Westland; **Purpose** Shipborne medium ASW; **Crew** 2 pilots, 1 observer, 1 rating sonar operator; **Maiden flight** 1980; **Service delivery** 2 October 1980; **Service entry** November 1980 (820 Squadron); **Squadrons** 706 (1981-), 810 (1983-), 814 (1982-), 819 (1984-), 820 (1980-), 824 (1982-), 826 (1981-); Still active; **Range** and **Max speed** as Sea King HAS 2; **Cruising speed, Endurance, Service ceiling, Rate of climb, Length, Height** and **Rotor diameter** as Sea King HAS 1; **Power plant, All-up weight** and **Empty weight** as Sea King HAS 2; **Weapons** 4 × Mk 44, Mk 46 or Stingray torpedoes; 4 × Mk 11 depth

Sea King HAS 2A, 819 Squadron, during joint operations with an 'Oberon' Class submarine off the Scottish coast (RN/Gannet).

charges or nuclear depth bombs; 7.62 mm machine gun in cabin; **Sensors** as Sea King HAS 2 but Sea Searcher radar and MIR-2 standard and LAPADS sonobuoy processing; some aircraft fitted with REL EW systems for MAD.

By 1986, all Sea King squadrons in the Fleet Air Arm in the ASW role had been equipped with the Sea King HAS 5. The main differences in this helicopter are the provision of the LAPADS processor, the Sea Searcher radar and the increased internal space made by moving a bulkhead; many HAS 5s are converted HAS 2 airframes.

Sea King HAS 6 This is a planned Fleet Air Arm version of the Advanced Sea King with increased all-up weight and other refinements which will enable it to operate from a frigate-sized warship. No orders had been made by 1987.

Sea King serials include HAS 1/2/2A/5 *XV370-XV373, XV642-XV677, XV695-XV714;* HAS 2/5 *XZ570-XZ582;* HAS 5 *ZA126-ZA137; ZA166-ZA170; ZD630-ZD637; ZE418-ZE420.*

Wasp HAS 1

Manufacturer Westland; **Purpose** Shipborne light ASW/ASVW; **Crew** 1 pilot (1 aircrewman), 1 observer for *Endurance,* up to 3 passengers; **Maiden flight** 28 October 1962; **Service entry** June 1963 (700W Squadron); **Squadrons** 700W (1963-64), 703 (1972-80), 706 (1964-75), 829 (1964-); 848 (1967-73); Still active; **Range** 263 nm (488 km);

Max speed 104 knots (193 km/h); **Cruising speed** 96 knots (177 km/h); **Endurance** 2.4 hours; **Service ceiling** 1,200 ft (3,720 m); **Rate of climb** 1,440 ft/min (7.2 m/sec); **Length** 30.3 ft (9.24 m); **Width** 8.67 ft (2.64 m); **Height** 8.92 ft (2.72 m); **Rotor diameter** 32.25 ft (9.83 m); **Power plant** 1 × Rolls-Royce Bristol Nimbus 503 (710 shp); **All-up weight** 5,500 lb (2,495 kg); **Empty weight** 3,425 lb (1,566 kg); **Weapons** 2 × Mk 44 torpedoes or 2 × Mk 11 depth charges or 1 × nuclear depth bomb, or 2 × AS 12 anti-shipping missiles (from 1968), or 1 × 7.62 mm machine gun in cabin;

Left *Sea King HAS 5, 814 Squadron, embarked in* Illustrious, *1985.*

Right *Wasp HAS 1, 829 Squadron, from the frigate* Londonderry, *during a patrol in Malaysian waters* (Rolls-Royce).

Below left *Wasp HAS 1, 829 Squadron, during land-away training in Germany.*

Below right *Wessex HAS 1 formation from Portland* (Westland).

Sensors SFIM roof sight (when fitted).

The diminutive Wasp was the result of a Saunders Roe contract to produce a small, turbine-powered helicopter for the British Army, the P 531. A wheeled version was developed for the Fleet Air Arm and the first ship's flight (*Leander*) embarked on 11 November 1963. Since then the Wasp has been part of the ship's weapons systems for 'Rothesay', 'Leander', 'Amazon' and 'Tribal' Class frigates, as well as survey ships, *Endurance* and various other craft as needs have dictated.

The standard operational role of the Wasp was to stand by at alert on the deck of a frigate, armed with a Mk 44 lightweight torpedo (ASW) or the Nord AS 12 wire-guided missile (anti-ship). As the threat situation increased so the alert sequence would be brought forward to Alert 5, with the helicopter crewed ready to launch. For ASW sorties, it would be the pilot only but for launching missiles the air-crewman would be carried in the left-hand seat to operate the SFIM roof-mounted sight and the AS 12 missiles.

In 1982, the Wasp had the distinction of firing the first missile from a Fleet Air Arm helicopter in anger when helicopters from *Endurance* and *Plymouth* attacked the Argentine submarine *Santa Fé* off South Georgia. *Endurance* also carried an observer in the flight's complement for over water and ice operations in the southern hemisphere.

The Wasp will remain in service until the last of her parent ships is paid off in 1988.

Serials *XS527-XS545; XS562-XS572; XT414-XT443; XT778-XT795; XV622-XV639.*

Wessex HAS 1

Manufacturer Westland; **Purpose** Shipborne ASW; **Crew** 1 pilot (2 pilots at night), 1 observer, 1 rating operator, up to 16 passengers depending on internal configuration; **Maiden flight** 17 May 1957 (S-55), 20 June 1958 (Wessex); **Service entry** June 1960 (700H Squadron); **Squadrons** 700H (1960-62, 1967), 706 (1962-71), 737 (1962-78), 771 (1963, 1969-79), 772 (1974-76), 814 (1961-67), 815 (1961-66), 819 (1961-68), 820 (1964-69), 826 (1966-68), 845 (1962-65); **Phased out of service** 1979 (*Ark Royal* Ship's Flight); **Range** 340 nm (630

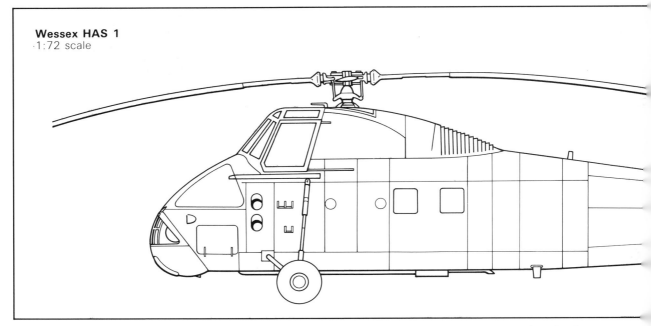

Wessex HAS 1
·1:72 scale

km); **Max speed** 120 knots (222 km); **Cruising speed** 90 knots (167 km/h); **Endurance** 2.5 hours; **Service ceiling** 7,000 ft (2,135 m); **Rate of climb** 1,750 ft/min (8.9 m/sec); **Length** 65.83 ft (20.1 m), 38.17 ft (11.6 m) folded; **Height** 15.83 ft (4.8 m); **Rotor diameter** 56 ft (17.1 m); **Power plant** 1 × Napier Gazelle 160 turboshaft (1,450 shp); **All-up weight** 12,600 lb (5,715 kg); **Empty weight** 7,600 lb (3,447 kg); **Weapons** 2 × Mk 44 torpedoes, 2 × Mk 11 depth charges; **Sensors** Type 195 sonar.

Developed from the Sikorsky HSS-1 anti-submarine helicopter, but powered by the Napier Gazelle free turbine engine, the Westland Wessex was a true workhorse of the Fleet Air Arm during the 1960s and 1970s. It was designed to a Naval Staff Requirement for a specially anti-submarine helicopter, following on the US Navy's requirement which had led to the HSS-1. Having an automatic pilot, coupled to the flight control system and kerosene fuel, the Wessex HAS 1 was favourably received by all.

The helicopter was originally used in aircraft carriers, embarking in *Ark Royal* during September 1961 (815 Squadron) and later in the early 'County' Class destroyers. As the helicopter's abilities were discovered it was developed into a commando lift helicopter, although the designation Wessex HAR 1 seems to have been unofficial despite being widely quoted. For discussion of the helicopter's contribution to the development of commando lift operations, please see page 172.

The Wessex HAS 1's last operational role was SAR from *Ark Royal* and Culdrose. A total of 129 were built.

Serials *XL722* (S-58); *XL727-XL729; XM299-XM301; XM326-XM331; XM832-XM845; XM868-XM876; XM915-XM931; XP103-XP118; XP137-XP160; XS115-XS128; XS149-XS154; XS862-XS889.*

Wessex HAS 3

Manufacturer Westland; **Purpose** Shipborne ASW; **Crew** 1/2 pilot(s), 1 observer, 1 rating sonar operator, up to 10 passengers depending on internal configuration; **Maiden flight** Not available; **Front line service entry** September 1967 (814 Squadron); **Squadrons** 700H (1967), 706 (1967-70), 737 (1967-82), 814 (1967-70); 819 (1968-71), 820 (1969-72), 826 (1968-70); **Phased out of service** 1982; **Range** 300 nm (556 km); **Max speed** 110 knots (204 km/h); **Cruising speed** 100 knots (185 km/h); **Endurance** 1.25 hours; **Service ceiling** 12,000 ft (3,658 m); **Rate of climb** 1,640 ft/min (8.3 m/sec); **Length, Height** and **Rotor diameter** as Wessex HAS 1; **Power plant** 1 × Napier Gazelle 165 (1,600 shp); **All-up weight** 13,500 lb (6,124 kg); **Empty weight** 9,350 lb (4,240 kg); **Weapons** as Wessex HAS 1, except Mk 46 capable; **Sensors** as Wessex HAS 1, but with MEL ARI 5955 radar in 'thimble'.

The ultimate ASW variant of the Wessex, the

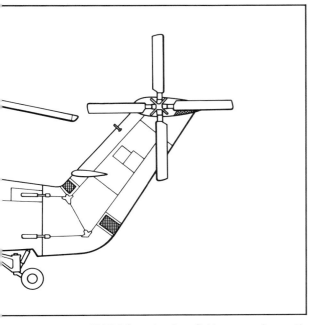

Below *Wessex HAS 3 formation from Culdrose; note the camel's hump radar.*

Above *Wessex HAS 3,* Antrim *Flight, during operations in South Georgia, 1982.*

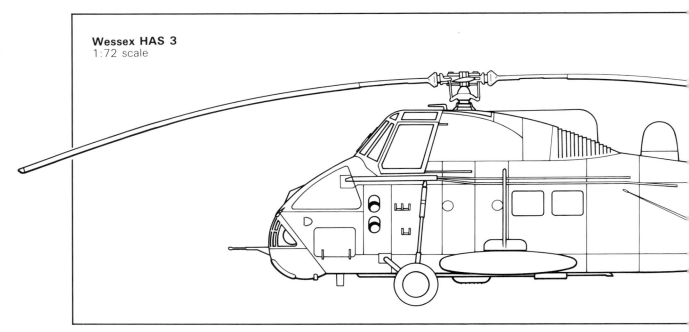

Wessex HAS 3
1:72 scale

HAS 3 had the visual recognition feature of the camel's hump which contained the aerial for the MEL ARI 5955 radar, used for plotting the progress of the anti-submarine battle and for tactical navigation.

Fifty helicopters were converted from the HAS 1 airframe to serve in aircraft carriers, 'Tiger' Class cruisers and 'County' Class destroyers (DLGs) in a front line ASW role, being replaced in the former two by the Sea King HAS 1. In addition, the helicopter was used for training observers and aircrewmen at Portland with 737 Squadron which also acted as the parent for the DLG flights.

In 1982, just before retirement, the Wessex HAS 3 was active in the Falklands, being flown by *Antrim* Flight in South Georgia, when it directed the attack on the *Sante Fé*, and Lieutenant Commander Ian Stanley, the flight commander, rescued the SAS off Fortuna Glacier; *Glamorgan* Flight was also operational. In the DLGs, it was replaced by the Wessex HU 5 and then the Lynx HAS 2/3.

Although a dated airframe, the Wessex HAS 3 was sophisticated in its use of automatic flight control systems and the sonar/radar fit was identical to the Sea King. It has been said that the only thing which the HAS 3 lacked as compared to the Sea King was endurance (it was half that of the Sea King HAS 1) and a second engine.

Serials include *XM327; XM331; XP103-XP105; XS119; XT255-XT257* were built as prototypes for the conversion programme.

Whirlwind HAS 7

Manufacturer Westland; **Purpose** Shipborne ASW; **Crew** 1 pilot, 1 observer, 1 rating sonar operator; **Maiden flight** 17 October 1956; **Service**

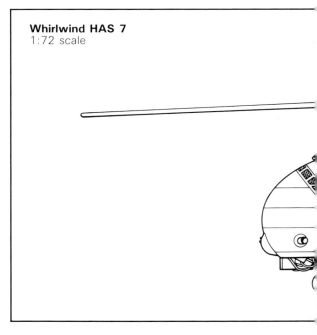

Whirlwind HAS 7
1:72 scale

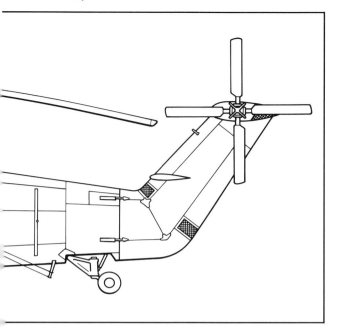

out of service 1976; **Range** 290 nm (537 km); **Max speed** 95 knots (176 km/h) at sea level; **Cruising speed** 75 knots (139 km/h); **Service hovering ceiling** 9,400 ft (2,865 m); **Rate of climb** 910 ft/min (4.6 m/sec); **Length** 41.71 ft (12.7 m); **Height** 15,375 ft (4.69 m); **Rotor diameter** 53 ft (16.2 m); **Power plant** 1 × Alvis Leonides Major 775 (750 hp); **All-up weight** 7,800 lb (3,538 kg); **Empty weight** 5,170 lb (2,345 kg); **Weapons** 1 × 53 cm Mk 30 torpedo (later Mk 44 Mod 0 introduced) or depth charge; **Sensors** 1 × AN/AQS-4 dipping sonar (alternative to weapons).

This helicopter resulted from a re-engining of the Whirlwind airframe with Alvis Leonides piston engine but the HAS 7 did not have a happy early life as there were a number of serious engine failures resulting in the total destruction of several helicopters. At one time, fixed-wing aircraft were brought back into service to cover for the lack of helicopter ASW at sea. All HAS 7s were grounded for six months in 1959.

Following the introduction of the Wessex HAS 1, the Whirlwind HAS 7 was converted for commando support duties in the Far East and served for many years as a training helicopter at Culdrose and other air stations. The SAR flights at Brawdy, Culdrose, Lossiemouth and Yeovilton were equipped with the Whirlwind HAS 7. The helicopter was phased out in 1976 after some 120 had been built and, despite initial engine problems, several million flying hours were flown. For details of the helicopter's service in

entry June 1957 (700H Squadron); **Squadrons** 700H (1957), 705 (1960-74), 737 (1959-62), 771 (1962-65, 1967-70), 814 (1960-61), 815 (1958-60), 820 (1958-60), 824 (1958-63), 845 (1957-59), 846 (1962-64), 847 (1963-64), 848 (1965-66); **Phased**

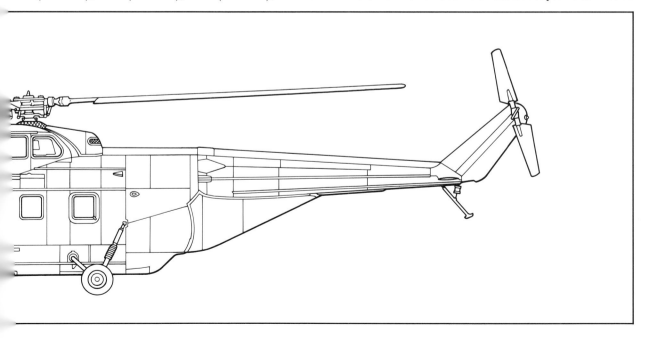

Above Whirlwind HAS 7, 820 Squadron, embarked in Albion, *1958* (RN/Culdrose).

Below Whirlwind HAS 22, VIP version, carrying HM The Queen Mother from Ark Royal *in 1955*.

commando support see page 173.

Serials include *XG586-XG597; XK906-XK912; XK933-XK945; XN299-XN314.*

Whirlwind HAS 22

Manufacturer Sikorsky; **Purpose** Shipborne ASW; **Crew** 1/2 pilot(s), 1 observer/aircrewman; **Maiden flight** 10 November 1949 (S-55); **Delivery** 20 November 1952; **Service entry** September 1953 (706 Squadron); **Squadrons** 706 (1953-54), 781 (1959-70), 845 (1954-57); **Phased out of service** 1970; **Range** 350 nm (650 km); **Max speed** 85 knots (157 km/h); **Cruising speed** 70 knots (130 km/h); **Service ceiling** 10,500 ft (3,200 m); **Length** 42.17 ft (12.85 m); **Height** 13.33 ft (4.06 m); **Rotor diameter** 53 ft (16.2 m); **Power plant** 1 × Wright Cyclone R-1300 piston engine (700 hp); **All-up weight** 7,900 lb (3,583 kg); **Empty weight** 4,795 lb (2,175 kg); **Weapons** Trials with Mk 30 torpedo; **Sensors** 1 × AN/AQS-4.

Supplied to the Fleet Air Arm under the Mutual Defense Assistance Program, the Wright Cyclone-engined Sikorsky S-55 (known as the Whirlwind HAS 22) was the forerunner of a series of helicopter variants for anti-submarine warfare, commando lift and SAR from a common airframe, built under licence by Westland.

Whirlwind HAS 22, 'Green Parrot' admiral's barge, advertising Lee-on-Solent Air Day in the late 1960s (RN/Daedulus).

The Whirlwind HAS 22 was tested aboard a number of aircraft carriers, including *Perseus, Theseus, Triumph, Albion* and *Centaur* during an intensive Fleet Air Arm programme to confirm that the helicopter would make a good anti-submarine search and destroy platform.

The helicopter designated the Whirlwind VVIP 22 was used by HRH Prince Philip as a personal transport in the late 1950s and the type was apparently used by 781 Communications Squadron from January 1959 to March 1970, painted green and white and known as 'Green Parrots'. For details of the helicopter's service in commando support see page 174.

Serials *WV199-WV205; WV218-WV225.*

Commando helicopters

Under the terms of the Mutual Defense Assistance Program between the United States and the United Kingdom following the end of the Second World War, ten Sikorsky HRS-2 helicopters were diverted from a planned operational use in Korea by the US Marine Corps and sent instead to the Fleet Air Arm's anti-submarine warfare development programme. The helicopters arrived at Southampton docks in November 1952, but owing to the problems being experienced in Malaya, the General Officer Commanding there, General Templer, requested troop carrying helicopters to be sent out from the UK. The ten Sikorsky S-55 helicopters would be ideal for the task.

The HRS-2s were unloaded, reassembled and formed into 848 Squadron at Gosport after the Chiefs of Staff in London had agreed to the change of role for the helicopters and resultant delay in the helicopter ASW programme. The Squadron embarked in *Perseus* in December 1952 for service in the Far East; a remarkable achievement by the Fleet Air Arm in view of the pressures for equipment and manpower from Korea and other requirements. The first troop and load lifting practice for the aircrew was undertaken at Malta and in the Suez Canal Zone en route to Singapore, where the aircraft carrier arrived in January 1953. The helicopters were flown off the ship in formation to Sembawang.

Initially, the Squadron undertook jungle flying practice and began working up with the resident Royal Air Force and British Army staffs, with command of the 'joint-service helicopter support unit' eventually passing to an RAF Wing Commander (who also controlled the RAF helicopter unit). A Royal Navy Commander was appointed to head the administrative side of the operation, reporting to the Captain of Sembawang.

Although 848 Squadron was operationally ready on 23 January 1953, the RAF commander was not prepared to sign off the unit as ready until an army request to extract thirty Special Air Service troopers from a jungle clearing in Johore, successfully achieved by the Squadron in difficult conditions, proved the point. It is almost certain that 848 Squadron was the world's first operational troop transport helicopter unit to fly over and into primary jungle cover, developing techniques still used today, around the world. By the end of 1953, the squadron's helicopters, by then named Whirlwinds, had become commonplace in the military tactics of the anti-Communist campaign.

Tasks undertaken by 848 Squadron included: troop transportation (with up to battalion strength lifts being flown); freight carrying; VIP transport; SAS parachuting into the jungle; aid to the civilian population and medical/casualty evacuation (casevac) by day or night. In 1954, the Squadron won the Boyd Trophy for, among other things, lifting 10,000 troops, evacuating 220 casualties and maintaining nearly 80 per cent helicopter serviceability.

The place of the helicopter in trooping and transportation roles had been established, but it was not until the Suez Crisis in 1956 that the commando assault, resupply and aircrew SAR roles became fully established in the minds of senior Admiralty figures. By then the helicopter was here to stay in the Fleet Air Arm.

Helicopters at Suez

Although the Fleet Air Arm had used helicopters, both British and US marked, during the Korea War and later during the Malayan emergency, it was not until the Suez Crisis that the Royal Navy was able to experiment in action with commando assault, battlefield reconnaissance and logistical resupply using helicopters. The helicopters involved in 'Operation Musketeer' were Westland/Sikorsky Whirlwind HAS 22 (845 Squadron) and a mixed group of Westland Sycamore HR 14s and Whirlwind HAR 2s from the Joint Experimental Helicopter Unit (JEHU) which had been set up at Middle Wallop, Hampshire, by the Royal Air Force and Army.

Although trials were still under way, JEHU helicopters were embarked in *Theseus* at Spithead in October 1956 as tension rose in the Middle East; a little later 845 Squadron embarked in *Ocean*. This

unit had been formed in March 1954 to perfect anti-submarine warfare techniques with the helicopter, prior to using it to replace the fixed-wing carrier-borne types then in service. The helicopters were Whirlwind HAS 22s taken over from the original trials unit, 706 Squadron at Gosport. By 1956, the unit was based at Lee-on-Solent, but it had worked up with Royal Marine Commandos in the Mediterranean earlier that year.

Tension dropped for a short period and both units disembarked, but when it became clear that there would be conflict in the eastern Mediterranean, the helicopters re-embarked, JHU (the 'experimental' had been dropped) to *Ocean* and 845 Squadron to *Theseus*. Both carriers arrived in Malta in late October and worked up with 45 Commando Group, Royal Marines. For assault operations, the Whirlwind HAR 2 could carry five fully-equipped marines as against the Fleet Air Arm's HAS 22's seven men in fighting order; the Sycamore could lift only three men.

The original plan, it is said, was to use the helicopters for casualty evacuation tasks only, but it soon became clear that 45 Commando Group would need to move ashore rapidly to take key positions. At first light on 6 November 1956, after Wyvern and Sea Hawk strikes had gone in, a single Whirlwind HAS 22, flown by Lieutenant Commander J. C. Jacob, CO 845 Squadron, made a reconnaissance and was fired upon, receiving considerable small arms fire damage, but managed to return to *Theseus* without incident.

The first helicopter assault was flown later that morning despite the hostile reception and all helicopters available assisted in landing 415 men and 25 tons of *matériel*; on the return trips, the helicopter brought the wounded back to the aircraft carriers offshore. Two days later, one of 845 Squadron's two Whirlwind HAR 3s suffered a forced landing when it ran out of fuel after sustaining fire on the beachhead. The crew and injured aboard were safely recovered aboard *Theseus* by another helicopter.

The success of the Suez assault in military terms led to the decision to convert *Albion* and later *Bulwark* into Commando Carriers for the transportation and support of Royal Marines and other allied forces, using helicopters for transportation, evacuation, load lifting and reconnaissance tasks. Later *Hermes* was converted for commando duties, although she later had a dual ASW and Commando Carrier role.

Effective as the Whirlwind had been at Suez, it was obvious that the payload was too small and the endurance too short. Nevertheless, 846 and 847 Squadrons were converted from ASW configura-

tion to commando duties for service in Borneo and Brunei in May 1962. 846 Squadron re-formed in the role at Culdrose, taking its helicopters aboard *Albion* in September 1962 for passage to the Far East, where it operated for nearly two years, eventually disbanding at Sembawang in October 1964. During 1963, the Squadron flew some 3,750 sorties. In May 1963, 847 Squadron, also at Culdrose with the same helicopter, formed to train pilots to operate in jungle conditions, operating from *Bulwark* in Malayan waters. The unit's training role was taken over by 707 Squadron in 1964, which had been equipped with the Wessex HU 5 commando support helicopter. This helicopter formed the backbone of commando assault operations and training during the next twenty years, until the first Sea King HC 4s were introduced to 846 Squadron (December 1979) and 707 Squadron (October 1983). By the end of 1986, 845 Squadron had relinquished its Wessex in favour of the Sea King as well.

845 Squadron had been flying the Whirlwind HAR 3 and HAS 22 until 1957, when it converted to the HAS 7 for a short period before the needs of jungle commando flying required the acquisition of a turbine-powered helicopter. In April 1962, the first Wessex HAS 1s were delivered, to be replaced by the twin-engined HU 5 in 1966. The unit was deployed to the Far East in November 1962 for service in the 'confrontation' with Indonesia over rights in Borneo; the successful operation of 10,000 flying hours, carrying 50,000 passengers and rescuing 500 wounded and injured assured the Squadron of receiving the Boyd Trophy for 1964. After returning home, 845 Squadron took its Wessex

Above *Wessex HU 5, 848 Squadron, loading Royal Marine Commandos from* Albion's *flight deck in 1972* (Mike Webber).

Below *Wessex HAS 1, 848 Squadron, in tropical commando camouflage, operating into a jungle pad in Borneo.*

Bottom *Trooping by helicopter; vehicles and pesonnel are transferred ashore by Wessex HU 5 helicopters of 848 Squadron,* Albion, *1972* (Mike Webber).

Below *Sea King HAS 2 and HC 4 helicopters, supporting the British forces ashore in the Falkland Islands, operate from* Canberra (RN).

HU 5s to Borneo for the end of the campaign.

With the decision to withdraw from the East of Suez theatres, made by the Wilson government in the United Kingdom during this period, the commando support helicopter force had to look to the defence of the NATO Northern Flank as its operational area from then on. This also meant that the *modus operandi* of the commando squadrons would change because the helicopters would spend more time flying operations ashore, actually bivouacked with the troops it was supporting. This diminishing role for the commando carriers saw the paying off of *Albion* and the decision not to convert *Centaur* to the role. At the same time, two new assault ships, *Fearless* and *Intrepid*, were commissioned but neither had adequate helicopter operating facilities, both lacking a hangar. In 1986 studies were begun into a new commando support ship design, but in the meantime commando logistical support, in the 'quick dash' role, would be provided by the 'Invincible' Class CVSs.

The South Atlantic

By 1982, the commando support helicopter squadrons had been reduced to two front line units — 845 (Wessex HU 5) and 846 (Sea King HC 4) Squadrons — supported by the training unit, also at Yeovilton, 707 Squadron. With the invasion of the Falkland Islands by the Argentine in April 1982, it was decided to transport British marine and naval forces to the South Atlantic in the hope of forcing a negotiated settlement without hostilities.

Various warships embarked helicopters and troops, including the aircraft carriers *Hermes* and *Invincible*. All available commando assault helicopters were organized and several units were formed using war reserve Wessex HU 5s from storage and converted Sea King HAS 2 training helicopters, with the sonics gear removed, from Culdrose. At Ascension Island, 845 Squadron established a logistical base, commanded by Lieutenant Commander Roger Warden, CO 845 Squadron, and from there other flights were deployed to the South Atlantic

with the Task Force.

Both Wessex and Sea King units operated well, moving vast quantities of *matériel* in terrain which was ideal helicopter country. 846 Squadron pioneered the operational use of night vision goggles for clandestine placing of SAS, SBS and other special forces. One Sea King HC 4 was lost from *Fearless* when it is thought the tail rotor was struck by an albatross and another arrived in Chile after a secret mission.

The Falklands conflict helped to confirm the role of the helicopter in naval operations, particularly the support of ground forces and useful training was undertaken for the Northern Flank role. Further developments will include the investigation of the EH 101 as a possible utility helicopter of the future and the eventual scrutiny of the advanced American tilt-rotor idea for the next century.

Sea King HC 4

Manufacturer Westland; **Purpose** Commando support; **Crew** 1/2 pilot(s), 1 aircrewman, up to 28 passengers; **Maiden flight** 12 September 1973 (prototype Commando), 29 September 1979 (HC 4); **Service entry** November 1979 (846 Squadron); **Squadrons** 707 (1983-), 845 (1986-), 846 (1979-); Still active; **Range** 664 nm (1,230 km); **Max speed** 113 knots (210 km/h); **Cruising speed** 95 knots (176 km/h); **Service ceiling** 10,000 ft (93,050 m); **Length** 55.81 ft (17.01 m); **Height** 15.5 ft (4.72 m); **Rotor diameter** 62 ft (18.9 m); **Power plant** 2 × Rolls-Royce Gnome H 1400-1 turboshafts (1,660 shp); **All-up weight** 21,000 lb (9,526 kg); **Empty weight** 12,566 lb (5,700 kg); **Underslung load weight** 7,500 lb (3,402 kg); **Weapons** Can mount 7.62 mm machine gun in cabin; **Sensors** None, but radar warning receivers planned.

Developed from the export model of the Westland Sea King for the Egyptian armed forces and marketed under the name Commando, the Sea King HC 4 was purchased by the Royal Navy to give extra support to the Royal Marine Commandos, especially during operations in the Northern Flank area. Unlike most previous commando support helicopters, the Sea King HC 4 is used in the field, rather than embarked in Commando Carriers and the like.

During the 1982 Falklands campaign, the helicopter proved to be exceptionally good at landing specialist teams under cover of darkness with the aircrew equipped with ANVIS night vision goggles. The helicopters are credited with lifting nearly 1 million lb (453.6 tonnes) of cargo during the first day of the landings at San Carlos, using just seven helicopters.

Sea King HC 4, 846 Squadron, demonstrates its lift capacity with a 105 mm Light Gun.

By 1987, all the Wessex HU 5 helicopters used for front line commando support had been withdrawn to second line tasks, being replaced by Sea King HC 4s; it seems that the Fleet Air Arm production line will continue until 1988.

Serials include *ZA290-ZA299; ZA310-ZA314; ZD476-ZD480; ZD625-ZD627; ZE425-ZE428; ZF116-ZF124.*

Sea King HC 4, 846 Squadron, working from an Army Air Corps helicopter landing site at San Carlos (UKLF).

Wessex HAS 1

Manufacturer Westland; **Purpose** Commando support; **Crew** 1 pilot, 1 aircrewman; **Maiden flight** See page 161; **Role service entry** April 1962; **Squadrons** 706 (1962-67), 722 (1974-76), 814 (1964), 845 (1962-65); **Phased out of service** August 1965; **Range, Max speed, Cruising speed, Endurance, Service ceiling, Rate of climb, Length, Height, Rotor diameter, Power plant, All-up weight** and **Empty weight** See page 161; **Weapons** 7.62 mm machine gun and 2 in (50 mm) rocket pods.

In the early 1960s, with the British fighting 'invasion' forces from Indonesia in Borneo, a number of Wessex HAS 1 anti-submarine helicopters were converted to troop carrying and underslung load support tasks. In this role, the Wessex could carry up to sixteen fully-equipped troops or a cargo load of 4,000 lb (1,814 kg). In 1962-63, the Wessex HAS 1 supported the suppression of the Brunei rebellion.

845 Squadron spent some thirty months operating in the Far East in support of British forces before the Wessex HAS 1 was phased out in August 1965. The HAS 1, despite being single-engined, was the first step to the development of an excellent commando support helicopter, the Wessex HU 5.

Wessex HAR 1 This often quoted version does not seem to have been recognized officially by the Fleet Air Arm and all commando versions of the Mk 1 were designated Wessex HAS 1.

Serials See page 161.

Wessex HU 5

Manufacturer Westland; **Purpose** Commando support; **Crew** 1/2 pilot(s), 1 aircrewman, up to 16 passengers; **Maiden flight** 31 May 1963; **Service entry** 5 December 1963 (700V Squadron); **Squadrons** 700V (1963-64), 707 (1964-84), 771 (1979-), 781 (1969-81), 845 (1966-1986), 846 (1968-75, 1976-77, 1978-81), 847 (1969-71, 1982), 848 (1964-76, 1982); Still active; **Range** 416 nm (770 km); **Max speed** 132 knots (245 km/h); **Cruising speed** 121 knots (225 km/h); **Service ceiling** 5,500 ft (1,676 m); **Rate of climb** 1,640 ft/min (8.4 m/sec); **Length** 48.36 ft (14.74 m); **Height** 16.17 ft (4.93 m); **Rotor diameter** 56 ft (17.07 m); **Power plant** 2 × Rolls-Royce Bristol Gnome H-1200 (1,350 shp); **All-up weight** 13,492 lb (6,120 kg); **Empty weight** 8,657 lb (3,927 kg); **Underslung load weight** 3,500 lb (1,588 kg); **Weapons** 7.62 mm machine guns, or 2 in (50 mm) rocket pods or provision for 2 or 4 AS 12 wire-guided missiles.

The twin-engined Wessex was designed for troop and underslung load transportation, resulting from the experiences of operating the Wessex HAS 1 in

Left *Wessex HU 5 during early trials with 70 mm rockets and SS 11 wire-guided missiles.*

Right *Whirlwind HAS 7, Lossiemouth Station Flight, during winter emergency re-supply operations in 1963 (via Brian Johnstone).*

Below *Wessex HU 5, Lee-on-Solent SAR Flight, during wet winching drill.*

the Borneo jungles. With two engine safety and an uprated transmission, the HU 5 was considered to be highly manoeuvrable, even with a full load of commandos, although this meant a loss of endurance because fuel had to be traded for payload.

The HU 5 was the first commando support helicopter to transport the standard 0.75 tonnes Land Rover or 3,500 lb (1,588 kg) of underslung cargo. This ability was used in Borneo (Confrontation), Aden (Radfan), Northern Ireland, Cyprus and the Falkland Islands.

In Northern Ireland, prior to 1982, Wessex HU 5 helicopters and later just aircrew were rotated to support the civilian power with the movement of troops and police units, as well as the resupply of bases in 'bandit' country near the border with the Irish Republic.

During the Falklands campaign, the Wessex HU 5 was used to support ship-to-shore stores transfer, especially from Royal Fleet Auxiliary ships and at the roulement centre on Ascension Island. Some forty HU 5s were deployed, including a number of aircraft from store at Wroughton. Armed Wessex were used in an attempt to destroy the Argentine command post at the Port Stanley police station, using the AS 12 missile. The Nord AS 12 was carried on the wheel struts and guided via a Ferranti roof sight through a wire command link.

Whirlwind HAS 7

Manufacturer Westland; **Purpose** Commando support; **Crew** 1 pilot, 1 aircrewman, up to 8 passengers; **Maiden flight** See page 164; **Service entry** November 1959; **Squadrons** (commando only) 846 (1962-64), 847 (1963-64), 848 (1959-63, 1965-66); **Phased out of role** 1966; **Range, Max speed, Cruising speed, Service hovering ceiling, Rate of climb, Length, Height, Rotor diameter, Power plant, All-up weight, Empty weight, Weapons** and **Sensors** See page 164.

Although the HAS 7 was the first British anti-submarine warfare helicopter, it was operational in a commando support role in the early 1960s. It was flown in Borneo and other Far Eastern locations, as well as assisting in the 1961 Kuwait emergency by flying RM Commandos and their equipment to the tiny sheikdom to prevent an invasion from neighbouring Iraq.

Whirlwind HAR 21

Manufacturer Sikorsky; **Purpose** Utility and support; **Crew** 1 pilot, 1 aircrewman; **Maiden flight** 1962; **Service entry** October 1962; **Delivery** 20 November 1962; **Squadron** 848 (1952-56); **Phased out of role** December 1956; **Range** 352 nm (652 km); **Max speed** 88 knots (163 km/h); **Cruising speed** 70 knots (130 km/h); **Service**

ceiling 10,500 ft (3,200 m); **Rate of climb** 700 ft/min (3.6 m/sec); **Length** 42.17 ft (12.85 m); **Height** 13.33 ft (4.07 m); **Rotor diameter** 53 ft (16.16 m); **Power plant** 1 × Pratt & Whitney Wasp (600 hp); **All-up weight** 7,900 lb (3,583 kg); **Empty weight** 4,795 lb (2,177 kg); **Internal cargo** 2,855 lb (1,295 kg).

This version of the US Marine Corps' HRS-2 was used operationally by 848 Squadron during the Malayan emergency in 1953 and although only 21 were delivered, the helicopter remained in service until 1956.

Serials include *WV189-WV198.*

Whirlwind HAS 22

Manufacturer Sikorsky; **Purpose** Utility (primarily ASW); **Crew** 1 pilot, 1 aircrewman (commando role), up to 10 passengers; **Maiden flight** See page 166; **Service entry** October 1953; **Squadrons** 701 (1957-58), 705 (1953-56), 706 (1953-54), 728 (1963-65), 737 (1960-61), 771 (1961), 781 (1959-70), 845 (1954-57), 848 (1958-59); **Phased out of service** March 1970; **Range, Max speed, Service ceiling, Length, Height, Rotor diameter, Power plant, All-up weight, Empty weight, Weapons** and **Sensors** See page 166.

The first commando support helicopter squadron in the Fleet Air Arm which carried out amphibious warfare trials with 45 Commando Group, under the title 45 Heliforce, was 848 Squadron which flew the HAS 22 from 1958-59. The HAS 22 was succeeded by the HAS 7, also in the commando role.

Serials include *WV199-WV205; WV218-WV225.*

Other types

It is believed that several other types of helicopter were examined for commando support helicopter work, including the Bristol Sycamore and the Sikorsky CH-53D Sea Stallion. In addition, during the early examination of the amphibious support helicopter doctrine several other types were operated including the Hiller HT 1 and the Wasp HAS 1.

General purpose helicopters

Dragonfly HR 1

Manufacturer Westland; **Purpose** Utility and SAR; **Crew** 1 pilot, 1 aircrewman, up to 3 passengers; **Prototype maiden flight** 5 October 1948; **Production maiden flight** 22 June 1949; **Service entry** January 1950 (705 Squadron); **Squadron** 705

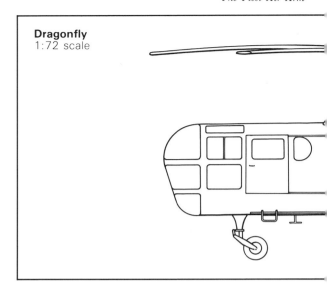

Dragonfly
1:72 scale

(1950-53); **Phased out of service** 1953; **Range** 300 nm (556 km); **Max speed** 80 knots (148 km/h); **Cruising speed** 65 knots (120 km/h); **Service ceiling** 9,000 ft (2,743 m); **Length** 41.15 ft (12.54 m); **Height** 12.96 ft (3.95 m); **Rotor diameter** 48 ft (14.63 m); **Power plant** 1 × Alvis Leonides 50

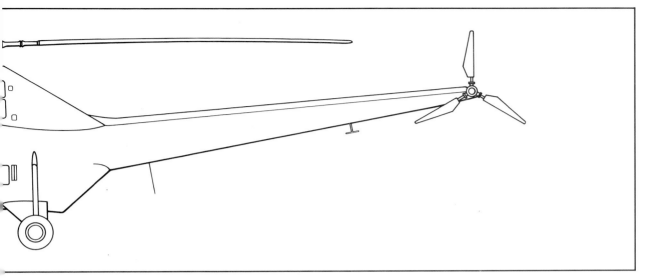

(520 hp); **All-up weight** 5,870 lb (2,663 kg); **Empty weight** 4,397 lb (1,994 kg); **Underslung load weight** 1,250 lb (567 kg).

Thirteen Dragonfly helicopters were purchased for the Royal Navy in the late 1940s to form the world's first all-helicopter unit outside the United States. The Dragonfly was the first licence production of a Sikorsky product by Westland Helicopters and was based on the S-51 helicopter which saw service in Korea, often supporting the British aircraft carriers on station with SAR cover.

One of the original Westland-Sikorsky S-51 was used for flight deck trials aboard *Vengeance* in 1949 and various tests were completed, including the problems associated with starting and shutting down the rotors, especially with high wind over the deck.

The helicopter served with 705 Squadron for operational trials before being superceded by the HR 3 (see below).

Serials *VX595-VX600; VZ960-VZ966.*

Dragonfly HR 3

Manufacturer Westland; **Purpose** Utility and SAR; **Crew** 1 pilot, 1 aircrewman, up to 3 passengers; **Maiden flight** 1952; **Service entry** July 1952 (705 Squadron); **Squadrons** 705 (1952-60), station SAR flights; **Phased out of service** 1960; **Range** 300 nm (556 km); **Max speed** 89 knots (166 km/h); **Cruising speed** 70 knots (130 km/h); **Service ceiling** 13,222 ft (4,030 m); **Length** and **Height** as Dragonfly HR 1; **Rotor diameter** 49 ft (14.9 m); **Power plant** 1 × Alvis Leonides 50 (520 shp); **All-up weight** 5,871 lb (2,663 kg); **Empty weight** 4,397 lb (1,994 kg).

Building on the initial operating experience of the HR 1, the Royal Navy took delivery of fifty HR 3 models, with all-metal rotor blades and better hydraulic controls which reduced pilot workload.

The HR 3 was active on various search and rescue tasks in 1952 and 1953, including the Dutch and East Anglian flood disasters when helicopters assigned to the various naval air stations at Brawdy,

Left *Dragonfly HR 1 during early personnel winching trials; note the determined effort to wear a cap!*

Right *Dragonfly HR 3s from* Theseus *and* Glory.

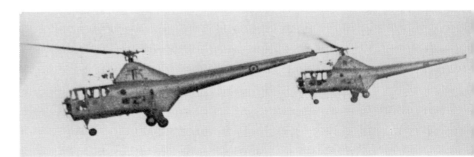

Culdrose and Lossiemouth were called in to assist.

In 1953, the Dragonfly led the Queen's Coronation Naval Review flypast over Spithead. After shipborne use in some of the Light Fleet aircraft carriers, the Dragonfly was assigned to helicopter requirement tasks and training duties.

Serials include *WG661, WG723* and *WP504.*

Dragonfly HR 5

Manufacturer Westland; **Purpose** Utility and SAR; **Crew** 1 pilot, 1 aircrewman, up to 3 passengers; **Maiden flight** 1956; **Service entry** 1957; **Squadrons** 701 (1957-58), 705 (1957-62), 727 (1958-60), 771 (1961-63), station SAR flights; **Phased out of service** 1963; **Range, Max speed, Cruising speed** and **Service ceiling** as Dragonfly HR 3 but with some marginal improvements; **Length, Height** and **Rotor diameter** as Dragonfly HR 1; **Power plant** 1 × Alvis Leonides 520; **All-up weight** as Dragonfly HR 3; **Empty weight** 4,400 lb (1,996 kg).

Some 25 to 30 earlier Dragonflies were brought up to HR 5 standard at Westland and the Naval Air Support Units. Issued to various requirements and training units, the Dragonfly was also used as a training and air experience helicopter at Britannia Royal Naval College, Dartmouth, during the 1960s and early 1970s.

Serials include *WG671.*

Dragonfly HR 7 According to Colonel John Everett-Heath's *British Military Helicopters* (Arms & Armour, 1986) there was a plan in 1957 to upgrade the Dragonfly to Widgeon standard with a larger cabin, but defence cuts meant a cancellation before work could begin.

Whirlwind HAR 1

Manufacturer Westland; **Purpose** Utility and SAR; **Crew** 1 pilot, 1 aircrewman, up to 10 passengers; **Maiden flight** 12 November 1952; **Service entry** July 1954; **Squadrons** 700 (1960), 705 (1954-60), 771 (1961), 781 (1961-62), 829 (1964-66), 848 (1954-55); **Phased out of service** 1966; **Range** 350 nm (650 km); **Max speed** 85 knots (157

Above right *Whirlwind HAR 1 factory trials during 1953.*

Right *Whirlwind HAR 3 factory trials before delivery to Gosport.*

Left *Dragonfly HR 5 during winching trials* (RN/Culdrose).

km/h); **Cruising speed** 70 knots (130 km/h); **Service ceiling** 10,500 ft (3,200 m); **Length** 41.71 ft (12.7 m); **Height** 13.21 ft (4.03 m); **Rotor diameter** 53 ft (16.1 m); **Power plant** 1 × Pratt & Whitney Wasp (600 hp); **All-up weight** 8,000 lb (3,629 kg); **Empty weight** 5,000 lb (2,268 kg).

The first Westland-built variant of the highly successful Sikorsky S-55 helicopter. Ten were delivered tot he Fleet Air Arm for utility and SAR.

Whirlwind HAR 3

Manufacturer Westland; **Purpose** Utility and shipborne SAR; **Crew** 1 pilot, 1 aircrewman; **Maiden flight** 24 September 1954; **Service entry** November 1955; **Squadrons** 700 (1958-61), 701 (1957-58), 705 (1956-66), 728 (1957-58), 737 (1959-60), 771 (1961-64), 781 (1963), 815 (1959), 845 (1955-57); **Phased out of service** 1964; **Range** 278 nm (515 km); **Max speed** 86 knots (159 km/h); **Cruising speed** 70 knots (130 km/h); **Service ceiling** 8,600 ft (2,620 km); **Length, Height** and **Rotor diameter** as Whirlwind HAR 1; **Power plant** 1 × Wright Cyclone R-1300 engine (700 hp); **All-up weight** 7,500 lb (3,402 kg); **Empty weight** 5,010 lb (2,277 kg).

First operational in the aircraft carrier plane guard role in September 1955, the Whirlwind HAR 3 was similar to the HAR 1 except that it was permanently equipped with a rescue winch and had the more powerful Wright Cyclone engine. The helicopter was used for the first vertrep (vertical re-

Whirlwind HAR 5
1:72 scale

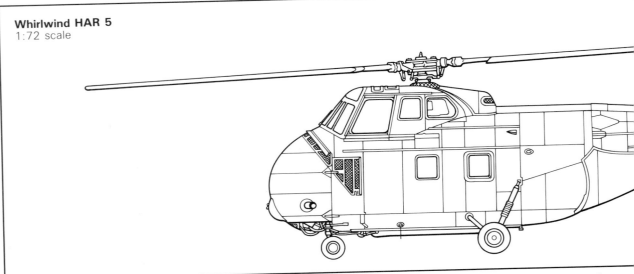

Far right *Whirlwind HAR 9, Culdrose SAR Flight, during a winching and lifeboat exercise off the Cornish coast in 1975* (Brian Johnstone).

Below *Whirlwind HAR 9, Culdrose SAR Flight, in 1975* (RN/Culdrose).

Below right *Gazelle HT 2, 705 Squadron, during a training flight from Culdrose.*

plenishment) trials between a warship and a Royal Fleet Auxiliary. Twenty were built for the Fleet Air Arm.

Serials *XG572-XG585; XG587-XG588; XJ393-XJ397.*

Whirlwind HAR 5

Manufacturer Westland; **Purpose** Utility and SAR; **Crew** 1 pilot, 1 aircrewman; **Maiden flight** 28 August 1955; **Service entry** 1956; **Squadrons** Served with ship's flights; **Phased out of service** 1960; **Range, Max speed, Cruising speed** and **Service ceiling** as Whirlwind HAR 1 with slight variations; **Length, Height** and **Rotor diameter** as Whirlwind HAR 1; **Power plant** 1 × Alvis Leonides Major (750 hp); **All-up weight** and **Empty weight** as Whirlwind HAR 3.

Developed from the basic Whirlwind airframe to include a modified tail cone for better survivor recovery which eventually led to the modified Sproule winch for the HAS 7 when that helicopter was transferred to station and aircraft carrier SAR duties.

Serials include *XJ396-XJ402; XJ445.*

Whirlwind HAR 9

Manufacturer Westland; **Purpose** SAR and utility; **Crew** 1/2 pilot(s), 1/2 aircrewman; **Maiden flight** 15 October 1965; **Service entry** 1966; **Squadrons** 829 (1967-76) and station flights; **Phased out of service** 1977; **Range** 300 nm (556 km); **Max speed** 92 knots (170 km/h); **Cruising speed** 73 knots (135 km/h); **Service ceiling** 16,600 ft (5,060 m); **Length** 44.17 ft (13.5 m); **Height**

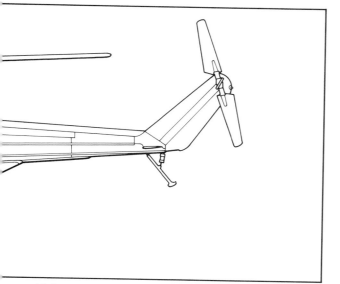

13.21 ft (4.03 m); **Rotor diameter** 53 ft (16.1 m); **Power plant** 1 × Rolls-Royce Bristol Gnome H-1000 turboshaft (1,050 shp); **All-up weight** 8,000 lb (3,629 kg); **Empty weight** 4,952 lb (2,246 kg).

Several piston-engined Whirlwind HAS 7 helicopters were taken in hand by Westland at Weston-super-Mare for conversion to a turbine engine; seventeen airframes were completed. The helicopters were embarked in the Ice Patrol Ships *Protector* and *Endurance,* as well as for SAR Flights at Brawdy, Culdrose and Lee-on-Solent. The latter

flight was the last in commission with the Wessex HU 5 taking over the SAR job in 1977.
   Serials include *XN387; XL875; XL899.*

Training helicopters

Gazelle HT 2

Manufacturer Aerospatiale/Westland; **Purpose** Training; **Crew** 1 instructor, 1 student, up to 3 passengers; **Maiden flight** 1973; **Service entry** 10 December 1974; **Squadrons** 705 (1975-); Fleetlands

Flight (1982-); Still active; **Range** 194 nm (360 km); **Max speed** 143 knots (265 km/h); **Cruising speed** 120 knots (222 km/h); **Service ceiling** 14,105 ft (4,300 m); **Rate of climb** 1,675 ft/min (8.5 m/sec); **Length** 31.27 ft (9.53 m); **Height** 10.45 ft (3.18 m); **Rotor diameter** 34.45 ft (10.5 m); **Power plant** 1 × Turbomeca Astazou XIV (592 shp); **All-up weight** 3,970 lb (1,800 kg); **Empty weight** 2,002 lb (908 kg).

One of the three helicopters which made up the Anglo-French helicopter agreement of the late 1960s, the Aerospatiale SA 341 Gazelle was purchased for the Fleet Air Arm and manufactured jointly between Aerospatiale and Westland. The helicopter replaced both the Whirlwind HAS 7 (see page 164) and the Hiller HT 2 (see below) in the helicopter pilot training role with 705 Squadron.

The helicopter is relatively simple to fly and gives the student a good introduction to rotary wing aviation after initial flying training with the RAF; operational training is undertaken by the front line units.

For many seasons since 1975, the operating squadron has formed the 'Sharks' display team with four Gazelle HT 2s flown by instructors at Culdrose.

Serials include many in the range *XW842-XW871; XW884-XW913;* nine from the range *XX370-XX419; XX431-XX462.*

Hiller HT 1

Manufacturer Hiller; **Purpose** Training; **Crew** 1 pilot, 1 student; **Maiden flight** 1950; **Service entry** May 1953; **Squadron** 705 (1953-63); **Phased out of service** 1963; **Range** 195 nm (362 km); **Max speed** 73 knots (135 km/h); **Cruising speed** 60 knots (111 km/h); **Service ceiling** 10,800 ft (3,292 m); **Length** 40.67 ft (12.4 m); **Height** 9.78 ft (2.98 m); **Rotor diameter** 35 ft (10.7 m); **Power plant** 1 × Franklin 6V4-200 piston (200 hp); **All-up weight** 2,500 lb (1,134 kg); **Empty weight** 1,755 lb (796 kg).

Ten Hiller HTE-2 helicopters were delivered to the Fleet Air Arm in 1953 under the Mutual Defense Assistance Program for training helicopter pilots. One helicopter was operated during trials from the Ice Patrol Ship, *Vidal,* using pontoon floats.

Serials include *XB474-XB481; XB513-XB524.*

Hiller HT 2

Manufacturer Hiller; **Purpose** Training; **Crew** 1 pilot, 1 student, 1 passenger; **Maiden flight** 1962; **Service entry** September 1962; **Squadron** 705 (1962-75); **Phased out of service** 1975; **Range** 195 nm (362 km); **Max speed** 83 knots (155 km/h); **Cruising speed** 60 knots (111 km/h); **Service ceiling** 15,000 ft (4,572 m); **Length** 40.67 ft (12.4 m); **Height** 9.78 ft (2.98 m); **Rotor diameter** 35.42 ft (10.8 m); **Power plant** 1 × Lycoming VO-540-A1B piston (305 hp); **All-up weight** 2,750 lb (1,247 kg); **Empty weight** 1,750 lb (794 kg).

Delivered under MDAP in 1962 to replace the earlier Hiller HT 1, the new version was remodelled by Hiller Aviation and designated the OH-23G Raven in US military service, The helicopter was used primarily for pilot training but some were diverted to commando support duties for a while, operating from the commando carriers *Albion* and *Bulwark.* Altogether 21 were delivered.

Serials *XS159-XS172; XS700-XS706.*

Left *Hiller HT 2, 705 Squadron, at Culdrose with Whirlwind HAS 7s in the background.*

Right *Hiller HT 2 underslung from a Wessex HU 5 of 845 Squadron* (Brian Johnstone).

Experimental helicopters

Bristol 173 Mk 1

A tandem rotor, twin-engined helicopter developed for various purposes. It first flew in January 1952 as a thirty seat utility helicopter and carried out three days of sea trials in *Eagle* during 1953.

Bristol 173 Mk 2

This development made its first flight on 31 August 1953. Completed with stud wings, it was Britain's first compound helicopter.

Bristol Type 191

Proposed to meet the Naval Staff Requirement HR 146 for a ship-based, utility, anti-submarine, anti-surface vessel and search helicopter to be powered by two Napier Gazelle turboshaft engines, this was cancelled in the 1957 Defence White Paper, leading to the development of the Wessex from the Sikorsky S-58 design.

Hoverfly I

Manufacturer Sikorsky; **Purpose** Utility; **Crew** 1 pilot, 1 co-pilot/observer; **Maiden flight** 13 January 1942 (US prototype); **Service entry** February 1945; **Squadrons** 705 (1947-50), 771 (1945-47), Gosport Station Flight (1946-47); **Phased out of service** 1947; **Range** 113 nm (209 km); **Max speed** 65 knots (121 km/h); **Cruising speed** 50 knots (93 km/h); **Service ceiling** 8,000 ft (2,438 m); **Length** 35.42 ft (10.8 m); **Height** 12.42 ft (3.8 m); **Rotor diameter** 38 ft (11.6 m); **Power**

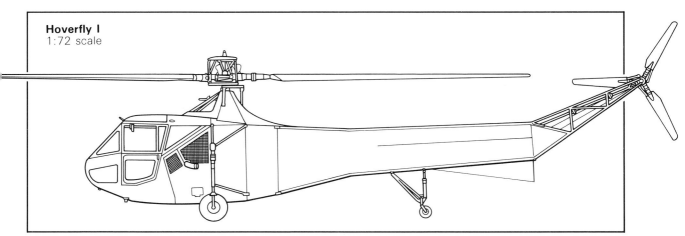

Hoverfly I
1:72 scale

Hoverfly I during trials and carrying a Flag Officer.

plant 1 × Warner Super Scarab radial piston (200 hp); **All-up weight** 2,530 lb (1,148 kg); **Empty weight** 2,020 lb (916 kg).

During the Second World War, the Fleet Air Arm worked closely with the US Coast Guard and Navy to develop the doctrine of shipborne helicopter operations and this led to the delivery of more than fifty Hoverfly I (the UK designation for the VS-316A) to the Royal Navy and some to the RAF.

The helicopter provided immeasurable experience and value to the Fleet Air Arm and various feats were carried out, including a landing on *Vanguard,* the battleship taking the Royal Family on a world cruise.

Serials include *KK969; KK984. KL113.*

Hoverfly II

Manufacturer Sikorsky; **Purpose** Utility and training; **Crew** 1 pilot, 1 co-pilot/observer; **Maiden flight** 15 October 1943 (US prototype); **Service entry** December 1945; **Squadrons** 705 (1947-50), 771 (1945-47); **Phased out of service** 1950; **Range** 150 nm (278 km); **Max speed** 83 knots (154 km/h); **Cruising speed** 61 knots (113 km/h); **Service ceiling** 10,000 ft (3,048 m); **Length** 47.92 ft (14.6 m); **Height** 12.49 ft (3.79 m); **Rotor diameter** 38 ft (11.6 m); **Power plant** 1 × Franklin piston engine (240 hp); **All-up weight** 2,600 lb (1,179 kg); **Empty weight** 2,100 lb (953 kg).

The VS-316B improved Hoverfly was delivered to the Royal Navy in 1945 for utility and pilot training experiments. The fifteen operated identically to the R-6A of the US military, but were not found successful enough to warrant an order for more helicopters.

Hoverfly II (Sikorsky R-6) during joint service trials.

The squadrons

Front line Naval Air Squadrons

The front line squadrons of the Fleet Air Arm have borne their 800-series numbers since the control of the naval air organization passed from the Royal Air Force to the Royal Navy in 1937. During the Second World War, the integration of Common-wealth (then Empire or Dominion) and Royal Netherlands Naval units into the Fleet Air Arm mean that today there are units with 800-series numbers in those forces. These are included in the listing below which gives a brief introduction to each squadron's post-1945 history, with particular reference to notable events.

800 Squadron

Except for a short period in the 1970s, 800 has been in commission since the end of the Second World War, flying fighter and strike aircraft. The unit pioneered the jet fighter into Fleet Air Arm service with the introduction of the Supermarine Attacker F 1 in August 1951, later operating Sea Hawks at Suez and carrying out trials with air-to-air refuel-ling; this work was carried out by 800B Flight flying Scimitar F 1s, whilst the Squadron was fully operational with Buccaneer S 1s. From March 1980, the unit has flown the Sea Harrier FRS 1, being operational in the South Atlantic in 1982.

801 Squadron

Always rivalling 800's claim to be the premier naval air squadron, 801 has also been in commission during the bulk of the post-war period, excepting the late 1940s and the 1970s. It brought the Sea Hornet F 20 twin-engined naval fighter into service, fought over Korea and pioneered the Buccaneer S 1 into service in July 1962; doing the same for the S 2 in 1965. After almost eleven years of disband-

Sea Harrier FRS 1s of 899 (furthest from camera), 801 and 800 Squadrons in formation for the camera. Note the different squadron markings and the carrier letters N (Invincible) and H (Hermes) (RN).

ment, 801 was recommissioned as Sea Harrier FRS 1 unit in 1981, taking part in 'Operation Corporate' (1982) and 'Orient Express' (1983-84).

802 Squadron

A unit of the 1940s and 1950s, 802 was to have been the third sea-going Sea Harrier unit in 1982, but plans to recommission the unit were apparently abandoned when it was decided to operate three CVSs and two air groups. Starting the post-war period flying the Seafire XV and FR 47, the unit was active over Korea with Sea Fury FB 11s, a flight of which destroyed the first jet, a MiG-15, in combat by any Fleet Air Arm aircraft. The unit also flew Sea Hawk and Sea Vampire jets.

803 Squadron

After the Second World War, the unit formed as a Canadian squadron and was transferred to the Royal Canadian Navy in 1951, taking up the 870 Squadron identity. 803 then became a jet fighter unit, including pioneering the first nuclear-capable naval aircraft, the Scimitar F 1, into service in 1958. The unit also operated Buccaneer strike aircraft before disbanding in 1969.

804 Squadron

When the unit re-formed after the Second World War as a Seafire unit, part of 14 CAG, it operated in the Far East, including Korea, re-equipping with Sea Hawk jets in 1953. It was active during Suez and operated Scimitar F 1s in the Far East. It disbanded in 1961.

Scimitar F 1, 804 Squadron, preparing to launch from Hermes *in 1961. When the FDO (Flight Deck Officer) drops his flag, the catapult will launch the aircraft into flight* (Brian Johnstone).

805 Squadron

Forming as part of the Royal Australian Navy in 1948, after immediate war service with Firefly FR 1 and Seafire F 17 fighters, the unit operated over Korea and then transferred to Australia. It was carrier-borne until the demise of *Melbourne* and disbanded in 1982, following the phasing out of front line fixed-wing naval aviation in Australia.

806 Squadron

The first unit to operate the Sea Hawk, 806 won the Boyd Trophy in 1955 for its work with night operations, but it was shortlived and disbanded in 1960.

807 Squadron

In 1947, 807 brought the Sea Fury to the Fleet Air Arm and began trials with the first British naval aircraft to have power-folding wings. Active over Korea, the unit's Scimitars played an important role in lessening tension in Kuwait in 1961, but the squadron disbanded the next year.

808 Squadron

Formed in 1950 to operate the Sea Fury FB 11 for the Royal Australian Navy, the unit later flew Sea Vampire and Sea Venom aircraft, before disbanding and transferring its aircraft to 805 Squadron.

809 Squadron

Famous for its 'firebird' emblem, 809's aircraft have seen action at Suez and, whilst recommissioned for a short period in 1982, the South Atlantic. The unit was the operational flying training squadron for all Buccaneer flying and operated the type in *Ark Royal* until the demise of conventional fixed-wing naval aviation in the Royal Navy in 1978. The 1982 recommissioning included a ferry flight from Yeovilton to Ascension Island by eight Sea Harrier FRS 1s of the squadron, about 4,000 nm, being the longest Fleet Air Arm flight on record.

810 Squadron

Being involved in anti-submarine operations from 1948-54, 810 then became a fighter squadron, being present at Suez. In 1959, it re-equipped with Gannet AS 4s for a short period. Since 1983, the unit has been the Advanced Flying Training and Operational Flying Training unit for helicopter observers and aircrewman in the Fleet Air Arm, flying Sea King HAS 5 helicopters.

811 Squadron

Flying the Sea Mosquito TR 33 immediately after the war, the unit disbanded in 1947, being reformed with Sea Fury FB 11s in 1953, until disbanding again in 1956.

812 Squadron

Experimenting with night fighter techniques in 1948-49, 812 operated over Korea before disbanding in 1953. From 1955-56, the Squadron operated the Gannet in the anti-submarine role.

813 Squadron

Never truly operating jets, this unit initially operated the troublesome Firebrand TF IV in 1945-46, before taking the TF 5 variant to sea between 1947-49. In 1953, the unit was re-equipped with the Wyvern S 4, the only operational variant of this type, but was again disbanded in 1958.

Above *809 Squadron operated the last Buccaneer S 2s in the Fleet Air Arm, embarked in* Ark Royal *(RN/Ark Royal).*

814 Squadron

This unit has been in commission for almost the whole of the post-war period and since 1950 has been involved in anti-submarine flying, first with Firefly and Gannet aircraft, later converting to helicopters. In September 1967, the squadron introduced the Wessex HAS 3 into service, later flying the Sea King HAS 1 from *Hermes* and *Tiger*. The Squadron went to war in 1982 in *Hermes* and is now part of *Illustrious'* air group.

815 Squadron

The unit has a liaison with a famous Irish brewery, bearing its harp motif on several of its post-war aircraft. Since 1945, the unit has been engaged in anti-submarine or torpedo reconnaissance roles with fixed-wing equipment until pioneering the use of helicopters from 1958. It was the first unit to fly the Wessex HAS 1 in front line service, but it was dormant from 1966-81, until the Lynx HAS 2 was

Right *815 Squadron Avengers ranged on deck for a free take off.*

introduced to the Fleet Air Arm; it now parents the operational Lynx small ships' flights.

816 Squadron

From 1948, this unit has been Australian (including a period of service in Korea), flying, amongst others, the Gannet, Tracker and Wessex HAS 31B. It is thought that this squadron will fly the Sikorsky S-70B Seahawk when it enters Royal Australian Naval service.

817 Squadron

Another Australian unit, 817 is still operational with Sea King HAS 50/50A helicopters, although it is now shore-based. It is destined to continue in service until the late 1990s.

818 Squadron

Not operational since August 1945.

819 Squadron

Post-war, 819 has been a helicopter unit for the whole of its career since re-forming at Eglinton in 1961. Being closely involved in anti-submarine operations, the unit now supports the Polaris submarine squadron. It is based at Prestwick and flies the Sea King HAS 5.

820 Squadron

Since 1951, the unit has been involved in anti-submarine operations, first with Firefly AS 5s and re-equipping with Gannet AS 1, before becoming the first helicopter ASW unit when it re-formed with Whirlwind HAS 7s in January 1958. Disbanded 1960-64, the unit then flew Wessex HAS 1 and HAS 3s, before being equipped with Sea King helicopters. The Sea King HAS 5 is the present equipment and the unit is part of *Invincible*'s air group, having been active in the South Atlantic in 1982.

821 Squadron

Operational only from 1951-53, the unit flew Firefly AS 6 for ASW duties and then FR 5s for a strike role in Korean waters.

822 Squadron

During 1945-46, the unit was equipped with Firefly FR 1s.

823 Squadron

Not operational since July 1944.

824 Squadron

An anti-submarine squadron since re-forming in 1952, 824 flew Firefly AS 6, Avenger AS 4, Gannet AS 1 and AS 4 aeroplanes, before receiving the Whirlwind HAS 7 in 1958. In 1970, it became the first Sea King unit and embarked in *Ark Royal* for the whole of the carrier's last eight years. In 1980, the unit took over support of the Royal Fleet Auxiliaries with, from 1982, some experimental

duties with AEW helicopters, before the re-formation of 849.

825 Squadron

Operating most marks of the Firefly post-war, the unit also flew the Gannet AS 1 and AS 4, as well as the Whirlwind HAS 7 in ASW roles. In the late 1940s the unit was attached to the Royal Canadian Navy, and in 1982 it re-formed temporarily to operate in the commando role in the Falklands.

826 Squadron

After a short spell with the Royal Canadian Navy (where 826 was renumbered 880 in 1951), the unit became an anti-submarine unit with Firefly AS 6s in May 1951. One of its major claims to fame happened in January 1955 when the first Fairey Gannet AS 1 ASW aircraft arrived at Lee-on-Solent, but although it was the first unit with the type, 826 disbanded in November the same year. In 1966 826 re-formed and the Wessex HAS 1 was

taken on strength and later the HAS 3, before the Sea King was introduced in June 1970. From 1983 to 1986, the unit flew the Sea King HAS 5 on detachment to the Falkland Islands and Royal Fleet Auxiliaries, the former role being given in November 1986.

827 Squadron

Strike and anti-submarine duties with Firefly FR 1 aircraft were the roles for the unit until 1950 when the Firebrand TF 5 was introduced. In 1954, the Wyvern was taken on strength and went to sea in *Eagle* during her first commission. The unit disbanded in November 1955.

828 Squadron

After VJ-Day the unit operated the Avenger III for a short period and has not been re-formed since June 1946.

829 Squadron

The unit did not re-form after the Second World War until 1964 when the Westland Wasp HAS 1 was introduced into service for small ships' flights and by 1985 there were 21 flights in commission. In 1986, operational Lynx HAS 2/3 flights from Type 22 frigates joined the remaining Wasps.

830 Squadron

During 1955-57, the unit flew the Wyvern S 4, including operational service at Suez in November 1956 when embarked in *Eagle*.

831 Squadron

Embarked in *Ark Royal* after re-forming in November 1955, the unit flew the Wyvern S 4 until the end of 1957. It re-formed again the next year with the Gannet and was then engaged in early electronic counter-measures (ECM) trials with various types, until these duties were taken over by the joint RN/RAF unit, 360 Squadron, in 1966.

832 Squadron

Not operational since February 1945.

833 Squadron

Not operational since September 1944.

834 Squadron

Not operational since November 1944.

835 Squadron

Not operational since March 1945.

836 Squadron

Not operational since 1945.

837 Squadron

The unit finished its war service in the Far East and sailed home in *Glory* to disband in October 1947.

838 Squadron

Not operational since February 1945.

839 Squadron

No record of any unit.

840 Squadron

Not operational since August 1943.

841 Squadron

Not operational since November 1944.

842 Squadron

Not operational since January 1945.

843 Squadron

No record of any unit.

844 Squadron

No record of any unit.

845 Squadron

Several times in its history, 845 has been the largest unit in the Fleet Air Arm, having been a helicopter unit since re-forming post-war in 1954 with the Whirlwind HAS 22. Its helicopters operated in a commando assault role at Suez, although officially it was still a training unit for helicopters. Since 1962 the unit has flown various marks of Wessex helicopter with great success in Brunei, Borneo, Malaya, Northern Ireland, Cyprus and the Falkland Islands. In 1983 the commando assault role was lost and until 1985 the unit provided logistical support at Ascension Island. Helicopters from 845 still operate each winter in Norway and provide vertrep (vertical replenishment support) for Royal Fleet Auxiliaries.

846 Squadron

Since 1962, the unit has been engaged in commando support helicopter operations with Wessex and Sea King helicopters, both afloat and ashore. In December 1979, 846 brought the Sea King HC 4 into Fleet Air Arm service. This aircraft has served in the South Atlantic and Lebanon on active duty.

847 Squadron

Formed to operate from trouble-plagued Cyprus in 1956, the unit flew Gannet AS 1 and AS 4s until 1959. When it re-formed in 1963 it flew Whirlwind HAS 7s in a commando role until 1964, taking up the same role with the Wessex in 1969-71 and in 1982 for 'Operation Corporate'.

848 Squadron

Famous as a commando support helicopter unit, the squadron flew helicopters from its post-war re-formation in 1952 until it was disbanded in 1976. Apart from a brief commissioning during the Falklands conflict in 1982, the unit has not been in service since, although it might be reformed in 1987 to operate as another Sea King HC 4 unit.

849 Squadron

Since the end of the Second World War and re-formation in 1952, 849 has been the Fleet Air Arm's airborne early warning (AEW) unit, first with Sky-raider AEW 1, then Gannet AEW 3 and in 1984 with the Sea King AEW 2, the world's first operational helicopter AEW platform. The unit has embarked flights of three to four aircraft in carriers since January 1953 when A Flight went to sea in *Eagle*. The latest A Flight re-formed in May 1985 for service in *Illustrious*.

850 Squadron

Having a brief post-war spell as a Royal Australian Navy squadron, the unit disbanded in 1954 after a year's service with Sea Fury FB 11s.

851 Squadron

A Royal Australian Navy unit which is still in commission.

852 Squadron

Not operational since October 1944.

853 Squadron

Not operational since May 1945.

854 Squadron

Not operational since December 1945, and from VJ-Day did not fly aircraft.

855 Squadron

Not operational since October 1944.

Above *845 Squadron Wessex HU 5 loading Royal Marines during an exercise on Salisbury Plain; the squadron relinquished this type in 1986.*

Below *846 Squadron Sea King HC 4 helicopters embarked in Hermes in 1983.*

Bottom *849 Squadron has been associated with airborne early warning since reformation after the Second World War; the Squadron's first aircraft was the Skyraider AEW 1.*

856 Squadron

Not operational since June 1945.

857 Squadron

Not operational since November 1945, and from VJ-Day did not fly aircraft.

858 Squadron

No record of any unit.

859 Squadron

No record of any unit.

860 Squadron

Formed in January 1946 as a squadron of the Royal Netherlands Navy, operating the Firefly, Sea Fury, Sea Hawk, Wasp and latterly the Lynx helicopter.

861 Squadron

Formed for a short period to operate Dutch Firefly aircraft.

862 Squadron

No record of any unit.

863 Squadron

No record of any unit.

864 Squadron

No record of any unit.

865 Squadron

No record of any unit.

866 Squadron

No record of any unit.

867 Squadron

No record of any unit.

868 Squadron

No record of any unit.

869 Squadron

No record of any unit.

870 Squadron

Formed as a Royal Canadian Navy squadron to fly the Sea Fury FB 11 and lastly the Banshee fighter from ashore and aboard *Bonaventure*.

871 Squadron

Formed to operate the Firefly and Banshee from *Magnificent* (and later *Bonaventure*) with the Royal Canadian Navy.

872 Squadron

No record of any unit.

873 Squadron

No record of any unit.

874 Squadron

No record of any unit.

875 Squadron

No record of any unit.

876 Squadron

No record of any unit.

877 Squadron

Not operational since December 1943.

878 Squadron

Not operational since January 1944.

879 Squadron

Operational in Malaya when the Second World War ended, the unit flew Seafire XVIIs on its return to the UK, but disbanded in January 1946.

880 Squadron

After the Second World War, this unit re-formed as a Canadian unit and was still operational in 1985 as a part of Maritime Command, Canadian Armed Forces. During its carrier days, it served in *Magnificent* and *Bonaventure*.

881 Squadron

Equipped with Avengers, the unit was commissioned into the Royal Canadian Navy and embarked in *Bonaventure*, but disbanded in July 1959.

882 Squadron

Not operational since October 1945.

883 Squadron

To be part of the Royal Canadian Navy, the unit formed in 1947 for sea service in *Warrior*, but was redesignated 871 Squadron in 1951.

890 Squadron flew the Sea Venom FAW 21 for a few months in 1956 before amalgamating with 893 Squadron (Fleet Air Arm Museum).

884 Squadron

Not operational since July 1943.

885 Squadron

Not operational since September 1945.

886 Squadron

Not operational since July 1944.

887 Squadron

Not operational since March 1946, having no aircraft after VJ-Day.

888 Squadron

Not operational after August 1946, having no aircraft after VJ-Day.

889 Squadron

Not operational since September 1945.

892 Squadron decorated its Sea Vixen FAW 1 aircraft with a witch on a broomstick.

890 Squadron

The witch on a broomstick emblem of the unit was a characteristic of the deployments to carriers of the unit's Sea Vixen aircraft, but before then it had pioneered the Sea Venom FAW 20 into service. The Sea Vixens flew on the Beira Patrol in 1966, but the unit was disbanded in 1971 with the demise of the type.

891 Squadron

The unit was closely involved with the development of night fighter tactics from 1945, when it formed with the Hellcat II(NF), later flying the Sea Venom and training Australian crews. The Sea Venom FAW 22 was its last aircraft type, disbanding in July 1961.

892 Squadron

This unit was the first to fly the Sea Vixen all-weather naval fighter and the last to operate conventional jets from a British carrier, the last Phantom FG 1 leaving *Ark Royal*'s deck in late 1978. The Sea Venoms of 892 were active during Suez, and the unit finally disbanded in December 1978.

893 Squadron

From 1956, when the unit re-formed after the Second World War, until its demise in July 1970, it was closely associated with the all-weather fighter, flying Sea Venoms and Sea Vixens. It took part in the Suez operations and the Kuwait crisis of 1961.

894 Squadron

During 1957-60 it flew Sea Venom all-weather fighters from *Eagle, Victorious* and *Albion*.

895 Squadron

During 1956 the unit was temporarily re-formed to operate the Sea Hawk, taking part in the Suez operations flying from *Bulwark*. It has not been operational since then.

896 Squadron

Not operational since November 1945.

897 Squadron

Another Sea Hawk unit of limited life, the unit re-formed with the Sea Hawk FB 3 in November 1955 and operated against targets ashore during the Suez crisis with the FGA 6, before disbanding in January 1957.

898 Squadron

After VJ-Day, the unit re-formed in July 1951 with Sea Fury FB 11s, being requipped with Sea Hawk F 1s in 1953. Various marks of the nimble fighter were then operated until the Squadron disbanded again in April 1959.

899 Squadron

'The bunch with the punch' began its post-war career in 1955 with the Sea Hawk FGA 6, participating in the Suez operations and then forming the Sea Vixen headquarters unit in 1961. The unit was the first to receive the Sea Vixen FAW 2 in December 1963, but disbanded in 1972. With the arrival of the Sea Harrier FRS 1, 899 was re-formed in 1980 as the first front line unit, tasked with operational training and headquarters work. It went to war in 1982, when its aircraft, aircrew and maintainers were embarked in *Invincible* and *Hermes*.

Second line units

The specialist, training and auxiliary tasks of the Fleet Air Arm have been carried out, since before the Second World War, by so-called second line units. These squadrons and flights are numbered in the 700-series. In the 1940s several 1700-series units appeared, whilst many 1800-series units were Royal Naval Volunteer Reserve (and more recently Royal Naval Reserve) air branch units. There were so many of these that space precludes detailed descriptions.

899 Squadron Sea Harrier FRS 1 manning up in the early morning off Norway in March 1984 (RN/Illustrious).

Royal Naval Volunteer Reserve Squadrons

Squadron	Dates	Role	Aircraft operated
1830	1947-57	ASW	Firefly I; Firefly AS 6; Firefly FR 3; Avenger AS 5
1831	1947-57	Fighter	Seafire XV/XVII; Sea Fury FB 11; Attacker FB 2
1832	1947-57	Fighter	Seafire FR 46; Sea Fury FB 11; Attacker FB 2; Sea Hawk F 1
1833	1947-57	Fighter	Seafire F 17; Seafire FR 47; Sea Fury FB 11; Attacker FB 2
1834	1953-55	Fighter	Sea Fury FB 11
1835	1953-57	Fighter	Sea Fury FB 11
1836	1953-57	Fighter	Sea Fury FB 11
1840	1951-57	ASW	Firefly FR 4; Firefly AS 6; Gannet AS 1
1841	1952-57	ASW	Firefly FR I; Firefly AS 6; Avenger AS 5
1842	1953-57	ASW	Firefly AS 6; Gannet AS 1
1843	1953-57	ASW	Firefly AS 6; Avenger AS 5
1844	1954-57	ASW	Firefly AS 5/6; Avenger AS 5

Air Division	Formation	Squadrons controlled
Scottish	June 1 1952	1830; 1843
Northern	June 1 1952	1831; 1841
Southern	June 1 1952	1832; 1834; 1835; 1836
Midland	June 1 1953	1833; 1844
Channel	June 1 1952	1840; 1842

Carrier Air Groups 1945-54

The Carrier Air Group concept was developed towards the end of the Second World War to ensure that the large Fleet carriers of the 'Illustrious' Class were provided with sufficient aircraft. With the end of hostilities in the Pacific against the Empire of Japan, the Royal Navy decided to maintain the system in the immediate post-war period, especially as the Commonwealth nations were then acquiring naval air power of their own to operate from Light Fleet Carriers. The Carrier Air Groups went to war in Korea, but by 1952 the Royal Navy ceased to have a need for them and they were only retained by Australia and Canada until 1954. The accepted abbreviation for Carrier Air Group is CAG, a term which is still used by the United States Navy.

Above right *781 Squadron provided the Royal Navy's Flying Clipper service around the United Kingdom in the 1970s, with the Sea Heron C 1 (nearest) and the Sea Devon C 20.*

Right *Carrier Air Group: Sea Fury FB 11s and Firefly AS 5s aboard Sydney off Korea (Australian War Memorial).*

Carrier Air Group	Dates	Carrier	Aircraft operated
1st CAG	1945	*Victorious*	849 (Avenger); 1834 and 1836 (Corsair)
	1947-50	*Implacable*	801 (Sea Hornet); 813 (Firebrand)
	1950-51	*Indomitable*	801 (Sea Hornet); 813 (Firebrand)
2nd CAG	1945	*Formidable*	848 (Avenger); 1841 and 1842 (Corsair)
3rd CAG	1945	RANAS *Nowra* (Australia)	854 (Avenger); 1843 and 1845 (Corsair)
4th CAG	Not formed		
5th CAG	Not formed		
6th CAG	Not formed		
7th CAG	1945-46	*Indefatigable*	820 (Avenger); 887 and 894 (Seafire); 1770 and 1772 (Firefly FR I)
	1950-51	*Vengeance*	809 (Sea Hornet); 814 (Firefly)
8th CAG	1945-46	*Implacable*	828 (Avenger); 801 and 880 (Seafire); 1771 (Firefly I)
9th CAG	Not formed		
10th CAG	Not formed		
11th CAG	1945	*Indomitable*	857 (Avenger); 1839 & 1844 (Hellcat)
12th CAG	Not formed		
13th CAG	1945-46	*Vengeance*	812 (Barracuda); 1850 (Corsair)
	1946-50	*Triumph*	800 (Seafire); 827 (Firebrand)
	1951-52	*Eagle*	800 and 803 (Attacker); 826 (Firefly); 827 (Firebrand)
14th CAG	1945-46	*Colossus*	827 (Barracuda); 1846 (Corsair)
	1946-47	*Theseus*	804 (Seafire); 812 (Firefly)
	1948-49	*Ocean*	804 (Seafire); 812 (Firefly)
	1949-52	*Glory*	804 (Sea Fury); 812 (Firefly)
15th CAG	1945	*Venerable*	814 (Barracuda); 1851 (Corsair)
	1945-46	*Venerable*	814 (Firefly); 1851 (Corsair)
	1946-47	*Venerable*	802 (Seafire); 814 (Firefly)
	1947-50	*Vengeance*	802 (Sea Fury); 814 (Firefly)
	1950	*Vengeance*	809 (Sea Hornet); 814 (Firefly)
	1950-51	ashore	802 (Sea Fury)
	1951-52	*Theseus*	802 (Sea Fury); 814 (Firefly)
16th CAG	1945	*Glory*	837 (Barracuda); 1831 (Corsair)
	1945-46	*Glory*	837 (Firefly); 1831 (Corsair)
	1946-47	*Glory*	806 (Seafire); 837 (Firefly)
17th CAG	1947-51	*Theseus*	807 (Sea Fury); 810 (Firefly)
	1951-52	*Ocean*	807 (Sea Fury); 810 (Firefly)
18th CAG	1947-48	*Warrior*	826 (Firefly); 883 (Seafire)
	1948	*Warrior*	826 (Firefly); 883 (Sea Fury)
	1948-51	*Magnificent*	825 and 826 (Firefly)
	1951	became 30th CAG, Royal Canadian Navy	
19th CAG	1947-48	*Warrior*	803 (Seafire); 825 (Firefly)
	1948-51	*Magnificent*	803 (Seafire); 883 (Sea Fury)
	1951	*Magnificent*	803 (Seafire); 825 (Avenger)
	1951	became 31st CAG, Royal Canadian Navy	
20th CAG	1946-48	*Ocean*	805 (Seafire/Firefly); 816 (Barracuda)
	1948-51	*Sydney*	805 (Sea Fury); 816 (Firefly)
	1951-53	*Sydney*	805 and 808 (Sea Fury)
	1953-54	*Sydney*	805 and 850 (Sea Fury)
21st CAG	1950-51	*Sydney*	808 (Sea Fury); 817 (Firefly)
22nd CAG	Not formed		
30th CAG	1951-54	*Magnificent*	871 (Sea Fury); 881 (Avenger)

Training Air Groups 1946-52

To prepare naval air squadrons to embark in aircraft carriers, a number of Training Air Groups (TAGs) were set up at various Naval Air Stations. Usually the result of combining two squadrons, with the senior squadron commander in overall charge, this system was operated from 1946 until almost the end of the Korean War, in 1952. Four TAGs were formed.

Training Air Group	Dates	Base
50th TAG	1948-52	Yeovilton
51st TAG	1946	Eglinton
	1948-50	Lee-on-Solent
52nd TAG	1946-47	Eglinton
	1950-51	Culdrose
53rd TAG	1950-51	Eglinton

Specialist units

Over the years, especially with the advent of new technology in the period since 1945, the Fleet Air Arm has formed, disbanded and re-formed a number of specialized units to complete important tasks. In more recent years individual squadrons, both front and second line, have taken over these tasks and in order to provide a more readily available force to national and NATO commanders, the more specialist units have been integrated into the normal force structure.

Between 1950 and 1959 and again in 1960-61, whilst the helicopter was being integrated in the anti-submarine community, the Naval Anti-Submarine School was in being as part of both 719 and 737 Squadrons. The School was not an establishment but usually operated from Eglinton.

With the advent of the jet fighter, the Fleet Air Arm formed the Naval Air Fighter School in 1950 and it operated (with 702 and 736 Squadrons) until 1954. In order to train pilots for front line service in the Scimitar F 1, the School was re-formed in 1960-61 to give practice with Sidewinder and Bullpup missiles and other weapons.

In May 1947, to develop naval photographic tactics and techniques, 739 Squadron was formed into the Photographic Development Unit, attached to the Royal Air Force centre at Benson. The unit disbanded in 1950.

At the end of the Second World War, night fighter tactics had been developed on an ad hoc basis and in order to standardize and improve on techniques, the Fleet Air Arm formed the Naval Night Fighter Development Unit which saw service in 1945-56. By this time the all-weather fighter had become operational and specialist night fighter operations were no longer undertaken.

The training of observers for the Fleet Air Arm has always been a special task as their work is demanding and requires a high degree of training. During 1955-59, 750 Squadron operated as the Observer and Air Signal School. By 1960 the title had changed to simply the Observer School as the Firefly T 7 was phased out and the Sea Prince confirmed as the observer trainer. In 1978, 750 Squadron was equipped with the Jetstream T 2, supplemented by the T 3 in 1986.

The Trials and Requirements Unit was formed from 703 and 771 Squadrons at Ford in 1955 to provide facilities for trials and to meet the needs of every aspect of naval operations. When Ford closed in 1958, the Unit moved to Yeovilton but was disbanded in 1961. By 1957, the requirements section had been taken over by Airwork Limited, flying naval aircraft including black-painted Sea Hawk FGA 6 and Scimitar fighters. The requirements section, including radar calibration and trials, has been formed into the Fleet Requirements and Air Direction Unit (FRADU), based at Yeovilton, flying Hunter aircraft. The contract was taken over by Flight Refuelling Limited in 1984 and the Fan Jet Falcon aircraft replaced the Canberras in 1985.

When new aircraft are brought into service the Fleet Air Arm has had a policy of forming an Intensive Flying Trials Unit with second line status. After completing its work it usually becomes the first (sometimes the headquarters) front line unit. It has become traditional to form an IFTU within 700 Squadron, which is commissioned for the purpose from time to time. 700 Squadron was, at the end of the Second World War, the Maintenance Test Pilot Training Squadron to prepare 'plumber pilots' from engineering officers turned pilot.

Squadron	Dates	Aircraft type
700A	1979-80	Sea Harrier FRS 1
700B	1965	Buccaneer S 2
700G	1959-60	Gannet AEW 3
700H	1957	Whirlwind HAS 7
	1959	Whirlwind HAS 7
	1960-62	Wessex HAS 1
	1967	Wessex HAS 3
700L	1976-77	Lynx HAS 2
700P	1968-69	Phantom FG 1
700S	1969-70	Sea King HAS 1
700V	1963-64	Wessex HU 5
700W	1963-64	Wasp HAS 1
700X	1957-58	Scimitar F 1
	1959-61	Wasp/P 531
700Z	1961-63	Buccaneer S 1

Before the first 700 Squadron re-formation to test and evaluate the Whirlwind HAS 7 for squadron

Early helicopter trials with the Hoverfly I.

embark in aircraft carries. The HTU was in being 1957-58 and, in 1967, 771 Squadron was re-formed as the Anti-Submarine Fleet Requirements Unit, equipped with Whirlwind helicopters, but it was disbanded in 1974.

When the new jet equipment, the Supermarine Attacker, was introduced to service, the Naval Jet Evaluation and Training Unit was formed at Culdrose in 1949 to evaluate jet techniques at sea. The Unit was 702 Squadron and was disbanded in 1952.

The Naval Air-Sea Warfare Development Unit was operational in 1945-50 and again in 1954-56, for joint work with the Royal Air Force in maritime air techniques, flying the Firefly AS 6 and Gannet AS 1 aircraft as 744 Squadron.

Other units included the Joint Warfare Establishment (1946-76), the Air Signal Squadron (1949-53) and the joint RN/RAF unit, 360 Squadron.

One of the most famous and valuable units of the early post-war period was the Naval Service Trials Unit which had been formed as 767 Squadron in September 1949. The principle task of the Unit was to train the deck landing control officers (the batsmen) of the aircraft carriers and to do this required a skilled aviator who could approach and land on a carrier's flight deck without the usual aid of bats. Because of the number of circuits and landings required the squadron soon acquired the name 'clockwork mice' and flew the Firefly FR 4 and Sea Fury FB 11s when 'mousing'. With the advent of the mirror landing aid, the 'clockwork mice' were employed training the landing signals officers (LSOs), with Avenger and Sea Hawk aircraft. The Unit disbanded at Stretton in 1955 and the practice deck at Hensbridge, laid out as an aircraft carrier, was abandoned. Deck landing was carried out in *Illustrious* and other training carriers.

service, it was the role of 701 and 705 Squadrons, as the Helicopter Trials Unit (which had been formed out of the Helicopter Fleet Requirements Unit), to work up small ships' flights at sea. Helicopters included those destined for the Ice Patrol ship, *Protector*, and the helicopter flights to

The 'clockwork mice' emblem can be seen on this 767 Squadron Attacker FB 1 at Stretton, 1954 (R.B. Wigg).

The aircraft carriers

Although aircraft carriers are not and never have been the only way in which the Royal Navy has taken aircraft to sea, they remain the major warship type for the embarkation of aircraft, both fixed-wing and helicopters. As such, they merit special treatment and the carriers which served post-1945 are listed below in their respective types and classes. Space has only allowed the barest of details to be included but this chapter should provide the basic source material for anyone wishing to undertake further research. An aircraft carrier is defined as a warship with an extensive flat topped deck on which to operate aircraft.

Fleet Carriers

Class *Illustrious*

Name *Illustrious*; **Pennant number** R87; **Flight deck code** Y, D; **Builders** Vickers Armstrong (Barrow); **Laid down** 27 April 1937; **Launched** 5 April 1939; **Commissioned** 25 May 1940; **Paid off** December 1954; **Broken up** November 1956.

Technical details (as built) Displacement (standard) 22,400 tons, (full load) 28,210 tons; **Overall length** 740.0 ft (225.6 m); **Overall beam** 95.75 ft (29.2 m); **Draught** 29.0 ft (8.8 m); **Machinery** 3 × shafts geared turbines (113,700 shp); **Speed** 29.25 knots (54.2 km/h); **Weapons** 16 × 4.5 in, 6 × 8 2-pdr AA; **Aircraft** 15 × fighters, 16 × Swordfish.

Technical details (1946) Displacement (standard) 25,940 tons, (full load) 31,360 tons; **Overall length** 748.5 ft (228.1 m); **Overall beam** as built; **Machinery** as built; **Speed** as built; **Weapons** 5 × 8 2-pdr AA, 3 × 40 mm, 52 × 20 mm; **Aircraft** 52.

Modernization and refits 1940-45 Many; **1946** To reduce armament and improve sensors; **1940-45** Many; **1947-48** Fitted for jet aircraft trials.

Service summary 1940-45 War service in Mediterranean (including Taranto raid and Malta convoys), refitted in USA, Madagascar landings, Eastern Fleet and British Pacific Fleet; **1945**

Illustrious *at sea in 1945* (Fleet Air Arm Museum).

Entered refit; **1946** Trials and Training Carrier; **1947** Temporarily withdrawn from service and trials; **1948** Trials; **1949** Deck-Landing Training Carrier; **1951** Trooping to Cyprus (Canal Zone crisis in November); **1952** NATO exercises; **1953-54** Deck-landing training.

Important dates 13 January 1937, ordered from 1936 Naval Estimates.

The first carrier built with the armoured box to protect the aircraft, now considered the primary weapon system. Armoured deck proved effective against 'kamikaze' attacks in 1945.

Name *Formidable*; **Pennant number** Not available; **Flight deck code** X; **Builders** Harland & Wolff; **Laid down** 17 June 1937; **Launched** 17 August 1939; **Commissioned** 24 November 1940; **Paid off** 1947 (into reserve); **Sold for scrap** May 1953; **Scrapped** November 1956.

Technical details (as built) Displacement (standard) 23,000 tons, (full load) 29,240 tons; **Overall length** 746.75 ft (227.6 m); **Overall beam** 95.75 ft (29.2 m); **Draught** 29.0 ft (8.8 m); **Machinery** 3 × shafts Parsons geared turbines (110,000 shp); **Speed** 31 knots (57.4 km/h); **Weapons** 16 × 4.5 in, 6 × 8 2-pdr AA; **Aircraft** 15 × fighters, 16 × torpedo bombers.

Modernization and refits 1940-45 Many; **1947** Prepared for modernization.

Service summary 1940-45 War service in Mediterranean, including Battle of Cape Matapan, Malta convoys, evacuation from Greece and Crete; refitted in USA; Eastern Fleet operations, invasion of Sicily and British Pacific Fleet; hit by kamikaze;

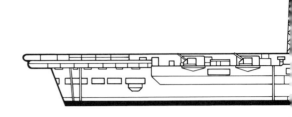

Victorious   1960
1:1000 scale

1945-46 Trooping and ferrying liberated prisoners of war; **1947** Returned to Home Fleet duties and later placed in Reserve at Motherbank; **1948-52** Awaiting reconstruction and modernization but plans cancelled; **1953** Paid off for scrapping.

Important dates 26 May 1941, hit by 2 × 1,000 kg bombs; 4-9 May 1945, damaged by kamikaze attacks; 9 August 1945, Lieutenant R. H. Gray RCNVR won posthumous Victoria Cross for attack on Japanese warships after launch from her deck in Corsair.

She played a useful part in war service but her subsequent modernization was not completed for cost and operational reasons.

Victorious at sea, showing her angled deck.

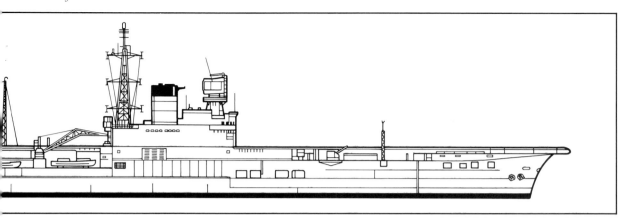

Name *Victorious*; **Pennant number** R38; **Flight deck code** V; **Builders** Vickers Armstrong (Newcastle); **Laid down** 4 May 1937; **Launched** 14 September 1939; **Commissioned** 15 May 1941; **Paid off** 13 March 1968; **Sold for scrap** July 1969; **Broken up** 1970.

Technical details (as built) Displacement (standard) 23,000 tons, (full load) 31,790 tons; **Overall length** 750.5 ft (228.8 m); **Overall beam** 95.75 ft (29.2 m); **Draught** 29.0 ft (8.8 m); **Machinery** 3 × shafts Parsons geared turbines (111,000 shp); **Speed** 29 knots (54 km/h); **Weapons** 16 × 4.5 in, 6 × 8 2-pdr AA; **Aircraft** 15 × fighters, 16 × torpedo bombers.

Technical details (1958) Displacement (standard) 30,530 tons, (full load) 35,500 tons; **Overall length** 781 ft (240 m) **Overall beam** 103 ft (31.4 m); **Draught** 31 ft (9.4 m); **Machinery** 3 × shafts Foster Wheeler geared turbines (110,000 shp); **Speed** 31 knots (57.4 km/h); **Weapons** 12 × 3 in AA, 6 × 40 mm, 4 × 3-pdr saluting; **Aircraft** 25 × fixed wing, 8 × helicopters.

Modernization and refits 1941-45 Many; **1951-57** Complete modernization with fully angled flight deck, lengthened flight deck, rearming and new sensors, including Types 984, 293 and 974 (cost £1 million); **1960** Mini-refit; **1962-63** Major refit; **1967** Major refit (during which ship caught fire).

Service summary 1941-45 War service with Home Fleet, Bismarck incident, and Russian convoys, North African landings, loaned to USN, Eastern Fleet, British Pacific Fleet; **1945-47** Trooping duties in the Far East; **1947** placed in Reserve; **1947-50** Training Squadron of Home Fleet; **1951-57** Modernization; **1958** Recommissioned as flagship of Flag Officer Aircraft Carriers in Home and Mediterranean Fleets; **1959** NATO exercises; **1960** Buccaneer trials; **1961** Kuwait crisis and Far Eastern duties; **1963-64** Far East; **1965** Tanganyika revolt; **1966-67** Far East and Mediterranean; **1968** Paid off as part of defence cuts; **1970** Broken up at Faslane.

Her major refit cost £20 million and was protracted as the Admiralty tried to keep up with technology. She was the first carrier to commission with fully (8.75 degrees) angled flight deck and Type 984 3-D radar and was basically rebuilt from flight deck level upwards. Most of her service life post-1958 was spent in the Far East during four commissions. She should have been replaced by CVA-01 in 1970-72, and was scrapped after minor fire damage in political gesture by Labour government of the day. Her original cost in 1941 was £6.5 million.

Name *Indomitable*; **Pennant number** R92; **Flight deck code** A, O, W; **Builders** Vickers Armstrong (Barrow); **Laid down** 10 November 1937; **Launched** 26 March 1940; **Commissioned** 10 October 1941; **Paid off** 21 September 1955; **Sold for scrap** 1955; **Broken up** 1955-56.

Technical details (as built) Displacement (standard) 23,500 tons, (full load) 29,730 tons; **Overall length** 754 ft (229.8 m); **Overall beam** 95.75 ft (29.2 m); **Draught** 29.5 ft (9.0 m); **Machinery** 3 × shafts Parsons geared turbines (110,000 shp); **Speed** 31 knots (57.4 km/h); **Weapons** 16 × 4.5 in, 6 × 8 2-pdr AA, 8 × 20 mm Oerlikon; **Aircraft** 24 × torpedo bombers, 24 × fighters (in two hangars).

Technical details (1950) Displacement (standard) 24,680 tons, (full load) 31,000 tons; **Overall length, Overall beam, Draught, Machinery** and **Speed** as built, except ship used for trials of USN fighter control radar; **Weapons** 16 × 4.5 in, 6 × 40 mm, 20 × 20 mm Oerlikon; **Aircraft** 12 × Sea Fury FB 11, 12 × Firebrand TF 5.

Modernization and refits 1941-45 Many; **1947-50** Extensive refit and modernization at Portsmouth, including new forward flight deck.

Service summary 1941-45 War service with Eastern Fleet, Madagascar expedition, Malta convoys, Home Fleet service, Sicilian landings, repairs in United States, Home Fleet, Eastern Fleet and British Pacific Fleet; **1945** Relief of Hong Kong; **1946** Far East trooping; **1947-50** Refit; **1950** Joined Home Fleet; **1951** Flagship, Home Fleet and first RN warship to carry a helicopter (Dragonfly); **1952-53** Flagship of Heavy Squadron, Home Fleet, Mediterranean exercise (including serious hangar fire 3 February 1953), present at Coronation Review at Spithead, 15 June, placed in Reserve after being towed from Portsmouth to the Clyde (October).

Important dates Reoccupation of Hong Kong, 30 August 1945; placed in Reserve 5 October 1953.

Damaged by enemy action on numerous occasions (3 × bombs in 1942, torpedoed 1943 and kamikaze 1945). *Indomitable* differed from others in her class because of the two deck hangar (lower 168 ft (51.2 m) long) to increase her air group to 48 aircraft. Deck height was reduced as a consequence and she carried less armour plate. She carried out helicopter trials during her time as Admiral Sir Philip Vian's flagship.

Class *Implacable*

Name *Implacable*; **Pennant number** R86; **Flight deck code** A, C, M, N; **Builders** Fairfield (Clyde); **Laid down** 21 February 1939; **Launched** 10 December 1942; **Commissioned** 28 August 1944; **Paid off** 1 September 1954; **Broken up** October 1955.

Technical details (as built) Displacement (standard) 23,450 tons, (full load) 32,110 tons; **Overall length** 766.17 ft (233.5 m); **Overall beam** 95.75 ft (29.2 m); **Draught** 29.33 ft (8.9 m); **Machinery** 4 × shafts Parsons geared turbines (149,598 shp); **Speed** 31.9 knots (59 km/h); **Weapons** 16 × 4.5 in, 6 × 8 2-pdr AA, 37 × 20 mm Oerlikon; **Aircraft** 21 × torpedo bombers, 33 × fighters.

Technical details (1950) Displacement (standard) 26,000 tons, (full load) 32,110 tons; **Overall length, Overall beam, Draught, Machinery** and **Speed** as built; **Weapons** 16 × 4.5 in, 12 × 40 mm, 21 × 20 mm Oerlikon, 6 × 8 2-pdr AA, 4 × 3-pdr saluting; **Aircraft** 13 × Sea Hornet F 20, 12 × Firebrand TF 5.

Modernisation and refits 1945-46 Few, including Sydney; **1947** Refitted for trials and modern aircraft; **1948-49** Refitted for flagship

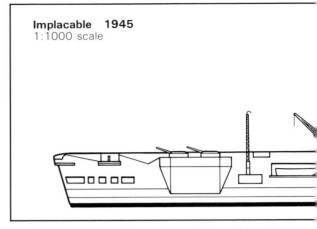

Implacable 1945
1:1000 scale

duties; **1950-52** Refitted for training ship role as unsuitable for jet aircraft.

Service summary 1944-45 War service, including operations against *Tirpitz* and British Pacific Fleet; **1945-46** Trooping and repatriation of allied POWs in Far East; **1946** Home Fleet's deck landing training ship; **1947** Mediterranean exercise then refit; **1948-50** Home Fleet flagship and Jet Fighter Evaluation Unit trials; **1952** Flagship of Home Fleet Training Squadron; **1953** Transportation of troops to Caribbean; **1954** Training ship; **1955** Paid off for scrapping at Inverkeithing.

Implacable was fifth in the series of armoured carriers designed before the Second World War, but modified to include more powerful engines, greater overall length, increased flight deck area, second hangar deck, two catapults, new crash barrier design and redesigned island. Construction was delayed to give priority to escorts. Her deck park could handle 81 aircraft (as for ferry passage to Far East in 1945), but the low hangar roof clearance

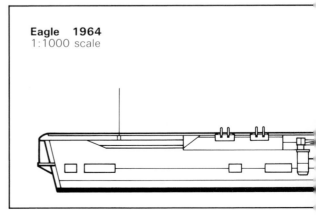

Eagle 1964
1:1000 scale

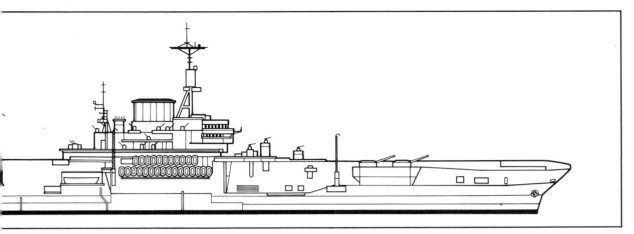

meant that the ship could not be modified for jets.

Name *Indefatigable*; **Pennant number** R10; **Flight deck code** B, D, S; **Builders** John Brown (Clyde); **Laid down** 3 November 1939; **Launched** 2 December 1942; **Commissioned** 3 May 1944; **Paid off** August 1954; **Sold for scrap** November 1956; **Broken up** 1956-7.

Technical details (as built) Displacement (standard) 23,450 tons, (full load) 32,100 tons; **Overall length** 766.5 ft (233.6 m); **Overall beam** 95.75 ft (29.2 m); **Draught** 26 ft (7.9 m); **Machinery** 4 × shafts Parsons geared turbines (148,000 shp); **Speed** 32 knots (59.3 km/h); **Weapons** 16 × 4.5 in, 6 × 8 2-pdr AA, 37 × 20 mm Oerlikon (10 × 40 mm Bofors added in 1945); **Aircraft** 54 (12 × Avenger, 36 × Seafire, 12 × Firefly FR I in 1945-46).

Modernisation and refits 1945 Repairs after kamikaze attack; **1949-50** Conversion to training role.

Service summary 1944-45 War service includ-ing air strikes against enemy targets in Norwegian Sea, operations against *Tirpitz* before transfer to British Pacific Fleet (as flagship FOAC BPF) and present for surrender of Japan; **1945** Evacuation of former POWs; **1946** Trooping to and from Far East; **1946-49** Reduced to Reserve at Portsmouth; **1949-50** Refit; **1950-54** Home Fleet Training Squadron, transferred to Reserve Fleet on the Clyde; **1955** Towed to Gareloch from Rosyth for scrapping and handed over to British Iron and Steel Corporation.

Despite a distinguished wartime career, *Indefatigable,* like her sister-ship, *Implacable,* was not suitable for the jet aircraft era and thus her last days were spent as a training ship. She was the saluting ship at Dover for members of foreign Royal Families who came to the United Kingdom for the funeral of HM King George VI.

Class *Audacious, Eagle* or *Ark Royal*

Name *Eagle*; **Pennant number** R05; **Flight deck**

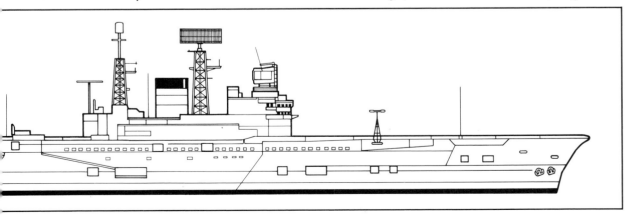

Above Eagle *at sea in 1956* (Fleet Air Arm Museum).

Below Eagle*'s two hangar decks, photographed from one of the aircraft lifts* (I.K. MacDonald).

code J (until 1957), E; **Builders** Harland & Wolff; **Laid down** 24 October 1942; **Launched** 19 March 1946; **Commissioned** 1 October 1951; **Paid off** 26 January 1972; **Broken up** October 1978.

Technical details (as built) Displacement

Ark Royal *passing the Liver Building in Liverpool after commissioning in 1955.*

(standard) 41,200 tons; (full load) 49,950 tons; **Overall length** 803.75 ft (245 m); **Overall beam** 112.75 ft (34.4 m); **Draught** 35.6 ft (10.9 m); **Machinery** 4 × shaft geared turbines (152,000 shp); **speed** 31.5 knots (58.3 km/h); **Weapons** 16 × 4.5 in (twin), 48 × 40 mm (octuple), 4 × 40 mm (twin), 9 × 40 mm, 4 × 3-pdr saluting guns; **Aircraft** 75; **Cost** £15.795 million.

Technical details (1971) Displacement (standard) 43,000 tons, (full load) 50,536 tons; **Overall length** 813.4 ft (247.9 m); **Overall beam** 112.75 ft (34.4 m); **Draught** 34.5 ft (10.5 m); **Machinery** as built; **Speed** 29.25 knots (54.1 km/h); **Weapons** 8 × 4.5 in (twin), 6 × Seacat quad SAM, 4 × 3-pdr saluting guns; **Aircraft** 34 fixed-wing and 10 helicopters.

Modernization and refits 1954-55 5½ degrees partial angled deck; **1959-64** 8½ degrees angled deck, forward 4.5 in batteries and 40 mm removed, Type 984, 963 (CCA) and 965 radars fitted, 6 × Seacat SAM fitted; **1966-67** Waist catapult installed for Phantom operations.

Service summary 1952 Trials, relieved *Indomitable* as flagship, Flag Officer Heavy Squadron (Home Fleet); **1953** Coronation Review and trials; **1954** 7,000th deck landing, search for Comet airliner wreckage and went into refit; **1955** Rejoined Home Fleet; **1956** with Mediterranean Fleet, 'Operation Musketeer' (Suez) and first use of nylon crash barrier; **1957** Fitted with interim mirror landing aid, operations with Home Fleet and NATO forces; **1958** Took part in naval exercises and the support operations for Jordan following the Iraqi coup; **1959** Extensive modernization began (similar to that of *Victorious*); **1964** Recommissioned as most up-to-date RN carrier, launched first Seacat from carrier and arrived on Middle East Station; **1965** Joined Far East Fleet before returning to Middle East Station; **1966** Beira

Patrol, during which at sea for 71 days, short spell in Singapore before returning to Devonport; **1967** Completed refit and proceeded to Aden; **1968** Returned to Devonport for NATO exercises; **1969** Phantom trials and Western Fleet deployment to USA and Mediterranean; **1970** Mediterranean and Harrier sea trials; **1971** Mediterranean and final Far East deployment (including covering withdrawal from Singapore); **1972** Paid off at Portsmouth and towed to Devonport for laying up.

Important dates 31 October 1951, completed builder's trials; 2 September 1952, first squadrons embarked; 26 January 1972, last squadron departed.

Eagle was originally ordered under the War Programme as an aircraft carrier of the 'Ark Royal' Class with the name of *Audacious*, with a design which would improve upon the existing 'Implacable' Class. This new design called for two armoured hangar decks, improved watertight construction internally, better underwater protection, and a better flight deck construction for the operation of 30,000 lb aircraft and to withstand direct hits by conventional bombs. Her construction was halted for three years whilst the Royal Navy considered its needs for aircraft carriers. Although refitted to allow for Phantom FG 1 operations, the 1966 Defence White Paper put paid to any further service beyond 1971. Her final years were spent at Devonport providing spares for her sister ship, *Ark Royal*.

Name *Ark Royal*; **Pennant number** R09; **Flight deck code** O (until 1957), R; **Builders** Cammell

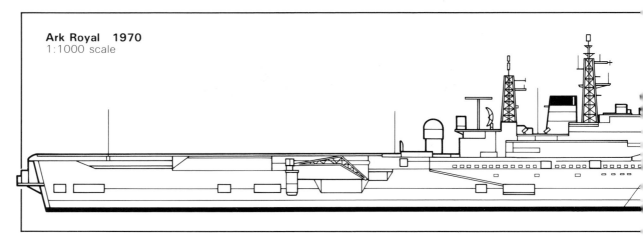

Ark Royal   1970
1:1000 scale

Laird; **Laid down** 3 May 1943; **Launched** 3 March 1950; **Commissioned** 25 February 1955; **Paid off** 13 February 1979; **Broken up** 1980.

Technical details (as built) Displacement (standard) 43,060, (full load) 49,950 tons; **Overall length** 808.25 ft (246.4 m); **Overall beam** 112.7 ft (34.4 m); **Draught** 33.25 ft (10.1 m); **Machinery** 4 × shafts Parsons single reduction geared turbines (167,000 shp); **Speed** 30.5 knots (56.5 km/h); **Weapons** 18 × 4.5 in (twin), 5 × 40 mm (sextuple), 2 × 40 mm Mk 5, 6 × 40 mm Mk 9, 4 × 3-pdr saluting guns; **Aircraft** 60; **Cost** £21.5 million.

Technical details (1975) Displacement (standard) 43,344 tons, (full load) 50,170 tons;

Overall length 845.7 ft (257.8 m); **Overall beam** 112.7 ft (34.4 m); **Draught** 36.0 ft (11 m); **Machinery** as built; **Speed** 29.25 knots (54.2 km/h); **Weapons** 4 × Seacat SAM, 4 × 3-pdr saluting guns; **Aircraft** 30 fixed-wing and 6 helicopters.

Modernization and refits 1956 Angled deck extended and 2 × 4.5 in turrets removed (port); **1959** Removal of deck-edge lift, 2 × 4.5 in (starboard) and 6 × 40 mm removed, 2 × 40 mm

Ark Royal *at 'recovery stations' in the West Indies soon after her 'Phantomization' refit with Phantom (892 Squadron) and Buccaneer (809 Squadron) jets embarked* (RN/PO Holdgate).

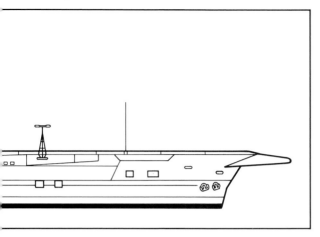

Bofors (twin) and Type 965 radar added; **1964** Fully equipped for Buccaneer, remaining 4.5 in turrets and remaining 40 mm removed, sponsons for Seacat added; **1967-70** Phantomization including strengthened deck, full 8½ degree angle, new catapults (including waist), Type 982/983 and CCA radars, Corvus and Seacat launchers, ESM/EW — cost £32 million; **1973-74** Long maintenance period.

Service summary 1955 Trials and Mediterranean Fleet; **1956** Mediterranean and refit; **1957** Mediterranean and Home Fleets, visit to International Naval Review, Virginia; **1958** Mediterranean and refit; **1959** Completed refit, NATO exercises; **1960** Home and Mediterranean Fleets, Sea Vixen trials; **1961** Refit, then general service with Mediterranean and Home Fleets, received first Wessex squadron in Fleet; **1962** Deployed to Far East; **1963** Returned to Devonport, again deployed to Far East; **1964** Refit; **1965** Exercises with Home Fleet before returning to Far East; **1966** Beira Patrol and returned to Devonport for refit; **1970** Allocated to Western Station and embarked Phantoms and Sea Kings, Mediterranean and NATO exercises; **1971** Harrier trials and Eastlant exercises; **1972** Westlant and Mediterranean exercises; **1973** Exercises and refit at Devonport; **1974** Home· waters and Mediterranean; **1975** Eastlant and South America; **1976** Westlant exercises, 'Sailor' television programme filmed aboard; **1977** Silver Jubilee Review and Mediterranean; **1978** Last operational deployment to Westlant and farewell cruise around United Kingdom; **1979** Paid off for disposal.

Important dates 1942, adopted by City of Leeds; 26 September 1955, first squadrons embarked; 13 November 1961, first warship to embark Wessex; 4-5 May 1971, RAF Harrier trials; 27 November 1978, last fixed-wing launch (Phantom of 892 Squadron).

Ark Royal was perhaps the most famous aircraft carrier of the post-war era and yet one which was apparently prone to mechanical problems. Originally named *Irresistible,* she was, like her sister ship *Eagle,* left dormant for three years whilst the Admiralty considered ̠its carrier policy. She was the last fixed-wing, conventional carrier to remain in service and is unique in not having been involved in any action. Attempts to have her preserved failed in 1980 and she was towed to Scotland to be broken up.

Cancelled designs Two other hulls were laid down as members of the class but were cancelled after the cessation of hostilities.

Name *Africa;* **Builders** Fairfields. **Ordered** 1943; **Cancelled** January 1946.

Name *Eagle;* **Builders** Vickers Armstrong (Tyne); **Ordered** 1943; **Cancelled** January 1946.

Class *Malta* or *Gibraltar*

Name *Gibraltar*; **Builders** Vickers Armstrong (Tyne); **Ordered** 1943; **Cancelled** November 1945.

Name *Africa*; **Builders** Fairfield; design transferred from 'Audacious' Class in 1944; **Cancelled** November 1945.

Name *Malta*; **Builders** Clydebank; **Ordered** 1943; **Cancelled** January 1946.

Name *New Zealand*; **Builders** Cammell Laird; **Ordered** 1943; **Cancelled** January 1946.

Technical details Displacement (standard) 46,900 tons, (full load) 56,800 tons; **Overall length** 916.5 ft (279.3 m); **Overall beam** 136.0 ft (41.5 m); **Draught** 34.5 ft (10.5 m); **Machinery** 4 × shaft Parsons geared turbines (200,000 shp); **Speed** 33 knots (61 km/h); **Weapons** 16 × 4.5 in, 55 × 40 mm (various); **Aircraft** 80.

This class was designed to have a large hangar, served by two deck-edge lifts and open-sided engine running areas, together with a large island structure to carry the radar suites then entering service. Some authorities only state that there were three designs, but recent research indicates that *Africa* was rescheduled to this class. Some authors give *Malta*'s builders as John Brown and *New Zealand*'s as Harland & Wolff. None of the four hulls was laid down.

Light Fleet Carriers

Class *Colossus*

Name *Colossus;* **Pennant number** R15; **Flight deck code** C (1945), J (1946), S (1946); **Builders** Vickers Armstrong (Tyne); **Laid down** 1 June 1942; **Launched** 30 September 1943; **Commissioned** 1 December 1944; **Transferred** 6 August 1946 (French Navy); **Sold** August 1951 (French Navy); **Paid off** November 1973; **Broken up** 1978.

Technical details (as built) Displacement (standard) 13,190 tons, (full load) 18,400 tons; **Overall length** 695 ft (211.8 m); **Overall beam** 80 ft (24.4 m); **Draught** 23.5 ft (7.2 m); **Machinery** 2 × shafts Parsons geared turbines (40,000 shp); **Speed** 25 knots (46.3 km/h); **Weapons** 6 × 4 2-pdr AA, 32 × 20 mm (later 19 × 40 mm); **Aircraft** 12 × Barracuda, 24 × Corsair.

Technical details (1951) Displacement (standard) 13,190 tons, (full load) 18,040 tons; **Overall length, Overall beam, Draught, Machinery** and **Speed** as built; **Weapons** 6 × 4 40 mm AA, 19 × 40 mm; **Aircraft** 12 × Hellcat, 12 × Helldiver (capacity for 43).

Technical details (1970) Displacement (standard) 14,000 tons, (full load) 18,500 tons; **Overall length** 694.5 ft (211.7 m); **Overall beam** 80.2 ft (24.4 m); **Draught** 23 ft (7.0 m); **Machinery** 2 × shafts Parsons geared turbines (40,000 shp); **Speed** 23.5 knots (43.5 km/h); **Aircraft** 24 × helicopters; **Pennant number** R95; **Flight Deck Code** H.

Modernization and refits 1946 (Simonstown, South Africa) as *Colossus;* **1951** as *Arromanches;* **1957-58** Reconstructed with 4 degree angled deck, mirror landing aid and increased armament; **1960**

Conversion to training aircraft carrier; **1968** Refit for anti-submarine duties with helicopters.

Service summary (*Colossus*) **1945** Joined British Pacific Fleet but did not see action, assisted in repatriation of POWs; **1946** Handed over to Marine Nationale on loan; (*Arromanches*) **1946-48** French Fleet; **1949** Supported Indo-China operations; **1956** Suez operations; **1960-68** Training carrier role; **1969-74** ASW carrier with helicopters.

The Light Fleet aircraft carriers, of which *Colossus* was the first, were designed to meet the growing needs for air support of the Royal and Commonwealth (then Empire) Navies on a world-wide basis. They were smaller and lighter than the 'Illustrious' and 'Implacable' Classes, thus easier to build in smaller yards, but had less potential. Most remained in service for many years after the war; some of the later 'Majestic' Class are still in overseas service. The design has a single hangar deck, no armour and only light AA defence.

Name *Glory*; **Pennant number** R62; **Flight deck code** L, Y and R (1946-54); **Builders** Harland & Wolff; **Laid down** 27 August 1942; **Launched** 27 November 1943; **Commissioned** 2 April 1945; **Paid off** 1954 and finally 1958; **Broken up** 23 August 1961.

Technical details (as built) Displacement, Overall length, Overall beam, Draught, Machinery, Speed and **Weapons** as for *Colossus*; **Aircraft** 12 × Firefly FR I, 20 × Hellcat (for night fighter duties with BPF).

Modernization and refits 1947-49 At Devonport; **1953-54** After Korean War service (short refit at Sydney in 1951).

Service summary 1945-47 With British Pacific

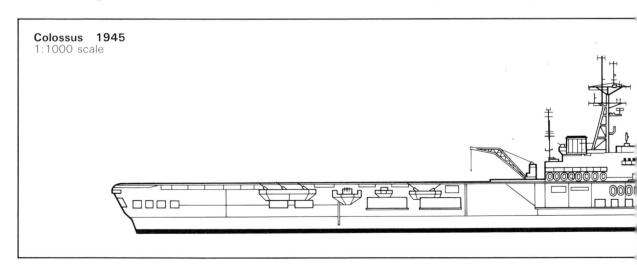

Colossus 1945
1:1000 scale

Glory *sailing in Japanese waters during the Korean War.*

Fleet but did not see war service; **1949-51** With Mediterranean Fleet; **1951-53** Korean War service; **1954** Mediterranean Fleet and as ferry carrier to Far East; **1955** Acted as helicopter base ship in Lock Eriboll during severe winter; **1956-58** In Reserve; **1958** Conversion to troop carrier abandoned; **1958-61** In Reserve.

She had operational periods in Korea from 25 April to 27 September 1951, 5 February to 1 May 1952 and 8 November 1952 to 19 May 1953 and also took part in attacks on Communist terrorists in Malaya on 27 October 1952. A total of 9,664 fixed-wing sorties were flown, plus 381 helicopter sorties (including rescue missions).

Name *Venerable*; **Pennant number** Not available; **Flight deck code** B (1945-46), N, T (1946), V (1946-48); **Builders** Cammell Laird; **Laid down** 3 December 1942; **Launched** 30 December 1943; **Commissioned** 17 January 1945; **Transferred** 28 May 1948 (Royal Netherlands Navy) as *Karel Doorman;* **Pennant number** Not available; **Flight deck code** D; **Withdrawn from service** 29 April 1968; **Sold** 15 October 1968 (Armada Argentina); **Commissioned** 12 March 1969 as *Veinticinco de Mayo* ('25th May'); **Pennant number** V2; **Flight deck code** D; In service.

Technical details (as built) Displacement, Overall length, Overall beam, Draught, Machinery, Speed and **Weapons** as *Colossus*; **Aircraft** 12 × Barracuda, 12 × Firefly FR I (later 12 × Seafire XV).

Technical details (1950) Displacement (standard) 13,190 tons, (full load) 18,000 tons; Overall length 693.17 ft (211.3 m); **Overall beam** as *Colossus*; **Draught** 23.42 ft (7.14 m); **Machinery** as *Colossus*; **Speed** 23.5 knots (43.5 km/h); **Weapons** 34 × 40 mm AA; **Aircraft** 6 × Avenger, 12 × Firefly FR I.

Technical details (1970) Displacement (standard) 15,892 tons, (full load) 19,896 tons; **Overall length** and **Overall beam** as built; **Draught** 25 ft (7.62 m); **Machinery** as built (but from *Leviathan*); **Speed** 24.25 knots (44.9 km/h); **Weapons** 10 × 40 mm; **Aircraft** 8 × S-2 Tracker, 6 × helicopter.

Technical details (1983) Displacement, Overall length, Overall beam, Draught, Machinery and **Speed** as 1970; **Weapons** 9 × 40

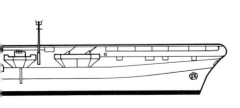

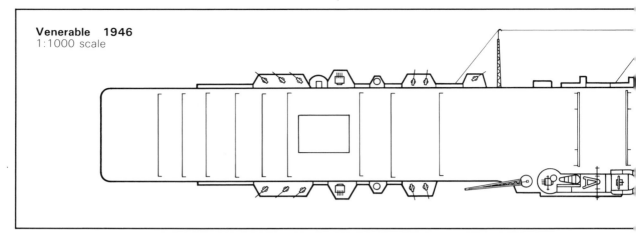

Venerable 1946
1:1000 scale

mm L70; **Aircraft** 18 × fixed-wing (Super Etendard or A-4Q Skyhawk and/or S-2E Tracker), 4 × helicopters (S-61D Sea King or Alouette III).

Modernization and refits 1948 For Dutch service; **1955-58** Reconstruction to operate jet aircraft, including 8 degrees angled deck, steam catapult, mirror landing aid, strengthened aircraft lifts, superstructure redesigned with tripod lattice mast, new funnel and Dutch radar; **1965-66** Reboilered using equipment from *Leviathan* (see below); **1968-69** Refitted for Argentine service in Netherlands, including new turbines from *Leviathan*; **1975** Armament reduced; **1980** Armament further diminished; **1983-84** Refit to operate Super Etendard aircraft, plus data link and new flight deck equipment.

Service summary (*Venerable*) **1945-46** Joined 11th Aircraft Carrier Squadron (with *Colossus, Glory* and *Vengeance*), British Pacific Fleet, but did not see war service; (*Karel Doorman*) **1948-68** Operated as light fleet escort carrier, later as anti-submarine warfare carrier assigned to NATO (eventually with helicopters and S-2 Tracker aircraft only); (*Veinticinco de Mayo*) **1969** sailed for the Argentine; **1970-75** Fleet service; **1975-80** Fleet service; **1982** Covered initial invasion of Falkland Islands but not used for offensive operations; **1984** Returned to commission with Super Etendard/Exocet strike potential.

This carrier has had a most interesting career and is destined to continue in service until 1990 (at least) carrying the latest aircraft, radar, electronic warfare and computer equipment. Her service during the Falklands conflict was undistinguished — she was unable to operate Super Etendard/Exocet strikes, as well as being unable to launch A-4Q strike against *Sheffield* because of lack of wind over the deck.

Ironically Harrier trials had been carried out aboard in 1970 when she was in European waters.

Name *Vengeance*; **Pennant number** R71; **Flight deck code** A (1945), N (1946), Q (1946-57); **Builders** Swan Hunter; **Laid down** 16 November 1942; **Launched** 23 February 1944; **Commissioned** 15 January 1945; **Transferred** 13 November 1952 (Royal Australian Navy) with same name; **Returned to RN** 13 August 1955 (Reserve); **Sold** 13 December 1956 (Brazilian Navy); **Named** *Minas Gerais* 6 December 1960; **Pennant number** A11; In service.

Technical details (as built) Displacement as *Colossus*; **Overall length** 693.75 ft (211.5 m); **Overall beam, Draught, Machinery** and **Speed** as *Colossus*; **Weapons** 6 × 4 2-pdr, 11 × 2 20 mm Oerlikon, 10 × 20 mm Oerlikon; **Aircraft** as

Vengeance served with the Royal Australian Navy, 1953-55 (Australian War Memorial).

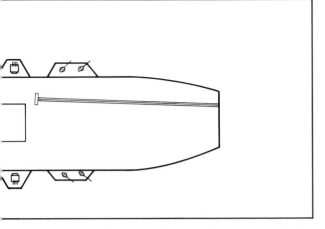

Colossus (later 8 × Sea Hornet NF 21, 8 × Firefly AS 6).

Technical details (1970) Displacement (standard) 15,890 tons, (full load) 19,890 tons; **Overall length** 695 ft (211.8 m); **Overall beam** as built; **Draught** (mean) 21.5 ft (6.6 m); **Machinery** and **Speed** as built; **Weapons** 1 × 2 40 mm, 2 × 4 40 mm, 2 × 47 mm saluting; **Aircraft** (21 maximum) 8 × S-2E Tracker, 4 × S-61D/ASH-61D Sea King.

Modernization and refits 1946 (at Sydney and Devonport) when insulation work completed; **1948** Refit prior to joining Home Fleet; **1948-49** Prepared for Arctic operations; **1949** Refit prior to rejoining Home Fleet; **1950-51** Repairs and refit for training role; **1951-52** Refit for Far East duties; **1952** Alterations prior to RAN service; **1957-60** Reconstruction in the Netherlands including 8

Warrior served in the Royal Canadian Navy, 1946-48 (Public Archives Canada).

degrees angled deck, steam catapult, mirror landing aid, new fire control and radar equipment, rebuilt superstructure and funnel; **1976-80** modernization and major refit.

Service summary (*Vengeance*) **1945-46** Joined 11th ACS (later 1st ACS), British Pacific Fleet, went to Hong Kong for anti-piracy operations, East Indies Station; **1947** Training carrier at Rosyth; then BPF; **1948** Returned to UK for Home Fleet exercises; **1949** 'Operation Rusty' Arctic exercise with jets and helicopters; **1950** Home Fleet; **1951** Trials and Training Carrier; **1952** Far East trooping to Singapore; **1952-55** Transferred to 5th ACS RAN; **1955** Paid off to Class III Reserve (extended notice); (*Minas Gerais*) **1956-60** Reconstruction (see **Modernization and refits**); **1961** Sailed for Brazil (13 January); **1961-76** Anti-submarine warfare carrier; **1981** Completed modernization for service until early 1990s.

Another active Light Fleet Carrier, again operating the US types primarily for anti-submarine duties. Such carriers are difficult to replace.

Name *Warrior*; **Pennant number** R31; **Flight deck code** W (1946-48), J; **Builders** Harland & Wolff; **Laid down** 12 December 1942; **Launched** 20 May 1944; **Commissioned** 24 January 1946 (Royal Canadian Navy) and 23 March 1948 (RN); **Placed in Reserve** February 1958; **Sold** 4 July 1958 (Armada Argentina); **Commissioned** 4 November 1958 as *Independencia*; **Paid off** 1971.

Technical details (as built) Displacement, Overall length, Overall beam, Draught, Machinery, Speed and **Weapons** as for *Colossus*; **Aircraft** 12 × Seafire XV (later 12 × Sea Fury FB 11), 12 × Firefly FR I (later 9 × Firefly FR 4).

Technical details (1954) Displacement (standard) 15,690 tons, (full load) 19,540 tons;

Overall length and **Overall beam** as built; **Draught** 25.08 ft (7.64 m); **Machinery** 2 × shafts Parsons geared turbines (36,000 shp); **Speed** 24.25 knots (44.9 km/h); **Weapons** 5 × 2 40 mm Bofors Mk 5; 7 × 40 mm Bofors Mk 7; 11 × 40 mm Bofors Mk 9; 2 × 3-pdr saluting; **Aircraft** (35 maximum) 8 × Firefly AS 5, 12 × Sea Fury FB 11.

Technical details (1970) Displacement, Overall length and **Overall beam** as 1954; **Draught** 21.3 ft (6.5 m); **Machinery** (40,000 shp); **Weapons** 8 × 40 mm Mk 7; **Aircraft** (21 maximum) including 8 × S-2 Tracker.

Modernization and refits 1948 For conversion for 'rubber' deck (see page 233); **1952-53** Limited modernization, including extended superstructure (bridge) and new lattice mast; **1954** Modified in Singapore to carry refugees; **1954-56** Refit including partial angled deck, new arrester gear and reduced armament; **1959-71** Various whilst in Argentine service.

Service summary (*Warrior*) **1946-48** Commissioned into Royal Canadian Navy as first carrier to be manned entirely by Canadians; **1948-49** 'Rubber' deck experiments; **1949** Placed in Category B Reserve at Portsmouth; **1950** Brought back into service as aircraft and troop carrier for the Korean War; **1951** Trooping to Cyprus; **1954** Relieved *Sydney* off Korea and joined Far East Fleet (assisted with refugee transfer in Vietnam); **1956-57** Flagship of Special Service Squadron for 'Operation Grapple' (the hydrogen bomb tests off Christmas Island); **1958** Placed in Reserve (extended notice); (*Independencia*) **1958** departed for Argentina (10 December); **1959-71** Operated in anti-submarine role.

The use of the carrier at Christmas Island as operational control ship in the target area, as well as an SAR centre, is interesting, as is the little known work whilst off Korea in 1954, but her later service was unspectacular.

Name *Theseus*; **Pennant number** R64; **Flight deck code** T; **Builders** Fairfield; **Laid down** 6 January 1943; **Launched** 6 July 1944; **Commissioned** 9 February 1946; **Placed in Reserve** 21 December 1956; **Scrapped** March 1960.

Technical details (as built) Displacement (standard) 13,350 tons; **Overall length, Overall beam, Draught, Machinery, Speed** and **Weapons** as *Colossus*; **Aircraft** 12 × Seafire XV, 12 × Firefly FR I (for Korean service, 21 × Sea Fury FB 11, 12 × Firefly AS 5); helicopters operated at Suez (Joint Helicopter Experimental Unit).

Modernization and refits 1947-48 Refit for flagship duties; **1950** Refit; **1951-52** Refit after Korean War service; **1953-54** Refitted for training role; **1955-56** Converted for helicopter trials.

Service summary 1946 Joined Rosyth Command for deck landing training duties, then 1st ACS BPF; **1947** Far East service; **1948-50** 3rd ACS Home Fleet, including first deck landings by jet at night (19 June 1950); **1950-51** Relieved *Triumph* off Korea, later rejoined 3rd ACS; **1952-54** Mediterranean Fleet duties; **1954** Home Fleet Training Squadron; **1956** Suez Crisis, operated helicopters (with *Ocean*) during 'Operation Musketeer'; **1956** placed in Reserve.

Her aircraft won the Boyd Trophy in 1950. Her role during the Suez crisis laid the foundation for the later Commando Carriers.

Name *Ocean*; **Pennant number** R68; **Flight deck code** O; **Builders** Stephen (Glasgow); **Laid down** 8 November 1942; **Launched** 8 July 1944;

Commissioned 8 August 1945; **Placed in Reserve** 5 December 1957; **Paid off** March 1958; **Scrapped** May-August 1962.

Technical details (as built) Displacement, **Overall length, Overall beam** and **Draught** as for *Colossus*; **Machinery** 2 × shafts Stephens geared turbines (36,000 shp/40,000 shp); **Speed** as *Colossus*; **Weapons** 6 × 4 2-pdr AA, 3 × 1 2-pdr AA, 10 × 40 mm Bofors; 2 × 40 mm Mk 9; **Aircraft** as *Theseus* (for Korean service, 21 × Sea Fury FB 11, 12 × Firefly AS 5), helicopters at Suez (Joint Helicopter Experimental Unit).

Modernization and refits 1947-48 Refit; **1950** Refit for Korean War service; **1954** Converted for training role; **1956** Converted for helicopter role.

Service summary 1945 Rosyth Command for first jet landing on any carrier; **1946-47** Mediterranean Fleet (including 2nd ACS); **1948-49** Covered withdrawal from Palestine; **1949**

Trooping to Far East; **1951** Mediterranean Fleet; **1952-53** Korean operations (9 May to 31 October 1952 and 15 May to 2 November 1953); **1954** Home Fleet Training Squadron; **1955** Trooping to Cyprus; **1956** Suez operations with *Theseus*; **1957** Exercises in UK waters.

Her aircraft won the Boyd Trophy in 1952.

Name *Triumph*; **Pennant number** R16 (later A108); **Flight deck code** P (1946-55); **Builders** Hawthorn Leslie; **Laid down** 27 January 1943; **Launched** 2 October 1944; **Commissioned** 9 May 1946; **Placed in Reserve** 21 December 1955; **Converted** January 1965 (to Fleet Maintenance Ship); **Paid off** 17 March 1972; **Placed in Reserve** 8 December 1975; **Scrapped** 1981.

Technical details (as built) Displacement, **Overall length, Overall beam, Draught, Machinery, Speed** and **Weapons** as *Colossus*;

Above *Firefly FR 5, with hook down, passes* Ocean (RN/FONAC).

Left Theseus *during trials with the Sea Vampire; note the Sea Otter ranged right aft* (Bruce Clark).

Right Triumph *with specialist trials aircraft ranged on deck; Sea Vampire, Sea Hornet, Firefly, Seafire and Barracuda* (Swan Hunter).

Aircraft 12 × Seafire XVII (later Seafire FR 47), 12 × Firefly FR I (later 8 × Firefly FR I, 4 × Firefly NF 1); Korean service 12 × Seafire FR 47, 12 × Firefly FR I.

Technical details (1970) Displacement (standard) 13,350 tons, (full load) 17,000 tons; **Overall length** 699 ft (213.1 m); **Overall beam, Draught, Machinery** and **Speed** as *Colossus*; **Weapons** 4 × 40 mm Bofors, 3 × 2-pdr saluting; **Aircraft** 3 × helicopters (flight deck hangar).

Modernization and refits 1946 Conversion for trails and training; 1948 Refit for Far East service; **1950-51** Post-Korea refit; **1953** Refit; **1961-65** Conversion to Fleet Maintenance Ship (Heavy Repair) at Portsmouth; **1968-69** Refitted for Far East service; **1973** Dehumidified at Chatham.

Service summary 1946 Training and trials carrier for twin-engined landings; **1947** Mediterranean; **1949** Far East station; **1950** Korean War service; **1951** Trooping to Middle East; **1953-55** Cadet Training Ship; **1955** Visit to USSR and placed in Reserve; **1965** Became Escort Maintenance Ship at Portsmouth; **1966-68** Far East; **1969-72** Far East service (total of 7 years); **1972-81** Laid up at Chatham; **1981** Towed to Spain for scrapping (26 November).

Triumph provided naval aircraft in Korea in a stop-gap role prior to being fitted as a Heavy Repair Ship. She was designed to take four destroyers or frigates alongside and fitted with comprehensive workshops especially for the Far East and Indian Ocean.

Class *Majestic*

Name *Majestic*; **Pennant number** R93; **Flight deck code** none; **Builders** HM Dockyard Devonport; **Laid down** 19 April 1943; **Launched** 30 September 1944; **Sold** 16 December 1948 (Royal Australian Navy); **Commissioned** 5 February 1949 as *Sydney*; **Pennant number** R17 (later A214 & P214); **Flight deck code** K (1949-58), S (1958-73); **Converted to trooping** 7 March 1962; **Paid off** 1973; **Sold for scrap** 1975; **Broken up** 1976.

Technical details (as built) Displacement (standard) 14,512 tons, (full load) 19,550 tons; **Overall length** 630 ft (192.0 m); **Overall beam** 80 ft (24.4 m); **Draught** 24.5 ft (7.5 m); **Machinery** 2 × shafts Parsons geared turbines (40,000 shp); **Speed** 25 knots (46.3 km/h); **Weapons** 30 × 40 mm Bofors, 4 × 3-pdr saluting; **Aircraft** 12 × Sea Fury FB 11, 24 × Firefly FR 4, 1 × Sea Otter.

Technical details (1970) Displacement (standard) 12,569 tons, (full load) 17,233 tons; **Overall length, Overall beam, Draught, Machinery** and **Speed** as built; **Weapons** 4 × 40

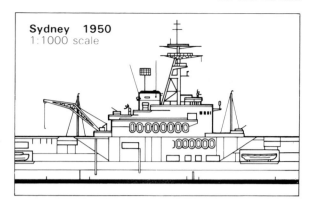

Sydney 1950
1:1000 scale

mm Bofors; **Aircraft** 6 × Wessex HAS 31 (when carried) or 3 × Bell UH-1B (when carried).

Modernization and refits 1948-49 Converted for Australian service; **1954-56** Conversion to Training Carrier; **1961-62** Converted to troop transport; **1968-69** Modified to carry six landing craft.

Service summary 1948 Admiralty agreed to transfer to RAN (16 February); **1949** Arrived in Australian waters (May); **1951-52** Korean War service; **1953-54** Korean UN patrol; **1957** Training Carrier role following commissioning of *Melbourne* (see below); **1962-73** Supported Australian presence and role in Malaya (later Malaysia and Borneo) and South Vietnam when known as 'Vung Tau Ferry'. Last Vietnam trip completed 12 March 1972.

She operated successfully off Korea with Sea Fury FB 11 and Firefly AS 5/6 aircraft and was involved in trials for complete ASW or strike CAGs.

Name *Magnificent*; **Pennant number** R21; **Flight**

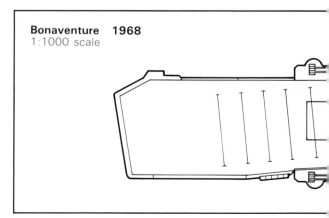

Bonaventure 1968
1:1000 scale

deck code X; **Builders** Harland & Wolff; **Laid down** 29 July 1943; **Launched** 16 November 1944; **Commissioned** 7 April 1948 (Royal Canadian Navy); **Returned to RN** 14 June 1957 and placed in Reserve; **Sold for scrap** 12 July 1965.

Technical details (as built) Displacement (standard) 16,000 tons, (full load) 20,320 tons; **Overall length, Overall beam, Draught, Machinery** and **Speed** as *Terrible*; **Weapons** 25 × 40 mm **Aircraft** 8 × Sea Venom FAW 53, 7 × Gannet AS 1, 2 × Sycamore helicopters.

Technical details (as built) Displacement, Overall length, Overall beam, Draught, Machinery, Speed and **Weapons** as *Terrible*; **Aircraft** 12 × Sea Fury FB 10; 9 × Firefly FR 4 (later 11 × Firefly AS 5); (1951) 7 × Avenger TBM-3E, 9 × Sea Fury FB 11 (later joined by 1 × Sikorsky S-55/HO4S-3 helicopter).

Modernization and refits 1949 Refit and repairs including fitting of DLCO sponson; **1950-51** Refit with new propellors; **1951-52** long refit; **1954** general repairs.

Service summary 1949-50 Atlantic exercises; **1950-51** More exercises, including Mediterranean in place of RN carriers; **1952-54** Atlantic exercises; **1955** Pacific training cruise; **1956-57** UN duties in Middle East; **1957-65** In Reserve.

Called 'Maggie' by the Canadians, she was arcticized to replace *Warrior* (see above) and was

Magnificent was a Light Fleet carrier which served with the Royal Australian and Royal Canadian Navies as well as the Royal Navy. This picture taken in Canada shows the ship with Canadian Sea Fury and Avenger aircraft embarked (Public Archives Canada).

herself replaced in service by *Bonaventure* (see below).

Name *Powerful*; **Pennant number** R95; **Builders** Harland & Wolff; **Laid down** 27 November 1943; **Launched** 27 February 1945; **Sold** 12 July 1952 (Royal Canadian Navy); **Renamed** *Bonaventure* 20

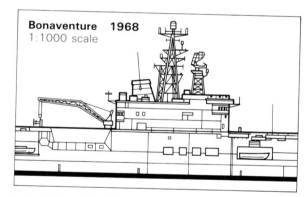

Bonaventure 1968
1:1000 scale

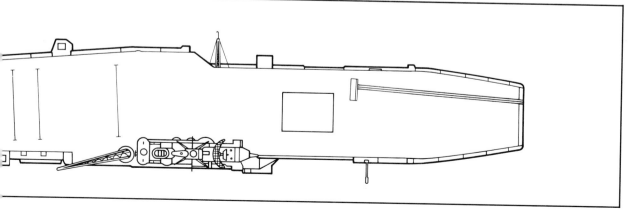

December 1952; **Commissioned** 17 January 1957; **Paid off** 3 July 1970; **Sold for scrap** 1978.

Technical details (as built) Displacement (standard) as *Terrible*, (full load) 18,000 tons; **Overall length** 720 ft (219.5 m); **Overall beam, Draught, Machinery** and **Speed** as *Terrible* but one propellor was three-bladed and the other four-bladed to give significant reduction in vibration; **Weapons** 4 × 2 3-in mountings; **Aircraft** 10 × CS2F-1 Tracker, 8 × McDonnell Banshee (later 10 × Tracker, 8 × SH-3 Sea King helicopters).

Modernization and refits 1952-57 Completed with 8 degrees angled deck, mirror landing aid, steam catapult, redesigned superstructure, lattice mast and modern radar; **1959** Long refit; **1962** Conversion to ASW carrier; **1963** Long refit; **1967** Half-life refit and modernization.

Service summary 1957-70 Atlantic service with RCN, initially as strike carrier, later (1962-70) as ASW carrier.

Name *Majestic*; **Pennant number** R77; **Flight deck code** None; **Builders** Vickers Armstrong (Barrow); **Laid down** 15 April 1943; **Launched** 28 February 1945; **Sold** 1946 (Royal Australian Navy); **Commissioned** 26 October 1955 as *Melbourne;* **Pennant number** 21; **Flight deck code** M; **Paid off** 30 June 1982; **Sold for scrap** November 1983.

Technical details (as built) Displacement (standard) 16,000 tons (full load) 20,320 tons; **Overall length, Overall beam, Draught,**

Machinery and **Speed** as *Terrible*; **Weapons** 25 × 40 mm; **Aircraft** 8 × Sea Venom FAW 53, 7 × Gannet AS 1, 2 × Sycamore helicopters.

Technical details (1970) Displacement, Overall length, Overall beam, Draught, Machinery and **Speed** as built; **Weapons** 4 × 2 40 mm Bofors, 4 × 40 mm Bofors; **Aircraft** 4 × A-4 Skyhawk, 6 × S-2E Tracker, 10 × Wessex HAS 31 helicopters.

Technical details (1982) Displacement (full load) 19,996 tons; **Overall length, Overall beam, Draught, Machinery** and **Speed** as built; **Weapons** 4 × 40 mm Bofors; **Aircraft** 8 × A-4G Skyhawk, 4 × S-2G Tracker, 5 × Westland Sea King HAS 50.

Modernization and refits 1949-56 Completed with 5½ degrees angled deck, direct-action arrester gear, mirror landing aid, port-side steam catapult; **1963** Converted for ASW helicopters; **1968-69** Converted for A-4 and S-2 aircraft, new radar; **1971** New catapult and flight deck lengthened; **1976-77** Refit for visit to UK waters; **1982** Removed 40 mm twins.

Service summary 1956 Flagship of RAN; **1957-74** SEATO service; **1975-82** General service (including visit to UK for Silver Jubilee review in 1977).

Melbourne in 1978 showing the bridge radar, bridle catcher and angled deck modifications. (Australian Department of Defence).

Melbourne was to continue in service until 1985 but the incoming Australian Labour government retired her early and she was not replaced. After building, *Melbourne* was modified with US radar and aircraft. During her career she was involved in two fatal collisions at sea (1964 and 1969). Air group composition: 10 × Sea Venom FAW 53, 10 × Gannet AS 1, 2 × Sycamore (1958), 4 × Sea Venom FAW 53, 6 × Gannet AS 1, 10 × Wessex HAS 31 (1963).

Name *Leviathan*; **Pennant number** R97; **Builders** Swan Hunter; **Laid down** 18 October 1943; **Launched** 7 June 1945; **Contract cancelled** May 1946; **Placed in Reserve** July 1946; **Scrapped** from 1968.

Technical details (as built) As for *Terrible* but work stopped when only 95 per cent structurally completed and 80 per cent fitted out.

Modernization and refits None but boilers and engines removed 1965-66 and used for other Light Fleet Carriers.

Name *Hercules*; **Pennant number** R49; **Flight deck code** None; **Builders** Vickers Armstrong (Tyne); **Laid down** 12 October 1943; **Launched** 22 September 1945; **Construction halted** May 1946;

Sold January 1957 (Indian Navy); **Commissioned** 4 March 1961 as *Vikrant*; In service.

Technical details (as built) Displacement (standard) 16,000 tons, (full load) 19,550 tons; **Overall length** 700 ft (213.4 m); **Overall beam, Draught, Machinery** and **Speed** as *Terrible*; **Weapons** 4 × 2 40 mm Bofors Mk 7, 7 × 40 mm Bofors; **Aircraft** 10 × Sea Hawk, 4 × Breguet Alize, 2 × Alouette III helicopters (Sea Harrier FRS 51 embarked in 1985 in place of Sea Hawks).

Modernization and refits 1957-61 Completed by Harland & Wolff; **1979-82** Major refit and modernization for Sea Harrier operations; **1983-84** Possible reconstruction with ski-jump apparently abandoned.

Service summary 1971 (December) War service against Pakistan with strikes against Chittagong (Sea Hawk) and inshore minelaying (Alize).

Last completed of the Light Fleets, *Vikrant* is similar to *Bonaventure* in appearance with reconstructed superstructure, lattice mast, steam catapult, 5½ degree angled deck, direct-action arrester wires and Carrier Control Approach radar. She is destined to continue in service until 1993 and due to be replaced then.

Class *Centaur*

Name *Centaur*; **Pennant number** R39 (later RO6); **Flight deck code** C; **Builders** Harland & Wolff; **Laid down** 30 May 1944; **Launched** 22 April 1947;

Centaur showing the painted partially-angled deck for trials (Rear Admiral Rolfe).

Commissioned 17 September 1953; **Paid off** 24 April 1970; **Sold for breaking** 11 August 1972.

Technical details (as built) Displacement (standard) 18,300 tons, (full load) 24,500 tons; **Overall length** 737 ft (224.6 m); **Overall beam** 90 ft (27.4 m); **Draught** 22 ft (6.7 m); **Machinery** 2 × shafts Parsons geared turbines (80,000 shp); **Speed** 29.5 knots (54.6 km/h); **Weapons** 2 × 6 40 mm Bofors Mk 6, 5 × 2 40 mm Bofors Mk 5, 4 × 40 mm Bofors Mk 7, 4 × 3-pdr saluting; **Aircraft** 12 × Sea Fury FB 11, 8 × Avenger AS 5 (later replaced by 20 × Sea Hawk FB 3, 9 × Gannet AS 1, 2 × Dragonfly helicopters).

Modernization and refits 1947-53 Completed with partial 5½ degrees angle painted on flight deck; **1956-58** Limited modernization at Devonport to complete angled deck, replace steam catapults and arrester gear; **1960-61** Refit at Portsmouth; **1962-63** Refit for new radar (Type 965) and some gun armament removed.

Service summary 1953-54 Trials; **1954-55** Work-up in Mediterranean; **1956** Far East Fleet duties; **1958** Flying trials for Home Fleet; **1959-60** Far East exercises and operations off Aden; **1960-61** Home Fleet exercises; **1961** Kuwait emergency and Aden, then Mediterranean Fleet duties; **1961-62** Middle East station; **1962** Far East and Mediterranean exercises; **1963-64** Far East and Indian Ocean, Radfan operations; **1966-67** Accommodation ship for *Eagle*'s refit at Devonport; **1967** Tender to shore establishment *Drake,* towed to Portsmouth; **1967-70** Portsmouth as accommodation ship; **1970-72** Plymouth as accommodation ship; **1972** Broken up at Queensborough, Kent.

Centaur was the first of a proposed class of eight to supplement the 'Colossus' Class by having more powerful machinery to keep pace with the Fleet Carriers. The class eventually suffered from being too small to operate second-generation jets, although *Albion* and *Bulwark* were redesigned in 1951 to amend certain faults. *Centaur* was used for angled deck trials with propellor-engined air group, later with jets, to experiment with increased flight deck usage and operational abilities. *Centaur* has the distinction of being the first angled-deck aircraft carrier to embark aircraft operationally.

Name *Arrogant*; **Pennant number** R14; **Builders** Swan Hunter.

Name *Hermes*; **Builders** Cammell Laird.

Name *Monmouth*; **Pennant number** R96; **Builders** Fairfield.

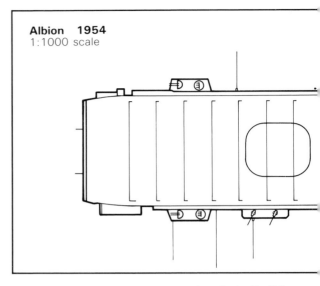

Albion 1954
1:1000 scale

Name *Polyphemus*; **Pennant number** R57; **Builders** HM Dockyard Devonport.

All four were cancelled in late 1945 when hostilities ceased and were dismantled on their slipways. The name *Hermes* was taken by *Elephant* (see below).

Class Modified *Centaur*

Name *Albion*; **Pennant number** R07; **Flight deck code** Z (1954-57), A (1957-72); **Builders** Swan Hunter; **Laid down** 23 March 1944; **Launched** 6 May 1947; **Laid up** 1947-54 (Rosyth); **Commissioned** 27 May 1954; **Recommissioned** 1 August 1962 as Commando Carrier; **Paid off** 2 March 1973; **Sold for conversion** July 1973 (to heavy lift ship for North Sea oil exploration); **Broken up** November 1973 onwards.

Technical details (as built) Displacement (standard) 20,260 tons, (full load) 26,118 tons; **Overall length** 737.8 ft (224.9 m); **Overall beam, Draught, Machinery** and **Speed** as *Centaur*; **Weapons** 2 × 6 40 mm Bofors Mk 6, 2 × 2 40 mm Bofors Mk 5, 4 × 40 mm Bofors Mk 7, 4 × 3-pdr saluting; **Aircraft** 16 × Sea Hawk FB 3, 8 × Gannet AS 1, 4 × Skyraider AEW 1 (later joined by 8 × Sea Venom FAW 21).

Technical details (1970) Displacement (standard) 23,300 tons, (full load) 27,705 tons; **Overall length, Overall beam, Draught, Machinery** and **Speed** as built; **Weapons** 4 × 2 40 mm Bofors Mk 5, 8 × 40 mm Mk 7; **Aircraft** 16 × Whirlwind HAR 7 (replaced by 16 × Wessex HU 5, 2 × Sioux AH 1); in addition room for 900 troops and carrier equipped with 4 × LCVP.

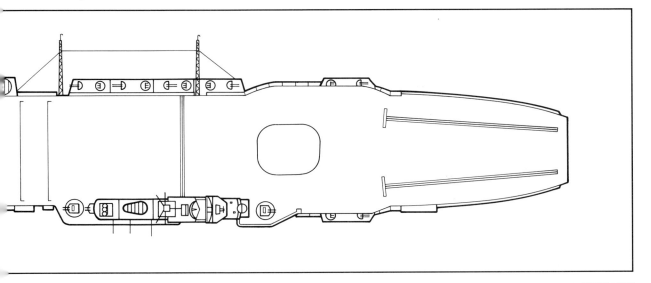

Albion *leaves the builders in May 1954* (Swan Hunter).

Modernization and refits 1951-54 Completed with interim 5 ¾ degrees angled deck with extended flight deck, hydraulic catapults and reduced armament; **1958** Refit; **1960-61** Conversion to Commando Carrier with deletion of catapults and arrester gear, but retaining equipment for possible anti-submarine role; **1964-65** Refit; **1966** Docked in Singapore for maintenance; **1966-67** Refit at Portsmouth; **1969-70** Final refit at Portsmouth.

Service summary 1954-55 Work-up and exercises before joining Home Fleet; **1956** Far East service before 'Operation Musketeer' off Suez; **1957** Home Fleet; **1958-59** Far Eastern service and commando support for Jordan; **1959-60** Far East and Mediterranean (Commando Carrier) **1962-63** Home waters and Mediterranean; **1963** Far East Fleet at Aden; **1963-64** Borneo campaign; **1965-66** Far East for 'confrontation' and general service; **1967** Withdrawal from Aden; **1968** SEATO exercises in Far East leaving Far East station on 14 July 1969; **1970-71** Far East commission for withdrawal from Singapore (October 1971); **1972** Mediterranean and home waters, plus exercise off Canada.

Name *Bulwark*; **Pennant number** R08; **Flight deck code** B; **Builders** Harland & Wolff; **Laid down** 10 May 1945; **Launched** 22 June 1948; **Commissioned** 29 October 29 1954; **Recommissioned** 19 January 1960 as Commando Carrier; **Placed in Reserve** April 1976; **Reactivated** 23 February 1979; **Paid off** March 1981; **Placed in Reserve** 1981-83 at Portsmouth; **Sold for scrap** April 1984.

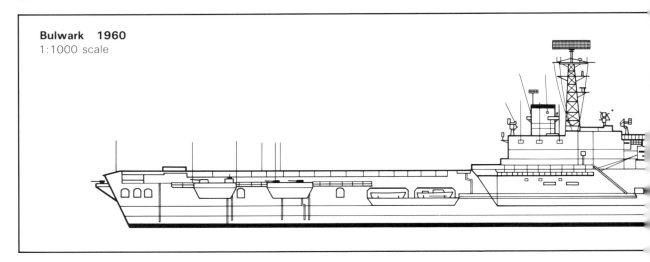

Bulwark   1960
1:1000 scale

Bulwark *enters Rosyth in 1979 with anti-submarine Sea Kings embarked in support of the ship's NATO role as a joint ASW and commando carrier* (RN/Bulwark).

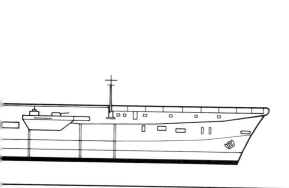

Technical details (as built) as *Albion*, except aircraft because of trials carrier role.

Technical details (1970) Displacement, Overall length, Overall beam, Draught, Machinery and Speed as *Albion*; Weapons 3 × 2 40 mm Bofors Mk 5, 2 × 40 mm Bofors Mk 7; Aircraft as *Albion*.

Modernization and refits 1954 Fitted with mirror sight deck landing aid for Trials Carrier role; 1957 Refit after Suez; 1959-60 Converted to Commando Carrier with removal of catapults, arrester gear and most of gun armament at Devonport; 1963 Refitted to same standard as *Albion* (see above), with variation in air conditioning for Far East operations; 1977-79 Refitted for joint ASW-Commando Carrier role.

Service summary 1954-56 Trials carrier with Home Fleet; 1956 'Operation Musketeer' and Mediterranean duties; 1957-59 Home Fleet duties and service in Caribbean, Indian Ocean and Persian Gulf; 1960-63 Far East Fleet in Commando Carrier role; 1964-76 Far East operations, including 'confrontation' duties in Borneo; 1979-81 Service as ASW Commando Carrier for NATO duties.

Bulwark was initially converted to operate 16 × Whirlwind HAS 7 helicopters (848 Squadron), and in 1962 further modified to carry 12 × Wessex HAS 1 helicopters, plus Sioux (Royal Marines), plus a full Commando of 900 men (as opposed to the previous 750). Her ship's boats had been replaced by Royal Marines-manned LCVPs on davits. In 1976-79 she was converted again to operate 12 × Wessex HU 5 and 4 × Sea King HAS 1/2/2A ASW helicopters (later joined by Sea King HC 4 Commando helicopters and Gazelle AH 1 and Scout AH 1 from the Royal Marines).

Class Improved *Centaur*

Name *Hermes*; Pennant number R12; Flight deck code H; Builders Vickers Armstrong (Barrow); Laid down 21 June 1944; Launched 16 February 1953; Commissioned 18 November 1959; Recommissioned 18 August 1973 as Commando Carrier; Recommissioned 10 December 1976 as ASW Carrier; Recommissioned 5 June 1981 as Sea Harrier Carrier; Paid off in Reserve 12 April 1984 (Preservation by Operation at Portsmouth); For disposal 1985 and sold to India as *Virato*.

Technical details (as built) Displacement (standard) 23,000 tons, (full load) 27,800 tons; Overall length 774.25 ft (236 m); Overall beam 90 ft (27.4 m); Draught 27.83 ft (8.5 m); Machinery 2 × shafts Admiralty geared turbines (76,000 shp); Speed 28 knots (52 km/h); Weapons 10 × 2 40 mm Bofors Mk 5 guns; Aircraft 6 × Scimitar (804 Sqn), 10 × Sea Vixen FAW 1 (890 Sqn), 3 × Gannet AEW 3 (849 C Flt), 8 × Whirlwind HAS 7, later 8 × Wessex HAS 1 (814 Sqn).

Technical details (1974) Displacement (standard) 24,900 tons, (full load) 29,000 tons; Overall length as built; Overall beam 90.25 ft (27.5 m); Draught 29.5 ft (9 m); Machinery and Speed as built; Weapons 2 × 4 Sea Cat launchers; Aircraft 14 × Wessex HU 5 (845 Sqn), 4 × Sea King HAS 1 (814 Sqn).

Technical details (1983) Displacement, Overall length, Overall beam, Draught,

Hermes at sea with Sea Vixen FAW 1, Scimitar F 1 and Gannet AEW 3 aircraft ranged on deck (Brian Johnstone).

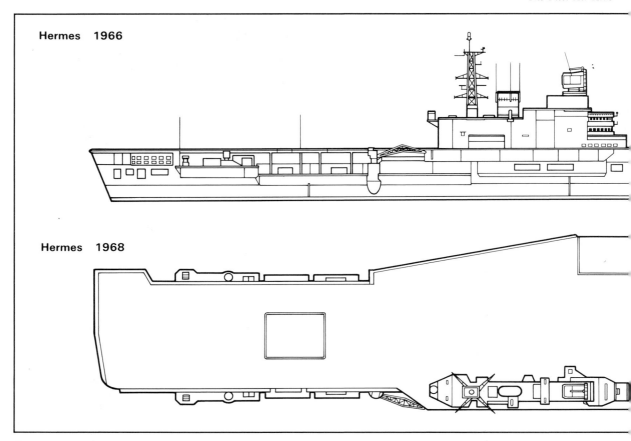

Hermes 1966

Hermes 1968

Hermes departs from Portsmouth in 1981 after her ski-jump refit and with an embarked air group of Sea Harrier fighters (800 Squadron) and Sea King HAS 5 helicopters (814 Squadron) (RN/Daedalus).

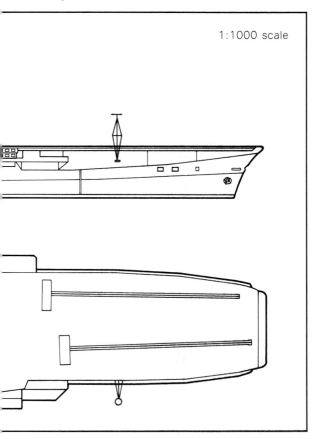

1:1000 scale

Machinery, Speed and **Weapons** as 1974; **Aircraft** 5 × Sea Harrier FRS 1 (800 Sqn), 9 × Sea King HAS 5 (814 Sqn) and now fitted with MEL Madge approach aid.

Modernization and refits 1945-52 Construction suspended; **1953-57** Completion suspended; **1961-62** Refit for Buccaneer trials; **1964-66** Refit to improve mirror landing aid (160 ft maximum width flight deck), add 'Alaskan Highway' around island, fit Sea Cat SAM launchers and better living accommodation; **1971-73** Conversion to Commando Carrier (to replace *Albion* — see above) with removal of all fixed-wing equipment, including radars, and provision for 750 RM Commandos, including LCVPs; **1976** Conversion for embarkation of ASW helicopters; **1980-81** Conversion for Sea Harrier operations, including the fitting of a 7½ degrees ski-jump ramp and state-of-the-art command, control and communications equipment.

Service summary 1959-61 First commission in Home and Far East waters; **1962-64** Buccaneer trials then joined Far East Fleet, followed by Sea Vixen trials; **1966-68** Far East Fleet; **1969-70** Last fixed-wing commission with Western Fleet and Mediterranean Fleet; **1973-76** Commando Carrier duties in NATO area, including Cyprus evacuation by embarked helicopters of 814 (Sea King HAS 1) and 845 (Wessex HU 5) Squadrons; **1977-80** ASW/Commando trials, Sea Harrier experiments, Silver Jubilee Review and NATO exercises; **1981-84** NATO duties, plus role as flagship for 'Operation Corporate', the liberation of the Falkland Islands.

When commissioned in 1959, *Hermes* represented the most modern RN carrier with 6½ degrees angled deck, deck-edge lift port-side, steam catapults, mirror landing aid and Type 984 3-D radar system. Her conversion to Commando Carrier cost £25 million (1973 value).

Light ASW Carriers

Class *Invincible*

Name *Invincible*; **Pennant number** R05; **Flight deck code** N; **Builders** Vickers (Barrow); **Laid down** 20 July 1973; **Launched** 3 May 1977; **Commissioned** 11 July 1980; **First major refit** 1986-87.

Technical details (as built) Displacement (standard) 16,000 tons, (full load) 19,500 tons; **Overall length** 677 ft (206.3 m); **Overall beam** 90 ft (27.4 m); **Draught** 24 ft (7.3 m); **Machinery** 2 × shafts, 4 × RR Olympus gas turbines (112,000 shp); **Speed** 28 knots (52 km/h); **Weapons** 1 × 2 Sea Dart launcher (36 missiles), 3 × 3-pdr saluting; **Aircraft** 5 × Sea Harrier FRS 1 (801 Sqn), 9 × Sea King HAS 5 (820 Sqn); (Commando lift role) 18 × Sea King HC 4/Wessex HU 5 (846 & 845 Squadrons).

Technical details (1982) As built, except for post-Falklands armament additions of 2 × Vulcan Phalanx 20 mm CIWS, 2 × 20 mm Oerlikon GAM-B01, counter-measures launchers.

Technical details (1985) Displacement (full load) 19,810 tons; **Overall length, Overall beam, Draught, Machinery, Speed, Weapons** and **Aircraft** as 1982.

Modernization and refits 1982 Post-Falklands modifications to fit additional close-in weapons; **1984** Post-Orient Express deployment repairs to shaft/propeller; **1986-87** First major refit (to equip for Sea Harrier FRS 2 and EH 101; additional work on weapons).

Service summary 1981 Declared operationally ready 16 June after work-up with Fleet and NATO units; **1982** South Atlantic Task Force duties and in

action off Falkland Islands in May, relieved by *Illustrious*; **1983-84** Orient Express deployment to Far East and Australia.

The 'Invincible' Class were initially designed to take 'large' numbers of medium ASW helicopters to sea but when ordered on 17 April 1973, the Admiralty included the provision of the Sea Harrier FRS 1; this meant the construction of the 7 degrees ski-jump ramp to allow the Sea Harrier to launch at maximum weight. The flight deck (550 × 42 ft/167.6 × 12.8 m) is angled at ½ degree to port to allow for the Sea Dart GWS 30 system which was a late addition to the design. For cost reasons the Sea Wolf SAM system was abandoned, but may be refitted later. Designed as a command and control ship, the CVSs will become flagships in time of war when the air complement will be increased to 9 × Sea Harrier FRS 1 and 18 × Sea King HAS 5/6. *Invincible* established many records on entering service, including being the largest gas turbine

warship in RN, having the largest propeller (the cause of vibration problems in 1981-84) and special scissor-action aircraft lifts.

Name *Illustrious*; **Pennant Number** R06; **Flight deck code** L; **Builders** Swan Hunter (Tyne); **Laid down** 7 October 1976; **Launched** 12 December 1978; **Completed** 18 June 1982 (for sea service in South Atlantic); **Accepted into service** 21 June 1982; **Commissioned** 30 March 1983.

Technical details (as built) Displacement, Overall length, Overall beam, Draught, Machinery, Speed and **Weapons** as *Invincible*, except 20 mm Mk 15 Vulcan Phalanx fitted prior to service; **Aircraft** 5 × Sea Harrier FRS 1 (809 Squadron), 9 × Sea King HAS 5 (814 Squadron), 2 × Sea King AEW 2 (824 D Flight).

Service summary 1982 Accepted for sea service to relieve *Invincible* in South Atlantic (28 August 1982), AEW helicopter trials; **1983-84** Fleet

Above left Invincible, *the first of the light anti-submarine aircraft carriers, firing a Sea Dart area air defence missile* (RN/FPU).

Above Illustrious *with Sea King HAS 5 (814 Squadron) and Sea Harrier FRS 1 (800 Squadron) embarked* (RN/ Illustrious).

Right Illustrious, *the second of the new breed of 'Invincible' Class light aircraft carriers.*

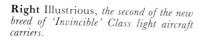

Ark Royal *and* Illustrious *(nearest camera) at sea.*

exercises in Atlantic; **1985** Further exercises and first operational deployment of AEW helicopters at sea.

Illustrious is basically the same as *Invincible* but with better command and control facilities from building.

Name *Ark Royal*; **Pennant number** R07; **Flight deck code** R; **Builders** Swan Hunter (Tyne); **Laid down** 12 December 1978; **Launched** 2 June 1981; **Completed** October 1984; **Commissioned** May 1985.

Technical details (as built) Displacement, Overall length and **Overall beam** as *Invincible*;

Draught 25 ft (7.6 m); **Machinery** and **Speed** as *Invincible*; **Weapons** 3 × Vulcan Phalanx Mk 15 CIWS, 2 × 20 mm Oerlikon GAM-B01, 2 × 2 30 mm Oerlikon GCM; **Aircraft** as *Illustrious.*

Service summary 1985 Work-up and AEW trials.

Ark Royal was built with a 15 degrees ski-jump ramp and fitted out following the operational experience gained by the previous sister ships.

Maintenance Carriers

Class *Unicorn*

Name *Unicorn*; **Pennant number** I72/F72; **Flight deck code** X (1945), U (1946), Y (1946-53);

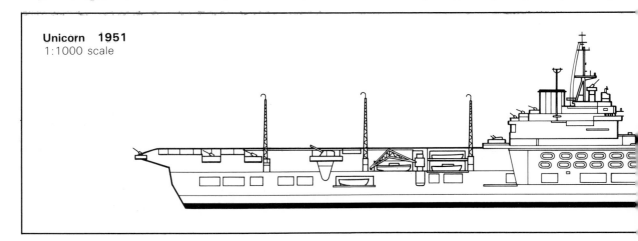

Unicorn 1951
1:1000 scale

Builders Harland & Wolff; **Laid down** 29 June 1939; **Launched** 20 November 1941; **Commissioned** 12 March 1943; **Placed in Reserve** 1953; **Sold for scrap** 15 June 1959.

Technical details (as built) Displacement (standard) 16,530 tons, (full load) 20,300 tons; **Overall length** 646 ft (196.9 m); **Overall beam** 90 ft (27.4 m); **Draught** 20.5 ft (6.3 m); **Machinery** 2 × shafts, 4 × Admiralty/Parsons steam turbines (40,000 shp); **Speed** 24 knots (44.4 km/h); **Weapons** 8 × 4 in, 4 × 4 2-pdr pom-poms, 13 × 20 mm Oerlikon; **Aircraft** 36 in wartime.

Technical details (1950) Displacement, Overall length, Overall beam, Draught, Machinery and **Speed** as built; **Weapons** 16 × 20 mm; **Aircraft** as built.

Modernization and refits Various refits and weapons changes.

Service summary 1943-44 Home and Mediterranean Fleets, operating as aircraft carrier with Seafire fighters at Salerno landings; **1944** Eastern Fleet duties as ferry and depot carrier; **1945** British Pacific Fleet duties, including invasion of Okinawa; **1946-49** In reserve; **1949-50** Far East Fleet Maintenance Ferry Carrier; **1950-53** Korean War service as Ferry Carrier working between Hong Kong/Singapore and Japan; **1953-59** Reserve.

Designed in 1938 for aircraft supply and repair duties, *Unicorn* was pressed into service as an operational carrier (Light Fleet type) for most of the Second World War. With increasing trouble in Far East, she was brought out of Reserve and proved invaluable during Korean conflict. Her hangar deck was designed for floatplanes, being 16.5 ft (5.1 m) high. She had two lifts and a hydraulic accelerator forward and workshop space below decks.

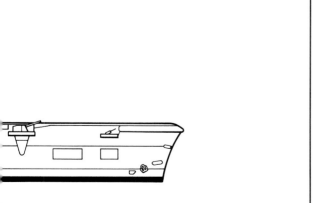

Class *Colossus*

Name *Perseus*; **Pennant number** R50; **Builders** Vickers (Newcastle); **Laid down** 1 June 1942 as *Elgar*; **Launched** 26 March 1944 as *Perseus*; **Commissioned** 19 October 1945; **Sold for scrap** May 1958.

Technical details (as built) Displacement (standard) 12,265 tons, (full load) 18,040 tons; **Overall length** 695 ft (211.8 m); **Overall beam** 80 ft (24.4 m); **Draught** 23.5 ft (7.2 m); **Machinery** 2 × shafts Parsons steam turbines (40,000 shp); **Speed** 25 knots (46.3 km/h); **Weapons** 6 × 4 2-pdr pom-poms, 32 × 20 mm; **Aircraft** None but could transport 50.

Technical details (1949) Displacement, Overall length, Overall beam, Draught, Machinery and **Speed** as built; **Weapons** 19 × 40 mm Bofors replaxing 20 mm Oerlikons but armament totally removed in 1950.

Modernization and refits 1950 Long refit.

Service summary 1945-49 Service as Aircraft Maintenance Ship; **1950** Catapult trials ship (Northern Ireland).

Intended as additional Light Fleet Carrier, *Perseus* was modified in light of experience with *Unicorn* (see above).

Name *Pioneer*; **Pennant number** D76; **Builders** Vickers (Barrow); **Laid down** 2 December 1942 as *Mars*; **Launched** 20 May 1944 as *Ethalion,* changed to *Pioneer*; **Commissioned** 8 February 1945; **Placed in Reserve** 1950; **Sold for scrap** September 1954.

Technical details (as built) as *Perseus*.
Technical details (1949) as built.
Modernization and refits 1950 Disarmed.
Service summary 1945-49 Served as maintenance support ship.

Name *Triumph* See 'Colossus' Class Light Fleet Carriers above.

Projected designs
CVA-01

Name CVA-01 (possibly *Furious* but not confirmed); **Proposed** 1959; **Cancelled** 1966.

Technical details Displacement (standard) 50,000 tons, (full load) 54,500 tons; **Overall length** 963 ft (293.5 m); **Overall beam** 191 ft (58.2 m); **Draught** 32 ft (9.8 m); **Machinery** 3 × shafts, 6 × Admiralty boilers for steam turbines (135,000 shp); **Weapons** 1 × 2 Sea Dart GWS 30 on quarter.deck (Type 909 radar); **Aircraft** 18 × Phantom FG 1, 18 × Buccaneer S 2D, 4 × Gannet AEW 3, 5 × Sea

CVA-01, *an artist's impression.*

King HAS 1, 2 × Wessex HAS 1 or Whirlwind HAR 9.

In 1966 the Labour Government's Defence White Paper announced the death of the fixed-wing aircraft carrier with the cancellation of the *Ark Royal, Eagle, Victorious* and *Hermes* replacement, the CVA-01 type. This carrier concept was highly rated and would have been amongst the best in the world. Service entry was expected in 1970-72. Features included a single hangar of 660 ft × 80 ft (201 m × 24.4 m), fifteen per cent increase in flight area over *Ark Royal,* two aircraft lifts away from 'runway', full-sized 'Alaskan highway' to starboard of the island, two new, long-stroke steam catapults, direct-acting water spray arrester gear.

Escort carriers

Class *Pretoria Castle*

Name *Pretoria Castle*; **Builders** Harland & Wolff; **Launched** 12 October 1938 as RMS *Pretoria Castle*; **Acquired by Admiralty** 1942; **Commissioned** 9 April 1943; **Sold** 1947 as merchant ship *Warwick Castle*; **Scrapped** 1963.

Technical details (as commissioned) Displacement (standard) 19,650 tons, (full load) 23,450 tons; **Overall length** 594.6 ft (181.2 m); **Overall beam** 75 ft (22.9 m); **Draught** 28 ft (8.5 m); **Machinery** 2 × shafts, diesel engines (21,869 bhp); **Speed** 18 knots (33 km/h); **Weapons** 4 × 4 in, 4 × 4 2-pdr pom-pom, 20 × 20 mm Oerlikon; **Aircraft** 21 (1945).

Modernization and refits 1939-40 Converted to armed merchant cruiser; **1943** Converted to trials carrier.

Service summary 1939-45 War service; **1946-47** Trials and training carrier.

Class *Campania*

Name *Campania*; **Pennant number** D48; **Builders** Harland & Wolff; **Laid down** 12 August 1941; **Launched** 17 June 1943; **Commissioned** 7 March 1944; **Reserve** 1952-55; **Scrapped** November 1955.

Technical details (as built) Displacement (standard) 12,450 tons, (full load) 15,970 tons; **Overall length** 540 ft (164.6 m); **Overall beam** 70 ft (21.3 m); **Draught** 22.83 ft (6.96 m); **Machinery** 2 × shafts, diesel engines (10,700 bhp); **Speed** 16 knots (29.6 km/h); **Weapons** 2 × 4 in, 4 × 4 2-pdr pom-pom, 16 × 20 mm; **Aircraft** 18 (wartime).

Modernization and refits 1941-43 Converted from merchant hull; **1945** Refitted as Ferry Carrier; **1949** Refitted for 'Festival of Britain'; **1952** Refitted for nuclear test headquarters role.

Service summary 1944-45 War service; **1945-49** Ferry Carrier and peace keeping in Baltic; **1950-51** Floating exhibition for the 'Festival of Britain'; **1952** British nuclear tests in Pacific; **1953** Placed in Reserve; **1955** Scrapped at Blyth (11 November).

Helicopter-carrying Cruisers

Class *Tiger*

Name *Tiger*; **Pennant number** C20; **Flight deck code** TG; **Builders** John Brown; **Laid down** 1

Right Blake *at sea; note the hangar and flight deck aft* (RN).

Below Engadine, *used for aviation training* (Mike Lennon).

October 1941; **Launched** 25 October 1945; **Commissioned** 18 March 1959; **Converted to helicopter role** 1970; **Paid off** 1978 and scrapped in 1986; **Aircraft** 4 × Wessex HAS 1/2 (826 Squadron).

Name *Blake*; **Pennant number** C99; **Flight deck code** BL; **Builders** Fairfield; **Laid down** 17 August 1942; **Launched** 20 December 1945; **Commissioned** 8 March 1961; **Converted to helicopter role** 23 April 1969; **Paid off** January 1980 and scrapped in 1982; **Aircraft** as *Tiger*, but Sea Kings from 820 Squadron.

Helicopter Support Ship

Class *Engadine*

Name *Engadine*; **Pennant number** K08; **Flight deck code** EN; **Builders** Henry Robb; **Laid down** 9 August 1965; **Launched** 15 September 1966; **Commissioned** 15 December 1967 into Royal Fleet Auxiliary; **Aircraft** Room for training helicopters, such as Wessex HAS 3 (four), Sea King HAS 1/2 (two) and Wasp/Lynx (four/six).

Engadine has been used for deck landing training by Fleet Air Arm helicopter pilots and will be replaced by *Argus* before 1990.

Aircraft carrier technology

Flight deck

In the twenty years immediately following the Second World War, the Royal Navy led the world in aircraft carrier technological development, but the decision to scrap the Fleet Carrier in the mid-1960s caused a decline in the conventional carrier technology directly related to the flight deck. Nevertheless the needs of the smaller aircaft carrier have bred its own technology and again the Royal Navy has developed equipment to fulfil today's high technology needs.

Angled deck

The angled deck was the invention of Professor Lewis Boddington, a British government scientist, and Captain Dennis Cambell RN, the then Assistant Chief Naval Representative at the UK Ministry of Aviation. Captain Cambell was a veteran naval aviator and former CO of a Skua squadron in *Ark Royal* (III).

A conference at RAE Bedford on 7 August 1951, chaired by Captain Cambell, considered the continued problems of eliminating the deadly barrier across the flight deck, and the alternatives after the flexible deck (see below). The chairman produced several pencil sketches of possible alternatives and the largest of these showed the flexible deck angled 10 degrees to port.

The idea produced no visible reaction at the time, but Professor Boddington, having pondered on the various schemes, came to the conclusion that the angled deck principle could be applied forthwith to the new carrier *Ark Royal* (IV), nearing completion, allowing 30,000 lb (13,610 kg) swept-wing jet

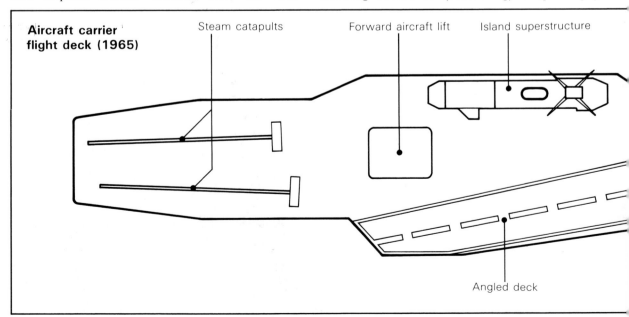

Aircraft carrier flight deck (1965)

Steam catapults

Forward aircraft lift

Island superstructure

Angled deck

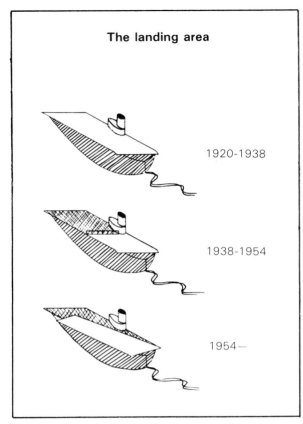

The landing area

1920-1938

1938-1954

1954—

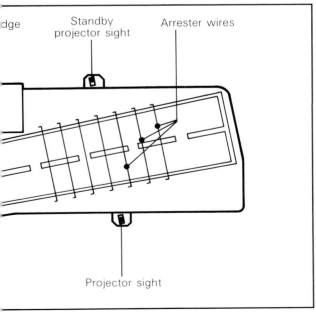

Standby projector sight

Arrester wires

dge

Projector sight

Above Ocean *off Korea with the conventional axial flight deck.*

Left *The co-inventor of the angled deck was Rear Admiral Dennis Cambell; these are his own drawings of the types of flight deck.*

Below Ark Royal *with her partial angled deck in 1961.*

Ark Royal *showing her fully angled deck* (via Derek Monsell).

aircraft to be embarked.

Trials were carried out in *Triumph* on a touch-and-go basis, the ship's centre line having been repainted at 10 degrees to port. The trials were very successful, but the Admiralty wanted to postpone fitting such a system (with its realignment of facilities, including the arrester gear) to the next generation of aircraft carriers. These in fact did not materialize and if it had not been for an exchange agreement with the US Navy the angled deck might not have been adopted.

In 1953, a US carrier carried out full scale demonstrations in the English Channel and showed the extra efficiency available. The Royal Navy immediately ordered conversions to be carried out and *Centaur* was the first aircraft carrier to be modified. *Ark Royal* (IV), of which Captain Cambell was the first captain, entered service in 1955 as the first carrier with an angled deck installed prior to commissioning. In actual fact it was a partial angle and the first full angle was not installed until her second refit in 1958-9. Nevertheless, even the half-angled deck eliminated the steel, and later nylon,

crash barrier (used to protect the aircraft park forward). The tension of deck landings had also been taken away as any aircraft – or 'bolter' – which did not take the wire could use the angled deck to go around again with no fear of crashing into the deck park, although of course there were still very spectacular accidents. The figures speak for themselves – in 1949 there were 200 accidents for every 10,000 deck landings, but after the angled deck had been installed there were fifty accidents in 10,000 landings. Other devices, improved aircraft performance and better training eventually brought the figure down even lower.

The angled deck contributed to the development of the side aircraft lift to transfer aircraft from the flight deck to the hangar below, and vice versa. Centre line lifts could not be operated during recovery operations, although some very slick operating procedures did allow the forward lifts of some carriers to be used very successfully in this operation. The landing aircraft could disengage from its hook, taxi forward under power, with wings folding, onto the lift (off the angled deck centre line) and be taken below immediately after the engine(s) had been shut down, the pilot still in the cockpit.

Above *A Scimitar F 1 (803 Squadron) about to catch an arrester wire on* Ark Royal*'s flight deck.*

Right *Time exposure shot of a Buccaneer 'bolter' on* Eagle *during the Beira Patrol — note the sparks as the hook hits the deck. With the angled deck, the Buccaneer could safely 'go round again'* (Brian Johnstone).

Arrester gear and barriers

Since the early days of naval flying, it has been vital to provide some form of arresting device to assist an aircraft landing on the deck, preventing it from going over the side and, until the advent of the angled deck, preventing it from crashing into the deck park of aircraft ranged forward.

In the post-war period, until the development of the modified Mark 6 system, naval aircraft were limited to a landing weight of 20,000 lb (9,070 kg) and a maximum entry (landing) speed of 60 knots (111 km/h); carriers such as *Indefatigable*, *Illustrious* and *Implacable* were fitted for such aircraft. With the development of the jet aircraft with weights up to 30,000 lb (13,610 kg) and higher entry speeds (in the region of 100 knots), naval engineering developments and those by industry, such as MacTaggart Scott, led to systems optimized for each type of aircraft carrier.

Type of carrier	Gear type	Landing weight	Max entry speed
Early Light Fleet	Mark 8	up to 16,000 lb (7,259 kg)	74 knots (137 km/h)
Eagle	Mark 10	up to 30,000 lb (13,610 kg)	88 knots (163 km/h)
Eagle (refit)	Mark 10 Mod 1	up to 30,000 lb (13,610 kg)	100 knots (185 km/h)
Later Light Fleet	Mark 11	up to 30,000 lb (13,610 kg)	88 knots (163 km/h)
Later Light Fleet	Mark 11 Mod 1	up to 30,000 lb (13,610 kg)	100 knots (185 km/h)
Canadian types	Mark 12	up to 20,000 lb (9,070 kg)	85 knots (157 km/h)
Post-1955 types	Mark 13	up to 30,000 lb (13,610 kg)	85 knots (157 km/h)*

To back up the arrester gear, naval engineers had developed a barrier which could be placed across the flight deck, at about the mid-island position, to prevent an aircraft which had missed the arrester wires in landing from crashing into parked aircraft or crashing over the side. Apart from normal flight emergencies, aircraft often returned to the ship with undercarriage or arrester hook problems.

However, the barrier was a deadly device itself, especially to the new breed of jet aircraft without much protection for the pilot. In piston and turbine-engined types, such as the Firefly or

Prior to the need of jet fighters and the introduction of angled decks, the standard method of stopping an aircraft which missed the arrester wires was a steel rope barrier. This could damage both aircraft and aircrew.

Firebrand, the nose, propellor and engine block provided some form of protection for the pilot; not so the forward cockpit of jets, like the Attacker or Sea Hawk.

The first barriers were constructed of three horizontal steel wires, connected by vertical and cross wires, or sometimes nets. They were first employed in *Ark Royal* (III) from 1938 with the capability of stopping an 8,000 lb (3,630 kg) aircraft, travelling at 40 knots (74 km/h) with a maximum of 1.5 g force. By 1945, *Colossus* was carrying the Mark 7/8 system with an improved performance of being able to take 15,000 lb (6,800 kg) aircraft travelling at the same speed but developing 4 g force. The last steel barrier to be developed was the Mark 11 (1951) for *Albion* and *Centaur*, which was capable of taking a 30,000 lb (13,610 kg) aircraft travelling at 88 knots (163 km/h) and developing 3.7 g force.

It was obvious that steel barriers were going to kill people, so nylon was introduced from 1956. The nylon barrier was used in conjunction with undrawn nylon packs, and the number of the packs used was dependent on the weight of the landing aircraft. All operational aircraft carriers after 1956 were fitted with the nylon barrier, capable of taking a 30,000 lb aircraft, travelling at over 88 knots and exerting an average force of 2 g. Barriers continued to be used in special circumstances after the introduction of the angled deck but the need to erect

Ark Royal, Centaur, Hermes and *Victorious* were refitted with this type of arrester gear which had a pull out of 220 ft (67 m), rather than the more usual 160 ft (49 m).

Even with angled decks, the barrier was still sometimes necessary to catch an aircraft with a major emergency. Note the nylon barrier ropes, and the fact that this Sea Vixen FAW 1 (890 Squadron) is carrying a Firestreak air-to-air guided missile (Brian Johnstone).

them for every landing when aircraft were ranged on deck was eliminated.

Flexible or rubber deck

This system was designed by Major F.M. Green RFC (Rtd), and was the result of a conference held at RAE Farnborough in January 1945 to determine the shape of future naval aviation in the jet age. Major Green's flexible 'carpet' was 150 ft x 40 ft (45 m x 12 m) and capable of taking aircraft up to 8,000 lb (3,630 kg), using a conventional arrester wire system, but the aircraft landing without wheels.

Trials were carried out at RAE Farnborough in late 1947 and the spring of 1948 before Commander Eric Brown took a Sea Vampire F 21 (with its undercarriage retracted) aboard *Warrior* on 3 November 1948. *Warrior's* rubber deck took up 190 ft (60 m) of the after end of the flight deck, the rest being conventional steel decking for normal aircraft operations. A crane was used to move the aircraft from the rubber deck and either onto a trolley or high enough for the undercarriage to be lowered. Tests continued aboard Warrior from November

Right *Modern naval helicopters are secured to the deck by means of a Fairey Harpoon deck lock carried on the aircraft which is 'fired' into the ship's flight deck grill, as illustrated by Birmingham Flight's Lynx.*

1948 to May 1949, with 200 accident free recoveries.

The conclusion of the study was that although there was a weight saving which could be passed on as extra endurance or speed, the lack of flexibility for normal land-based operations would prove too inconvenient for operational service. The costs of providing flexible decks around the world and on all carriers in service was too high. Eric Brown was however awarded the 1948 Boyd Trophy for the finest feat in naval aviation in 1947.

Harpoon

This simple system developed by Fairey Engineering ensures that a helicopter is secured to the parent ship's flight deck even in the most severe conditions. A probe is lowered from the helicopter

and attaches to a grill in the ship's flight deck; it can be retracted immediately prior to launch. Helicopters equipped are the Lynx HAS 2 and 3; the EH 101 will have the equipment fitted.

MADGE

A simple yet highly effective microwave landing system for Sea Harrier and helicopter aircraft carriers, fitted to the 'Invincible' Class CVSs Sea acceptance trials were carried out in *Ark Royal* (V) in 1985. The system was designed and is manufactured by MEL.

The system is mainly used for Sea Harrier operations, providing the pilot with a microwave landing system to enable recovery to continue in marginal conditions. It also gives the FlyCo (Flying Control) data on the identity of the aircraft, its distance and bearing from the ship, height, fuel state, air speed and angle of attack.

Deck landing mirror sight

To eliminate the human error possible in the 'batsman' (or Deck Landing Control Officer) on the aircraft carrier deck, especially with the new jet aircraft entering service in the early 1950s, an invention of Lieutenant Commander (E) Nick Goodhart was incorporated into *Ark Royal* and

subsequently all aircraft carriers with angled decks. This was completed within one year.

Commander Goodhart considered that a steadily descending jet aircraft approach to the flight deck at 3 degrees or so would allow for the pitch of the carrier's deck but could still result in an overshoot or impact on the flight deck 'round-down'. The pilot had to be given an opportunity of correcting his approach to the deck and with the mirror he was likely to do it much quicker than the 'batsman' could signal it.

The deck landing mirror sight (DLMS) was a horizontal concave mirror with a datum line of converted airfield approach lights and studio floodlights modified to act as source lights to provide a blob of white light – the 'meatball' – which moved relative to the aircraft's position, above, on or below the glide path indication from the green datum line. Six datum lights were placed each side of the mirror to cover the final approach angles of some 60 degrees. Initial trials were carried out in *Albion*.

By 1957, an entirely new lighting system had been developed by GEC Lighting Laboratories for service in *Centaur, Hermes* and *Victorious*. It was known as the Mark 1A and developed for naval service by RAE Bedford and John Curran Ltd of Cardiff. For initial deck landings and some operations in bad weather, the Landing Safety Officer (also a pilot) would monitor the approach

Deck Landing Mirror System.

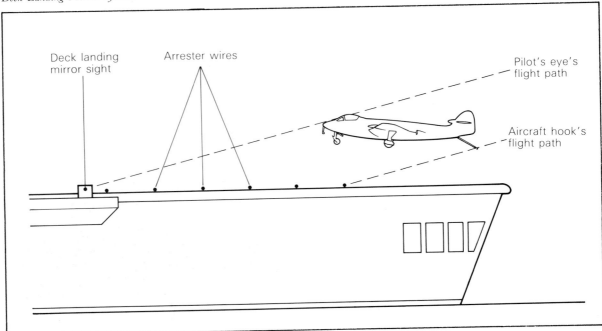

Right *Projector sight in use for a Sea Vixen FAW 1 approaching* Ark Royal's *flight deck; note the plane guard Whirlwind alongside the arrester wires.*

Below right *Ski-jump ramp in operation, with Sea Harrier FRS 1 of 800 Squadron in ballistic trajectory* (RN/ Illustrious).

and landing from a platform adjacent to the DLMS.

Projector landing system

A development of the deck landing mirror sight, the projector system did not use the mirror but relied instead on a projected beam of graduated light which allowed for even more accurate recoveries to be achieved. The system, like many of the British aircraft carrier equipment developments, was adopted by foreign navies for aircraft carrier service.

Modern CVSs use the deck approach projector sight, situated adjacent to the Flying Control (or FlyCo) position, whereas the DLMS and projector sight were situated adjacent to the arrester wires. A vertical series of lights are aligned with the horizontal bars by the pilot of the Sea Harrier, thus obtaining the correct angle of approach to the hover and thence deck recovery.

Ski-jump ramp

A special feature of the 'Invincible' Class CVSs, the ski-jump ramp is now being developed for aircraft carriers of other nations. It is basically a means of giving short take-off and vertical landing (STOVL) aircraft, like the Sea Harrier, a capability of launching irrespective of wind conditions with full fuel and ordnance. *Ark Royal* was completed with a 12 degrees ramps and *Invincible* and *Illustrious* (built with 7 degrees ramps) will be refitted with the greater angle by 1990.

The ski-jump was the brain-child of Lieutenant Commander Doug Taylor, the Flight Deck Engineering Officer in *Victorious* during the

'confrontation' period in the Far East (when Indonesia had territorial designs on the newly independent Malaysia). During hot weather, the catapult runners expanded and aircraft could not be launched. This problem caused Commander Taylor to consider a 'runway in the sky' which would allow jet aircraft to operate from smaller ships, following the demise of the aircraft carrier.

Although there is a penalty of the launched Sea Harrier being in a semi-ballistic, non-flying trajectory for several hundred yards after launch, the system of a free take-off ramp at the end of a deck runway of 480 ft (146 m) or thereabouts was mathematically possible. On land, a fully fuelled and armed Sea Harrier FRs 1 is thought to require 980 ft (300 m) to take off, even with wind down the runway. With the decision late in *Invincible*'s building to equip the ship with Sea Harriers as well as Sea King helicopters, the need for a ski-jump ramp resulted in a design change before completion.

Steam catapult

Second World War fighter and torpedo-strike-reconnaissance aircraft needed only wind over the deck (WOD) of some 30 knots (56 km/h) to achieve a free take-off from an aircraft carrier deck. Accelerators seem to have been generally used for a large range of aircraft (with limited free deck space for take offs) or when the WOD was low. The accelerator was moved by compressed air acting through the medium of hydraulic fluids and could cope with a maximum take-off weight of 10,000 lb (4,536 kg) with a launch velocity of about 65 knots (120 km/h).

Some propeller-driven aircraft were fitted with rocket assisted take-off gear (RATOG) if especially heavily loaded with ordnance or fuel; examples

Left *'Hot to trot', this Buccaneer S 2 from 809 Squadron illustrates the steam catapult at work* (RN).

Above right *Before the steam catapult, heavily-loaded naval aircraft like this Firefly FR 5 from* Theseus *used the RATOG system.*

Below *Royal Navy skills allowed for ripple launches of aircraft by steam catapult, as shown by these two Scimitar F 1s of 803 Squadron.*

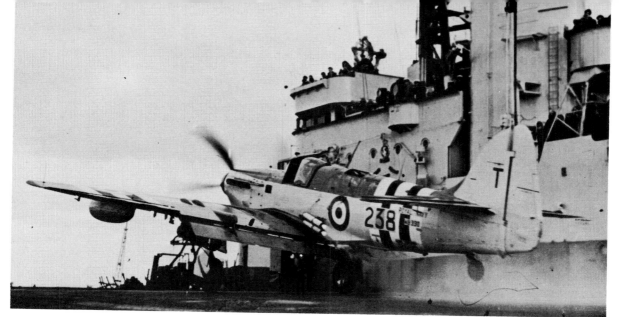

include the Firefly AS 5s flown from Light Fleets during the Korean War.

With the coming of larger jet-powered naval aircraft, a better propulsion method than the accelerator catapults was required to launch them into the air. In 1947, the late Commander (E) C.C. Mitchell developed the direct-acting steam catapult, known as the BS 4, which entered service in *Ark Royal* in 1955, after trials in *Perseus* with the BXSI experimental system in Belfast Lough. The end speed was in excess of 90 knots (167 km/h), dependent on the weight of the aircraft.

The steam catapult still required the aircraft's engines to run up to full throttle, causing heat for the flight deck, noise for the deck crew and jet efflux which could easily blow men or machinery into other aircraft ranged on deck, or over the side. Water cooling devices were installed, efficient deck-loop radio communications took over from shouts or hand-signals and blast deflector screens were necessary.

With two steam catapults in operation, a large aircraft carrier like *Ark Royal* or *Eagle*, with a fully worked up deck crew and air group, could launch an aircraft every 20 seconds, one aircraft per catapult every 40 seconds. Recovery rates with angled deck and direct acting arrester wires could be as short as 30 seconds, and were often carried out simultaneously with a single catapult in operation.

Development of aircraft carrier sensors

The development of the aircraft carrier's own sensor suite has paralleled that of other surface warships although there has been an obvious plan to ensure that the aircraft direction and control sensors have been optimized for the ship's roles. Underwater sensors – sonars – have played a less important part in the sensor suite development programmes because the ships have been designed to carry aircraft, initially fixed-wing and later helicopters, with proficient systems for anti-submarine warfare. Emphasis has therefore been placed on the long range warning, surveillance and air control radar systems; thermal imagery (for low light conditions) and electronic warfare systems have been comparatively recent developments.

During the Second World War, there was rapid technical development of radar and radio direction finding systems; these were important for aircraft carriers although operational tactics, following the losses of carriers sailing alone, would mean that the carrier could also rely on cover from escorts' systems as well. Later in the war, American technology was being developed for use by the Royal Navy, including the adoption of USN's SM-1 fighter control radar.

The Escort Carriers commissioned during the war seem to have been fitted primarily with High Frequency/Direction Finding (HF/DF) gear for the British-built ships, but the American-supplied vessels came with the characteristic lattice surface warning sets. By the time that the 'Colossus' Class Light Fleet aircraft carriers were being built, radar was a standard fit from new, including types for long-range air warning.

Fighter control sets had been developed although one carrier was still fitted with a heavy but effective

Controlling the aircraft on the carrier's flight deck and immediate area is Little F (Lieutenant Commander Flying) in Flyco (Flying Control).

SM-1. As the Pacific War progressed, it was obvious that good, long-range radar coverage of the air threat was essential as the Japanese launched raids aimed against the aircraft carriers alone; radar picket destroyers were introduced to protect the

carriers which led to the development of the airborne early warning aircraft within the decade.

For the design of the new Fleet Carriers, *Eagle* and *Ark Royal*, serious attention was now paid to the sensor suite, allowing for all weather operations, night and day, against comprehensive threats. Long range air warning radar was now capable of reaching out to 150 m (278 km) in optimum conditions, with associated systems providing height information and fighter direction and control. Gun directors had become sophisticated, especially with the introduction of several USN systems, like the Mark 37.

Post-war improvements

The immediate post-war period saw the introduction of the fruits of wartime research on both sides of the Atlantic for surface warning (like Types 293 and 982) with ranges approaching 60 nm (111 km). With the advent of jet-powered aircraft in air groups (and as adversaries), sensor performance improved to match the air power requirements. When *Victorious* was taken in hand for modernization between 1950-58, she emerged with some interesting systems, including Type 984 (three-dimensional long-range radar), 974 (surface warning) and 293Q 30 nm (26 km) height finding systems, useful for carrier controlled approaches. Carrier controlled approach (CCA) allowed for low light, adverse weather recoveries of jet aircraft without their own radar systems. *Eagle* emerged from her refit in 1959, with Type 965 long-range 'bedstead' air warning radar on a new high lattice

A great boon to air defence and air direction for aircraft carriers was the Type 984 3-D radar, the large 'dustbin' on Hermes' *superstructure.*

mast, supplemented by the three-dimensional 984 and CCA system, Type 963. As *Eagle* and subsequent carriers now sported Seacat short-range air defence guided missile systems, the directors were also fitted; initially these were optical guidance only but radar control options were offered later. *Ark Royal* appeared in 1969, ready for Phantom operations with Type 965 long-range radar, height finding and CCA systems.

Albion and *Bulwark* were fitted with air warning radars, height finders and fighter direction sets during their lives as fixed-wing Light Fleet Carriers, whilst their near-sister ship *Hermes* was completed with the three-dimensional radar also fitted to *Victorious* and *Eagle*.

CVA-01 would have mounted an impressive suite of Anglo-Dutch type search, tracking and illumination systems, Sea Dart missile control and CCA systems. When the programme was cancelled and later the 'Invincibles' were partly substituted, the radar suite was altered to reflect the basically helicopter (VTOL) role of these new ships – they retain the Sea Dart's radar system, but have been fitted with an Anglo-Dutch development for long-range air warning, navigation and helicopter control. Electronic warfare suites include ESM (electronic surveillance measures). During refits, a new three-dimensional radar from Plessey will be fitted.

Sonar systems have been fitted to the 'Invincible' CVSs to reflect the carriers' anti-submarine role; other previous carrier designs have basically relied on the surface escorts and air groups for such data. *Hermes* in her ASW role was also fitted with hull-mounted sonar.

Aircraft carrier defensive armament

Although primarily designed to operate aircraft, both in offensive and defensive roles, the aircraft carrier has always carried some form of defensive armament. As the threat environment grew and changed, so the weapons systems carried were amended, improved and upgraded to meet that threat, sometimes not as successfully as others. There has always been a problem of accommodating the weapons and their directors at the expense of deck space and top weight.

The first ship designed to carry aircraft, *Ark Royal*, was armed with conventional 12 pounder guns to defend itself against surface threats because in 1914, when the ship was purchased, the air threat had yet to fully be realized. In fact, the first carriers

were also primarily concerned with being attacked by surface ships, rather than either submarines or aircraft. It took just a few years for the air threat to be recognized so that by the time *Furious* was commissioned as an aircraft carrier, 4 in (102 mm) anti-aircraft gun batteries had been fitted but the 12 pounder guns were retained.

In the early 1920s, the multi-barrelled pom-pom 2 pounder mounting provided the first real air defence system to support the less rapid 4 in guns. Following her 1934 refit, *Hermes* was fitted with 50 calibre (12.7 mm) machine gun mountings with four barrels. At the same time, most carriers were being refitted without the larger calibre surface gunnery systems, such as the 5.5 in (140 mm) low-angle guns.

Second World War

With the loss of *Courageous* to a submarine in the early days of the war, the decision was made to protect aircraft carriers within task groups but the air threat still had to be fully envisaged. Nevertheless, the Admiralty had begun to fit medium and close range air defence batteries, including the fitting of high-angle gunnery directors. *Ark Royal (III)* was built with six 2 pounder and eight multiple 12.7 mm mountings around the flight deck, in addition to 16 4.5 in (114

Until the 1960s, aircraft carriers were equipped with large calibre guns for self-defence, like these 4.5 in (114 mm) mountings in Indomitable *(Captain Jack Button).*

The Falklands campaign showed just how important close-range light defensive guns could be in combat; here is one of Invincible's *Oerlikon 20 mm mountings.*

mm) mountings. The same weight of defensive gun power was designed into the 'Illustrious' Class.

Rearming the carriers with the highly effective 20 mm Oerlikon cannon (still in use in the 1980s) and the 40 mm Bofors gun proved a reliable and effective mix for close-range defence. *Victorious* boasted 45 of the Oerlikon guns and 21 Bofors by the time she sailed for the Pacific in 1945.

In the Pacific War, the aim became the classic

'Invincible' Class aircraft carriers are armed with the 30 mm Gatling-system Phalanx gun system which can be used against sea skimming missiles (RN/Illustrious).

'wall of lead' technique which seems to have proved effective in the Falklands conflict. The 4 in gun continued in service for some time, although the 'Colossus' Class was fitted with 2 pounder pom-poms and a selection of different 20 mm mountings, dependent upon availability; the design for this class had restricted the defensive armament to anti-aircraft close-range only, the first carriers so to be armed.

The design of *Eagle* and *Ark Royal,* the 1942-type Fleet Carriers, included 4.5 in (114 mm) weapons as well as the now standard 40 mm mountings, although the armament changed as the design progressed after the initial early peacetime delay. The pom-pom was going out of favour and being progressively replaced by the single 20 mm (sixty in the *Eagle* design), the 40 mm and the twin 20 mm. By the end of the war, the six barrelled 40 mm mounting had appeared, linked to good gunnery directors.

Post-war systems

As the Fleet Carriers were refitted in the course of their post-war service, the 4.5 in and 40 mm systems were reduced and then deleted. This not only saved top weight but eventually allowed for the fitting of a surface-to-air guided weapon system, Short Seacat. When *Hermes* was commissioned in 1959, her defensive armament had been reduced to ten 40 mm guns, showing how much the defence of the carrier had been shouldered by the escorts and the air group.

Victorious was rearmed during her modernization in the 1950s, receiving 40 mm guns and twelve 3 in (76 mm) mountings, which she kept until decommissioned prematurely in 1967. The post-war Light Fleets generally carried 40 mm guns for self-defence.

When CVA-01 was designed in the early 1960s, the area air defence missile, Sea Dart, was proposed for the ship, linked to the Type 909 missile control radar. The aircraft carrier had moved into the missile era and in no way could be considered a stand-alone ship.

Sea Dart was the primary weapon system designated for the 'Invincible' Class, but originally close-range Sea Wolf point defence missiles were to have been fitted; in the South Atlantic, a close-range defence system was found most necessary. In 1982, *Illustrious* and then *Invincible* were fitted with additional 20 mm Oerlikon guns, countermeasure launchers and the American Phalanx gatling gun close-in weapons system. *Invincible* will be fitted with the Goalkeeper system during her 1986-87 refit, followed by her two sister ships.

Air equipment

Airborne sensors

During the Second World War it became very clear that there was a major need for equipment to look 'over the horizon' or 'through weather'. This was particularly so in the Battle of the Atlantic where aircraft had succeeded in closing the Black Hole of mid-Atlantic and were able to attack surfaced U-boats at night and in bad weather using air-to-surface vessel radar (ASV) and the famous Leigh Light for localizing the target.

The Fleet Air Arm had been at the forefront of these developments, especially with aircraft like the Fairey Swordfish and later the Grumman Hellcat equipped with airborne interceptor (AI) radar to engage night prowlers keeping watch on a convoy or task group. Obviously with the cessation of hostilities the pace of development slackened, only to recover with the conflict in Korea and the threat of East-West conflict. Again the threat was mainly that of the submarine although the kamikaze attacks of the late Pacific War had also increased the pressure on airborne early warning radar which continued to be developed, in tactical terms, by the British, with the US supplying the equipment.

Air interception

The naval aviation radars appear to have been used for interception during the Second World War, but with the coming of the jet age developments increased to today's high technology standards.

AI Mk V Entered service in 1945 for night fighter interception, combat air patrol and air/surface search, mounted in Firefly NF 1 and Barracuda 5 aircraft.

AI Mk X Developed by Western Electric Company in the late war years and experimentally fitted in the Firefly NF 5 before seeing service as the Sea Venom FAW 20's first centrimetric radar. The observer used a 30 in (76 cm) display. Replaced by the AN/APS-57.

AI Mk 15 Developed from ASV Mk 9 for the Sea Hornet NF 21 and some Firefly models in a fighter role; manufactured by Western Electric Company.

Sea Hornet NF 21's thimble-nosed AI Mk 15 radar (Fleet Air Arm Museum).

Replaced by AN/APS-6 for the Sea Hornet.

AN/APS-57 First manufactured in 1948 by Westinghouse, this radar was fitted to the Sea Venom FAW 20 and later to the FAW 21 as the search/detection element of the AN/APS-35 system.

Blue Fox This radar, designed by Ferranti, was developed for the Sea Harrier FRS 1's single crew cockpit for air search, surface search and air interception. It is linked to the inertial navigation system and head-up display. It is frequency agile.

Blue Vixen A development of Blue Fox for the Sea Harrier FRS 2 update programme giving look-down, shoot-down capability. It is a multi-mode, coherent pulse-Doppler system giving beyond visual range all-weather capability.

Airborne early warning

AN/APS-20A Developed under the auspices of the Anglo-American Scientific Committee as an over-the-horizon radar to detect low flying enemy aircraft, the radar was fitted to the Skyraider AEW 1 aircraft from 1952.

AN/APS-20F Various in-service modifications to the original radar culminated in the F model for the Gannet AEW 3 carrier-borne aircraft and the system was operational 1959-78. On the demise of the Gannet from Fleet Air Arm service, the radars were passed to the Royal Air Force for the Shackleton AEW 2 programme and destined to remain in service for a further ten years.

Searchwater Derived from the fixed-wing surface surveillance radar for the Royal Air Force, Searchwater was rapidly installed in the Sea King Mk 2 during the Falklands conflict in 1982. Manufactured by Thorn EMI Electronics, Searchwater is an I-band radar which can be used for detecting and tracking sea skimming missiles and low flying aircraft over a wide area of sea. Advanced processing and classification equipment

allow for identification of targets against sea clutter and it is thought that data can be passed to interceptor aircraft or the command ship by secure speech or data link. Used in conjunction with Cossor Jubilee Guardsman IFF and Racal Avionic MIR-2 Orange Crop ESM.

ASW and surface search

ASV Mk 9 Also known as ARI 5607 and developed from AN/APS-4 by Western Electric Company, this radar's 14.5 in (37 cm) dish was mounted in a pressurized 'bomb'. It was flown in the Barracuda 5, Sea Mosquito TR 33 and Firefly 4, 5, 6 and 7.

ASV Mk 11 Developed from the RAF Lancaster H2S Mk III system, this roll stabilized radar had been mounted between the Swordfish's undercarriage during the battle of the Atlantic and was fitted to the Barracuda III.

ASV Mk 13A Developed as a roll stabilized surface search radar for the Barracuda III and later

Sea Mosquito TR 37; replaced by ASV 21 in 1962. The radar was an Anglicized version of the American AN/APS-6 which was licence-built by E.K. Cole and Kelvin-Hughes from 1944.

ASV Mk 13B The tropical version of 13A, fitted to the Sea Hornet NF 21 from 1949 and again having 360 degrees sector scan from the 18 in (46 cm) dish.

ASV Mk 15 Also known as ARI 5578, this radar was used for trials in the Spearfish and later the Anson but tests showed a performance only slightly better than Mk 13A. Features included continuous rotation or sector scan, as well as early miniaturization of components.

ASV Mk 19A Another Cole and Kelvin-Hughes development, being both roll and pitch stabilized as well as having a tilt control. Again using the 18 in dish, the radar's range in the Avenger AS 5 and Sea Prince C 1 was limited to 40 nm (74 km) by the display.

ASV Mk 19B The version developed for the Gannet AS 1 series from 1954.

ASV Mk 25 A system carried by the Spearfish in

Wessex HAS 3 with ARI 5955 radar in the 'hump' (RN/Culdrose).

a retractable radome under the fuselage.

ARI 5955 A development of preceding radars for a helicopter mounting in the Wessex HAS 3 and Sea King HAS 1 and 2. The radar was used for surface search, anti-ship surveillance and anti-submarine warfare, said to have the ability to detect small targets on the surface at a range of up to about 50 nm (93 km). It entered service in 1968 and was replaced by Sea Searcher in remaining Sea Kings in 1983.

Blue Kestrel An advanced radar from Ferranti which is being offered for the EH 101 programme. Flight trials in an RAE Bedford Sea King began in 1986.

Blue Parrot The attack/strike radar for the

Buccaneer S 1's radar was called Blue Parrot (Rolls-Royce).

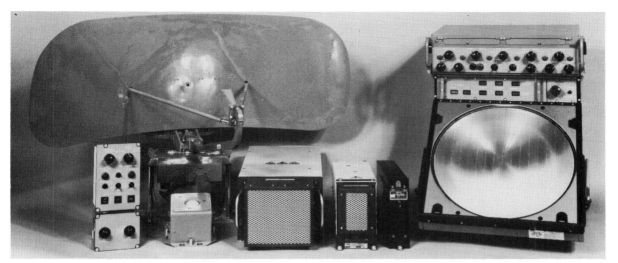

Above *MEL's Sea Searcher radar carried by Sea King HAS 5 helicopters.*

Right *Lynx helicopters carry Sea Spray Mk 1 radar (aerial shown).*

Buccaneer, later fitted to the Canberra T 22; from 1979 if was used for radar training.

Sea Searcher Manufactured by MEL for the Sea King HAS 5 helicopter, this radar is a lightweight 360 degrees system, giving high definition and over-the-horizon targetting capability. It is interfaced with the Racal Avionics Tactical Air Navigation System and Type 195M sonar.

Sea Spray Mk 1 Developed by Ferranti for the Lynx HAS 2 and its Sea Skua anti-shipping missiles. The system weighs less than 60 kg with search/track and transponder modes. It illuminates the target for the Sea Skua missile.

Sea Spray Mk 3 Offered as an update of the Mk 1 for the Lynx HAS 8 programme with a 360 degrees ability, it is virtually a new radar giving track-while-scan, digital scan conversion, variable picture scale and picture freeze abilities. It is data-bus integrated and has a high interval between failures.

Super Searcher A development of Sea Searcher which could be used for the Sea King HAS 6 update and is a contender for the Lynx HAS 8 update. By 1986, the Lynx programme's radar had still to be selected and a special version of Super Searcher was being offered by MEL.

Training radar

ASR 360 An X-band maritime patrol radar,

developed by Racal Avionics and fitted to the Jetstream T 3 training aircraft which entered service in May 1986. It is classed as lightweight and relatively clutter-free, using the Clearscan video processing system.

Underwater systems

To track and identify submarine contacts, aircraft (and ships) use high and low frequency sound waves called sonar. Today there are two main categories,

Left *Whirlwind HAS 7 from 815 Squadron (Hermes), dunking its American-built sonar during an exercise. Note the surface submarine, top left (Brian Johnstone).*

Below *The observer and sonar operator's positions in a Sea King HAS 5.*

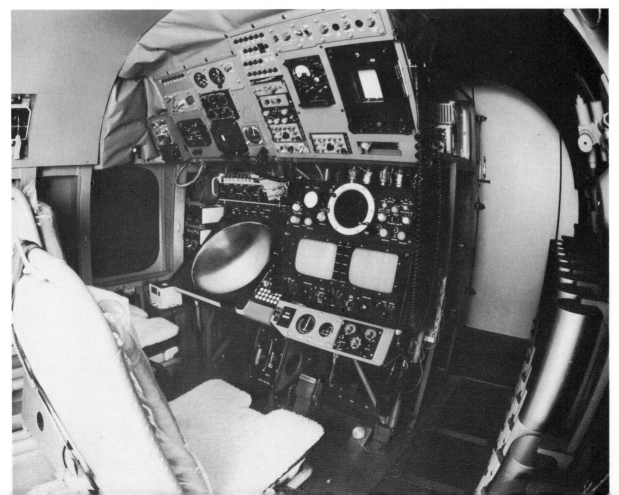

active and passive. Most naval ASW aircraft have been equipped to operate both although passive systems have been developed as a result of the threat generated by Soviet nuclear-powered submarines.

AN/AQS-4 This was the first dipping sonar system installed in a British helicopter, being used with the Whirlwind series programmes in the early 1960s.

AN/UYS-503 This is the Computing Devices of Canada onboard processor system which was cut from the Lynx HAS 8 programme due to British government spending cuts in 1968. It gives the helicopter the ability to process sonobuoy data rather than rely on ship-relayed data for ASW targetting.

Cormorant This is a lightweight active/passive dipping sonar for helicopters which has been developed by Plessey Marine for possible use with the proposed Lynx dipping sonar version which has apparently been abandoned. It has been ordered for the future Canadian maritime helicopter.

HELRAS This is a new long range 'strategic' sonar developed for the EH 101 by British Aerospace and Bendix Oceanics, with FIAR of Italy. It is a low frequency active system with some 1,500 ft (457 m) cable to enable the operator to use the sonar body to penetrate thermal or saline layers in the sea under which submarines might be hiding.

LAPADS Standing for lightweight acoustic processing and display system, this system is carried in the Sea King HAS 5 and used to update the tactical plot from sonobuoy transmissions. It is manufactured by GEC Avionics under the designation AN/AQS-902 and an updated version, AQS-903, has been selected for the EH 101 programme. AQS-902 entered service in 1980.

MAD Used to localize submarine contacts, the magnetic anomaly detector used for a limited number of Lynx HAS 2/3 and Sea King HAS 5 helicopters is produced by Texas Instruments under the designation AN/AQS-501.

Onboard MAD Mk3 This is a French developed system from Crouzet, who have teamed with Dowty Electronics in the United Kingdom to sell the system to the Royal Navy for the Lynx HAS 8 update. The system does not require that a MAD 'bird' is flown behind the helicopter but has the full system on the helicopter.

Sonobuoys The use of passive sonobuoys has been developed to counter the nuclear-powered submarine threat and the ideal deployment is by screens of buoys across the ocean. The air droppable sonobuoy is deployed from a helicopter flying at between 150 and 9,850 ft (45 and 3,000 m), at about 100 knots (185 km/h). The buoy's

Above *Lynx helicopter MAD 'bird' installation.*

Below *For sonobuoy processing, Sea King HAS 5s use the GEC Avionics LAPADS system (GEC Avionics).*

Bottom *British-developed sonobuoys for helicopters.*

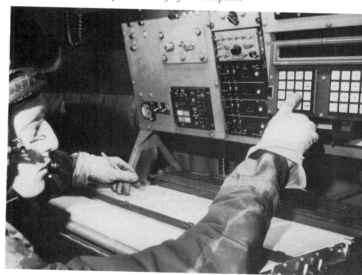

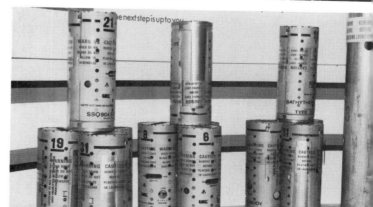

equipment listens for noise and relays the data via radio to a processor on board the helicopter. The operating time is from 1.4 to 8 hours depending on the type. Various sonobuoys have been used by the Fleet Air Arm including the Dowty Ultra mini-Jezebel which weighs 10 lb (4.5 kg).

Type 195M This dipping active sonar was developed by Plessey Marine and equipped the Wessex HAS 1 and HAS 3, Sea King HAS 1, 2 and 5. The transducer is lowered up to 55 m into the water and is controlled by the helicopter's aircrewmen. It has a range of about 8 nm (13 km) and gives bearing and range data to the helicopter's observer.

Other sensors Various systems have been deployed by naval aircraft since 1945, including the Dowty Ultra bathythermal buoy (AN/SSQ-936) which can transmit water temperature data up to 1,410 ft (430 m) below the surface.

Passive systems (non-EW)

Sea Owl Known as PIDS (passive identification system) and developed by GEC Avionics for the

Above *Wessex HAS 3 lowering Type 195M sonar* (Westland).

Below *Buccaneer S 2 weapons suites: rockets and practice bombs (front), rockets and SNEB pod with nuclear weapon (centre), 1,000 lb bombs, bomb-bay tanks and Martel missiles.*

Lynx HAS 8 programme, the Sea Owl is used for passive search at night. It has a thermal imaging module fitted to the nose of the Lynx, above the 360 degrees radar (an active system), and allows the aircrew to identify surface targets at night, perhaps prior to attack with Sea Skua missiles. It is an aid to the MIR-2 Orange Crop system which can only operate if the target is emitting radar/radio signals. Service entry 1988.

Air weapons

Certainly since the First World War and even before then, naval aircraft on operational and active service duties have been armed. Over the years the sophistication of the weaponry has improved out of all recognition as compared to the early machine guns and bombs of the Royal Naval Air Service. Nevertheless there is still a place for machine guns and bombs in modern state-of-the-art naval aircraft.

For the purpose of this book, naval air weapons have been divided into the following categories: missiles, guns and free-fall weapons.

Missiles

Missiles replaced unguided rockets in the air defence role and later for ground attack and anti-shipping purposes. As the threat has grown in sophistication, so has the capability of the missile systems employed to counter it.

AIM-9C The first Sidewinder missile supplied to the Royal Navy was part of the Phantom FG 1's armament suite but was limited to tail chase and certain other restricted angle engagements.

Above right *AIM-9L Sidewinders being carried by a Sea Harrier FRS 1.*

AIM-9L Used extensively in the Falklands where it was very successful, the Lima version of the Sidewinder equips the Sea Harrier FRS 1 and is capable of all aspect engagement.

ALARM Standing for air-launched anti-radar missile, this British Aerospace product will be included in the Sea Harrier FRS 2 suite.

AMRAAM Developed by Hughes Aircraft, the AIM-120A AMRAAM (advanced medium range air-to-air missile) is another update system for the Sea Harrier force.

AS/SS 11 The first helicopter-launched air-to-ground guided weapon was designed in France and supplied for the Wessex HU 5 for close support of Royal Marine commando operations. The target

Right *Wessex HU 5 with two SS 11 missiles mounted (Brian Johnstone).*

Wasp HAS 1 launching an AS 12 missile.

was tracked through the optical sight and guided via a wire command link.

AS 12 The improved French wire-guided missile which was supplied for the Wasp HAS 1 in an anti-ship role and small numbers were supplied for commando support Wessex HU 5 helicopters, both using the SFIM M260 optical sight mounted on the cabin roof. Used in anger against the *Santa Fe* off South Georgia, the weapon in now obsolescent and will retire with the Wasp in 1988/89.

ASRAAM The advanced short-range air-to-air missile is being tested for service with the Sea

Harrier FRS 2 to replace the AIM-9L Sidewinder for air defence duties.

Bullpup An American supplied air-to-surface guided weapon which was used to arm carrier-borne Scimitar F 1, Buccaneer S 2 and Sea Vixen FAW 2 aircraft in the 1960s and 1970s.

Firestreak An air-to-air missile, tested on the Sea Venom FAW 22 and in service with the Sea Vixen FAW 1, it was designed for tail-chase engagements. It remains in RAF service.

Martel An Anglo-French development for anti-radar strikes and for air-to-ground targets, using television link guidance. An expensive missile, it was nevertheless effective and armed the Buccaneer S 2D variant. It remains in RAF service.

Red Top The successor to the Firestreak, Red Top was used to arm the Sea Vixen FAW 2 for all aspect air-to-air combat. It remains in RAF service.

Sea Eagle A new generation anti-shipping missile

Buccaneer S 2 carrying Bullpup missiles (Fleet Air Arm Museum).

Above *Sea Vixen FAW 1 with four Firestreak missiles in 1959* (Brian Service).

Right *First prototype Sea Vixen FAW 2 showing four Red Top missiles and underwing fuel tanks* (Gordon Roberts).

which entered service in 1987 for the Sea Harrier FRS 1 and later will arm the FRS 2 version. It was tested successfully in 1984.

Sea Skua A helicopter-launched short-to-medium range anti-shipping missile which was operationally tested during the Falklands conflict. Part of the Lynx HAS 2/3's primary weapon load, the missile was designed by British Aerospace. It is guided by Sea Spray Mk 1 radar.

Below *Sea Harrier FRS 1 during Sea Eagle trials in 1984* (RN).

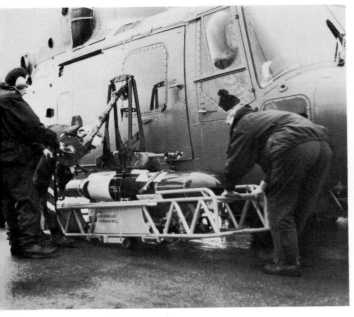

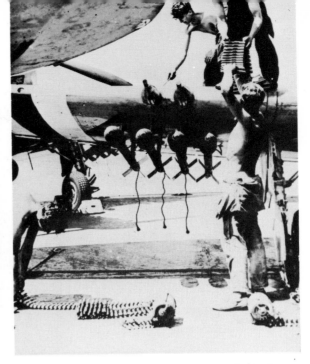

Above *Loading Sea Skua missiles to* Hermione's *Lynx HAS 2.*

Right *20 mm Aden cannon and underwing rocket projectiles, 1952.*

Sparrow III Purchased as part of the Phantom carrier-borne fighter package, the AIM-7 Sparrow (still operational with the RAF) was in service from 1969-78 with the Fleet Air Arm.

Aircraft ordnance

Fixed and moveable guns have been carried by many naval aircraft, but since the Second World War there has been a movement towards the larger calibre cannon rather than the machine gun. Cannon have greater 'punch' but fewer rounds can normally be carried.

Helicopters have not been armed with fixed guns by the Fleet Air Arm, relying instead on unguided 68 mm rockets and guided weapons. However, during the Falklands conflict Sea King HC 4 helicopters were fitted with the 7.62 mm General Purpose Machine Gun L7A2 which has an effective range of about 800 m (0.43 nm). Other naval helicopters also have the ability to mount the GPMG.

For many purposes, including air-to-air combat,

Calibre	Date	Aircraft	Remarks
20 mm	1945	Firebrand TF 4/TF 5	Hispano design
20 mm	1947	Sea Fury FB 10/11	Hispano design
20 mm	1948	Sea Hornet F 20	
20 mm	1949	Sea Hornet NF 21	
20 mm	1953	Wyvern S 4	
20 mm	1953	Firefly AS 6	
20 mm	1953	Sea Hawk F 1	
20 mm	1958	Hunter GA 11	Aden
20 mm	1979	Sea Harrier FRS 1	Aden (ROF) design

guns went out of fashion in the 1960s, but the lessons learned by the US forces in Vietnam resulted in their reintroduction in fixed-wing strike aircraft like the Sea Harrier. Again during the Falklands campaign, the Sea Harrier proved that the 30 mm Aden cannon was an effective weapon.

30 mm Aden cannon packs carried underfuselage by the Sea Harrier FRS 1.

under licence by Marconi in the UK. It was effective against Second World War-designed submarines.

Air droppable weapons

Naval aviation has also been involved with air droppable ordnance, from the days of the 20 lb (9 kg) Cooper bombs of the Royal Naval Air Service to the Stingray anti-submarine torpedo of the Sea Kings of today. Since the Second World War, the bulk of the weapons have been linked to anti-submarine warfare although the Sea Harrier still retains its ability to carry 'iron' bombs.

Mk 11 depth charge A conventional high explosive depth bomb, updated by British Aerospace in 1985 to provide a warning and last resort weapon for anti-submarine warfare. Its original role was against Second World War-designed submarines in shallow water, dropped from fixed-wing aircraft like the Firefly and Gannet.

Mk 44 torpedo A limited range, shallow water torpedo which entered service shortly after the Korean War. Carried by all helicopters from the Whirlwind HAS 1 to the Sea King HAS 5, the torpedo was designed by Honeywell and made

Mk 11 depth charge on a Sea King HAS 1 of 706 Squadron.

Above *Sea King HAS 2, 824 Squadron from Ark Royal, drops a Mk 44 torpedo. Note the aircrewman preparing to throw a smoke marker from the open cabin door* (RN/Ark Royal).

Left *Two Mk 46 Mod 2 torpedoes loaded on a Lynx HAS 2.*

Top right *Sea King HAS 2 drops a Stingray trials round during initial Royal Navy tests* (MOD PE).

Middle right *Sea Vixen FAW 1, 890 Squadron, firing a pod of 2 in folding fin aerial rockets (note the acquisition Firestreak missile under the port wing)* (Brian Johnstone).

Right *60 lb warhead rocket projectile with a 500 lb bomb underwing on a Sea Fury FB 11.*

Mk 46 torpedo Three versions have been used by helicopters of the Fleet Air Arm for deeper diving submarines with speed in excess of 40 knots. Mod O used a solid propellant (1965-67); Mod 1 was a liquid propelled version (1967-72); Mod 2 has an improved motor (1972 to date).

Aerial torpedoes Several Second World War types including the 18 in (45.7 cm) and 22 in (56 cm) were carried by fixed-wing aircraft, including the Spearfish and the Sea Mosquito.

Stingray torpedo An advanced design for the Lynx HAS 2/3 and Sea King HAS 5 from Marconi Underwater Systems Ltd, the Stingray was subject to the largest defence contract of the time in 1986. It is designed to hunt, track and destroy the advanced, high speed, double-hulled nuclear-powered submarines which could pose a threat to the United Kingdom. It is intelligent and can dive to at least 300 m.

Unguided weapons

For close air support, and previously to break up the threat of large bomber aircraft formations, naval aircraft have been equipped with unguided rockets, usually the fin folding type developed from American sources and using French launcher technology.

2 in RP A development of the Second World War, especially useful against surface submarines, the rocket projectile (RP) was developed after 1945 with new motors and better warheads. It was carried by several types of aircraft, including the Sea Fury FB 11 and Firefly series, and was used operationally by Sea Hawk and Wyvern units during the Suez operations and later in Aden and the Indonesian confrontation.

60 lb RP This developed rocket projectile was carried by the Gannet AS 1 and other surface strike

Right *Sea Harrier FRS 1 bombing up with 1,000 lb iron bomb prior to raid on Argentine positions in the Falkland Islands* (RN/FPU).

Below right *This Sea King AEW 2 carries a Jubilee Guardsman IFF aerial in the Searchwater radome and Orange Crop ESM on the nose and rear fuselage.*

Below *Sea Vixen FAW 1, 890 Squadron, bombing up aboard* Hermes *in 1961* (Brian Johnstone).

aircraft in the late 1940s and 1950s.

68 mm SNEB A rocket pod developed in France for fixed-wing and helicopter platforms. The SNEB pod has been used operationally by Scimitar and other aircraft. From 1980 it equipped the Sea Harrier FRS 1.

Iron bombs From Korea onwards, conventional free-fall 'iron' bombs have been used by naval aircraft. Even during the Falklands conflict, Sea Harrier aircraft were operational with 500 lb iron bombs whose design had altered relatively little since 1945.

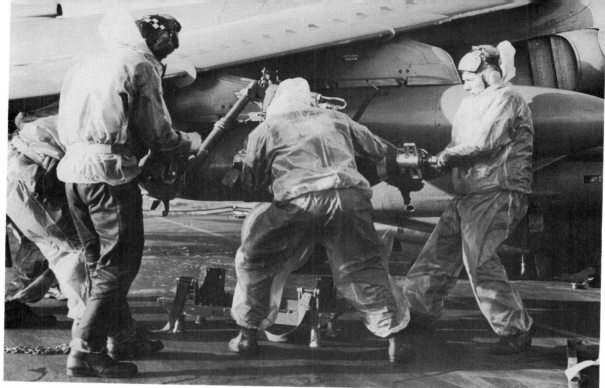

Electronic warfare systems

Radar not only helped the United Kingdom to win the Battle of Britain in 1940 but also played a vital part in the successful war against the U-boat in the Atlantic Ocean. As with all military systems, once something has been developed, there will be countermeasures developed. So it was with radar.

From the early 1950s, the Royal Navy has taken the threat of electronic warfare (EW) very seriously, and over the years British industry has developed systems to assist in countering enemy radar

emissions and to train own force countermeasures operators, ashore and afloat.

In 1951, aircraft were carrying out radio-direction trials to detect and acquire early sonobuoys which previously had used smoke markers. Sonobuoy development has been continued to a high state of art (see page 247).

As early as June 1955, 744 Squadron's X Flight was formed to evaluate radar jamming devices, operating the Firefly AS 6 and other contemporary types, mainly linked to anti-submarine operations. In April 1956, the unit was redesignated 745 Squadron to carry out the tactical evaluation of the Orange Harvest ECM (electronic countermeasures) system, using Culdrose and Eglinton amongst its bases. Detachments went to sea in *Albion* and *Bulwark*.

In May 1958, front line squadron status was achieved by EW aircraft when it is believed that the Fleet Air Arm's first specialist unit, 831 Squadron, was formed at Culdrose. The initial equipment was the Sea Venom ECM 21/22 modification of the standard all-weather fighter, joined in 1959 by the Gannet ECM 4 (later by Gannet ECM 6 modifications).

To a large extent the Squadron's role remains classified even after disbandment in 1966 when the role became joint-service with the RAF and 360 Squadron was formed. The basic task seems to have been the training of radar operators in an electronic warfare environment and later the retraining of those operators in an electronic countermeasures situation. 831 Squadron took its aircraft to various naval air stations and aircraft carriers, throughout home, Mediterranean and Far Eastern waters.

In the age of sea skimming and homing missiles, most operational naval aircraft have some form of EW equipment fitted, being either passive (ESM – electronic surveillance measures) or active (ECM – electronic countermeasures). Following the Falklands conflict additional emphasis has been given to the various facets of EW training and operation, all of which are highly classified, although basic details of some of the known systems are included below.

ARI 18228 A development by Marconi Defence Systems to give radar warning to Buccaneer S 2 and Phantom FG 1 carrier-borne aircraft. A display in the aircraft's cockpit gave a simple indication of the direction and type of radar threat – missile, gun and so on.

Chaff Hotel This is the chaff (thin metal strips cut to a wavelength pattern to confuse enemy

Phantom FG 1s were equipped with fin-top radar warning receivers (RN/LA, Steve Pratt).

Used for surveillance and other reconnaissance tasks, the Marconi Heleteli is carried by the Lynx helicopter, seen here from Newcastle *alongside a Soviet 'Kresta II' cruiser in the Barents Sea.*

radars) which is carried by helicopters and released through chutes or through cabin doors. In the Falklands, Chaff Hotel was used against the radar seeking heads of enemy missiles.

Guardian A new, still secret electronic warfare system being developed by Thorn EMI Electronics for the Sea Harrier FRS 2.

Jubilee Guardsman This is an IFF (identification, friend or foe) developed by Cossor Electronics for the Sea King AEW 2 helicopters for use in concert with the Thorn EMI Electronics Searchwater radar. Details are secret.

Kestrel ESM The proposed passive fit for the EH 101, under development until it enters service in 1990. It gives 360 degrees coverage in azimuth and elevation.

Orange Crop Developed by Racal Avionics for the Lynx HAS 2/3 and Sea King AEW 2/HAS 5 helicopters for passive operation. First deliveries were made in 1978 for the Lynx fleet and the system entered service in the Sea King immediately prior to the Falklands invasion, operational trials being carried out in action.

Orange Harvest An early electronic warfare system.

REL EW mounting A decoy device carried by Lynx and Sea King helicopters, mounted on the weapons pylon of the helicopter. Thought to be the so-called 'Exocet decoy' device from the Falklands campaign.

Simulation and training

The use of ground-based training aids has increased tremendously over the past twenty years and today the Fleet Air Arm has two of the most advanced flight simulators in the world and several of the best procedural trainers currently available. It is important to train aircrew on the ground to save costs and to prevent unnecessary flying accidents during pilot training and refresher courses.

Helicopters Current simulator training equipment includes the Rediffusion Sea King Mk 5 full flight simulator with the world's most advanced visual system, giving day, dusk and night scenes. This replaced the Singer Link-Miles Sea King Mk 2 simulator in mid-1986 and has been linked to the Ferranti rear crew trainer to give a complete ground-based helicopter training package.

At Portland, one of the most modern combat mission and full flight simulators has been commissioned by Rediffusion Simulation of

Crawley, Sussex. In addition to this system, which was updated in 1983, there is a Ferranti-built Lynx Observers' Procedural Trainer with two static cockpits, operational from October 1984.

Fixed-wing At Yeovilton, a Singer Link-Miles Sea Harrier FRS 1 simulator has been built with special emphasis being given to the shipboard and weapons side of training, whilst at Culdrose, for navigational training a radar procedural ground trainer has been built by Ferranti for the Jetstream (in which helicopter observers learn their trade).

Specialist equipment

Ejection seats

The first Fleet Air Arm aircraft to be equipped with ejection seats was the Westland Wyvern S 4 and in November 1956, during the Suez campaign, the system was successfully used by pilots of crippled aircraft. Steadily over a period since then, the Martin Baker ejection seat has been developed to world-leading standards.

Flying helmets

The development of the aircrew flying helmet has mirrored the development of the naval aircraft. Immediately after the Second World War, the leather skull-cap type helmet was in regular use, having the radio-telephone ear pieces integrated with the head covering, and a clip across radio microphone and oxygen mask. With the development of jet aircraft (and aircraft with ejection seats) and the increased risk to pilots of barrier engagements, a plastic resin helmet was introduced with the Attacker, Wyvern and the Sea Hawk. These first helmets were large and cumbersome, giving rise to the adoption of the US Navy term 'bonedome'. Medical requirements now mean that helmets are lightweight, have good noise prevention and good crush resistance. The Royal Navy has used the products of Helmets Limited for many years.

Night vision goggles

These devices are lithium battery powered and fit over the front of aircrew flying helmets with the suitable modification. Using image intensifying tubes, the goggles give sufficient light for night flying operations to be conducted. The first US-designed ANVIS sets were introduced to the Fleet Air Arm in 1981 and were used successfully by helicopter crews in the Falklands. In 1986, Ferranti Electro-Optics won the tender for ASR 1011 for new lighter-weight goggles for both fixed-wing and helicopter operations. The key to the success of NVG is a compatible cockpit.

Safety equipment

Fleet Air Arm safety equipment, which encompasses the full range of survival and safety equipment for aircrew, passengers and ground-crew, is controlled from Seafield Park near Lee-on-Solent. Modern liferafts have not changed greatly in principle from those of the 1940s, but the quality of material is greater, the equipment carried is greater and more attention has been paid to such items as personal distress radios and beacons. Aircrew carry personal strobe lights and one such device was used to locate a downed Sea Harrier pilot during the Falklands conflict.

Sproule net

This special air-sea rescue device was developed by Lieutenant Commander John Sproule who had joined the Fleet Air Arm as a pilot in 1940. By the time he retired in 1960 he had produced a number of helicopter search and rescue equipment and helicopter operating improvements for the Fleet Air Arm. The device was to recover injured or otherwise incapable survivors by dragging a net across the surface of the water, with one end attached to the helicopter's rescue winch.

Wessex HAR 1 of 771 Squadron netting of Portland with a Sproule net.

Select bibliography

The Admiralty-Air Ministry debate: 1935-39, by Paul Lewis (MA thesis for King's College, London, 1985). Gives the reader a good understanding of the feeling of conflict between the FAA and the RAF.

Aircraft Carriers, Norman Polmar and others, Doubleday. In this book Captain Eric Brown describes some of the most important developments in British carrier aviation and other authors identify other nations' successes.

Aircraft Carriers of the World, Roger Chesneau, Arms & Armour Press, 1984. An excellent reference work on aircraft carriers.

Aircraft of the Royal Navy, Paul Ellis, Jane's, 1982. Good illustrations of the major naval aircraft.

The British Aircraft Carrier, Paul Beaver, Patrick Stephens Ltd, 1982, 1984, 1987. Details the development of the British conventional aircraft carrier and how the needs of the 1970s and 1980s altered the concept.

British Naval Aircraft since 1912, Owen Thetford, Putnam, 1977. The standard work since the 1950s, but is lacking in detail about the post-1945 types in particular. Goods photographs and line drawings.

Encyclopaedia of the Modern Royal Navy, Paul Beaver, Patrick Stephens Ltd, 1982, 1985, 1987. Deals with the current situation of the Fleet Air Arm.

The Squadrons of the Fleet Air Arm, Ray Sturtivant, Air Britain, 1984. Must be considered the most detailed and complete work on the Fleet Air Arm yet published. Without Mr Sturtivant's book, the author would have been hard pressed to check the facts for this book.

Societies

British Aviation Research Group, c/o 8 Nightingale Road, Woodley, Berkshire RG5 3LP. Produces two excellent private circulation newsletters — *British Aviation Review* (current aircraft) and *Roundel* (historic aircraft) — which contain valuable information for the FAA enthusiast.

Fleet Air Arm Officers' Association, 94 Picadilly, London W1V 0BP. An organization which maintains contact between officers with a direct connection with the Fleet Air Arm all over the world.

Society of Friends of the Fleet Air Arm Museum, RNAS Yeovilton, Somerset BA22 8HT. Open to anyone with an interest in British naval aviation, the society undertakes important work in historical research.

Telegraphist/Air Gunners' Association, c/o Fairhaven, Haseley Knob, Warwickshire. Run by and for former TAGS and has close connections with the Aircrewman's Association and the FAAOA.

Index

The following index combines a brief glossary of abbreviations. Where an abbreviation is common, eg RN, it is not indexed as it would be of no value as a reference. Similarly, entries such as *Ark Royal* which appear throughout the book are indexed only under their main entry and illustrations to avoid overlong strings of numbers. Entries in italics are ships' names and numerals in italics refer to illustrations. (*Index compiled by Lyn Greenwood.*)